Geography Teachers'
HANDBOOK

Geography Teachers'
HANDBOOK

Edited by Patrick Bailey and Peter Fox

THE GEOGRAPHICAL ASSOCIATION

Acknowledgements

In addition to the main contributors, we are also deeply indebted to many other people: those whose advice, given in respect of this book or long ago and now come to fruition, informed our decisions about what to include; those whose skill and talent have moulded the shape of the book; those who have supplied photographs, free of charge, to illustrate the text. Altogether, a full list of names would cover several pages, but we wish particularly to acknowledge the enormous help we have had from Fran Royle and Diane Wright, the Geographical Association's production team, without whose detailed, patient and imaginative work this book could not have been constructed. Others we wish to mention are Bill Marsden, for compiling the bibliography; Chris Lowe of Oundle School, who checked legal aspects of Chapter 3; the members of the GA Publications Advisory Panel, for making many helpful suggestions when the manuscript was in its first draft; Adrian Cook of Itchen College, Southampton, for help with the Resources sections; Roger Trend of Exeter University for help with cross-curricular links and John Castleford of Leicester University for advice about IT matters; Paul Coles and Linzi Henry, for the maps and cartoons respectively; and Margaret Binns, for compiling the index – at top speed! Also for their splendid work at top speed we would like to thank the staff at Armitage Typo/Graphics, who are responsible for the design and layout of the book. Finally, but far from least, we are indebted to Rose Pipes, whose clear and sustained editorial guidance helped everybody through the long journey towards publication.

Patrick Bailey and Peter Fox
January 1996

Frontispiece: **Margaret Roberts**

ISBN 1 899085 30 0

First published 1996. Paperback edition 1997.

Published by the Geographical Association, Solly Street, Sheffield S1 4BF. The views expressed in this publication are those of the authors and do not necessarily represent those of the Geographical Association. The Publications Officer of the GA would be happy to hear from other potential authors who have ideas for geography books. You may contact the Publications Officer via the GA at the address above.

The Geographical Association is a registered charity no. 313129

Edited by Rose Pipes
Index by Margaret Binns
Design and typesetting: Armitage Typo/Graphics, Huddersfield
Printed and bound in Hong Kong by Colorcraft Limited

The contributors

The *Geography Teachers' Handbook* could not have come into existence without the generosity of the following people, who freely gave their time, talent and experience to their contributions to this book:

Patrick Bailey is a past President of the Geographical Association and a Senior University Teacher at Loughborough University

Dr Hazel Barrett lectures at the School of Natural and Environmental Sciences, Geography Subject Area, Coventry University

Trevor Bennetts was formerly Staff Inspector for Geography in Her Majesty's Inspectorate. He is Visiting Fellow in the University of Southampton School of Education

Dr Tony Binns is a past President of the Geographical Association and lectures at the School of African and Asian Studies at the University of Sussex

Ken Bland is Head of INSET at Nene College of Higher Education, Northampton

Dr David Boardman was formerly Senior Lecturer in Education at the University of Birmingham and is editor of *Teaching Geography*

David Burtenshaw is Director of Collaborative Programme Development, Academic Development Centre, University of Portsmouth

Gary Cambers is First Deputy Principal at Guthlaxton College, Leicester. He is to be Chief Examiner for MEG GCSE Geography (Avery Hill) in 1998

Roger Carter is County Inspector for Geography, Staffordshire LEA

Bill Chambers is Head of Environmental and Biological Studies Department, Liverpool Hope University College

John Davidson is Head of Geography, Exeter School

Karl Donert is Senior Lecturer at Liverpool Hope University College

Chris Durbin, formerly Advisory Teacher in Derbyshire, is now Education Officer at the BBC

Peter Fox is Head of the Faculty of Development and Guidance at Chilwell Comprehensive School, Nottingham

Keith Grimwade is Head of Geography, Hinchingbrooke School

Colin Harris was a geography inspector in Hertfordshire and is now an OFSTED-trained inspector of secondary schools

David Lambert is Senior Lecturer at the University of London Institute of Education

Kevin Luker is Head of Humanities, Rossington High School, Doncaster

Paul Machon is Director of Studies at Wyggeston and Queen Elizabeth I College, Leicester

Fred Martin is Head of Humanities at Grange School, Kingswood, near Bristol

Wendy Morgan is a consultant in primary geography and was founder-editor of *Primary Geographer*

Keith Orrell is an Educational Consultant and GCSE Chief Examiner. Formerly he worked in teacher education

Andrew Powell is Senior Lecturer in Geography and Education at Kingston University

Graham Ranger is Geography and Environmental Education Adviser for Derbyshire County Council

Dave Richardson is Head of Centre/ Geography Tutor at Lancashire County Council's Field Centre, Hothersall Lodge

Margaret Roberts is Lecturer in Education at Sheffield University, Division of Education

Ewa Sawicka is Head of Geography at King Edward VI Camp Hill School for Girls, Birmingham

Alan Sutton is Lecturer in Education at the School of Education, University of Leicester

Tony Thomas is Director of the Field Studies Council, Preston Montford, Shrewsbury

Rex Walford is University Lecturer in Geography and Education, and a Fellow of Wolfson College, Cambridge

Patrick Wiegand is Senior Lecturer in Education at the University of Leeds and atlas adviser to Oxford University Press

Pat Wilson is an Educational Consultant and OFSTED Inspector. Formerly she was a Professional Officer with SEAC

Foreword

PATRICK BAILEY AND PETER FOX

January 1996

We have had two principal aims in preparing this book. First, we have tried to bring together ideas and materials which will give specific and immediately useful advice to teachers working within National Curriculum and assessment frameworks in English and Welsh schools. Such practical help is needed in many schools; perhaps in all. In pursuing this aim we have endeavoured to address the professional needs of experienced teachers, especially heads of departments who are responsible both for meeting National Curriculum and assessment requirements in their schools and for representing geography in the wider context of the whole curriculum. We have also tried to offer practical help on lesson planning and teaching methods to student teachers and those in their first few years of teaching.

We are keenly aware that National Curriculum geography in England and Wales is only one way among many of constructing a school geography programme. Implementing National Curriculum regulations and assessment procedures has been a monumental task which has focused the attention of the teaching profession on the letter of the law rather than its spirit, leaving little time and energy for thinking ahead. Moreover, we are in danger of concentrating so enthusiastically on the ever-developing technology of education that its ultimate purpose is overlooked. Our second principal aim, therefore, has been to reaffirm the nature and value of a geographical education. At its best, this can offer young people many insights into their world of increasing global interdependence, international competition and environmental concern.

The book is divided into sections, the content of which is signalled in their titles, and each opens with a summary of the constituent chapters. The bulk of the book relates to the early and middle years of secondary school, but there are also chapters on the primary stage, A level, post-16 education, teacher training and job opportunities for geographers. Issues of general concern to all teachers, such as gender, multi-ethnicity and cross-curricular themes are addressed in the opening section, which also looks at recent and likely future changes in geography. Some of the most recent changes are the subject of separate chapters – the revised GCSE syllabuses, for example, and recently revised OFSTED guidelines. A chapter is devoted to Information Technology, though references to IT permeate the whole book – this in itself reflecting the pace of change since the mid-1980s, when CD-ROMs and the Internet were unheard of in schools.

The Geographical Association cannot speak with one voice on such things as priorities, methods or content. Nevertheless, we hope that the content of this book is broadly representative of the current and future concerns of geography teachers. In selecting from and ordering the contributions received, we have worked from the assumption that the majority of readers will live in the UK, and in particular England and Wales, but that much of the content will be relevant and applicable to anyone, anywhere, whose interest and concern is the teaching of geography at the turn of the century.

Geography is all around us; it remains only to be learned and taught

Photo: **Chris Garnett**

Contents

Section One

The context for secondary geography

SUMMARY OF CHAPTERS

'The future is unpredictable...Thus a study in 1937 missed not only the computer but atomic energy, antibiotics, radar and jet propulsion, nearly all of which had been around in principle and waiting for development.'

Herman Kahn and Anthony J Wiener (1967), *The year 2000: a framework for speculation on the next 33 years.*
New York, Macmillan, page 21

This section deals with the context within which geography is now being taught and learned in secondary schools. The characteristics of primary school geography are essential background: a geographical education is a continuum from the age of five to fourteen and beyond. The many and varied contributions which geography can make to the wider curriculum are discussed, and then some guidelines for ensuring that geography lessons are free from prejudice and bias are outlined. Finally, recent and likely future developments in the geography curriculum are related to the methodology of geography in the secondary phase.

Chapter `1`

What happens in the primary phase?

WENDY MORGAN

'Work in primary school geography…must be thought of in terms of activity and experience rather than knowledge to be acquired and facts to be stored.'

Sir W H Hadow **et al** *(1931),* **Report of the Consultative Committee on the Primary School (The Hadow Report)**. *HMSO*. p. 93.

A new subject for many schools

Teaching geography is a fairly new experience for the majority of primary teachers. Until the National Curriculum made geography a statutory foundation subject in key stages 1 and 2, few schools had a recognisable geographical component in their integrated curricula. Now, however, the geography that is taught in the first two key stages forms the foundations on which the rest of geographical education builds, or crumbles.

Geographical work is taking shape in different forms and in a variety of contexts in infant and junior classes. The speed and success of its introduction has been largely dependent on the knowledge and expertise of teachers and heads, and on the support provided by advisory staff and other agencies.

Primary teachers are also specialists

Specialist geography teachers need to be aware that primary teachers are specialists too. Their specialism is in the pedagogical practices related to an age group, as opposed to a subject, but it is a specialism nevertheless. Many primary teachers have been trained or have evolved as specialists in infant or junior practice or even as Year 2 or Year 6 specialists.

In terms of subjects, primary teachers tend to concentrate on language, mathematics and the basic skills related to social and educational development. For infant teachers, reading has traditionally taken up a high proportion of teaching time each day. Beyond these basics, the topic or project, based on children's perceived interests, has frequently catered for the broader curriculum, sometimes including a geographical element.

Subject specialism in primary schools is not widespread and is generally limited to music and some aspects of PE. It is very rare for geography to be taught by a specialist, except in independent schools and some middle schools.

Secondary teachers may not be aware of the scale and quality of the geography taking place in some primary schools; the important thing is to liaise closely with the staff in your feeder schools

Photo: **Jo Hughes**

The class teacher is generally responsible for a class of a limited age range for a full school year, teaching every subject, with limited support from special needs teachers. Ancillary staff may be available to assist teachers, particularly those of younger children. It has become customary to invite parents to help in certain capacities, and this is common practice for fieldwork trips away from the school site.

The introduction of National Curriculum geography

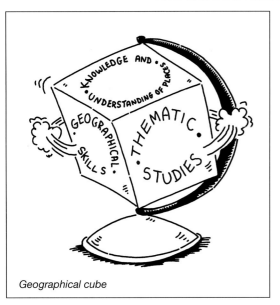

Geographical cube

The phased introduction of the National Curriculum gave a high priority to science as a core subject, resulting in many schools organising their topics around original science Attainment Targets. When geography and history subsequently came on stream this framework was found to be inadequate. One common solution was to introduce history study units as discrete topics and tack onto the science topics those parts of geography which fitted. Term-long topics were frequently reduced to half-term units, one of which was based on the local area and incorporated aspects of both history and geography.

This solution frequently neglected important parts of the geography curriculum. Studies of distant localities were often omitted and little provision was made for the acquisition of locational knowledge and the systematic introduction of mapping skills. The rationale behind National Curriculum geography, the combination of aspects of place with themes and skills (the geographical cube), was unclear to the majority of teachers who had typically received only a brief geographical education.

Teachers' geographical background

Half the current teaching force in primary schools stopped studying geography at fourteen. All teachers will have received a brief introduction to the subject during their training, amounting to about ten hours on a PGCE course, and a little longer as part of a BEd. This introduction may have been through an integrated course in which geography was combined with history and perhaps religious education. A minority will have studied geography as a main subject, but many of these will have adopted other semi–specialisms in school, perhaps because they consider such a shift to be more favourable to their career advancement.

Co–ordinating geography

Most schools have now appointed a teacher to co-ordinate geography. Although in an average-sized school most teachers have responsibility for co-ordinating only one subject, geography is frequently linked with history, often additionally with RE, and one co-ordinator is responsible for both or all subjects. Also typically, the more senior teachers co-ordinate the core subjects and receive responsibility allowances; geography is frequently co-ordinated by the least experienced newcomer who receives no responsibility allowance. Superior subject knowledge is not necessarily a criterion for the choice of a co-ordinator. In some cases, particularly in small schools, geography is co-ordinated by the Head or Deputy in addition to a multitude of other responsibilities.

Non-contact time in primary schools is very rare. Co-ordinators are only infrequently, if ever, released to work alongside class teachers or to teach as specialists. More often they are responsible for writing a policy, gathering resources, attending courses and possibly leading school-based INSET. Unless well qualified and confident in the subject, they have little chance of influencing colleagues to any extent.

Support for primary geography

Many LEAs have traditionally provided support by means of humanities teams in which primary geography expertise was not very prominent. Since the introduction of the National Curriculum, appropriate expertise has been bought in or developed to such an extent that support by means of courses and consultancy is often of a high order. Valiant efforts have been made in many cases to equip teachers, usually co-ordinators, to promote geography in their schools, and the provision of GEST-funded courses, in conjunction with HE departments, has been a major factor in raising teacher confidence. The GA, too, has been an important source of support for teachers, both through its publications and through its courses and Annual Conference.

Influence of published materials

To boost teacher confidence in geography, and to provide support, many schools have purchased elaborate schemes which purport to deliver the subject for a given key stage. Despite the fact that many excellent primary geography practitioners have been involved in writing these resources, they are not always entirely appropriate.

National Curriculum geography at key stages 1 and 2 is designed to maximise the use of the local area to lay the foundations for geographical learning. By definition, no published scheme can meet this requirement. In addition, National Curriculum geography requires the study of distant localities in considerable depth. Currently, the choice of these localities is largely resource-led, with much valuable material made available by the aid agencies and charities, including the GA, as well as the BBC and ITV. Commercial publishers now acknowledge the need for detailed, flexible resources of this kind, which can be used in a variety of ways with different age groups, and many recent publications now include case studies of real people and places.

The nature and timing of the curricular reforms meant that commercial publishers and their authors were faced with unprecedented uncertainty and change, and with a curriculum whose content and aims could not easily be provided for through commercially viable formats. In their rush to prepare new material in time, publishers inevitably operated more on hunch than certainty, and as a result, some of the first phase publications were wide of the mark. Many were thematically structured and failed to achieve the balance between places, themes and skills that was envisaged by the original curriculum designers.

Assuming a sustained period of stability in education, it is likely that more appropriate published material will become available, but teachers will always need to produce resources of their own, both to provide for the 'local' element in the curriculum, and to meet the highly variable demands of a mixed-ability audience.

Early stages of implementation

The National Curriculum for geography had only run for two full years when Sir Ron Dearing's review of the whole curriculum began. At that point it was only necessary for half of key stage 2 to study it, but in fact many schools had set up provisional structures which attempted to deliver the subject through all years. Laudable though these efforts were, imperfect understanding of the Order, and confusion due to the way it was presented in the ring binder, often resulted in inadequately planned structures.

In the first two years, OFSTED reported an over-emphasis on local geography and a neglect of distant localities. It was also reported that human and environmental geography were often neglected, while weather and mapwork received more attention. Schools where good planning was evident, and the influence of a co-ordinator was felt, were the most successful in delivering geography.

There was strong evidence that the complexity of the Order was to blame for much inadequate planning. Planning for the delivery of a multitude of fragments of Programmes of Study, plus the impossible task of assessing every Statement of Attainment, caused many teachers to give up in despair.

The Dearing Review

The review of the National Curriculum resulted in a much simplified and reduced primary geography curriculum. More manageable than its predecessor, the current curriculum is judged by some to be flawed in several respects. For example, the presentation of content under the headings 'skills', 'places' and 'themes' does little to encourage the combination of these three elements in units of geographical work. Setting out the content in relation to each key stage is certainly a great advantage, but the wording of the document is often remote from the reality of primary classrooms. In addition, there is little encouragement to teachers to realise the geographical potential of common topics such as 'Shopping' and 'Ourselves'. Neither is there any guidance on ways of linking geography with other subjects.

Post-Dearing, assessment procedures have been totally changed. Formative assessment based on the Programmes of Study is now left to teachers and schools to organise. Another innovation is end-of-key-stage teacher assessment, whereby pupil achievement is matched against Level Descriptions.

Features of current good practice

Currently, the best work in primary school geography occurs where the subject is treated as such. This does not preclude links with other subjects, but geography rarely flourishes in contexts where it is not the subject receiving most attention.

Where primary geography is well established, exciting innovative work occurs. This is characterised by effective planning at key stage, unit and lesson level and by an investigative approach guided by key questions. It often includes work outside the classroom, around the school site and local area, or on day or residential visits to other places.

Some of the most successful local geographical investigations are those in which pupils seek to model or map their locality, to make a brochure or guidebook, develop a video or slide/tape presentation and make use of the views of local people. Enquiries into local land use issues, in which pupils investigate a number of viewpoints and form and defend their own, can be a potent introduction to citizenship and environmental education as well as good geography.

The use of maps, aerial and ground level photographs and appropriate geological language are all features of developing good practice in primary geography.

Studies of places beyond the local area are frequently made in the context of day visits, school journeys and twinning schemes initiated by schools or the LEA. Some schools had already developed fruitful links and visits through which to study a European locality when the 1995 Dearing Review removed this obligation. Studies of distant places are more often based on the resources which prompted their selection, and more and more of these are being produced.

Geography in key stage 1

Teachers of infants are recognising that many of their traditional topics provide opportunities for developing geographical education. Thus, we find pupils responding to carefully worded directional instructions, modelling landscapes as part of sand and water play, and designing and mapping road systems using miniature toys and playmats. Infants can also learn geography by means of visits to farms, high streets and

nearby villages, and by developing IT skills through map overlays on concept keyboards or honing directional skills with programmable floor robots. Teachers may be surprised at the interest shown by very young children in people and places far away, but such studies can be very successful, especially when approached through the activities of families and school children in the locality concerned. Another opportunity for developing geographical concepts and language is through the use of story books, which, if carefully selected, can stimulate much discussion and ideas relating to geography.

Programmable robots help primary children to learn directional skills
Photo: **NCET**

Change and development

Integrated topic work, particularly where history and geography are linked, can result in geography being marginalised. In the early stages of its development, National Curriculum geography generally flourished best when treated as a separate subject. However, as teacher confidence increases, and geographical expertise becomes more widespread, it is likely that subject integration will reappear in a better managed and more balanced form. This is to be welcomed, as geography provides the ideal bridge between many subjects studied in the primary school. It offers one of the best contexts for language development, provides real situations for the application of mathematics, can be combined satisfactorily with scientific and historical investigations, and offers a stimulus for the use of technology and IT. At its best, integration can bring increased 'relevance' to the whole curriculum, while freeing up more time overall for worthwhile geographical investigations.

There are signs that researchers are taking more interest in the origins of children's geographical understanding. Too long overshadowed by inappropriate interpretations of aspects of Piaget's work, primary geography is now emerging as a valid research field. The work of Matthews and Wiegand concerning children's understanding of place, and of Boardman and Catling on the origins of map understanding, are notable. In addition many teacher educators are conducting small-scale research projects, the results of which will eventually illuminate the subject. It will be stimulating for primary geography practitioners to have research studies backing up their pragmatic assumptions about the best way to approach the subject with young children.

On a more negative note, it must be a cause of concern that as a consequence of the Dearing Review, geography in the primary key stages has been much reduced in content, so much so that teachers may be tempted not to fill the 5% of curriculum time allotted to it. Also, the loss of detailed specification has left generalist teachers ignorant of the nature and extent of the subject. It is unlikely that more widespread specialist teaching of geography will occur in the primary sector. While specialist teaching may become more common, it is improbable that geography will be amongst the first subjects to receive such treatment.

The need for cross-phase liaison

Few would argue against the need for liaison between primary and secondary schools, and, in particular, for secondary geography teachers to become familiar with the primary school context from which they will inherit their pupils. Inevitably, this context will vary from school to school, but the constraints of the class-teacher system, the demands of the whole curriculum and the novelty of geography as a compulsory subject are common to most, as are the freedom from rigid timetabling and the opportunity for class teachers to integrate content from different subjects. Another feature of most primary schools is the relative ease (compared with secondary schools) with which they can arrange for fieldwork to take place away from the school site, even though more adult helpers are needed.

Equally important is the need for teachers of older primary pupils to be aware of the expectations of their secondary colleagues and of the way in which geography will be presented in the first term of secondary education.

The National Curriculum, with its improved record-keeping and assessment procedures, will encourage a smoother transfer from primary to secondary than in the past, when ignorance and lack of contact characterised the primary/secondary relationship. Regular meetings between teachers from clustered schools, and goodwill on both sides, can break down barriers and yield many practical benefits. For example, specialists can offer their advice and expertise to non-specialists, and resources can be exchanged between schools. Teachers of Years 6 and 7 can teach one another's classes and arrange fieldwork which spans the phases. Secondary pupils can tutor primary groups in appropriate class or field-based work: this has been done successfully with sixth form A level geographers working alongside groups of Year 6 pupils. At the very least, secondary teachers can be invited to view the outcomes of topic work in primary classes, and primary pupils can visit secondary schools to see displays of older pupils' work.

Information required from feeder schools

At the time of transfer it is essential that secondary geography teachers receive information from feeder primary schools about options within the curriculum which have been taken up, in addition to detailed information about individual pupil achievement. For instance, information must be passed on about:

- localities in the UK studied in depth at KS1 and KS2,
- localities overseas studied in depth at KS1 and KS2,
- fieldwork undertaken beyond the school locality,
- residential experience of fieldwork in the UK and abroad,
- any geographical work which has been particularly significant for the class in question,
- the last major unit of geographical work undertaken by the class before transfer.

Summary

Geography is a new subject in many primary schools and is only gradually being planned and implemented. Local geography, weather and maps are more firmly established than 'distant' locality studies, human and environmental geography. Fieldwork frequently features the school grounds and immediate vicinity. Teachers' confidence is growing, although many start from a limited knowledge base, but support from specialist colleagues, LEA advisory staff and the Geographical Association is still vital if the foundations for 'good geography' are to be firmly laid at the primary school stage.

Chapter 2

Geography in the whole curriculum

In this chapter *Roger Carter* raises issues and questions relating to geography in the whole curriculum. *Patrick Bailey* then explores how our subject may be developed in relation to the cross-curricular themes.

ROGER CARTER AND PATRICK BAILEY

'There is an entitlement to a balanced and broadly based curriculum which promotes the spiritual, moral, cultural, mental and physical development of pupils at the school and of society; and prepares such pupils for the opportunities, responsibilities and experiences of adult life.'

Education Reform Act.

A DEFINITION OF THE CURRICULUM
'The curriculum: All the opportunities for learning provided by a school. It includes the formal programme of lessons in the timetables; the so-called 'extra-curricular' and 'out-of-school' activities deliberately promoted or supported by the school; and the climate of relationships, attitudes, styles of behaviour and the general quality of life established in the school community as a whole.'

Her Majesty's Inspectors of Schools (1980). **A View of the Curriculum.** *HMSO.*

Issues and questions

Children in schools today will have an adult life which may stretch beyond the middle of the next century. Will the revised National Curriculum provide the framework within which they may be prepared for it? Are the prescribed subjects the right ones? A glance at Figure 1 would indicate how stable the subject-based curriculum has been over almost a hundred years. We would need to know more about content within subjects and the teaching and learning process to judge whether today's content is capable of fulfilling the entitlement; and we need to consider what abilities and understandings will best equip today's youngsters for tomorrow's world.

The most hopeful aspect of the revised National Curriculum is that it moves us away from tight prescription, and creates both space and opportunity for teachers and schools to think creatively about the teaching and learning experiences to be offered to tomorrow's adults. It is a good time for us all to take stock of what we teach and why we teach it. A key starting point is to consider the potential contribution of geography to broad educational objectives, and how the subject links and relates to the whole

Issues of health, environmental protection and economic and industrial understanding have to be considered in geography lessons about Sellafield

Photo: **Bill Guest**

curriculum. The curriculum a school offers will need to go far beyond the sum total of the subject parts as specified in the National Curriculum. Geography, like all other subjects, will need to consider not only what it can offer distinctively within itself, but also how through the subject pupils may be better prepared as future world citizens.

Board of Education Regulations: 1904	National Curriculum: 1995
English	English
Mathematics	Mathematics
Science	Science
History	History
Geography	Geography
Foreign language	Modern foreign language
Drawing	Art
Physical exercise	Physical education
Manual work/housecraft	Technology
	Music
	Information technology

Figure 1: *The stability of the subject-based curriculum*

Making connections

Management of the curriculum in most secondary schools is not particularly conducive to the development of an holistic approach. Historically, secondary schools have developed stronger vertical than horizontal structures to support curriculum planning. Departments plan largely in isolation from each other, and opportunities to plan coherently across a range of subjects are relatively limited. Consequently it is often the pupil who must make the necessary connections between slabs of learning punctuated by bells and delivered through a range of teaching styles, learning demands and working conventions. To follow a pupil in, say, Year 7, through a day's work can be a salutary and often confusing experience!

The reduced subject content of the revised National Curriculum makes it more important than ever that connections are explicitly planned in across the years and key stages. If content in each subject is reduced to a smaller core, there is a risk of greater incoherence. It will be important for schools to come to a collective view of the learning needs of pupils at each age and key stage, and the responsibilities of various subjects in meeting them. This calls for stronger management and planning across departments – the more so since the cross-curricular themes received virtually no attention in the Dearing proposals and lie outside the statutory Orders.

However, geography has always had good potential for links across the curriculum. There are logical and natural connections with both arts and science subjects, and the range of content is such that pupils are drawn into learning experiences which can enhance their physical, social, emotional and intellectual development. The subject can help pupils make connections with other learning – and between their learning and their lives outside the school. This is important: pupils must be able to perceive the relevance of their work to themselves as individuals. We need to ask two questions of any programme we offer:

- how relevant is this work to these pupils?
- how will it enhance their capability as individuals?

Motivation to learn is likely to relate to the degree to which pupils perceive relevance to themselves, and can relate their learning to real situations in their own lives. As we begin to plan it is worth returning to the NCC series of documents on the whole curriculum and the cross-curricular themes (NCC: *Curriculum Guidance*, 1989/90), even though their publication was badly timed and presented great problems for teachers when they were introduced. Circular number 6 (NCC, 1989) provides a useful definition of whole-curriculum elements – dimensions, skills and themes. These are summarised in Figure 2.

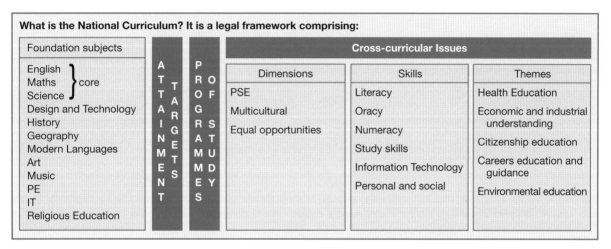

What is the National Curriculum? It is a legal framework comprising:

Foundation subjects	A T T A I N M E N T	T A R G E T S	P R O O F G R S A T M U D E Y S	Cross-curricular Issues		
				Dimensions	Skills	Themes
English Maths } core Science Design and Technology History Geography Modern Languages Art Music PE IT Religious Education				PSE Multicultural Equal opportunities	Literacy Oracy Numeracy Study skills Information Technology Personal and social	Health Education Economic and industrial understanding Citizenship education Careers education and guidance Environmental education

Figure 2: Elements comprising the whole-school curriculum

Whole-curriculum elements

DIMENSIONS
Commitment to providing equal opportunities, and a recognition that preparation for life in a multicultural society is relevant to all pupils, are dimensions which should permeate all aspects of the curriculum.

SKILLS
A range of core skills are identified which should be fostered across the whole curriculum in a measured and planned way. Geography departments need to consider the extent to which they develop skills of communication, numeracy, study skills, personal and social skills, and Information Technology through their programmes.

THEMES
The NCC identified five themes which it considered reasonable to assume are essential parts of the whole curriculum. These are listed in Figure 2: they are discussed more fully in the second part of this chapter. Each theme was developed in the NCC series of guidance publications. The booklets varied in quality and style, as well as in the demands they made. They were introduced alongside increasing subject-based

prescription which was growing in complexity by the day. Given the pressure that teachers were under at that time it is small wonder that the documents were often consigned to the top shelf whilst teachers set about developing the statutory programmes.

Part of the problem is that the themes were presented and perceived as extra content to be taught, rather than as a practical means of making the subject relevant and coherent. Eleanor Rawling (*Teaching Geography*, October 1991) proposed a much more helpful approach. She identified a number of common characteristics to the cross-curricular themes which point us more towards teaching and learning styles than content in their delivery. She listed a range of skills, abilities and values such as:

- skills to analyse, evaluate, review evidence, solve problems, make decisions, learn from first hand experience

- abilities to explore values and beliefs and to empathise with other people

- values such as respect for evidence and concern for others

- development of personal values and commitment, and social/moral responsibility.

These characteristics are vital to the rounded education of young people, but they may not stand out in the Programmes of Study of the first or the revised statutory Orders. For example, the Order for geography sets out only the content, skills and ideas of the subject that are to be taught and assessed, but pupils will need opportunities to apply and respond to the stipulated content. It must be made relevant to the learner by relating it to the real world and real people within it. We need to provide real contexts if these common characteristics are to develop in a meaningful way, and this shifts us away from what we teach to a closer consideration of how we teach it.

The cross-curricular themes can provide a personal focus for much of the geography programme. Pupils need to be able to personalise learning situations and relate them to their own lives as individuals and as members of the larger community. Thus the cross-curricular themes may be seen as a vehicle to enhance pupils' capability to operate in the world outside school as citizens, users of the environment, potential employees, and so on. A stronger focus upon the learner's needs as an individual and a member of larger groups is called for. These relationships are set out in diagram form (Figure 3), and explored in the INSET activity below.

INSET activity on cross-curricular themes

- Is what I teach relevant to my pupils?

- Will it enable them to apply skills and understandings to new situations?

- Do I recognise the full potential of the topics I teach to develop the cross-curricular dimensions, skills and themes?

- Does my teaching encourage pupils to think through their own attitudes and value positions?

- Where, and in what ways, does my geography programme prepare pupils for their role as an employee; a user of the environment; a global citizen?

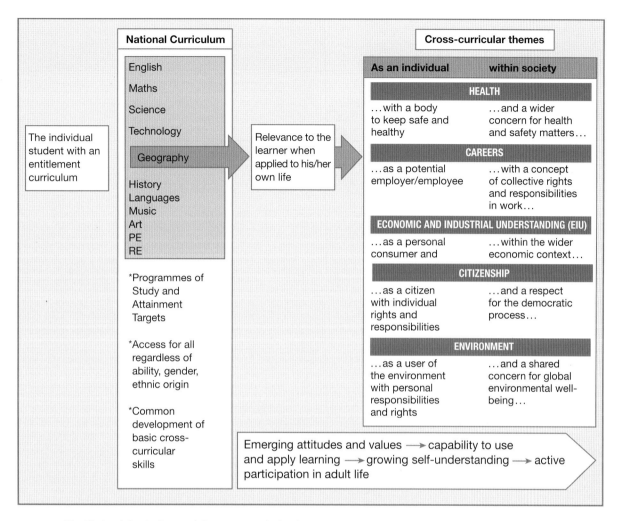

The individual student with an entitlement curriculum

National Curriculum

English
Maths
Science
Technology
Geography
History
Languages
Music
Art
PE
RE

*Programmes of Study and Attainment Targets

*Access for all regardless of ability, gender, ethnic origin

*Common development of basic cross-curricular skills

Relevance to the learner when applied to his/her own life

Cross-curricular themes

As an individual	within society
HEALTH	
…with a body to keep safe and healthy	…and a wider concern for health and safety matters…
CAREERS	
…as a potential employer/employee	…with a concept of collective rights and responsibilities in work…
ECONOMIC AND INDUSTRIAL UNDERSTANDING (EIU)	
…as a personal consumer and	…within the wider economic context…
CITIZENSHIP	
…as a citizen with individual rights and responsibilities	…and a respect for the democratic process…
ENVIRONMENT	
…as a user of the environment with personal responsibilities and rights	…and a shared concern for global environmental well-being…

Emerging attitudes and values ⟶ capability to use and apply learning ⟶ growing self-understanding ⟶ active participation in adult life

Figure 3: The National Curriculum and the cross-curricular themes

How can we contribute to the wider aims of education?

If we keep the learner's needs to the forefront in our planning we will present the prescribed content in such a way that pupils may apply and respond to it actively. One approach is to consider how in our geography lessons we can widen the range of questions that we encourage pupils to raise and pursue. I want to suggest three directions in which we might extend our enquiry questions.

1 QUESTIONING ONE'S VALUES AND ATTITUDES

All the Programmes of Study for geography stress the importance of the enquiry approach. If young people are to learn how to enquire about issues, questions and problems in geography, to consider a range of perspectives, and to think through their own position in relation to them, they need constant practice in their geography lessons. Questions which take pupils into describing and explaining activities are particularly important in developing geographical skills and understanding. Of equal importance, and far less explicit in the National Curriculum Order, are those questions which move pupils towards imagining, empathising, predicting, hypothesising, anticipating and responding. We need to challenge pupils to respond to questions such as:

- Why is this important to me?

- What would it be like if…?

- What is likely to happen?

- What would I like to happen?

- What do others think and feel about this?

- What do I think and feel about this?

- Why do I think this way?

- What can I do?

2 QUESTIONING ONE'S PLACE IN THE WORLD

An education for adult life must of necessity concern itself with the future. We have ample scope through the content of geography lessons to give pupils alternative outcomes and scenarios, both in relation to their known world, and through various scales of study. Most of the cross-curricular themes are essentially about educating for the future, and we need to encourage pupils to consider those aspects (political/social/environmental) of the future which are desirable and those which are not. They should also consider their capacity to influence and to act, both individually and collectively, at a variety of scales.

Our home address is a universal way of placing us all on earth. Each pupil has a name, and an address comprising dwelling, street, town, region and country. Beyond that our pupils are European citizens and will become increasingly conscious of this during their lifetime. Finally, and perhaps most importantly, they are global citizens. Each layer of the address represents the next larger tier of organisation and decision-making. At each level decisions are made which may affect us directly or indirectly. Equally we may make decisions (if only by voting) which may affect other people and places. Pupils, to be active citizens, will need some concept of their place within a global system and of how decisions are made and may be influenced at a variety of levels. We should encourage them not to accept the status quo, but to question, challenge and participate.

In exploring any issue it is worth asking:

- Who has the power in this situation and how will they use it?

- Who will decide?

- How will the decision be made?

- Who will gain or lose from the situation?

- How can the decision-making process be influenced?

- What can I do?

3 QUESTIONING FOR DEEPER UNDERSTANDING

Geographers are of course familiar with the compass rose. It is a basic tool of the subject, capable of use at any place and time to provide us with directions. The Development Education Centre in Birmingham (DEC, 1992) has explored the idea of a developmental compass rose (Figure 4) which, like its more familiar counterpart, may be set down over any place and used to enable the pupil to investigate the geographical features, processes and relationships at work in that location. The cardinal points of the developmental compass rose identify the natural, economic, social and political dimensions which may be pursued. Intervals between the cardinal points may explore the interface between (for example) the natural and economic dimensions. Such an approach is very versatile in widening the scope of an investigation and supporting pupils as they grapple with economic, political, social and environmental factors. It may be used with a photograph or other stimulus, in relation to a locality study, or as part of a theme investigation applied to a region or country. The rose also encourages the use of a similar set of questions as applied to a range of place studies, thus indirectly stressing the parallels that exist between people and geographical issues across the globe. It also enables pupils to approach issues in their own locality from perspectives gained by looking at the wider world. The range of questions, once internalised, may be reworked in relation to any new situation.

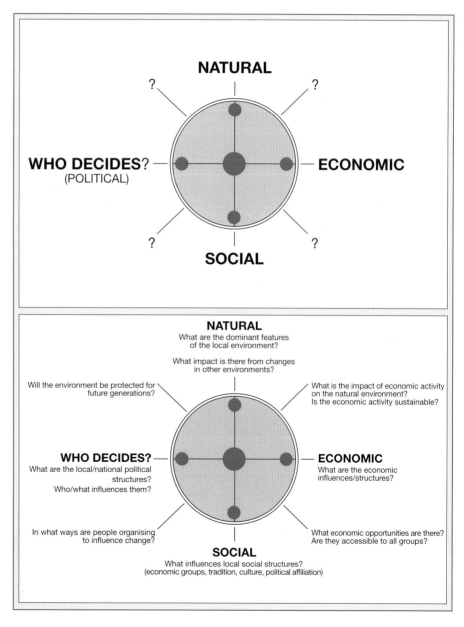

Figure 4: The developmental compass rose

Content and applications

In this part of the chapter, four of the five cross-curricular themes (see Figure 2) are considered in terms of their content and applications in geography. The fifth theme, careers education and guidance, is considered elsewhere (see Chapter 31). Each theme is explored in relation to the five Attainment Targets that were identified in the original (1991) geography National Curriculum which, although no longer specified in the curriculum, provide useful aids to planning.

Geography and education for citizenship

Society can only work to the benefit of everybody if all its members act with consideration towards others. The central message of geography is complementary: it is that all human beings are dependent upon one another because all share a globally inter-connected environment. What people do in one place may therefore affect people even in faraway places. An extreme case is the detonation of an atomic bomb in the atmosphere, which affects everyone on earth: we all breathe the same atmosphere and drink from one water supply. Geography also teaches the absolute dependence of everyone, even supermarket shoppers, upon the natural world and reminds us that the delicate balances of that world may easily be upset.

Both geography and citizenship education are ways of ordering a child's experience and drawing useful conclusions from that ordering. The very young child soon realises that the home environment is both social and spatial. (It is, of course, also set in time,

World citizens?
Photo: **Betty Press/ Panos Pictures**

and this realisation is the beginning of history). The spatial environment is found to have size, shape and boundaries and it has to be shared with others. Indeed, parts of it may be 'owned' by others, and others determine how the child may use different parts of space. Some places and areas prove more suitable than others for certain activities. So, gradually, the child's perceived environment takes shape and extends into the wider spaces beyond the family. Normally the child learns to live in this expanding environment with increasing freedom and independence; unless, that is, the environment is stultified by fear, hatred, disease, drought and famine, as it is for many children today.

In a well-ordered family the growing child learns lessons which also apply to global society: that if all members are to prosper they must practise give-and-take in the use of their resources, care and conservation rather than destructive exploitation of what is available, collaboration instead of unbridled competition. Help must be given if help is to be expected.

Together, geography and citizenship education teach us the conditions for a harmonious, humane family and for a harmonious, humane world.

GEOGRAPHICAL SKILLS

Specific geographical skills relate mainly to making, using and interpreting maps. There are also the skills of interpreting photographs and graphical presentations, linked with the handling of simple statistics. Maps are essential tools for making sense of social and economic information, in one's own town, for example. Some recent books on urban geography contain maps, tables of statistical data and photographs which make ideal starters for citizenship discussions. Topics such as the nature of inner city decline and possibilities for regeneration at once suggest themselves.

In addition, geography lessons make use of general learning skills (*Education for Citizenship*, NCC (1990), pp. 3-4). Investigatory and reporting skills are especially important, because geography is a 'finding out' subject. All geography begins with somebody, somewhere, going out to discover what some aspect of the world is like and why. The geographical approach is to observe, record, assemble information into usable forms, pose and test hypotheses, draw conclusions and present findings. This approach lies at the centre of geographical education and begins with the youngest children. Such investigatory methods give ample scope for collaborative work, the discussion of ideas and information and the development of oral, visual and written presentations – all citizenship skills.

PLACE KNOWLEDGE AND UNDERSTANDING
One very important purpose of geographical teaching is to ensure that young citizens leave school with a systematised knowledge of the configurations of their own country and of the world. They need an outline knowledge of their own country so they can decide where to look for work, where to try to locate a business, where to go for holidays. A basic knowledge of the relative positions, sizes, populations and resources of countries and continents of the world is part of the mental equipment of all competent citizens.

The requirement for good locational knowledge has intensified since the end of the Cold War because of the break-up of the political monoliths into small units, each pursuing its own policies. Situations which call for citizens to respond in informed ways to world events appear likely to multiply, as United Nations interventions increase and become ever more costly. One important task for geographers is to provide these citizens with an accurate and up-to-date information base.

PHYSICAL GEOGRAPHY
Citizens of an urban society urgently need reminding that *all* world citizens, whether desert nomads, traditional farmers or city dwellers, depend absolutely upon the atmosphere, soils, water and the 'web of life' for their very existence. Studies in natural geography are an essential foundation for learning and teaching about the world of people.

HUMAN GEOGRAPHY
Human geography explores the ways in which human beings occupy and use the earth's surface. They also consider the migration of people within and between countries and continents and the consequences of such migrations. Ways of forging links with citizenship studies abound in all these topics; for example, almost any industrial study will bring out Britain's dependence upon selling goods and services abroad, while studies of British farming will show that subsidies determine land use, rather than soil quality and climate. Citizens need to know these facts.

Human geography offers many opportunities for investigations by individuals and groups, for debates and the arguing of cases, for the preparing of reports and the evaluating of evidence. Inevitably it raises ethical questions about what is being done.

ENVIRONMENTAL GEOGRAPHY
Human studies are linked with the natural world through environmental studies. These show how attempts to intervene in natural environments have to take proper account of the processes at work in the natural world, otherwise disaster may ensue. Examples of such induced disasters include the creation of 'dust bowls' in North America and Central Asia and the drying out of the Aral Sea through ill-judged irrigation schemes.

The modern industrial world can cause environmental damage on an unprecedented scale. If citizens are to press their governments to put matters right, they have to understand what responsible environmental management entails – and be ready to pay for it. Here the lessons of citizenship and geography are complementary.

The Aral 'Sea' dried out through environmental mis-management

Photo: **Marcus Rose/ Panos Pictures**

Geography and health education

Some parts of the world are healthier than others; some of its 5.3 billion people enjoy better health than others. People's states of health and un-health powerfully affect their actions and their relationships with others; this is as true of nations as of individuals. Because geography attempts to explain human actions, it follows that studies of health and un-health and their causes must be included in geographical research and teaching.

Attempts to account for the distributions and areal variations of phenomena over the earth's surface, including those of health and un-health, lead into studies of the complicated and finely-balanced relationships which exist between human actions, the conditions and processes of the natural world and the economic, social, political and other environments which human beings generate for themselves. These environmental unravellings show, more often than not, that relationships between the quality and resource endowments of natural environments and the well-being of their inhabitants are extremely indirect. Economic and political considerations commonly intervene, so that some naturally well-endowed areas exhibit wretched living and working conditions (Britain's rich coalfields in the nineteenth century were an example; the Silesian coalfields are another) while areas with difficult environments and few natural resources may achieve extremely high standards of income and well-being. In the modern world, Japan is surely the prime example of such an achievement. Its resources consist almost entirely of an ingenious and industrious people and a culture which supports hard work. Most material resources have to be shipped in from overseas.

Geography is full of opportunities for exploring relationships between health and other aspects of human activity, and despite the many problems it reveals, the geography of health is a hopeful study, reminding us that health is a normal state: that everyone could have it. Unfortunately, it also demonstrates why they do not: that poverty, bad government, exploitation, greed and war are far more potent causes of un-health than difficult natural environments. Above all it is a call to action, an appeal to the young to go out and do more to secure good health for all than their elders have managed to do.

Coal mining is still unhealthy, dirty and dangerous

Engraving: **Mary Evans Pictures**

GEOGRAPHICAL SKILLS

For more than a century, mapping skills have been applied to medical research, and are useful aids to the teaching of many health-related topics. The mapping of information about health and disease probably began in Britain with John Snow's demonstration that cholera was transmitted by infected water (Snow, 1855). Since that time, similar techniques have been used with much success to help isolate the causes and methods of transmission of diseases in many parts of the world (see Jarcho, 1970).

A National Curriculum geography course can include the mapping of many kinds of health-related information in the local area, town and region. Possible enquiries include the distribution of open spaces in towns offering fresh air, exercise and safe places for children to play. Environmental assessment mapping can reveal and quantify variations in healthful and harmful conditions between one street and another, or one district and another. Maps of pedestrian and traffic density can show up planning problems and perhaps suggest possible solutions. Heavy concentrations of walkers, cars and lorries in the same streets can be unhealthy, uncomfortable and dangerous.

At the wider scales of country, Europe and world, levels-of-health maps can give a very instructive and thought-provoking picture of the general well-being (and otherwise) of the human race. Examples of such maps are to be found in good school atlases. They include those which show levels of national income, nutrition, clean water provision; numbers of doctors per thousand of the population; proportion of national income spent on health; and so on.

PLACE KNOWLEDGE AND UNDERSTANDING

Links between 'place' studies and health education can be made by asking questions about any place being studied such as:

- What conditions make some places healthier than others?
- Are these conditions natural, or are they mainly produced by people?
- Which places and areas are more or less healthy and why?
- How can unhealthy conditions be improved and why is this not always done?

PHYSICAL GEOGRAPHY

An understanding of how the natural world 'works' is basic to an understanding of human activities which relate to health and well-being. The life-sustaining and health-giving processes of the natural world are founded on the hydrological cycle, the continuous exchange of energy and water between atmosphere, ocean and all living things. Good health can only be maintained by keeping this circulating water clean and its supply uninterrupted.

Undertaking a local survey of water movements on and beneath the surface and of actual and possible causes of pollution is a compelling way of introducing a unit in physical geography, and it offers many opportunities for health issues to be discussed.

HUMAN GEOGRAPHY

Human geography brings in ideas and information about population, levels of urbanisation, migration (and it may be noted that there are more than 20 million enforced migrants and displaced persons in today's world); also about resources and their use, about farming, industry, power supplies, trade and other kinds of exchange. By relating this information to natural environments it is possible to construct an 'identikit' of healthy, and what may be termed optimistic, locations and to compare this ideal model with selected places, near home and further afield.

ENVIRONMENTAL GEOGRAPHY

Studies in environmental geography pull physical and human themes together and remind us, once again, that the well-being, even the survival, of the human race depends upon our maintaining the health of the paper-thin life-layer at the earth's surface within which we live: the atmosphere, oceans, soils, plants, animals and other living creatures which comprise the biosphere. Pupils can discuss developments which may upset the fine balances within the life-layer, such as atmospheric pollution and the poisoning of lakes and even whole seas, such as the Black Sea. A less obvious cause for concern, but an excellent topic for study, is the impact of mass tourism caused by the jumbo jet, perhaps to be superseded soon by the giant super-jumbo, if indeed any nation or international consortium can afford to build it.

In his novel *Paradise News* (1991), David Lodge reminded us that 'tourism is wearing out the planet'. Mass tourism has brought intolerable pressures to bear upon once isolated places and communities, with profound consequences for the health and well-being of individuals and groups. The island of Grand Canary is a case in point. A huge increase in tourist numbers to this small, mountainous island has caused whole new towns to be built in a desert environment, water supplies to be depleted and agriculture to be abandoned. Workers have moved to the towns, usually to find poor housing, menial work or – all too often – unemployment.

Mass tourism is drying out Gran Canaria, an island in desert latitudes

Photo: **A. Garrido/ Spanish Tourist Office**

Geography and the development of environmental understanding

Geographers are concerned with the mechanisms and interacting processes of the world's natural systems, and also with the means by which human beings adapt the natural world to suit their own purposes. Today, human activity is shaped mainly by the environments which humans themselves generate, notably their social, economic, political and cultural systems. These systems operate at every scale, from that of the home and immediate locality to the global marketplace.

World thematic maps in atlases are a particularly rich source of environmental information which can give substance to discussion about environmental issues, as are larger-scale maps, such as the OS 1:50 000 series. Such maps attempt to portray complete landscapes, that is everything one can see in a given area of the earth's surface.

It is illuminating to think of a familiar countryside as a kind of precipitate, in the chemical sense, of natural and human events and processes, past and present. In the countryside of lowland England, for example, we see a landscape of hedged fields, the result of enclosures in the eighteenth and nineteenth century; this is now being transformed in many areas into the hedgeless landscapes of highly capitalised, highly mechanised commercial farming. There is also set-aside land, caused by over-production and paid for by subsidies from the European Union. Industry too leaves its mark of change in the form of new and old quarries and mines, power stations, factories and areas of derelict land. The imprints of old and new transport systems are to be seen almost everywhere.

With the help of maps, landscapes can be 'read' as documents. They are the ultimate source materials for environmental education.

GEOGRAPHICAL SKILLS

School geography develops the skills of observing and recording information out-of-doors. Much of this recording takes the form of maps. Environmental education also begins with observation, usually in the local area. Methods of recording and presenting information and ideas are common to both kinds of study.

Local surveys which sharpen pupils' observations of environmental quality are very important. It is easy to take familiar environments for granted, as being 'normal'. It is the business of the geographer to help children look afresh at their surroundings

Local fieldwork is often a way into global studies

Photo: **Helen Sail**

and encourage them to ask questions about what they see around them. This kind of enquiry can lead into discussions about who might make improvements; pupils could also explore the ways in which local residents or shoppers may be able to influence those responsible for the local environment. It may be found that environmental issues in the wider world are echoed in the local area: effective traffic management is a global problem, yet local aspects are eminently mappable at the school gates. At continental or world scales some recently published atlases provide a wealth of information and ideas for environmental enquiry.

PLACE KNOWLEDGE AND UNDERSTANDING

Places *are* environments. An important purpose of geographical education is to help young people build up a bank of accurate information about where places are and what they are like. Such information is part of the essential framework within which environmental issues can be discussed constructively.

No environmental issue is *exclusively* local; they all have to be examined in wider contexts. Thus, for example, a debate about the expansion of roadstone quarrying in an area has to take account of the distribution of suitable rocks locally and further afield, and the relative costs, advantages and disadvantages of developing the various sources. A file of press cuttings can be built up on such a topic, which might also be studied through fieldwork.

PHYSICAL GEOGRAPHY

For many town dwellers, the natural environment is hidden beneath buildings and streets. Another important purpose of geographical education is to restore the visibility of the natural world.

One useful way of attempting this is to investigate local relief and drainage patterns and their relationship to building. Most towns and villages were originally located and have developed in response to relief and drainage features. In all but the flattest towns there are perceptible variations in height and slope which can be used to trace the courses of streams, even when these have been piped. Street names, such as Brook Street and Hill Street, large scale maps, aerial photographs, old editions of OS maps, interviews with residents can all help with this fascinating detective work.

HUMAN GEOGRAPHY

The most influential environments today are human organisations. A striking illustration of this is provided by the Russian aluminium industry. In 1995, workers' life-expectancy in this industry was about 47 years. Their living and working conditions were appalling. The aluminium they produced was sold on the world market at about half the price of the next-cheapest producers, Australia, Canada and Venezuela. Yet even these countries were low-cost producers compared with Britain, Germany, the United States and Spain. The Russian industry's effective environment was its country's absolute need to obtain 'hard' currency at almost any human and environmental cost.

ENVIRONMENTAL GEOGRAPHY

A powerful idea to be developed through studies in combined human and physical geography is that of intervention. Human life itself is an intervention in natural systems. Merely by eating, drinking, requiring clothes and shelter and producing wastes, even one family or one small village makes demands upon and modifies the natural world. How much greater is the impact of a growing megalopolis such as Mexico City, predicted to reach a population of 25 million by 2020!

There are many other kinds of intervention. Building on former farmland produces an instantaneous run-off of precipitation into local rivers, exacerbating flood control problems. The replacement of natural vegetation by crops over most of the habitable earth has led to a dramatic decline in biodiversity with unknown long-term effects. Burning fossil fuels produces toxic discharges into the atmosphere which may contribute to the 'greenhouse effect' and result in acid rain.

Geography and education for economic and industrial understanding

Much of geography is concerned with economic affairs; that is, with how people make their living in the world's mosaic of natural and human-made environments. Economic maps in atlases are invaluable sources of information and ideas for devising lessons about how economic theories relate to commercial practice in the real world.

Much 'pure' economic discussion takes insufficient account of environmental conditions; yet to be successful, the manufacturer, the marketing director, the would-be investor or the banker have to know what social, economic and political conditions obtain in any area where it is proposed to do business. Similarly, it is essential to be properly informed about natural and part-natural conditions, such as a chronic water shortage; or the probability of war or civil disturbance.

An out-of-town shopping centre: a microcosm of world economics?

Photo: **Meadowhall**

GEOGRAPHICAL SKILLS

All economic information can be mapped, and all competent school atlases include a selection of economic and economics-related maps. The explanation of these maps can provide many good geography lessons.

Economic mapping can often begin locally. As part of the process of analysing local geography, it may be possible to map the locations and distributions of different retail outlets, of manufacturing and commercial enterprises and of empty properties. Movements of people, traffic and goods can be mapped, showing perhaps the relative accessibility of different parts of a town to heavy goods vehicles, cars and people dependent upon public transport. The internal geography of out-of-town shopping centres can teach lessons about the selection of the most advantageous sites by the richest companies; overtones here of international economics.

Economics-related world maps are particularly important educationally because they remind us that, increasingly, our economic community is world-wide. Among the very important world maps young people need to encounter as part of their general education are those which show population numbers and trends and world food supplies. Both have massive implications for the changing balance of political power between countries.

PLACE KNOWLEDGE AND UNDERSTANDING

An account of the geography of any place will include references to how its people make their living. The geography National Curriculum requires the study of a representative selection of places, showing how people live and work in different parts of the world and in 'developed' and 'less-developed' countries.

A useful teaching device is to think of places as locations for future development, asking questions like:

- What do people do there now?

- Could new things be done, and is it likely that they will be?

- Who is likely to invest capital or establish new industries or services in this location?

- Why may they be attracted to do so?

- Do local people benefit from what is done there now, and is it likely that they would benefit from new developments?

- Why should we be interested in what happens in this place?

- If *we* had money to invest, would we invest it in this place, and for what purposes?

PHYSICAL GEOGRAPHY

All economic action involves interventions in natural systems, as for example when forests are cut down in a river basin and soil erosion and flooding follow. Before intervening in any natural system it is highly desirable to discover how it works. This is why the study of physical geography is so important, especially in a society which sometimes acts as though the natural world had been reduced to insignificance. The fundamental importance of the hydrological cycle has already been mentioned; despite our rapidly growing global population and the need for industrial development, we have to find ways of not polluting our water supply. Pollution results from industrial discharges into rivers, seas and the atmosphere; intensive farming leaks pesticides into rivers; raw sewage damages fragile environments.

Technically it is perfectly possible to eliminate most causes of pollution, but it is not cheap. If people understood the damage caused by pollution, they might be willing to pay to have things put right. Studies in physical geography may help develop this essential understanding.

HUMAN GEOGRAPHY

Geography highlights the complicated relationships between human behaviour and the natural world of nature, emphasising that every human activity has its cost. Often, those costs are borne by somebody else.

Population increase in Nepal provides an example. As population in the Himalayan valleys increases, cultivation terraces are pushed higher and higher up the mountainsides. Productivity declines with altitude, so each extension uphill produces proportionately less food. To make the new terraces trees are felled, leaving the soil liable to erosion. Soil begins to slide downhill, reducing upland productivity still further

Himalayan rains flood Bangladesh. Natural events and processes ignore national boundaries

Photo: **Trygve Bølstad/ Panos Pictures**

and clogging the rivers with silt. Further downstream in Bangladesh, where population growth has forced people onto low-lying land, flooding results.

The most fertile areas of the earth have long since been fully populated, and population growth pushes poorer and poorer land into food production. Further extensions will be technically difficult and expensive. Geography reminds us that increasingly there is only one economic world; large aircraft, bulk carriers and electronic communications have contracted the once-great distances. This contraction has caused its own tensions. For example, workers in the South China growth pole of Hong Kong-Shenzhen-Guangzhou receive about one-fifth of the wages customarily paid in Western Europe, but their factories are only 24 hours' flying time from Western markets. Barriers between low- and high-wage areas are breaking down. How will Western wage levels respond to one-world competition?

Geographical studies also bring out the uncertainty of economic planning, if only because natural events cannot be predicted for certain. Nobody can forecast a harvest precisely, therefore nobody can know the price of coffee next year. Equally unpredictable and perhaps more powerful in shaping the economic fortunes of countries is what Dennis Healey (1989) referred to as the 'atomic cloud' of footloose money which is moved around the world by international investors in pursuit of the highest dividends. To ignore the role of these vast sums when discussing any aspect of national or international economics is unrealistic, even at the elementary levels of the National Curriculum. Young people should at least know about the causes of our uncertainties in the economic field.

ENVIRONMENTAL GEOGRAPHY

Environmental impact studies offer many opportunities for broadening young people's understanding of economic and industrial matters; and especially for reminding them of the fact that few people act at any time from purely economic motives. Alternative uses of resources and opportunities, and conflicts of interest – all normal facts of life – emerge from environmental impact studies, as for example when discussing the pros and cons of china clay extraction and army battle training in the Dartmoor National Park.

Impact studies and associated environmental quality studies may be developed at all scales, beginning with the local and immediate. Examples might range from discussions of the probable effects on traffic of pedestrianising a local street, through attempted evaluations of the effects on London and south-east England of the Channel Tunnel road and rail links, to considerations of such long-term, global questions as 'What might be the effects of a major earthquake in Tokyo on the world's economic systems?' or 'Will Australia be a Japanese economic colony a quarter of a century from now?'

Conclusion

Half a century ago, in *For Whom the Bell Tolls*, Ernest Hemingway predicted that the evil powers unleashed in the Spanish Civil War would shortly pursue their ambitions on a wider stage; and that therefore what was happening to Spain was the whole world's concern. So it turned out to be. Hemingway prefaced his book with a quotation from John Donne:

> 'No man is an *Iland*, intire of it selfe;
> every man is a peece of the *Continent*,
> a part of the *maine*...any mans *death* diminishes *me*,
> because I am involved in *Mankinde*...'

The one-ness of humanity is the central message of geography and of the four cross-curricular themes discussed here. Whatever we do is liable to affect somebody else; what others do will almost certainly affect us. This is also a central message of religious education, with which both geography and the four themes have close and compelling links.

References and further reading

Archer, M. (1991) *Aspects of Applied Geography: Development and Health.* Hodder and Stoughton.

DEC (1992) *Developing Geography.*

Dorling, D. (1995) *A New Social Atlas of Britain.* Wiley.

Edwards, J. & Fogelman, K. (eds) (1993) *Developing Citizenship in the Curriculum.* David Fulton.

Goodall, S. (ed) (1994) *Developing Environmental Education in the Curriculum.* David Fulton.

Harrison, J. & Edwards, J. (eds) (1994) *Developing Health Education in the Curriculum.* David Fulton.

Healey, D. (1989) *The Time of my Life.* Penguin.

Jarcho, S. (1970) 'Yellow fever, cholera and the beginning of medical cartography', *Journal of the History of Medicine and Allied Sciences*, 25, 131-42.

Kerr, D. (ed) (1994) *Developing Economic and Industrial Understanding in the Curriculum.* David Fulton.

Kidron, M. & Segal, R. (1987) *The New State of the World Atlas.* Pan Books.

Mackay, J. (1993) *The State of Health Atlas.* Simon and Schuster.

NCC (1989) *Circular 6: The National Curriculum and Whole-Curriculum Planning.*

NCC (1990) *Curriculum Guidance 3: The Whole Curriculum.*

NCC (1990) *Curriculum Guidance 4: Education for Economic and Industrial Understanding.*

NCC (1990) *Curriculum Guidance 5: Health Education.*

NCC (1990) *Curriculum Guidance 6: Careers Education and Guidance.*

NCC (1990) *Curriculum Guidance 7: Environmental Education.*

NCC (1990) *Curriculum Guidance 8: Education for Citizenship.*

Rawling, E. (1991) 'Geography and cross-curricular themes', *Teaching Geography*, 16, 4, pp. 147-154.

SCAA (1996) *SCAA Discussion Papers: No. 6. Education for Adult Life. The Spiritual and Moral Development of Young People.* SCAA.

Snow, J. (1855) (2nd edition) *On the Mode of Communication of Cholera.* Churchill. British Library reference: BL 7560 and 67.

Chapter 3

Education without prejudice

HAZEL BARRETT

What is equal opportunity?

Until recently the terms 'equal opportunity' and 'multicultural education' were buzz words within the teaching profession. 'Equal opportunity' dealt with gender, whilst 'multicultural education' dealt with race and ethnicity. However, this distinction excludes considerations such as ability/disability, socio-economic background and age, and considerable evidence exists to show that a broader definition is justified.

> i   Social origins strongly affect life chances. The *Times Education Supplement* in 1990 reported that 57% of the population are working class, but only 18% of university students are working class. Of course the term 'working class' needs clarification, but such statistics – however crude – raise serious concerns.
>
> ii In many curriculum subjects girls out-perform boys, and in the traditional 'male' subjects of science and computing they are catching up. Yet their achievements in the workplace do not yet reflect this progress.
>
> iii The Swann Report *Education for all* (1985) produced evidence that, as a group, children of West Indian origin were achieving at lower levels than their white peers.
>
> iv The Fish Report *Educational opportunities for all* (1985) gave evidence that many children continued to be educationally disadvantaged because of disabilities.
>
> Source: Staffordshire Education Authority, no date

Harvesting rice – over 70% of Africa's food is produced by women
Photo: **Tony Binns**

Geography as a subject area, with people as its focus, has unrivalled potential for breaking down prejudices, questioning stereotypes and broadening cultural understanding. The wide range of geographical studies, from global to local level, should give the subject a head start in terms of providing equal educational opportunities.

This chapter will first examine the legal framework for equal opportunities in education, then the responsibilities of schools and teachers, and then explore issues such as language and stereotypes. Finally, teaching strategies, resources and assessment will be evaluated in terms of their contribution to the equal provision of geographical education.

The legislative framework

A number of Acts of Parliament provide for equal opportunities for pupils in our schools. Under the terms of the Sex Discrimination Act (1975) and Race Relations Act (1976), schools have a duty to ensure that facilities for education are provided without sexual or racial discrimination. The Education Acts (1944, 1981, 1986), the Education Reform Act (1988) and the Children Act (1989) state that pupils are entitled to efficient full-time education suitable for their ages, abilities and aptitudes. Children are also entitled to receive help for any special educational needs they may have.

The Education Act (1944) imposes a duty on local authorities to ensure that children receive education in accordance with their age, ability and aptitude.

The Education Act (1981) outlines the duty of authorities to identify and assess the special educational needs of those pupils for whom they have a responsibility. The Act also directs that children and young people with special educational needs should be educated in mainstream education where appropriate.

The Education (No. 2) Act (1986) sets out the role of governors in admissions and exclusions, and the constitution, powers and duties of governing bodies. This includes the power to co-opt members of the local community: this could include women, disabled people and members of minority ethnic groups. Section 44 of the Act also forbids partisan political activities and views in schools.

The Education Reform Act (1988) affirms that every pupil registered in maintained schools, including maintained special schools, is entitled to a balanced and broadly based curriculum which:

a   promotes the spiritual, moral, cultural, mental and physical development of pupils at the school and of society; and

b   prepares such pupils for the opportunities, responsibilities and experiences of adult life.

The Sex Discrimination Act (1975) makes it unlawful to discriminate directly or indirectly on the grounds of sex or marital status, or to apply requirements or conditions which have a disproportionately disadvantageous effect on people of a particular sex or marital status where this cannot be justified.

The Race Relations Act (1976) makes it unlawful to discriminate directly or indirectly on the grounds of colour, race, nationality, (including citizenship) or ethnic or national origin, or to apply requirements or conditions which have a disproportionately disadvantageous effect on people of a particular racial group, and which cannot be justified on non-racial grounds.

The Children Act (1989) requires local authorities to meet the needs of children defined as being in need. This Act has important implications for questions of equality of opportunity; Section 22, for example, refers to 'the race, religion, culture and language of the child' in determining care.

The Education Act (1993) also makes substantial amendments to exclusion laws following disquiet about the number of pupils, especially black pupils, on indefinite exclusion.

Figure 1: Legislation relating directly to equal opportunities in education. Source: Ensuring Equality in Staffordshire Schools

By law, therefore, schools are responsible for ensuring equal opportunities in the classroom. Along with the local education authority (LEA), schools must ensure that all pupils, whatever their ability, ethnicity, gender or social background, have access to the curriculum and that their progress is commensurate with their abilities. Schools must also meet the requirements of the Sex Discrimination Act (1975) and Race Relations Act (1976). At the present time British schools are not covered by any European Union directives on equal opportunities.

Responsibilities of schools and teachers

All education is an exercise in the elimination of prejudice

Photo: **Sally and Richard Greenhill**

The law is in place to ensure equal opportunities for all pupils in British schools, and it is the responsibility of schools and individual teachers to ensure that the law is upheld. To this end, the Office for Standards in Education (OFSTED) recommends that schools should have a clear policy on equal opportunities. This helps protect both pupils and teachers. The OFSTED evaluation criteria are as follows:

i)   All pupils, irrespective of gender, ability (including giftedness), ethnicity and social circumstances have access to the curriculum and make the greatest possible progress.

ii) The school meets the requirements of the Sex Discrimination Act (1975) and the Race Relations Act (1976).

Source: Staffordshire Education Authority

Whatever the age of pupils and the composition of the school population, all schools need equal opportunities policies. Different schools approach equal opportunities in different ways, some embracing all areas in the same policy, others focusing on one at a time. The basic components of such a policy are shown in Figure 2.

Schools and teachers should strive to:

1   Address and remove obstacles which prevent pupils and pupils from gaining access to appropriate learning opportunities and benefiting from them.

2   Offer a curriculum which is free from the stereotypes which can lead to low or restricted expectations, prejudice or discrimination, and which recognises, celebrates and values all cultures in the community.

3   Take positive action on behalf of those who begin from a disadvantaged position or under-achieve.

4   Conduct affairs in ways which positively assert people's rights to equality of consideration and opportunity.

Figure 2: Principal components of a school-based equal opportunities policy.
Source: Guidance for equal opportunities, Support and Advisory Service, City of Coventry

If an equal opportunities policy is to be accepted in a constructive and positive way extensive consultation is essential: parents, pupils, governors, teachers and the LEA must all be involved in the process. Once agreed, the policy document should be practical, realistic and drafted in terms that everyone can understand. A policy document composed of jargon will alienate some and amuse others: either result is counter-productive. Once a policy has been adopted teachers, parents and pupils should be made aware of it, with copies freely available. It may be appropriate for the policy document to be published in more than one language, depending on local circumstances and needs.

Words alone do not ensure equal opportunities. Although many schools already have an equal opportunities policy, they do not always produce satisfactory practice. The HMI Annual Report on Education in England (1990-91) states: 'Progress on equal opportunities is best described as patchy. In some schools awareness of the take-up of educational opportunities as between the sexes and among ethnic minority groups is high; in others it is totally inadequate. Most institutions have policies for promoting equality of opportunity but too often the gap between policy and practice is unacceptably wide.' (paragraph 28). The successful implementation of an equal opportunities policy within a school depends upon the active co-operation of everybody in the management hierarchy, from the head to the classroom teacher; each

Management role	Responsibilities with equal opportunities implications
Headteacher	Implementation and evaluation of Equal Opportunities Policy Resource allocation Staff development
e.g. when planning capital expenditure, are the needs of pupils with disabilities and learning difficulties considered?	
Senior management	Deployment of staff and resources Monitoring the curriculum Assessment and record keeping Groupings of pupils Cross-curricular skills and themes
e.g. How often is a curriculum audit undertaken with regard to equal opportunities issues and does it inform the Equal Opportunities Action Plan?	
Head of department/curriculum leader	Teaching groups Learning structures Resources Assessment Time management
e.g. Is time allocated within the training programme for equal opportunities issues to be discussed?	
Teacher	Teaching styles Organisation of classroom materials, space and time Resources Classroom relationships
e.g. Does the teacher encourage pupils to discuss issues of gender, ethnicity and disability?	

Figure 3: School management roles with respect to equal opportunities issues. Source: Guidance for equal opportunities, Support and Advisory Service, City of Coventry

member of staff has a different contribution to make. Figure 3 illustrates the responsibility of the different management roles for the successful implementation of an equal opportunities policy.

Once in place, an equal opportunities policy must be monitored regularly and a report on equal opportunities progress should be included in the school's annual report to parents, governors and the LEA. Where practice is unsatisfactory, under-achievement will be evident: in such circumstances managers must ensure that resources are made available to help remedy the situation.

Language, stereotypes and role models

LANGUAGE

Language is the most powerful means of conveying attitudes and values, and as such is crucial to equality of opportunity.

Clearly the most important way of communicating concepts and ideas in the classroom is by word of mouth. The misuse of language, whether intentionally or not, can distort reality, convey stereotyped images and ultimately reinforce prejudice. Mental images, once formed, are very hard to replace or alter: it is very important, therefore, to use words that do not stereotype or give biased images.

One example is the term 'man', commonly used in geography in the 'man and environment' era of the 1970s. Research has shown that gender-specific terms such as 'man' are rarely interpreted generically, and most people do not appreciate that the male form may include the female form. The use of such language, often labelled 'sexist', reflects and reinforces sex-role stereotypes. The use of 'man' as a generic term is ambiguous and can convey an implicit message that women are of secondary importance – as, for instance, in the term 'man and wife', which implies differences in the freedom and activities of each and may prompt the reader to evaluate the roles inappropriately. Thus 'husband and wife' and 'man and woman' are preferable in this case; in other contexts the terms 'people', 'humankind' or 'human beings' avoid introducing negative images of women. It is important therefore to monitor our own use of language to ensure that we are not inadvertently conveying incorrect or negative images to pupils (source: *The Psychologist*, 1988).

It is also important that our teaching reflects the changing nature of society. For example, we should question the use of the word 'housewife' to identify an occupation. It is a term that indicates sex and marital status and excludes men. Yet many men are in fact 'homemakers'. Likewise many men engage in 'parenting' or 'nurturing', rendering the word 'mothering' inappropriate in many domestic situations in the 1990s.

Language can also be racist. Styles and preferences for nouns referring to ethnic groups may change; in some cases, even members of the same group disagree about the preferred name at any given time. Teachers should try to ascertain the most acceptable current terms and use them. It is also important to avoid language that suggests evaluation of one culture against an assumed universal standard; better to compare two or more groups of cultures or cultural groups, rather than judging each against a standard. Avoid the negative connotations of the term 'non-white'; be positive and use terms such as 'black' or 'British Asian'.

The avoidance of language misuse has been encouraged by the Institute of British Geographers, which in June 1989 published 'Guidelines for the use of non-sexist language' in *AREA*. This was followed up in December 1991 with a discussion of the British Sociological Association's draft guidelines on anti-racist language. Some examples of commonly used words and phrases with non-biased alternatives are given in Figure 4 (*AREA*, 1989, 1991).

An issue that teachers have to deal with daily is the misuse of language by pupils. The above principles should apply to pupils as well as to teachers. The use of language should be openly discussed in the classroom, and teachers should give reasons for any corrections. Teachers should also discourage the use of discriminatory and abusive language such as 'spastic', 'Paki', and 'slag' by pupils. Schools should have procedures for dealing with racist, sexist, ignorant or insensitive comments and actions made by pupils, and all staff, both teaching and non-teaching, should be aware of these procedures.

Teachers should be aware of the home language of pupils and able to pronounce pupils' names correctly. The value of bi-lingualism should be recognised; at the same time, support in English should be given to those who need it.

man, mankind	people, humanity, human beings
manpower	workforce, personnel
man-made	artificial, synthetic
foreman, postman, policeman	supervisor, postal worker, police officer
handicapped	disabled
coloured	black people, British Asians
native	native born
host society	industrial society

Figure 4: Examples of biased terms, plus alternative terms which communicate accurate unbiased information. Source: AREA, 1989, 1991

STEREOTYPES
It is important to avoid perpetuating incorrect or out-dated stereotypes in the classroom; rather, we should give pupils positive role models to emulate. Displays and resources should contain positive, non-stereotypical and challenging images in relation to gender, ethnicity, nationality, culture, disability, age and religion.

Teaching strategies

How the curriculum is delivered in the classroom has a direct impact on equality of opportunity. Girls have better verbal and written skills, whereas boys do better with practical and technical tasks. Boys are more confident in the classroom and often overestimate their abilities, whereas girls work harder both in class and at home but are often less confident. These rather general and simplistic differences are, however, complicated by culture, disability and social background. People from ethnic minority groups and children with disabilities consistently have low personal esteem and academic confidence. There is also evidence that many children from lower social classes under-achieve (Gold, 1995). To meet all these different needs a variety of teaching styles and approaches should be adopted.

The classroom should be managed in such a way that all pupils feel engaged in learning and are all motivated to persevere and contribute. The teacher should foster a positive atmosphere of mutual respect and trust amongst pupils. Teaching styles should aim to motivate pupils and give them a sense of personal worth by drawing on their own personal experience. Practical tasks and activities, objects and artefacts, pictorial and visual materials and pupils' work are all valuable when introduced at appropriate times. Access should also be provided via a range of languages or means of communication, both verbal and non-verbal, to help bi-lingual pupils explore and express ideas.

Geography, with its fieldwork, maps and IT-based practicals, role play exercises as well as traditional verbal and writing components, is ideally placed to foster equal opportunities in terms of teaching variety. However, these activities must be carefully planned to ensure equal opportunities.

FIELDWORK

Are all pupils able to get first hand experience through fieldwork? How do we ensure disabled children get the most from fieldwork? How do we ensure that girls from some ethnic minorities can participate, especially in residential field classes? Do we ensure that pupils, especially teenage girls, are given enough 'comfort stops' whilst in the field? Do we use a variety of techniques to bring out the best in all pupils?

PRACTICAL WORK AND IT

Traditionally, boys perform well on practical tasks and IT, although girls are catching up, if not overtaking, boys in some of these areas (Gold, 1995). How do we ensure that girls receive encouragement and gain confidence with practical tasks and modern technology without neglecting the needs of boys? How do we ensure that disabled pupils are given access to these resources? Can we ensure that pupils from poorer homes have access to IT facilities out of school hours?

ROLE PLAY EXERCISES

Many role play exercises have been heavily criticised for their use of gender based stereotypes (Connolly, 1993). How do we select groups for these exercises? How do we ensure that disabled pupils participate? How do we encourage respect for alternative views?

WRITTEN AND VERBAL COMPONENTS

In general, girls out-perform boys in written and verbal skills. How can we encourage boys to do better? Do we provide extra classes for under-achievers? Do we provide support for bi-lingual children? How can we help all pupils fulfil their potential? Some schools have tried quite radical and controversial methods (Gold, 1995).

There are no simple answers to these questions, but an awareness that such issues must be addressed is an essential beginning. Each teacher needs to consider the relationship of the school's equal opportunities policy to all areas of classroom practice, and teaching and learning strategies should be selected to ensure that all pupils are able to reach their full potential.

Resources

The content of resources, the way they are used and pupil access to them can have a direct impact on pupils' learning experiences and their views of the outside world. Resources should be deployed as equitably as possible, for example by band, set or age-group. A school's resources should reflect its equal opportunities policy and should therefore be as free as possible from bias and stereotyping.

TEXTBOOKS

Much progress has been made since the publication in 1984 of the report of a working party on sexism in geography (*LEA Geography Bulletin* number 19). This report found that 'geography books, almost without exception, displayed some degree of sexist bias. In some cases the bias displayed is so great as to appear almost wilful'. It went on: 'More recent texts show some attempt to reduce or eliminate sexist bias, at least as far as language is concerned [although] the situation regarding illustrations and roles in which women are portrayed is less encouraging' (quoted in Connolly, 1993). In a more recent survey of thirteen National Curriculum textbooks for key stage 3 (Connolly, 1993) it was found that the issue of sexist and ethnically biased *language* was at least being addressed: analysis of the *illustrations,* however, was less encouraging. Of the 430 photographs that showed people, 51% featured males or were mixed with males dominant, 21% showed females or were mixed with females dominant, and 28% were mixed with neither dominant. There were very few photographs of British black women or girls. There were many positive images of women and girls which challenged the common stereotypes; however, more positive images of groups of people who are marginalised or discriminated against is needed.

We must be alert to bias in textbooks, and look into the reasons for it. For example, who wrote the book? Who collected the figures? For what purpose? Who took the picture? Who edited it?, etc. A matrix for this purpose is given in Figure 5. It is equally important to make sure that pupils are aware of any bias in textbooks; they could be asked to carry out their own appraisal of materials based on a simplified version of the matrix. This would help them to recognise and challenge bias for themselves.

Title:			Publisher:			ISBN:	
(1) AUTHOR(S)	SEX:		EDITION DATE:				
(2) ILLUSTRATIONS	Male only	Female only	Black only	White only	Mixed		Illustrations without any people
Photographs							
Sketches							
(3) ROLE OF PEOPLE IN ILLUSTRATIONS	Male roles		Female roles		White people's roles		Black people's role
Photographs							
Sketches							
(4) Are the sketches lifelike or stereotyped?							
(5) Language: Use of sex specific terms in general situations (add to list)	He	She	His	Her	Man		
(6) ROLE PLAY AND EXERCISES	Male roles		Female roles		White roles		Black roles
	Total		Total		Total		Total
(7) OMISSIONS							
(8) WOMEN AS AN IDENTIFIABLE GROUP							
(9) How are black people generally depicted as an identifable group?							
(10) Are there any people with physical disabilities shown? In what situations?							

Figure 5: *Textbook evaluation matrix for geography teachers. Source: Connolly, 1992*

MOVING IMAGES

All the issues raised above concerning books apply also to moving images. It must be stressed that just because images are 'real' it does not necessarily make them value-free. We must ask questions. Who made the film? Why did they make it? Who was their intended audience? What point are they trying to make? Who edited the film? Are there any censorship issues? How are sub-titles or voice-overs handled? We should note the sex and ethnicity of the experts presented on the film and whether people with accents or disabilities are given prominence. A matrix similar to that presented in Figure 5 can be devised and used both by teachers and pupils to encourage the critical evaluation of television or film materials.

TALKS

Parents and members of the local community could be invited into school to give talks, and contribute to story telling and oral history. They should also be encouraged to give classroom support and assistance with careers advice. Such activities will provide pupils with positive role models and may dispel unfounded myths.

Assessment

Assessment is a continuous process that is both formative and summative. The focus should be on achievement as opposed to 'failure'. Different groups of pupils perform better with different forms of assessment; for instance, girls tend to be better at written work and boys do better practical work. It is therefore important to use a whole range of assessment types, thus enabling all pupils to demonstrate their achievements. Geography is a subject which lends itself well to diversity of assessment, including written, practical and fieldwork. All pupils should have access to assessment activities which should be free from bias and stereotypes. Teachers should seek advice concerning assessment for bi-lingual pupils.

No approach to assessment is entirely objective. Assessment procedures and teacher attitudes and expectations are subject to bias built upon stereotypical views. Teachers must examine their own views and expectations of different groups of pupils and try to be objective when marking their work. It is important to monitor assessment and progress of pupils according to the school's equal opportunities policy; then action can be taken if one group of pupils is not achieving its full potential. After all, equal opportunities are there to ensure that all pupils, no matter what their gender, economic and ethnic background or ability/disability, can achieve their full potential at school. We are preparing young people to enter the adult world with an understanding and tolerance of cultural and societal diversity. Geography is an excellent medium through which to achieve these aims.

References

AREA (1989) 'Guidelines for the use of non-sexist language', *AREA,* 21,2, pp. 115-116.

AREA (1991) 'Editorial: non-sexist and non-racist writing', *AREA,* 23, 4, pp. 289-294.

City of Coventry (no date) *Guidance for Equal Opportunities.* Support and Advisory Service.

City of Coventry (1994) *Preparing for the inspection of equal opportunity: identifying and presenting evidence of good practice.* Education Service.

Connolly, J. (1992) 'Geography: equal opportunities and the National Curriculum' in Myers, K. (ed) *Genderwatch,* pp. 143-146. Cambridge University Press.

Connolly, J. (1993) 'Gender balanced geography: have we got it right yet?', *Teaching Geography,* 18, 2, pp. 61-64.

Gold, K. (1995) 'Hard times for Britain's lost boys', *New Scientist,* 4 February, pp. 12-13.

Staffordshire Education Authority (no date) *Ensuring Equality in Staffordshire Schools'.*

The Psychologist (1988) 'Guidelines for the use of non-sexist language', *The Psychologist,* 1, 2, pp. 53-54.

Chapter 4

Change in school geography

PAUL MACHON AND GRAHAM RANGER

What we teach in school geography courses, as well as to whom and how we teach it, are determined by a range of factors and forces, many of which are in a constant state of change. Even when policy changes are plain and easy to define, and formal structures attempt to guide change, informal and chance factors will always intrude (Ham and Hill, 1984; Hogwood and Gunn, 1984). Figure 1 shows one way of expressing the major influences that affect our decisions; it is not a definitive statement, but more a model, or framework. We hope that this framework will be useful to school geography departments, for INSET and in Teachers' Centres as colleagues look to the future and the kind of geography that they will be teaching at the turn of the century.

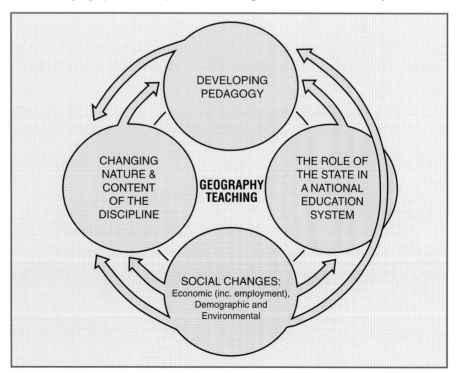

Figure 1: *A framework for analysing past and future changes in the geography we teach*

Back to the future

It is instructive to compare the present situation, with its welter of changes driven by agencies outside both education and geography, with the last upheaval to affect geographical education, namely '…the torrent of quantitative, conceptual and theoretical revolution(s)' (Tidswell, 1990, p. 309) of the 1960s and early 1970s. These earlier changes were driven from within the discipline, and were largely the result of an invigorating dialogue between geographers in higher education and in schools; Rex Walford's personal account (1989) pointedly illustrates the informality of this dialogue. The immediate impact of these changes was most clearly seen in A level geography, but these changes are representative of what took place elsewhere. A dramatic early effect of this paradigm shift was to sweep away some long-established content (Marsden, 1988, p. 327) – for example, much regional geography went; in its place came a search for order (Abler *et al*, 1972), rules and even laws! Syllabuses were heavily modified; for example London's popular 210 lost both its cartography and regional geography papers and gained a 'modern' human geography paper. This contained models of rational behaviour which were said to underpin economic decision-making, together with statistical tools and process-based accounts of geographic forms. In making these changes, the examination boards acted entirely consistently as responsive suppliers in a free market, without referring to the Government or its agents as now they must. However, in an effort to appeal to the largest possible audience, they sometimes pursued both *continuity* and *change* by combining questions from ideologically distinct eras in the same papers.

Consider for instance the following two questions:

---

17. (a) Distinguish between the terms 'site' and 'situation' as used in urban geography.

    (b) Assess the significance of site and situation to the geography of a town which you have studied.

18. Why is it that some areas of the inner city suffer from social deprivation?

London University A level Geography, Paper 2, June 1980

Number 17 could have been asked, and answered, between the wars; Number 18, however, is clearly more recent: it is looking for process, not form, and the best answers would be expected to reflect upon a theoretical account of urban structure, although usually only from the Chicago School of Burgess and others. But the critical potential of these new approaches failed to materialise: the models were seen simply as 'something else to learn', certainly not to be employed in a search for explanation.

Geography in schools and higher education

For mainstream A level syllabuses, like London Board's 210, once these content changes had been established there followed a de-coupling of geography in schools from geography in higher education. The causes of this, and the consequent fragmentation of the geographic community, would repay further study (Bale, 1995). A partial explanation for the change exists in the attention that had to be paid in school geography to the National Curriculum, particularly for younger pupils; here we have evidence of the State's increasingly interventionist role after 1979. The de-coupling was accelerated by the reduction in numbers of university lecturers writing school textbooks, and serving as examiners (Haggett, 1972).

The impact of the de-coupling was, and is, significant on a number of counts. First, in the mid-1990s it is very hard to imagine a repetition of the exchanges between different educational sectors that took place at the Madingley Conferences in the 1960s, and the 'underground press' that followed (Walford, 1989). Second, and most strikingly, there has been almost no conceptual development in school examination syllabuses, the content of which has remained largely unaltered since the mid-1970s. Even the most modern modular version of London's syllabus 210 has essentially the same content as the syllabuses that were developed in the mid-1970s, with the exception perhaps of some gentle environmentalism (Martell, 1994), although not of a type that looks for structural causes (and structural solutions) in the non-sustainable exploitation of nature. This de-coupling has left most school geography largely untouched by the structuralist, humanist and realist critiques of the positivist revolution so, for example, pupils are *still* taught explanatory models in geography without being able to challenge them, to be aware of their implications or to grasp their intellectual pedigree in any fundamental way. As the example below shows, these things matter because there is a moral cost (Walford and Haggett, 1995, pp. 10-11), laying the discipline open to the charge that its pursuit of 'science' avoids real debate and that as a discipline it uncritically serves the status quo (here, the recent growth of Travel and Tourism within geography departments is very telling).

Example: Models of urban structure

The account of urban structure by E. W. Burgess (1925) continues to dominate pupils' answers on this core topic. Even in otherwise exhaustive school textbooks, such as Waugh's *Geography: an Integrated Approach* (1995) the model is described without reference to its social-Darwinist pedigree or to the fact that Burgess was a sociologist, not a geographer, or to the implications of that fundamentally racist model. Consequently, criticisms of the model tend to be facile, dealing with failures of 'goodness of fit' against the real world rather than an exploration of its primary, and idealised, assumptions. Such an approach may meet the requirements of the examination boards but certainly fails on other counts, for instance against all three of Marsden's (1988, p. 327) criteria – 'good geography...good pedagogy...good social education' – and in spite of profound warnings about the use of theories themselves (Harvey, 1969, pp. 96-99 and pp. 119-121).

How may we as geography teachers improve matters? In other disciplines, particularly politics, psychology and sociology, an examination of key texts from key authors provides pupils with a knowledge of how the discipline has developed and in what context. This biographical approach captures a sense of intellectual activity being a living thing and not just something capable of being reduced to a static body of facts to be learned. Using this approach pupils would be able to read, think about and discuss their key texts in context. Thus, pupils would find Burgess noting:

> By what process does a person become an organic part of his society? The natural process of acquiring culture is by birth (p. 53)...Yet interesting occupational selection has taken place by nationality, explainable more by racial temperament or circumstances than by old-world economic background, as Irish policemen, Greek ice-cream parlors, Chinese laundries, Negro porters, Belgian janitors, etc. (p. 57)

(Burgess, 1925).

Which takes some explaining away!

Finally, it should also be a matter of considerable concern that geography in the classroom has so many difficulties dealing with contemporary events. The wholesale economic, social and political changes that have marked the 1980s and early 1990s were met, by and large, by ignoring them. Britain's economic restructuring, for example, cannot be dealt with adequately by using normative models of industrial location. Endeavouring to account for the changes in the former Soviet Union and Central Europe cannot (assuming they are taught at all) be started, even at A level, by a school geography that has virtually no political content (Machon, 1991). How many geography lessons have you seen, or taught, that unravelled in a revealing way the fragmentation of the former Yugoslavia?

Developing pedagogy: geography, social change and 'vocationalism'

Changes within the discipline in the 1970s were accompanied by more obviously pedagogical changes, particularly those which centred more on enquiry by pupils than upon changes in the subject content (although any distinction between the two should not be drawn in too hard a way). Much of the force of these pedagogical changes came from a wider social change. There are clear contrasts here with the present changes, in which the role of the State is dominant.

The enquiry/problems-based approach that developed in the 1970s was echoed in many curriculum areas, notably in maths (the *Schools Mathematics Project*) and science (the *Nuffield Sciences Projects*). School geography projects were developed in the UK and elsewhere, e.g. *Geography for the Young School Leaver* (GYSL) for the last two years of compulsory schooling and *The American High School Geography Project* (FitzGerald, 1969). These curriculum initiatives, innovative in both content and pedagogy, originated from within the educational establishment itself. Evidence of this exists in the expansion in the number of Mode III syllabuses at CSE level in the late 1970s; projects piloted by teachers in schools able to work with an autonomy that now seems unthinkable. As implied by the name of the GYSL project (later renamed the Avery Hill project), these initiatives were also being driven by changes in schools, particularly those resulting from raising the school-leaving age, which led to an increase in the number of students completing courses with external examinations at 16 + . This in turn advanced the comprehensivation of sixth forms – the so-called 'New Sixth' – and also the Colleges of Further Education.

Geography's premier enquiry-based project was *Geography 16-19*. This was one of the last major curriculum development projects funded by the Schools Council and in terms of market share has been one of the most successful. From its start in 1974 (Naish *et al*, 1987) the project aimed to help teachers reflect on the objectives, content and teaching methods of their geography courses. The project was not without its critics; for example, concern was expressed about the balance between 'content' and 'enquiry' – a debate that developed a political dimension around what pupils should *know* and what they should be able to *do* that was repeated in the troubled first phase of the National Curriculum. However, the project did make it possible for teachers to reflect in their courses contemporary events (sometimes termed 'relevance') and developments in the discipline. At its best this essentially critical approach produced work of a high order but there was also a risk of the 'long distance work sheet masquerading as the enquiry approach. Teachers...[becoming]...managers of resources rather than stimulators of people.' (Tidswell, 1990, p. 309).

The most conspicuous social change, underpinning all 'reform' in schools, was the deterioration in employment prospects that accompanied economic restructuring. Throughout the 1980s arguments surrounding restructuring were often re-cast in free-market terms. Britain was seen as 'slipping behind' in an international league table of competitiveness, and schools were frequently implicated in the search for a cause of this. The Government responded by developing policies that moved schools towards 'preparing students for the world of work'; policies that we now recognise as the start of the 'New Vocationalism' (Bash and Colby, 1989). These policies were linked with others, such as a reduction in the powers of local authorities, that sharpened the impact of the changes, particularly by isolating schools competitively and so fragmenting collective behaviour amongst subject teachers. For many geography teachers the Geographical Association became their only contact with the wider community of specialist geography teachers.

The mid-1990s see vocationalism fairly well established in schools and colleges with the introduction of General National Vocational Qualifications (GNVQs) at a variety of levels. Advanced GNVQs co-exist with A levels and both are expected to enable the UK to reach national targets for post-16 participation in education by the end of the century. Concerns regarding the gulf between the two routes to qualifications may be addressed by changes of name, 'vocational A levels', for example, or the transfer of awarded credits (an outcome of modular A levels), but such changes should not conceal other, potentially more problematic issues for geography departments. Of these we identify the following: the difficulty geography may experience in identifying a clear vocational content; the lack of geographical substance and rigour in vocationally orientated areas such as Travel and Tourism; the conflict between geography as an essentially critical enquiry and vocationalism; and finally the undesirability of fragmenting the discipline so that, for example, 'difficult' areas like climatology are abandoned.

The State and its agents

After 1979 state intervention in education increased sharply. The major battleground was the National Curriculum, but the changes to A level syllabuses, pedagogy, departmental organisation and inspection – every bit as dramatic – have taken place with virtually no public debate. How may we explain this, and what are its implications?

A partial explanation can be found in the transformed power relationships between central and local government and, through the latter, into schools. This resulted from the establishment of *bureaucratic control systems* (Edwards, 1979, p. 48) that were administered through quangos – the surrogates of central government. These state-appointed agencies operated with state-imposed targets and performance indicators that were then replicated in schools and colleges. In this way *responsible autonomy* (Friedman, 1977, p. 134) is reproduced by a bureaucratic form of *technical control* (Edwards, 1979) working through hierarchical management and inspection systems. The phrase 'replicated in schools' should be emphasised: the day-to-day work of the quangos is in fact done in schools and colleges by teachers who, because they must grapple with cost-unit funding, balancing budgets and integrating modular courses into 'linear'-organised college systems, are being deflected from paying attention to geography itself. Perhaps in these circumstances, the tired nature of much of the debate about the discipline itself is not surprising.

The quangos themselves are not unaffected by change; it is clearly easier for central government to deal with fewer and larger agencies, especially if their senior officials are government appointments, and over the period there has been a steady shift towards their consolidation and centralisation. Two examples will show how this process works.

The first example is the *Schools Council*, an early quango which is now defunct. In the late 1980s this innovative and influential Council was reined in, evolving first into the *Schools Examination and Assessment Council* (SEAC), before being merged with the *National Curriculum Council* (NCC) to form the *Schools Curriculum and Assessment Authority* (SCAA). SCAA is now charged with the scrutiny of the Examination Boards which, as noted earlier, once exercised much greater autonomy than is the case today; their offerings now have a national uniformity which presages fewer and larger providers. Here again, the logic of increasing size, control and power exerts itself and with it the loss of choice for schools and colleges and an ossification of the geography that is available for pupils to study. In the end the key question remains: if you wished to teach something different, could you?

The second example centres on important changes in the management of institutions providing A level courses, changes which followed the creation of the *Further Education Funding Council* (FEFC), the quango that administers all Colleges of Further Education, all Sixth Form Colleges and a number of other vocationally dedicated colleges. Rushed into existence and working against deadlines that made consultation hollow, the FEFC has produced, and continues to produce, a succession of circulars determining policy in this sector. These policies are enforced by a combination of inspection, cash penalties and recondite funding mechanisms. To illustrate the last point, geography falls into a low funding band that does not reflect the real cost of geography courses, for example in the provision of fieldwork. The FEFC's imperative is growth with a reduced per capita spend in order to meet government targets. Such imperatives frequently conflict with moves elsewhere in the sector, for example increasing staying-on rates while capping public spending. Much of the pedagogy originates from yet another group, the *Further Education Unit*, whose own circulars inform the work of the FEFC's inspectorate. Again the logic of size applies, for the FEU was amalgamated in 1995 with the Staff College to form the *Further Education Development Agency* (FEDA), though their INSET courses have a familiar focus: funding, management and mechanisms of appraisal. The teaching of geography in this sector is covered in Chapter 29 by Andrew Powell, who also begins to map out some of the connections between the New Vocationalism and geography teaching.

And the future?

In looking to the future, we start from the position outlined above, so once again Figure 1 on page 39 provides a useful framework.

We have voiced our concerns about those tendencies that in recent years have limited the development of geography in schools, in particular its quiet divorce from the new work in higher education, its lack of self-scrutiny and its avoidance of a genuinely critical stance. Pressures from the other agencies shown in Figure 1 have done much to promote these tendencies and, as they seem likely to continue, our concern remains. Consequently the task facing those who want to move the discipline forward is a hard one. Their efforts are likely to be marginalised by a National Curriculum that reinforces the status quo, by vocationalism, and by a dwindling number of large, centrally dominated examination boards. However, the prizes for making such an advance would be high. One route forward would be to approach geography biographically, to come to grips with the roots of its intellectual activity. This biographical approach is the one taken by such immensely successful recent A level arrivals as politics, psychology and sociology, and has the bonus that it would place geography firmly among those disciplines that together constitute social enquiry.

It is difficult to predict the role of the State in education, and particularly in reforms in schools. Such changes have been driven by a Government determined to reduce public expenditure, however ideologically clothed, and have had a direct impact on the population at large. The effects of this are hard to predict, but the impact has not been a facile one ('my child's school'); it is more complex, concerned with the loss of opportunity, the dangers of too much bare-faced inequality and the acknowledgement that we all, finally, share in 'common endeavours' (Hutton, 1995, p. 310). Some of the recent reforms may be 'rolled back', but the continuing existence of the largely unaccountable quangos may be expected to slow the process.

'Social change' is a complex concept and given the limited scope of this chapter we shall confine ourselves to a single observation. Contemporary educational restructuring has prompted questions to which 'vocationalism' has been offered as the educational answer. We have already indicated our scepticism that vocationalism is the best answer, but note that the question remains valid: how are we to educate and train young people and, as important, sustain the process throughout people's working lives? Vocationalism may satisfy immediate needs – and will underpin low-wage economies – but the real prizes will go to nations who do something more.

The crucial question for any developing pedagogy is: how can the way we teach geography help prepare our pupils to become responsible and reflective citizens and creative workers? We reject any distinction between education for life and training for work – such a supposed distinction is destructive of education; through our teaching we must strive to develop personal autonomy within social limits.

Already, crises of citizenship press upon us, in the form of de-skilled adults and disaffected, unemployed and hopeless youngsters. As teachers of geography we cannot of course solve these problems, but we can contribute to their solution through what we teach, how we teach it and how we expect our pupils to learn.

Conclusion

At the start of this chapter we invited colleagues to consider four forces which we argued act upon the geography we teach. If the brief account that followed has stimulated discussion then it will have served its purpose. The geography that we teach at the turn of the century matters and, as a thinking community, geographers teaching at whatever level must have an input into what that geography should be. If debates about how the discipline is to develop, or how its pedagogy is to progress, or how it is to deal with contemporary social change and (finally) what influence state agencies are to have on your discipline are abandoned to others, then the discipline is in trouble. The stakes here are high.

References

Abler, R., Adams, J.S. & Gould, P. (1972) *Spatial Organisation*. Prentice Hall. This book can stand for the many textbooks of the period that ambitiously sought to present an overview of the discipline in a single volume. In its preface the authors noted: 'Underlying our approach to the analysis of human activities in terrestrial space is our belief that human geography is a social and behavioral science.'

Bash, L. & Coulby, D. (eds) (1989) *The Education Reform Act*. Cassell.

Edwards, R. (1979) *Contested Terrain*. Heinemann.

Fitzgerald, B.P. (1969) 'The American High School Geography Project and its implications for teaching in Britain', *Geography*, 242, 54, pp. 56-63.

Friedman, A.L. (1977) 'Responsible autonomy versus direct control over the labour process', *Capital and Class*, No. 1.

Haggett, P. (1972) *Geography: A Modern Synthesis*. Harper and Row. The title was, for once, accurate, for here was a 'synthesis' in the best sense of the word. The point being made here, however, is to note Peter Haggett's place on the borders between geography taught in universities and schools.

Ham, C. & Hill, M. (1984) *The Policy Process in the Modern Capitalist State*. Wheatsheaf.

Paul Hamlyn Foundation (1995) *Learning to Succeed: The Way Ahead*.

Harvey, D. (1969) *Explanation in Geography*. Edward Arnold. This groundbreaking book's fortune has somehow become connected to the revolution in the discipline already referred to, in part perhaps because of its clear exposition of scientific methodology. However, it continues to be worth reading on a huge range of other counts.

Hogwood, B.W. & Gunn, L.A. (1984) *Policy Analysis for the Real World.* Oxford University Press.

Hutton, W. (1995) *The State We're In.* Jonathan Cape. Will Hutton's dazzling book reviews Britain in the mid-1990s and reminds us all of what was nearly forgotten: that there is another way.

Machon, P. (1991) 'Geography' in Conley, F. (ed) *Political Understanding Across the Curriculum,* pp. 55-57. The Politics Association.

Marsden, W.E. (1988) 'Continuity and change in geography textbooks: Perspectives from the 1930s to the 1960s' *Geography,* 73, 321. Marsden opens with a revealing account of the textbook *Foundations of Geography* which was written in 1938 and was still, in 1988, selling over 100,000 copies a year!

Martell, L. (1994) *Ecology and Society.* Polity.

Naish, M., Rawling, E. & Hart, C. (1987) *The Contribution of a Curriculum Project to 16-19 Education.* Longman.

Park, R.E., Burgess, E.W. & McKenzie, R.D. (1925) *The City.* University of Chicago Press. Reprinted in 1957, from which edition these page numbers are noted.

Taylor, P. (second edition, 1989) *Political Geography.* Longman. First published in 1985, *Political Geography* straddles a discipline gap with real style and has played a significant part in the resurgence of political geography in universities. There is not a school parallel, and as a consequence any remotely political geography in schools is a poor bedraggled thing, largely underpinned by 'common-sense notions' of what political enquiry actually is.

Tidswell, V. (1990) 'Capes, concepts and conscience: continuity in the curriculum' *Geography,* 75, 329, 4, pp. 302-312.

Walford, R. (1989) 'On the frontier with the new model army: geography publishing from the 1960s to the 1990s' *Geography,* 74, 325, 4, pp. 308-320.

Walford, R. & Haggett, P. (1995) 'Geography and Geographical Education' *Geography,* 80, 346, 1, pp. 10-11.

Waugh, D. (second edition, 1995) *Geography: An Integrated Approach.* Nelson.

Section Two

Courses and lessons

SUMMARY OF CHAPTERS

'Diversity in unity: this is the nature of the
earth's surface on which we live and with
which our lives are so closely interwoven.
It should be reflected in any syllabus in the
secondary school, but it should be reflected
differently; for pupils, teachers and schools,
like the landscapes themselves, thrive
in their variety and will, within a certain
broad unity, find their satisfaction in a
variety of ways.'
Her Majesty's Inspectors of Schools (1961),
Geography and Education.
Education Pamphlet No. 39
(written by E C Marchant, HMI).
HMSO, page 41.

The aim of this section is to provide a sound
and detailed theoretical and practical
foundation for course design and lesson
planning. Particular attention is given to
ways of preparing work suitable for learners
of different abilities and aptitudes, also to
systematic skills development, with cross-
curricular links.

Chapter 5

Planning your courses

TREVOR BENNETTS

Introduction

This chapter is concerned with the formulation of departmental policies, the development of structure plans, and the planning of units of study in geography. Curriculum planning is a dynamic activity, in the sense that the curriculum is not a fixed format, but develops as a result of decisions and changing practices within a school, often in response to external influences and requirements. Even without the latter, curriculum planning is necessary to ensure that courses are directed towards worthwhile goals, that they are structured to facilitate learning, that lessons are adequately resourced and that pupils make satisfactory progress. The introduction of a National Curriculum and its revision have focused attention on curriculum planning as a means of ensuring that both statutory requirements are met and the aspirations of parents and pupils are respected. While OFSTED inspections add to the pressure on schools to give some priority to planning, and to produce documents which display clearly how they intend to achieve their curricular goals, these policy statements, structure plans and more detailed plans for study units should be working documents which help teachers to devise and implement a sound curriculum.

Curriculum planning in a secondary school takes place at a range of levels, each of which has well-defined purposes and clear outcomes. Figure 1 outlines a hierarchical scheme, in which general decisions affecting the whole curriculum are made at a school level; while specific decisions, which focus on lesson planning, are made by individual teachers in relation to particular groups of pupils. In between is a range of activities which are best undertaken by a department or team, and which ideally should involve all those who teach a specific subject or course.

Formulating departmental policies

Departmental policies should address matters which require a common approach and consistency in practice across a department. They should articulate the purposes, priorities and principles which the members of the department have agreed should underpin the geography curriculum. The policy document should explain the rationale for the curricular provision in the subject.

Photo: **John Birdsall Photography**

LEVEL	ACTIVITY	INITIAL OUTCOMES
School	1. Formulate general policies for the whole curriculum	General policy statements Guidance on specific aspects School timetable
Subject department or course team	2. Formulate policies for geography 3. Devise structure plans for courses 4. Plan and prepare units of study	Policy statements and guidelines for geography Structure plan and rationale for each course Plans for units of study
Individual teachers	5. Plan and prepare lessons	Lesson plans and teaching materials

Figure 1: *A planning hierarchy for the curriculum*

General policy statements can usefully include:

1. an outline of the teachers' views of the nature of their subject, and a summary of the aims of geographical education to which the teachers are committed;

2. a summary of the course provision which the department makes, with an explanation of any differences in provision for pupils of the same age;

3. criteria for the allocation of staff, accommodation and resources to teaching groups; and

4. the broad principles which the department applies to the choice of content, methods of teaching and assessment within courses.

More specific policy statements might focus on such matters as:

- meeting the requirements of the National Curriculum;
- the contribution of geography to cross-curricular themes, especially environmental education, economic and industrial understanding, and citizenship;
- links between geography and other subjects;
- continuity and progression in the geography curriculum;
- differentiation in the geography curriculum – catering for the disparate interests, experiences and capabilities of pupils;
- equal opportunities in the geography curriculum;
- marking pupils' work and recording their progress.

While some policies need to be determined before engaging in the details of course planning, it is unrealistic to expect a subject department to produce a whole range of carefully considered policy statements in advance of curriculum development or revision. It is more practical for a department to develop a rolling programme, at any given time focusing its attention on a few matters while recognising the relationships between many of the issues to be addressed. The incentive to produce a departmental policy may come from within the geography team or from a school initiative. In the case of the latter, geography teachers may benefit from exchanging experiences and exploring ideas with specialists in other fields. By being involved in school working parties, geographers can ensure that they contribute to the development of general policies, as well as gaining a better appreciation and understanding of them.

There is no single, simple, way of formulating policies. Much depends on the style of leadership of the head of department and the working relationships between members. However, the more that curriculum policies are formulated by discussion and agreement among the teaching staff, the more likely it is that they will be effective. Among the activities which can facilitate the development and articulation of policies are:

- preparing thoroughly, so that discussion within the department can be well informed (read relevant documents, such as those issued by official bodies (e.g. SCAA), by professional organisations (e.g. GA) and in professional journals);

- reporting to colleagues ideas gained from INSET;

- generating and exploring ideas through regular discussion within the department;

- drafting and revising statements, in order to produce an articulation of policies that all can understand and support;

- analysing the implications of policies, in order to anticipate any serious difficulties and assist the process of translating policies into practice; and

- monitoring the implementation of policies, so that any necessary adjustments can be made.

Figure 2 presents a list of key questions which need to be addressed in relation to a subject department's curricular policies.

---

1. On what curricular matters do we require departmental policies?

2. Who is to be involved in the formulation of these policies?

3. How are we to go about the task of developing policies?

4. What form should the policy statements take, in order to be most useful?

5. Do we all fully understand the implications of the policies?

6. Are we in agreement about the policies? If not, how do we resolve differences?

7. Are our policies consistent with legislative requirements and with the school's general curricular policies?

8. How shall we monitor the implementation of our policies?

Figure 2: Key questions about curricular policies

Curricular aims for geography

Curricular aims are general statements which give an overall sense of direction to a programme of teaching and learning. The aims should reflect the educational values of teachers, by indicating the nature of the geographical learning which they consider to be most worthwhile; and will often reveal assumptions about the sort of learning their pupils can achieve. There is a risk that educational aims will be taken for granted, rather than thought about constructively and critically. While statements of aims for geographical education can be taken from a variety of sources, a geography department will benefit from using such statements as stimuli, to help it reflect on its own goals and determine its own priorities. A carefully conceived statement of aims, which genuinely reflects the values and intentions of the teachers who use it, should support the development of more precise objectives for individual courses and units of study.

External examination syllabuses have their own statements of aims and objectives, those for GCSE being modelled closely on National Criteria (DES/WO, 1985; SCAA, 1995). While the statutory requirements for geography in the National Curriculum are not prefaced by any statement of aims, it is useful to refer to those formulated by the Geography Working Group (DES/WO, 1990). These aims remain pertinent to geographical education. Four very broad aims were proposed that clearly express values which the Working Group considered should not be linked to assessment. These were to:

- stimulate pupils' interest in their surroundings and in the variety of physical and human conditions on the earth's surface;

- foster pupils' sense of wonder at the beauty of the world around them;

- help pupils to develop an informed concern about the quality of the environment and the future of the human habitat; and

- thereby enhance pupils' sense of responsibility for the care of the earth and its peoples.

More particularly, and perhaps with assessment in mind, the Group suggested that the study of geography should aim at leading pupils to:

- acquire a framework of knowledge about locations and places that will help them to set local, national and international events within a geographical context, and that will support their development of geographical understanding;

- understand some of the important characteristics of the earth's physical systems – its landforms, weather and climate, hydrological and ecological systems – and the interaction between those systems;

- understand the significance of location and distribution patterns in human activities and physical processes; how places are linked by movements of people, materials and information, and by physical, economic, social and political relationships; and the interdependence of peoples, places and environments throughout the world;

- understand some of the relationships between people and environments, including both:

  a. the influence of environmental conditions on human activities, and

  b. the varied ways in which societies with different technologies, economic systems and cultural values have perceived, used, altered and created particular environments;

- develop a sense of place: a feeling for the 'personality' of a place and what it might be like to live there;

- acquire knowledge and understanding about the physical and human processes that bring about changes in place, space and environments, and a critical appreciation of the consequences of those changes;

- develop awareness and appreciation of the ethnic, cultural, economic and political diversity of human society, and its geographical expression;

- acquire the knowledge and develop the skills and understanding necessary to identify and investigate important cultural, social and political issues relating to place, space and environment, with sensitivity to the range of attitudes and values associated with such issues;

- acquire techniques and develop skills and competencies necessary for geographical enquiry, and of value for other purposes, especially the making and interpreting of maps, the use of information technology and the conduct of fieldwork; and

- develop intellectual and social skills, including the ability to observe, analyse and communicate.

These aims are wide-ranging and draw upon various traditions in the subject, in particular the study of: places; the relationships between people and environments; and the significance to human activities and physical processes of location, spatial patterns and spatial interactions. They are concerned with the processes which bring about change, and with important issues which have a geographical dimension. The aims encompass knowledge, understanding, skills and competencies; although there is only one explicit reference to attitudes and values, a reflection perhaps of the Government's priorities for the National Curriculum. Other formulations of aims can suggest alternative ideas and different emphases. For example, while most of the aims for the 11 to 16 curriculum proposed by HMI (1986) are very similar in spirit and tone to those of the Working Group, the following statements have rather different emphases:

- to help pupils to develop a sensitive awareness of the contrasting opportunities and constraints facing different peoples living in different places under different economic, social, political and physical conditions;

- to help pupils develop an understanding of the nature of multicultural and multiethnic societies and a sensitivity to cultural and racial prejudice and injustice;

- to help pupils to act more effectively in the environment as individuals and as members of society.

A more recent statement of aims, which is well worth considering, is that proposed by the Commission on Geographical Education of the International Geographical Union (1992). The Commission suggests that students should develop **attitudes and values** conducive to:

- interest in their surroundings and in the variety of natural and human characteristics on the surface of the earth;

- appreciation of the beauty of the physical world, on the one hand, and of the different living conditions of people, on the other;

- concern for the quality and planning of the environment and human habitat for future generations;

- understanding the significance of attitudes and values in decision making;

- readiness to use geographical knowledge and skills adequately and responsibly in private, professional and public life;

- respect for the rights of all people to equality;

- dedication to seeking solutions to local, regional, national and international problems on the basis of the Universal Declaration of Human Rights.

A geography department's statement of aims may be broader than what is required for the National Curriculum or for external examinations. It should not be limited to what can easily be assessed. However, the value of this statement lies in the extent of its influence on what is taught and how it is taught. It should provide signposts to help teachers maintain the general directions they intend. But maps must be constructed to plot the routes by which the various goals are to be reached; these curricular 'maps' are the documents which are usually called 'schemes of work' or 'teaching syllabuses'. Schemes of work should be tackled at two levels: first there needs to be a structure plan, which outlines the overall programme; and then more detailed plans for each unit of study within that programme.

Devising a structure plan

A structure plan describes the framework for the programme of content and activities which constitutes a course, or courses, within a particular school. Most geography courses consist of a sequence of units of study which are defined primarily by content, although some units may focus on a particular type of activity, such as mapwork, a fieldwork visit or a geographical enquiry. Specifying the units of study and arranging them in a suitable sequence are important initial steps in the process of transforming broad intentions and principles into a plan of implementation. Such planning cannot be tackled in a vacuum (Figure 3).

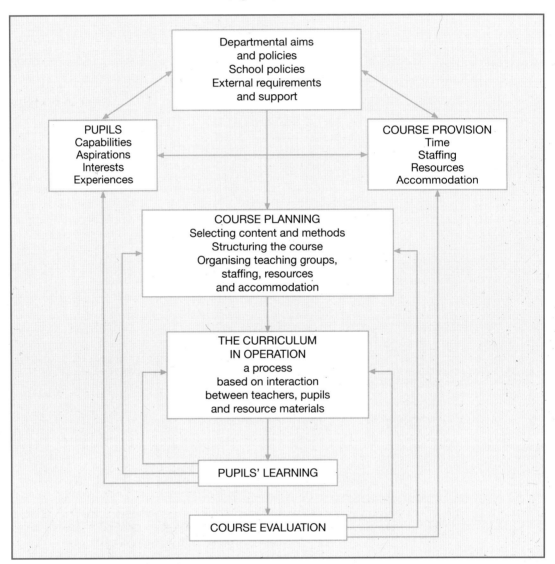

*Figure 3: **Course planning in context***

While course planning should set out to satisfy the curricular aims of the subject department, the policies of the school and department, and the requirements of the National Curriculum and of examining boards, this must be done in the context of:

a. the capabilities, aspirations, interests and experiences of pupils; and

b. the provision made for the course.

The implementation of the National Curriculum means pupils arriving from primary schools should already have considerable geographical knowledge, understanding and skills. It is, therefore, essential that teachers of geography in secondary schools be familiar with the Programme of Study (PoS) for key stage 2, and know what has been tackled in their feeder schools, so that they can take account of their pupils' previous experience of the subject (see Chapter 1). Whatever their experience, however, it is inevitable that pupils will vary in their levels of attainment. The question as to how the geography curriculum should be differentiated to cater for the range of pupils' experience and attainment is relevant from the time that pupils enter a school.

The essential components of the provision for a course are the time, staffing, resource materials and accommodation allocated to it. While in most respects the overall provision to a department will be determined at school level, the head of department may be delegated responsibility for the deployment of staff and allocation of accommodation and materials to individual teaching groups. There may be considerable scope for the department to obtain or create suitable teaching materials for a new or revised course. The organisation of teaching groups and of provision for a course must be planned alongside the curricular content and activities.

The planning of the structure of a course should be undertaken at an early stage, so that the more detailed planning and preparation of individual units of study can take account of the rationale for the course and where each unit lies within the total scheme. The Curriculum Council for Wales, in its *Non-Statutory Guidance* (CCW, 1991), recommended that 'developing a scheme of work should be a collaborative venture involving all staff teaching geography'. Quoting from the *GCSE Avery Hill 14-16 Geography Project Teachers' Handbook* the Council commented that:
'The benefits of participating in this process include:

■ a shared sense of direction and values;

■ a share in the decision-making process and a feeling of ownership;

■ an environment in which constructive feedback and evaluation are encouraged;

■ an opportunity for personal development for everyone.'
(WJEC, 1990)

While the task of designing the structure of a course may not require a strict sequence of steps, teachers need to:

1. familiarise themselves with the external requirements (e.g. in the case of key stage 3: the PoS; the Level Descriptions; and the arrangements for assessment);

2. in the light of these requirements, review:

    ■ the aims and policies of the department and their implications for the course,

    ■ the capabilities and previous experience of the pupils,

    ■ the resources available for the course, including allocation of time, and

    ■ the current geography programme, identifying which parts can be retained and how much alteration is necessary;

3. clarify the principles which should be applied when developing the structure of the course;

4. draft alternative frameworks, in order to explore different possibilities;

5. check the extent to which the most promising alternatives meet the requirements and satisfy the principles that have been identified;

6. select the most suitable framework, making any adjustments which could improve it.

When developing a structure plan for a particular course, it will be helpful to formulate a statement of aims which is written in terms specific to that course. While this statement should accommodate external requirements, it should also be consistent with the curricular aims of the department. It would, for example, be reasonable to expect a department's aims for an examination course to be slightly broader than those presented in the examination syllabus, if only because it might include some elements which are not assessed in the examination. Content and methods should be selected to further the aims of the course, and a structure devised to facilitate pupils' learning. Among the principles and criteria to be considered when undertaking these tasks are those related to coverage, breadth and balance of content, relevance, depth of study, coherence, progression and differentiation. They can be exemplified in relation to key stage 3.

Constructing a plan for key stage 3

Qualities of coverage, breadth and balance within key stage 3 geography are closely related to the requirements of the PoS. As far as **coverage** is concerned, these requirements are in terms of places, themes and skills. Pupils are expected to study the general geographical characteristics of two countries (excluding the UK), which are in significantly different states of development, and to compare two regions within each. In addition their thematic studies are to involve work at a range of spatial scales (local, regional, national, international and global) and in a range of contexts, including the local area, the UK, the EU and parts of the world in various states of development. The themes specified are:

Tectonic processes – earthquakes or volcanic eruptions

Geomorphological processes – landforms and landform processes associated with rivers or coasts

Weather and climate

Ecosystems – one type of vegetation

Population

Settlement

Economic activities

Development

Environmental issues

The skills include various techniques, in particular those associated with the use of appropriate instruments, maps, diagrams, atlases, aerial photographs and satellite images; and more general competencies, to do with the use of primary and secondary source materials, and the identification and description of patterns, relationships and changes. Pupils should also be given opportunities to use IT to gain access to additional information sources and to assist in handling, presenting and analysing data.

The PoS for key stage 3 does not define the units from which courses have to be constructed. Various elements of the PoS can be brought together within individual units. For instance, most of the skills can be developed in association with specific content and some aspects of the themes can be taught in the context of the specified place studies. This gives flexibility to the planning of key stage 3 courses in geography.

The coverage required by the PoS ensures some degree of **breadth** and **balance**, for example, in the attention given to places and themes, to aspects of both physical and human geography, and to environmental issues. If the time allocated to geography is sufficient, a department could decide to include elements which are not specified in the PoS. It could, for example, include a unit on the home region and use this as a vehicle for the delivery of a variety of goals, which may be related directly to the lists of required content and skills. A department could decide to assign greater emphasis to the general geography of the UK; with specific attention to such themes as 'communications and movements' and 'the use and misuse of natural resources', which are not highlighted in the PoS. A department might wish to ensure that the structure of its curriculum will enable geography to contribute to particular cross-curricular themes (see Chapter 2). Such provision would not necessarily require additional units of study, but might be accommodated within units which are designed with the PoS in mind. However, the decision might have implications for the way in which these units are developed.

The idea of balance can be applied to each of the three years of key stage 3 as well as to the key stage as a whole, thereby influencing the structure of the course. For example, each year could be planned to include a substantial study of a place and of themes in both physical and human geography, and through these incorporate a range of spatial scales.

Relevance can be interpreted in personal and social terms, through the attention given to:

- pupils' experiences and interests – which can influence the choice of places and topics to be studied;

- skills which pupils recognise as being useful;

- economic, social, political and environmental issues; and

- current situations and events which impinge directly on the lives of the pupils, or are 'in the news'.

Pupils' interests and experiences may be especially pertinent to geography when their families and community have close links with other parts of the world, or when they have visited distant places. Pupils can be helped to recognise the wider relevance of particular skills and techniques through the ways in which these are taught and applied.

Issues appear in the key stage 3 PoS in the context of 'Environmental Issues', and are central to the investigation of 'Development'. There is also abundant scope for attention to be given to various issues in other themes and topics. It is for a geography department to determine what emphasis to give to which issues, and how to approach them. Opportunities for good geographical teaching are often provided by events which cannot be anticipated. While the geography curriculum needs a strong structure, it should not be so rigid that advantage cannot be taken of such opportunities. An overloaded curriculum discourages such flexibility.

The development of pupils' understanding and skills often requires **depth of study** and this demands time. Consequently, there is always a potential conflict between breadth and depth in the curriculum. Both qualities are desirable and should be viewed as complementary; the studies which are tackled in greater depth provide the understanding and competencies which enable pupils to make better sense of those topics which receive lighter treatment. Here, again, there is a need for balance, which should be reflected in the allocation of time to different parts of a course.

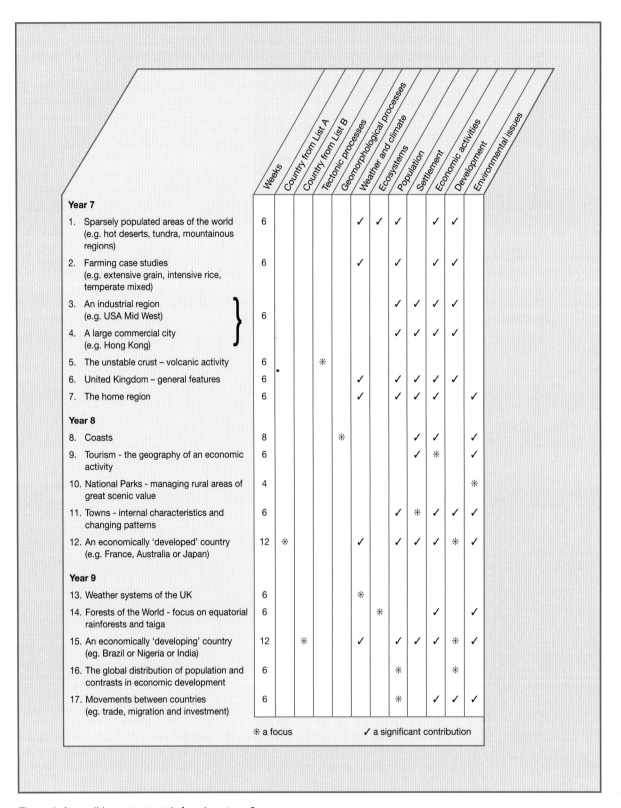

	Weeks	Country from List A	Country from List B	Tectonic processes	Geomorphological processes	Weather and climate	Ecosystems	Population	Settlement	Economic activities	Development	Environmental issues
Year 7												
1. Sparsely populated areas of the world (e.g. hot deserts, tundra, mountainous regions)	6				✓	✓	✓		✓	✓		
2. Farming case studies (e.g. extensive grain, intensive rice, temperate mixed)	6				✓		✓		✓	✓		
3. An industrial region (e.g. USA Mid West)	6						✓	✓	✓	✓		
4. A large commercial city (e.g. Hong Kong)							✓	✓	✓	✓		
5. The unstable crust – volcanic activity	6			✱								
6. United Kingdom – general features	6					✓	✓	✓	✓	✓		
7. The home region	6					✓	✓	✓	✓			✓
Year 8												
8. Coasts	8				✱				✓	✓		✓
9. Tourism - the geography of an economic activity	6								✓	✱		✓
10. National Parks - managing rural areas of great scenic value	4											✱
11. Towns - internal characteristics and changing patterns	6							✓	✱	✓	✓	✓
12. An economically 'developed' country (e.g. France, Australia or Japan)	12	✱				✓		✓	✓	✓	✱	✓
Year 9												
13. Weather systems of the UK	6					✱						
14. Forests of the World - focus on equatorial rainforests and taiga	6						✱			✓		✓
15. An economically 'developing' country (eg. Brazil or Nigeria or India)	12		✱			✓		✓	✓	✓	✱	✓
16. The global distribution of population and contrasts in economic development	6							✱			✱	
17. Movements between countries (eg. trade, migration and investment)	6							✱		✓	✓	✓

✱ a focus   ✓ a significant contribution

Figure 4: *A possible content matrix for a key stage 3 course*

As the content of key stage 3 is wide ranging, the **coherence** of a course depends on the strength of recurrent elements which bind the parts together. Prominent among these are the geographical perspectives which figured in the aims proposed by the Geography Working Group, and which resulted in the emphases outlined earlier. The recurrence of particular methods of study, such as the use of maps, and of an approach which emphasises enquiry are also important for cohesion.

Progression refers here to features in the structure of a course which enable pupils to advance their learning in an orderly manner. Although sometimes discussed in relation to the sequence in which topics are taught, the way in which the key stage 3 PoS is organised does not require one particular sequence rather than another. There is no single precise order in which to teach the places, themes and groups of skills which are identified in the Programme. Furthermore, the shift from content-specific Statements of Attainment to more generalised Level Descriptions has freed geography teachers from the association between specific content and levels, a feature of the 1991 Order which was such a serious source of difficulties for planning courses and for assessment. Progression is more usefully conceived as the gradual development of pupils' understanding, skills and appreciations, elements of which may be envisaged as threads running through the sequentially organised units of study. The qualities which characterise progression in geographical learning will be considered in Chapter 7.

The case for **differentiation** is based on the practical need to match curricular provision to the experience and capabilities of pupils. It is, for example, essential that more-able pupils are suitably extended, and that pupils who are not making adequate progress are given appropriate support. The National Curriculum PoS can be regarded as an entitlement for all pupils. The nature of the key stage 3 geography PoS is such that there is no strong reason to suppose that many, if any, pupils need be excluded from it. The challenge for teachers is to develop the curriculum in ways which make it accessible to all pupils and enable them to attain their potential. This means that it may be necessary to provide different learning materials and set different learning tasks for different pupils tackling the same topic. On some occasions, it will be appropriate to differentiate assessment tasks to ensure that pupils are given suitable opportunities to demonstrate what they have learnt. The Level Descriptions make it possible to recognise different qualities of performance within the same broad area of content. Differentiation can be introduced within units of study rather than in the framework of a course.

Curriculum planners need to check that the structures that they are creating can accommodate the various elements which they intend to include. This can be done with the help of matrices, such as that presented in Figure 4. Here a content framework is checked against the places and themes specified in the PoS. This particular scheme is one of many which could be suitable for key stage 3. Each of the three years has a major place study (Year 7 – the home region; Year 8 – an economically developed country; Year 9 – an economically developing country); and at least one study which focuses on physical geography (Year 7 – volcanic activity; Year 8 – coasts; Year 9 – UK weather systems). The matrix shows which units provide a focus for, or make a significant contribution to knowledge and understanding of the required places and themes. A similar approach can be used to identify which units have a fieldwork component, and which contribute to the development of particular types of skills. A third matrix might be used to display the contribution of the various units to cross-curricular themes. Such matrices not only provide a general check on coverage, breadth and balance, but also indicate opportunities to develop progression in learning.

The Key Questions in Figure 5 can be applied, in varying degrees, to designing a new structure plan; reviewing an existing plan; or revising a plan, following a departmental review or changes in external requirements.

Figure 5: **Key questions about a structure plan**

Planning and preparing units of study

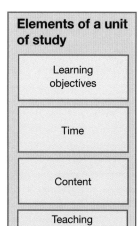

A unit of study is a coherent section of a course which has a clear identity. It is a basic building block in curriculum planning. The main elements to be considered are similar to those which figure in a structure plan, but at a greater level of specificity. The plan for a unit of study should focus on the sequence of **content** and **activities** which structure the teaching and learning. It should specify the **learning objectives** which the content and activities are intended to serve, the **resource materials** which will be available, and the **methods** which will be used to **assess** pupils' learning. The allocation of **time** to sections of the unit, even if only approximate, provides a guide for implementation and a check on progress. Any adjustments can then be made in the full knowledge of their implications for the remainder of the unit. The plan should also make provision for the evaluation of the unit. These components are closely inter-related and significant change to any one component has implications for others.

Because the inter-relationships between these components have to be kept in mind, there is much to be said for delegating the responsibility for designing an individual unit of study to one or two teachers. This need not preclude an initial pooling of ideas from a larger number of teachers, or encouraging all members of the department to comment on a first draft. However, to ensure that the unit adequately satisfies the aims of the course and fits into its overall structure, the head of department or a course leader should retain final responsibility. The discipline of preparing a formal plan and discussing it with another specialist is valuable, even when only one person is teaching a particular unit. This is often the case with A level geography courses. The isolation of the subject specialist in a small secondary school can sometimes be broken down by co-operating with colleagues in other schools.

There are various ways of presenting a unit plan. Figure 6 illustrates one possible framework which accommodates the example of a Year 7 unit on volcanic activity. The **learning objectives** for this unit are related directly to subject content and, in the case of the last objective, to a teaching strategy favoured by the department. They are fairly specific without being in the form of behaviourial statements. In this case, most of the

Elements of a unit of study

- Learning objectives
- Time
- Content
- Teaching methods/learning activities
- Resource materials
- Assessment and evaluation

GEOGRAPHY TEACHERS' HANDBOOK

Course	Geography KS3	Year	7	Unit of Study	Volcanic Activity	Time	6 weeks

Learning objectives

1. know about the scale of volcanic activity;
2. recognise and describe volcanic landforms - lava flows, volcanic cones and craters;
3. explain how particular types of landforms are related to types of eruption;
4. understand the nature and impact of hazards associated with volcanic eruptions;
5. explain how the global distribution of active volcanoes is related to the pattern of crustal plates;
6. make effective use of a range of source materials.

Contribution to cross-curricular themes

Information Technology: using IT to obtain, select, organise and present information

Links with other subjects

English: writing for different purposes – description (volcanic landforms); reporting (an eruption, hazards); explanation (causes of volcanic activity)

Science: some links with the earth science component in AT3 'Materials and their Properties'.

Time	Content	Learning activities and Teaching methods	Resource materials
2 wks	1. case studies of 3 volcanic eruptions illustrating contrasts (e.g. . . . .)	Watch video; examine photographs and maps; read accounts of the eruptions. Compare the eruptions; identify the types of materials emitted; describe landforms.	video film (. . . . .) textbook (. . . .) rock specimens
1 wk	2. volcanic landforms – lava flows, volcanic cones and craters	Identify and make notes on the factors which influence the shape of volcanoes; draw and annotate diagrams.	display of photographs and newspaper reports
2 wks	3. volcanic eruptions as natural hazards; the possibilities and difficulties of predicting eruptions. Why do people live in volcanic areas?	Use IT to produce a newspaper report of an eruption – small groups.	IT software (. . . .)
1 wk	4. global distribution of active volcanoes	Examine world maps to compare distributions of earthquakes, volcanoes, fold mountains and crustal plates.	maps textbooks
	5. explanation of distribution pattern	Teacher leads pupils towards simple explanation; pupils record the explanation with guidance.	differentiated worksheets

Methods of assessment

Routine monitoring of pupils' work, with particular attention given to the newspaper report, and to pupils' explanations of volcanic landforms and the global distribution pattern

Evaluation of unit

(Evaluation to be written soon after the completion of the unit, and following discussion between teachers)

Figure 6: A plan for a unit of study

learning objectives are derived directly from the key stage 3 PoS. However, the plan indicates that the unit is also designed to contribute to a **cross-curricular theme** (information technology) and it recognises potential **links** with two other subjects, English and science. The inclusion of such details facilitates cross-curricular strategies and liaison between subject teams, and thereby supports the development of a more coherent school curriculum.

The layout of the document is intended to highlight the close relationship between **content, learning activities/teaching methods,** and **resource materials**. Content can range from general concepts, for example, the nature of particular types of volcanic eruptions and types of volcanic landforms, to the specification of the examples to be studied. A unit plan might indicate scope for choice in the selection of case studies, resources and learning activities, to take account of the preferences of individual teachers and to make efficient use of the resources available. In this example some differentiation of resource materials has been planned, in the form of worksheets, to cater for the different levels of understanding which pupils can be expected to achieve. The need for differentiation is more likely to be apparent when the objectives focus on pupils' ability to explain geographical patterns, relationships and processes. This is simply because an explanation, and the understanding which it reveals, can so often be developed at a range of levels. An explanation of the global distribution of volcanic activity can be fairly simple, requiring limited knowledge, or very sophisticated and dependent on a depth of understanding.

While in this unit (Figure 6) **assessment** of pupils' progress is to be carried out by routine monitoring of their work – using methods which could be described in a departmental policy statement on assessment – other units could make use of tests or other formal methods of assessment. Such assessment should be designed to help pupils' learning, and to inform the teachers' **evaluation**, and subsequently their improvement, of the unit.

As with formulating policies and devising a structure plan, planning a unit of study can be helped by identifying key questions (Figure 7).

- What is the unifying theme or focus for this unit?

- What are the learning objectives for the unit?
  Are they consistent with the aims of the course?

- What content will best serve these objectives?
  Are there any particular ideas (concepts, generalisations or models) which should be introduced and developed? Should explicit attention be given to attitudes and values?

- Which learning activities and teaching methods are likely to be most productive?
  Will they help to motivate the pupils?
  What skills can be developed through such activities?

- What resource materials are available or could be produced?
  Do they influence the choice of content and methods?

- Can the unit contribute to any cross-curricular themes?
  Are there potential links with any other subjects?

- How is the unit to be structured?
  What would be the best sequence of content and activities?

- Should any of the content, learning activities or resource materials be differentiated to cater for the different interests, experiences and capabilities of pupils?

- How, when and for what purposes should the pupils' learning be assessed?

- How should the unit be evaluated?

*Figure 7: **Key questions about a unit of study***

Conclusion

Course planning is a complex activity which involves decisions at different levels. The hierarchical model emphasises the close links which must be maintained between these levels. Lesson planning is undertaken in the context of units of study, and units of study are planned in the context of an overall course structure. At all three levels, practice should be consistent with the curriculum policies of the subject department and of the school. Such planning is more likely to be of a high quality, and effective when it is supported by regular discussion and close co-operation between teachers.

References

Commission on Geographical Education. International Geographical Union (1992) *International Charter on Geographical Education.*

Curriculum Council for Wales (1991) *Geography in the National Curriculum. Non-Statutory Guidance for Teachers.*

DES/WO (1985) *General Certificate of Education. The National Criteria: Geography.*

DES/WO (1990) *Geography for Ages 5 to 16.*

DFE (1985) *Geography in the National Curriculum.*

HMI (1986) *Geography from 5 to 16.* Curriculum Matters 7, HMSO.

School Curriculum and Assessment Authority (1994) *Geography in the National Curriculum. Draft Proposals,* SCAA.

Welsh Joint Examining Council (1990) *GCSE Avery Hill 14-16 Geography Project Teachers' Handbook.*

Chapter 6

Planning your lessons

EWA SAWICKA

In Chapter 5, Trevor Bennetts outlined ways of planning geography courses. Once that crucial stage has been completed, the next step for teachers is to plan their lessons. This chapter offers some guidance on lesson planning and includes some examples of plans which have been followed successfully in the classroom.

Long gone are the days when pupils sat quietly, accepting what the teacher said, making copious dictated notes or taking notes from textbooks. As they hardly ever varied, such lessons did not require much planning. Young people now are unlikely to remain passive; they are accustomed to receiving information via many different media and resources, so they expect more stimulating lessons. Lessons need to challenge pupils so they want to start questioning and finding things out for themselves. In order for this to occur every teacher needs to plan his/her lessons in detail, focusing on individual objectives and criteria, and bearing in mind the abilities and experiences of the pupils in the classroom. The importance of planning lessons cannot be overstated, and is clearly identified in OFSTED reports.

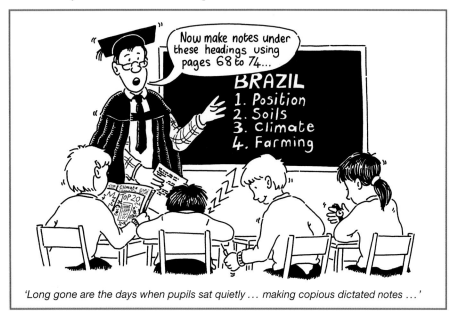

Only a well-planned course can produce effective lessons

Photo: **John Birdsall Photography**

'Long gone are the days when pupils sat quietly … making copious dictated notes …'

Planning

All teachers are faced with similar questions:

- What information do I use to plan lessons?
- How shall I use this information to develop lessons suitable for my particular group?

The obvious starting point is the departmental schemes of work which should be set out for key stages 3 and 4 and A level courses.

In any geography department handbook, schemes of work should include key questions for each theme; teaching and learning strategies; the knowledge and understanding that should be gained from a particular topic; the skills to be learned; and the resources to be used. Teachers can devise their own lesson plans from this framework. Questions which often arise at this stage are:

- Well – this is the theme, these are the suggested teaching and learning strategies, these skills need to be taught and I have these resources – this is my framework, but how shall I teach this topic?
- Where shall I start to plan this lesson?
- Which resources can I use with this particular group?
- How can I measure its success?

Lesson planning requires the consideration of a number of aspects:

- aims and objectives
- content
- methods and resources
- evaluation.

For each lesson it is important to realise what we are trying to achieve, what information we are trying to cover and how we are going to assess the success of the lesson. In other words, have the aims and objectives been covered?

Aims are broad statements of purpose. For example, the aim of a key stage 4 lesson on industry may be to introduce the idea of industry as a system which operates at a variety of scales. The aim may relate to one or two lessons, as the example, or a complete theme. Aims are, however, too general to plan lessons effectively; more specific objectives are necessary to develop precise teaching and learning strategies.

Objectives are specific statements, best defined in terms of what pupils will do or what they will achieve in a lesson. Objectives cannot be set as an after-thought. Before the lesson starts, teachers need to be clear in their own minds as to what they expect it to achieve, so that they can guide and direct pupils to specific goals. It is useful, though not essential, to share objectives with the pupils; this enables them to see progress being made.

Content or subject-matter forms the basis of the lesson and is arguably the most important element in planning a lesson. The subject-matter should be clearly stated in the schemes of work, but how it is taught will depend on resources available, time, the nature of the class, as well as the background, experience and character of the teacher.

Teaching **methods** will be influenced by the subject-matter and available resources. The availability of audio-visual materials, photographic packs, appropriate computer programs, CD-ROMs, satellite images, etc., will all affect the choice of methods. In devising teaching and learning strategies, teachers must ensure that progress is made in the lesson by all pupils. Different methods can be used to teach the same topic with equal effect, as long as they achieve the objectives of the lesson.

Evaluation should not be confused with 'assessment'. *Assessment* is the measurement of what the pupils have learned, and is usually expressed as a number, letter or a Level Description, depending on the marking policy of the department (see Chapters 16-18). *Evaluation* is a reflection by the teacher of how the lesson was received by the pupils; which strategies worked well for the group and which did not; what learning occurred; and, more importantly for the teacher's own personal development, what improvements could be made if the lesson was taught again. Evaluation is therefore mainly subjective, based on the teacher's own perceptions. However, there are some simple measures by which teachers can evaluate a lesson; for instance, how many pupils paid attention and for how long? This kind of evaluation should be done as soon as possible after the lesson with a few points jotted down for future reference. Evaluation of lessons should be an integral part of the planning process, a regular activity, not kept in reserve for crisis situations, such as an OFSTED inspection or a staff appraisal.

Although the four main aspects of planning a lesson have been considered here in isolation it is important to remember that they influence each other directly and indirectly. For example, the methods to be used for a particular lesson depend on the subject matter, the class and the resources available (as well as other constraints, such as the physical layout of the classroom), but they are also influenced by the aims and objectives. This inter-relationship is clearly presented by Boardman (1986) in his interactive planning model (see Figure 1). The bi-directional arrows indicate the interactions between the elements. For example, the evaluation will be based on the aims, objectives, content and methods used and will in turn influence them. Objectives may need to be re-determined as a result of evaluation. Content may need to be varied.

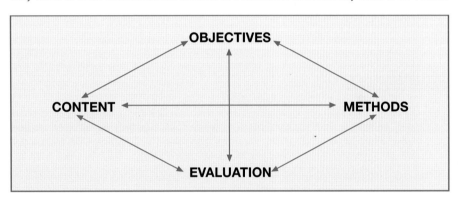

Figure 1: An interactive lesson planning model (after Boardman, 1986)

What, then, should the lesson plan look like? How long should it be? To be effective, lesson plans do not need to be long or complicated. The easiest approach is to have a proforma which has been prepared and agreed by the whole department. This permits compatibility to be achieved within the department as well as allowing lesson plans to be shared, for instance, during a departmental INSET day devoted to a review of lesson planning. An agreed departmental proforma also allows senior staff, advisers and inspectors to have access to information they may need. Figure 2 shows a proforma (one side of A4 paper) which was devised for one geography department. It has been completed for the final lesson in a series for Year 7 comparing two regions of the British Isles, in this case the West Midlands and Wales. The class of 32 pupils was split into two; one half considered the development of the green belt around the West Midlands and the other half the development of the Snowdonia National Park. Previous lessons had been spent discussing what a green belt is, why green belts have been established and reasons for the establishment and importance of National Parks in Britain.

Lesson plan

Date/period

14 February   1
15 February   2 + 3
21 February
22 February

Year group

Year 7 (11-12 years)

Aim of lesson

To hold a debate concerning the development of Snowdonia and the Green Belt

Objectives

1. Pupils to prepare speeches for particular roles chosen.
2. Pupils to be able to deliver speeches in these roles and to answer questions from the floor.
3. Pupils to vote for the development or the protection of Snowdonia and the Green Belt.

Unit of work/Content of lesson

Comparison of the West Midlands and Wales: looking at issues from different points of view about the development of the Green Belt around Birmingham or Snowdonia.

Resources

Cards made at home relating to specific roles (written on coloured card).

GREEN BELT (Green)	SNOWDONIA (Orange)
Members of local conservation group	Second-home owner
Leisure centre developer	Weekend visitor
Local residents	Local shopkeeper
Hypermarket manager	Snowdonia Tourist Board representative
Long-distance lorry driver	Hotel owner
Property developer – new housing estate	Forestry Commission officer
Birdwatcher	Local farmers
Local farmers	Dwr Cwmri – Welsh Water Board representative

Methods planned

1. Split the class into two. Pupils then asked to get into pairs.
2. The cards to be placed role side downwards and one pupil from each pair to choose a card.
3. Once the logistics are completed, pupils to be told to discuss with their partner whether they thought the role they had chosen would be for or against the respective development. Pupils to prepare short speeches (two–three minutes) putting their case. The pupils to be given the rest of a 35 minute lesson to do this, plus a homework.
4. The pupils to be told that the Green Belt people could then ask questions of the presenters of the case for or against the development of Snowdonia and that they would eventually vote, based on the presentations made. The same would then apply, with roles reversed, for the other group.
5. At the beginning of the double lessons pupils to be given ten minutes to finalise their speeches with their partners.
6. The presentations of two to three minutes to be followed by three minutes of questions.
7. Once all the presentations have been made, the pupils are asked to vote as to whether or not the Green Belt is to be developed.
8. Discuss with pupils the presentations, and the importance of their accuracy and audibility.

Homework (if applicable)

Preparation of speech, taking on a particular role in relation to the development of the Green Belt or Snowdonia.

Evaluation

Pupils produced very imaginative presentations: banners, rosettes, leaflets, etc. Some of the pupils were very articulate – especially some who are not gifted academically (pupils' names noted). Some pupils had difficulties with oral presentations: mumbling, lack of logical thought. Again, names noted and discussed with head of English.

NB. In order to do the work justice another double lesson was devoted to role-playing for and against the 'development' of Snowdonia. The single lesson on 21 February was a one-off devoted to producing a sketch from a photograph. This technique had previously been discussed and taught.

The proforma has been completed in much greater detail than is usually needed in order to show all aspects of the planning.

Figure 2: Lesson plan

Key stage 3: A lesson on local river work

In recent years, because of increasing pressure on the curriculum and an increase in school visits by other departments, fieldwork time for geography has been severely curtailed. What was possible a few years ago has had to be radically rethought. Often field visits are limited to lesson times and so have to occur within the surrounding area of the school. Problems most frequently occur when the work relates to physical geography. For example, how does one teach about river landforms to a Year 7 group in a large city?

The first part of the planning process is to think about the area surrounding the school. Questions to consider are:

- Are there any rivers or water courses within walking distance of the school?

- If so, are they easily accessible?

- Would it be possible for pupils to make measurements?

- Could they draw sketches, or do 'rivers' have to be taught from slides, photographs, textbooks or video?

Hands-on experience, when possible, is the most desirable method of teaching knowledge, understanding and geographical skills in the case of this topic. Before any lesson planning can start, a visit by the teacher to the chosen river is essential (see Chapter 14 for details on fieldwork planning).

Week	Work to be covered
Week 1	Mapwork - how height is shown on maps Identification of relief features – valleys, slopes, etc.
Week 2	Definition of features associated with river basins – using sand tray and watering can – words like source, mouth, channel, watershed, tributary, meander, erosion, transportation and deposition
Week 3	Preparation of fieldwork
Week 4	Fieldwork and exchange of information
Week 5	Exchange of information continued and preparation of poster presentation
Week 6	Causes and effects of river floods and methods used to reduce flood risks

Figure 3: Unit of work: rivers (1)

The plan for a unit of work, including the fieldwork, is shown in Figure 3. Figures 4 and 5 show the lesson plans for two double lessons in this unit of work. The preceding two weeks' lessons focused on mapwork, including ways in which height is shown on maps and on identification of relief such as steep and gentle slopes, valleys, etc., and on definitions relating to river basins, using a sand tray and watering-can to show different features.

What follows is a set of examples of lesson plans for different key stages and topics, all of which have been followed successfully in school.

Lesson plan

Period	**Year group**
4 + 5	Year 7 (11-12 years)

Aim of lesson

To prepare pupils for river study measurements in the field.

Objectives

1. Pupils to: suggest and discuss fieldwork tasks to be completed;
2. Pupils to: decide on how measurements to be taken for each task;
3. Pupils to: collect fieldwork equipment needed and to ensure they know how to use it;
4. Pupils to: present information to rest of class.

Unit of work

Rivers (1)
Fieldwork techniques for collecting information on rivers. Aspects covered:

> River width
> River depth
> Valley sides
> Speed
> Load
> Pollution

Resources

> Stop-watches
> Measuring tapes
> Rulers
> Ranging poles
> Card
> Stone size index boards
> Litmus paper
> Clinometers

Methods planned

1. Group work: pupils to be put into six groups using letters on cards.
2. Class discussion on fieldwork to be completed.
3. Main tasks suggested. Put on blackboard or OHP. Tasks allocated to groups.
4. Group discussion regarding methods to be used to complete task. Decision by group on best method and how it will be executed. Fieldwork equipment needed to be collected by group. Difficulties over methods and equipment to be discussed with teacher. Groups to decide who will do the measuring and who the recording.
5. Group to make card with specific instructions about fieldwork task. To be handed in at end of lesson.
6. One person from each group to present information to rest of class.
7. Brief class about the arrangements for fieldwork during next lesson – meeting time and place, clothing needed. Some groups will complete only one task, some two, because of time required for tasks.

Homework

To write a brief summary of all the measurements to be made on the river in exercise book and how these measurements to be taken.

Evaluation

Group worked well – but weaker pupils were not as fully involved in discussion as hoped. In future, perhaps groups need to be thought about more carefully. Groups more even in ability? Good ideas generated and good judgements made. Some groups worked faster than others, completing all work set, others a little slow.

Presentation to class enabled groups to see the need for clear instructions and organisation.

Figure 4: Lesson plan 1: key stage 3

Lesson plan

Period

1 + 2 (70 minutes)

Year group

Year 7 (11-12 years)

Aim of lesson

To obtain information on a specific river by taking measurements and completing an annotated sketch.

Objectives

Pupils to collect measurements on a river. (Note: Decide on which measurements before field trip).

Unit of work

Rivers (1)

Collection of fieldwork data on rivers.

Speed
Width
Load
Angle of valley sides
Pollution

Resources

Stop watches – speed
Measuring tapes – speed/width
Rulers – depth
Ranging poles – valley sides
Cards – with instructions for each group
Stone size index boards – load
Litmus paper – pollution
Clinometers – valley sides

Methods planned

1. Assemble pupils into six groups as in previous lesson in the classroom. Parents met over breaktime and taken up to classroom. Parents briefed regarding fieldwork tasks.
2. Collection of fieldwork materials/equipment needed for investigation by each group.
3. Pupils to be taken down to fieldwork site, with help from parents.
4. At fieldwork site parents given specific groups to look after.
5. Work to be carried out by each of the groups as decided in previous lesson.
   a) Measurement of speed on a 10m stretch of the river – on left, right and middle of river. Ten measurements to be taken at each position.
   b) Measurement of river width in ten different places across river.
   c) Measurement of river depth every 10cm across river in five different locations.
   d) River load measurement – removal of ten samples of stone from river in three different places. Stone boards used to measure length, width and depth of stones.
   e) Measurement of angle of valley sides using ranging poles and clinometer.
   f) Pollution of river measured using litmus paper, sediment test and visual assessment, on five sections of river.
6. Groups brought together and briefed about homework.
7. Groups return to school at end of double lesson accompanied by parents and member of staff.

Homework

All members of groups to write up method used to carry out fieldwork and to have a copy of the results of their group to bring to next lesson.

Evaluation

Groups generally worked sensibly and well although there were some instances when pupils had to be reprimanded for not carrying out tasks set. Fieldwork tasks proved successful with great team spirit. Recording of results not as successful as hoped despite briefing on accuracy. More time needs to be spent on this in future. As usual some pupils did not complete homework tasks - perhaps it would be better to set this in class before carrying out the fieldwork.

Figure 5: Lesson plan 2: key stage 3

Practical river studies
begin with measurement:
you need a small safe
stream

Photo: **Helen Sail**

The collection of data in the field was followed by a single lesson when the data were exchanged between groups so that all the groups had data relating to all tasks set. One double lesson was then allocated to preparation of a poster presentation of all the results by each group. This produced an amazing variety of excellent display work.

Local river found to be polluted

Pupils from a local school used a desk-top publishing package to write a newspaper report on the pollution they found in a local river they recently investigated on geography fieldwork.

Computer takes the strain

Pupils used a simple spreadsheet to log information collected on geography fieldwork. The computer then produced simple graphs and diagrams to illustrate a class display.

Fieldwork generally creates stimulating lessons because the pupils thoroughly enjoy collecting their own information and producing exciting displays from their results. This is evidenced in their work when newts, frogs, ducks, etc., appear alongside geographical data! The majority of lessons, however, have to be taught using only classroom resources and it is up to individual teachers to ensure that all pupils obtain stimulus and a sense of achievement in each lesson. As part of the work in Year 8 on Rivers (2), lessons were devised to encourage co-operation between pupils and improve independent learning (Figure 6).

Week	Work to be covered
1	Use satellite images to identify and interpret patterns relating to physical geography
2	Processes associated with the formation of river channels and river valleys: erosion, transportation and deposition
3/4a	Landforms associated with river valleys and channels: Stages 1, 2 and 3
	Identification of main sources of fresh water and methods used to provide people with reliable supplies of fresh water
5/6	Reasons why rivers, lakes and seas become polluted; ways in which the problems of pollution have been and tackled; and ways it could be prevented

Figure 6: Unit of work: Rivers (2)

The lesson plan shown in Figure 7 took time and careful planning. First, the pupils were consulted as to which people were good at art in their class and these individuals were assigned the task of producing a sketch for a wall display on river, lake or sea pollution. The pupils were shown exactly how much wall space was allocated.

The rest of the class was divided into groups with a team leader in each one, the team leader then assigns specific tasks to group members. These groups had the task of finding out as much information as possible for the next lesson on river, lake or sea pollution, and possible solutions to the various problems associated with this pollution. The pupils were asked to bring this information to the next lesson. The lesson plan for the subsequent lesson is shown in Figure 7.

Lesson plan

Day/period		Year group
Thursday	1 (35 minutes)	Year 8 (12-13 years)
Friday	7 and 8 (70 minutes)	
Thursday	1 (35 minutes)	
Friday	7 and 8 (70 minutes)	

Aim of lesson

To produce a wall display on sources of river, lake or sea pollution and the possible solutions to the pollution caused.

Objectives

1. Pupils to: brainstorm their ideas about the pollution of a river, lake or sea (and possible solutions to the pollution problems, depending on which aspect they had been allocated);
2. Pupils to: discuss sketch produced for display and how their ideas of the causes of pollution and possible solutions could be included in the sketch, and suggest any changes needed to the sketch;
3. Pupils to: work on set tasks allocated to them by the team leader;
4. Pupils to: produce the display.

Unit of work

Rivers (2)
Pollution of rivers, lakes and seas and ways in which problems of pollution could be tackled or prevented.

Resources

Library books – brought in by pupils
Use of school library and CD-ROM in library
Poster paper – variety of colours
A4 card – 2 colours available
Variety of felt tip pens
Sugar paper – variety of colours

Methods planned

1. Pupils to get into groups allocated in previous lesson.
2. The team leader to lead brainstorming session on the topic allocated, e.g. sources of pollution; possible solutions to the problem in rivers, seas or lakes.
3. The team leader, in consultation with the group, to allocate specific tasks from brainstorm for each pupil to produce written work for display – to include a specific source of pollution using the resources gathered by the group together with any resources available in the classroom or library.
4. Once pupils have completed this task then team leader to allocate specific aspects of the display work to specific group members.
5. Display to be put together involving all pupils including titles, sub-titles, drawings, etc., and mounted on display board.

Homework

Pupils to work on individual tasks set by team leaders.

Evaluation

Pupils found all over the classroom and in corridor. Working at desks, on the carpet, at display board. A real hum occurred throughout this work. All pupils engaged on task. Weaker pupils were helped by brighter pupils. Real team spirit. A very good approach to the subject, although great care needed in setting up the work. Pupils extremely resourceful in finding information – more information was brought in than an individual teacher could seek out on his/her own.

Figure 7: *Lesson plan 3: key stage 3*

CD-ROM used to investigate river/lake/sea pollution
After consulting the librarian and finding suitable CD-ROM disks, pupils were encouraged to investigate pollution saving the material on their own disks for incorporation into a word processed account.

Italy North: long-established industries, inward imigration

Photo: **Fiat Mirafiori**

Italy South: once poor, now transformed by natural gas and tourism

Photo: **Russell King**

Differentiation

Planning differentiated tasks is vital to ensure that the brightest pupils, as well as those who find academic work more challenging, are given learning activities which match their abilities. It would be difficult to plan differentiated tasks without a good working knowledge of individual pupils and their abilities. At no stage must the lower-ability pupils feel that their tasks are not as valid as those for the more able groups. No matter how classes are split into groups, whether by allocating letters or numbers or by using pupils' names, the pupils themselves will know which group consists of the 'more academically able' and the 'least able' pupils. Therefore, work has to be set which is valid, challenging in different ways, and which allows pupils to feel a sense of 'real' achievement.

Two important things must be remembered when planning lessons for key stage 3:

1. **Do not overload the lessons** – plan carefully what pupils need to know or be able to do at this stage.

2. **Frequently change the approach to lessons** – the unexpected creates excitement and produces excellent work from the pupils.

Figure 8 shows a series of activities planned for a class of Year 9 pupils on the North-South divide in Italy. This work was set at the end of a unit of work based on Italy – a European country (selected from List A in the key stage 3 Programmes of Study). The class was split into five ability groups and each group allocated a different task.

Pupils design Italian poster
Using a graphics package and CD-ROM images, pupils produced a variety of posters designed to develop the tourist potential of southern Italy.

Key stage 4: A unit of work on contrasts in development

Pupils at key stage 4 (ages 14-16+) have opted to do geography and frequently show a keen interest in the work. Although the content of lessons depends on the GCSE syllabus chosen, teachers should broaden the pupils' interest in the subject and lead them towards independent learning in the topics studied.

What follows is an example of a unit of work developing the topic of 'contrasts in development'. This is one of the topics included in the Southern Examining Group Syllabus A.

This work naturally leads into a study of widely used indicators of development. Figure 10 shows the lesson plan for work on GNP within this framework. Pupils were asked to focus on three more-developed and three less-developed countries.

Great care needs to be taken when planning lessons about different indicators if repetition is to be avoided. A variety of teaching and learning strategies need to be employed, as shown in Figure 11.

ACTIVITY 1

Resources *Access 1*, pages 40-53
Interactions, pages 56-57
Geoactive, No.80

Your task is to study the information in the *Geoactive* pamphlet, to answer Questions 2, 3, 4, 5 and 6 and prepare your answer in the form of a display under the heading 'Italy's North-South divide – does it still exist?' This will mean that you will need to add explanatory notes or comments to the diagrams, etc., which you produce.

ACTIVITY 2

Resources *Access 1*, pages 40-53
Interactions, pages 56-57

Your task is to prepare the script of a documentary programme for radio, assessing the effectiveness of the Cassa per il Mezzogiorno. Use the information in the resources to give you some ideas. Your programme is likely to include some straight factual information, but also items to illustrate the points such as interviews with industrialists, local people, farmers, young people who may be thinking of moving away, etc. Try to make your script 'flow', with some connection between one item and the next. Write or word-process your script in a way that could be displayed. You will have a chance to 'broadcast' your programme to the rest of the group.

ACTIVITY 3

Resources *Access 1*, pages 40-53
Interactions, pages 56-57

Your task is to assess the success so far of the Cassa per il Mezzogiorno and to make some suggestions as to how in the future it could narrow the gap between North and South still further.

Present your ideas and findings in the form of a display. Base your work on the four activities on page 47 in the *Access* book.

ACTIVITY 4

Resources *Access 1*, pages 40-53
Interactions, pages 56-57
Brochures of Italy

The Mezzogiorno could improve its economy by fuller development of its tourist industry. Your task is to produce a magazine poster advertisement to encourage people to develop the tourist potential in this part of Italy. It needs to be designed to appeal to all types of people who may get involved, e.g. hoteliers, farmers, property developers, sportspeople. Think in terms of job opportunities, what the area has to offer, potential new attractions, etc. A magazine advertisement, as well as looking attractive, should include quite a lot of factual information.

ACTIVITY 5

Resources *Access 1*, pages 40 - 53
Interactions, pages 56 - 57
Travel brochures featuring Southern Italy

One of the likely future developments to improve the economy of southern Italy is the further development of tourism. Your task is set out in *Access 1*, page 53, Activity 1.

Figure 8: The North-South divide in Italy

Week	Work to be covered
Week 1	Introduction: looking at development data in atlas, pupils work independently, disproving a number of statements written on the blackboard and giving reasons for their decisions
Week 2	Pupils work in groups of three/four using a computer program based on development data research. This involves pupils making correlations between different sets of data, including GNP, literacy rates, diet, health care, etc.

Figure 9: Unit of work on contrasts in development

A level

A level students should be able to work independently; however, the skills they need to do this must be developed systematically as they progress through school. The grounding for a really successful A level course is laid in the primary school! It can be rewarding for students and staff alike if the students themselves prepare and deliver a small section of an A level course. For this to work, the teacher must undertake some careful planning, with particular reference to available resources, e.g. textbooks, slides, photographs, maps, videos, computer programs, satellite images. The teacher must also

---

Lesson plan

Day/period	Year group
Monday 1 + 2 (70 minutes)	Year 11 (15-16 years)

Aim of lesson

To consider particular indicators as contrast in development.

Objectives

1. Pupils to know definition of GNP;
2. Pupils to use resource sheet of social and economic indicators to show contrasts in GNP and to give reasons for the contrasts;
3. Pupils to take on different roles in groups and complete a decision making exercise. (See examples in Figure 12.)

Unit of work

1. Contrasts in development – GNP as an indicator of development.
2. Decision-making exercise including role play – about using money to increase development.

Resources

Atlases
Textbooks
Information sheets of activities
Role cards
Computer data
CD-ROMs

Methods planned

1. Recap on previous lesson on indicators of development and types of correlation pupils found between different types of data.
2. Use of textbooks or geographical dictionary to find out definition of GNP. Pupils to write it out in exercise books.
3. Pupils to use resources sheet to find GNP values for the three more-developed and three less-developed countries. Values to be written out and commented on – giving as many reasons as possible why GNP values may be high or low.
4. Decision-making exercise: pupils given a list of activities which could help development and boost GNP in a developing country. Pupils to be allocated to a group and each group given a role. Each group has to decide on how to allocate funds supposing they had £3 million to spend, choosing from the activities indicated in Figure 12.
5. Pupils to prepare information for presentation to the whole class. Form of presentation left for pupils to decide. Work to be continued in next lesson with a view to each group doing a presentation.

Homework

A letter to be written to the Ministry of Development explaining the decision(s) reached by their group on how to spend the £3 million and why particular projects were chosen.

Evaluation

Use of atlases and textbooks as resource material good as it enabled pupils to use their own information. Work on GNP took longer than expected, more able pupils made perceptive comments, less able pupils just commented on the obvious. Group work generated interesting discussion. Need to remember to discuss various roles, attitudes and judgements with the whole class after the presentations.

Figure 10: Lesson plan: GCSE

---

ensure that the tasks set are within every student's capabilities; it is often easiest if the work is completed in pairs. An example of a unit of work that could be carried out using this method of teaching is one which concerns the processes involved in glacial and fluvio-glacial erosion, transport and deposition and the associated landforms. An enquiry approach can be adopted to answer basic questions, such as:

- What are the processes involved in glacial/fluvio-glacial erosion, transport and deposition?

- What landforms result and how are they formed?

Topic	Method
GNP	Resources sheet Role-play and decision-making exercise
Literacy	Worksheet containing specific questions
Health	Brainstorming Case study work: comparison between UK and The Gambia – OHP work
Diet	Comparison of diet of someone in the UK and in India Discuss relative merits of each diet. Video presentation Discussion and textbook work on undernourishment and malnutrition

Figure 11: Variations in methods used to teach topics

Roles

Role 1 – Minister for Planning in the government of the country.
Role 2 – A wealthy citizen of the country, who wants to make more money, and would also like to see the country develop.
Role 3 – An executive of a transnational company, who wishes to invest in the country.
Role 4 – A worker from a charity, such as Oxfam, involved in sending aid to the country.
Role 5 – A representative from the Overseas Development Department of the British Government.

Some of the activities which would help development and boost GNP in a developing country
(with their approximate cost)

- Build primary schools, for 200 pupils in each, in 50 villages (£2 million).
  Train 100 high school graduates to teach in village schools and run adult literacy classes (£300,000).
- Build and equip centres for basic health care in 30 villages (£2 million).
- Equip 20 minibuses to provide health care and family planning services in remote villages; train and pay salaries of workers on buses (£500,000).
- Install water supply systems in 200 villages (£1 million).
- Make funds available to banks, so that they can make loans of £2,000, with low interest charges, to 500 farmers (£1 million).
- Train 50 village field workers and pay their salaries for a year. Each will teach 100 farmers how to use new seeds and more efficient methods, to increase production (£250,000).
- Build a small factory to make bicycles in a capital city; develop a programme to train shanty town dwellers as workers (£1 million).
- Make a preliminary survey of energy resources as a first step to reduce oil imports (£100,000).
- Resurface and broaden a road carrying timber from a forest to a port, from which it can be exported (£2 million).

Figure 12: Contrasts in development

Students need to be given research time in the classroom and at home and then asked to plan their presentation to the rest of the group. This plan should be discussed with the teacher. More homework time should then be allocated to producing materials, whether OHPs, worksheets or information sheets, which may need to be duplicated before the lesson. The teacher should check whether students will require any equipment for the lesson, e.g. video, OHP, computer, slide projector. Student-led lessons are particularly rewarding because they do far more research than for teacher-led lessons. Students also have to ensure that they fully understand the work before presenting it to the rest of the group. It is amazing how well-researched, well-documented and resourceful student-led lessons can be and how their true abilities emerge. For lessons planned in this way it is essential that the aims and objectives are clearly stated; if possible students should work these out for themselves.

The main drawback of this method is time – both the extra time a teacher needs to devote to ensuring that materials are produced, presentations are planned and equipment is available – and the time taken for each of the presentations (most teachers could cover the topic in half the time).

Student presentations, if well-prepared and well-presented, can accelerate learning

Photo: **Margaret Roberts**

Conclusion

Planning lessons is an essential element in every teacher's schedule, no matter how long the teacher has been in service. At every level, effective teaching in geography begins with detailed planning which is adjusted to the capacities in the class and which allows all pupils in the classroom to make progress in their learning. This is the ideal. Sometimes we achieve it!

Reference

Boardman, D. (ed) (1986) *Handbook for Geography Teachers.*
The Geographical Association.

Chapter 7

Progression and differentiation

TREVOR BENNETTS

Introduction

Progression and differentiation are features of a curriculum which arise from the ways in which a school attempts to match its provision to the capabilities and needs of its pupils. Provision here includes the content and structure of courses, the organisation of teaching groups, the resources made available to pupils and the actual teaching which takes place. In the case of progression, the focus is on how the quality of attainments of pupils advance as they move through the school system. This advance is influenced by the ways in which pupils mature, as well as by the education which they experience. One of the challenges for teachers is to design courses which take due account of, and foster, pupils' intellectual, social and physical maturation. In the case of differentiation, the focus is on matching provision to the differences in interests, experience and capabilities of pupils of roughly the same age.

When planning for progression, teachers have to design routes along which their pupils can acquire knowledge and develop understanding, skills, attitudes and values. Such planning requires a clear sense of direction, as well as good knowledge of the terrain over which they will lead their pupils. To cater for a wide range of capabilities, they may decide to construct different routes for different groups of pupils – perhaps leading to different destinations; or to plan itineraries which recognise that different pupils will travel at different rates and will benefit from engaging in different activities, even when moving along the same route. Whichever strategy teachers adopt, they need to monitor their pupils' progress, to enable them to adjust their day-to-day programmes to meet the needs of individuals, while maintaining the general directions which they intend.

Most geography curricula in secondary schools have to satisfy the requirements of external frameworks. For Years 7 to 9, these are the requirements of key stage 3 of the National Curriculum; for Years 10 and 11, those of GCSE courses; and for Years 12 and 13, they are, in the main, the requirements for A and AS levels. To what extent the new GNVQ courses will affect this pattern remains to be seen. While these external frameworks (which are themselves subject to change) specify the sort of content and skills which must be attended to, and provide guidance on standards in relation to assessment, it remains the responsibility of teachers to design courses, organise provision and develop learning activities appropriate for their pupils and for the particular circumstances of each school. Teachers of geography in every secondary

Learning is individual. Discussions in small groups, perhaps helped by PGCE students, go some way towards achieving the ideal of individual teaching

Photo: **Margaret Roberts**

school have to face the challenges posed by the need for progression and differentiation in the curriculum.

Planning for progression

Among the more general principles which can guide planning for progression are:

- whenever possible, teaching should build on pupils' existing knowledge and previous experience;
- learning tasks should be matched carefully to pupils' capabilities;
- the overall scheme for a subject should take account of the ways in which pupils mature (intellectually, socially and physically) over their period of secondary education; and
- special attention should be given to progression in those aspects of a subject which are likely to be important to pupils' future learning, for example, ideas and skills which have wide application and which underpin more advanced learning in that subject.

Planning for progression should, therefore, take account of the past, present and future: what pupils have already experienced and achieved; what they can reasonably be expected to do at the time; and what will best serve their future needs.

Ideas to help us devise courses which promote progression in geographical learning can be sought from:

- geography as an academic discipline, the source of much of the understanding and methods of enquiry which underpin the geography curriculum in schools;
- educational research about the development of pupils' capabilities, in relation to their age and maturation; and
- the practical experience of teachers, gained from using a range of content, activities and learning materials with pupils of different ages and abilities.

While geography, as a research field and academic discipline, is a rich source of ideas for the school curriculum, it does not offer ready-made structures for the planning of progression in schools. Geographical content can often be organised in a variety of ways, and any theme or place can be explored at a range of levels. For example, most of the themes specified in the key stage 3 Programme of Study, such as geomorphological processes, weather and climate, population, settlement, economic activities and development, are also common components in GCSE and A level syllabuses. They are recurrent elements within the geography curriculum. To plan for progression within a theme, it is necessary to consider how the understanding and skills which are associated with it can be developed within and across the stages. Knowledge of the discipline can help us to:

- identify aspects of a theme which are worth exploring;
- select the concepts, principles and models which are likely to be most useful;
- analyse what is involved in understanding particular ideas and relationships; and
- consider what different forms of understanding and misunderstanding are possible.

THE MATURATION OF PUPILS

As pupils progress through the various stages of education, they not only broaden their experience and acquire a great deal of information, but also develop ways of thinking which enable them to better interpret their experiences and the wealth of information available. Much of the research which focuses on the cognitive development of young people has been influenced by the work of Piaget (Beard, 1969; Turner, 1984). According to Piagetian theory, secondary schooling covers a period during which many pupils advance from concrete operational to formal operational modes of reasoning.

During the phase of concrete operations pupils can develop a wide range of ideas about objects, activities and situations that they can identify in the 'real' world. They can reason logically, provided that what they are thinking about has meaning for them in physical terms. This is one of the potential benefits of helping younger pupils to explore their local environment and extending their direct experience through fieldwork. While pupils in this phase of development become more adept at classifying and ordering, they remain dependent on the evidence of their senses and find it difficult to contemplate possibilities that appear to contradict or go beyond their direct experience. Their reasoning is essentially inductive in character. In other words, while pupils may be capable of reaching general conclusions from the study of particular cases, it is hard for them to reason deductively from given principles.

Pupils who are capable of formal operations can extend their thinking from the world they have experienced to other possibilities. They can reason from propositions, accepting premises and working logically from them. This enables them to adopt a hypothetical-deductive approach to enquiry and problem solving. Pupils who engage in formal operational thinking can make sense of more abstract concepts and generalisations; their thinking extends beyond an understanding of relations between objects or events to an understanding of relations between ideas which themselves represent relations. For example, while a pupil at the level of concrete operations may be able to make sense of the ideas of soil erosion and soil protection (because these can easily be illustrated in physical terms), the concept of soil conservation (which requires some understanding of a state of dynamic equilibrium) would appear to be dependent on formal reasoning. A similar advance is implied in the difference between describing the land use patterns in a specific town and understanding the assumptions underpinning different models of urban structure.

Much Piagetian research is concerned with the cognitive development of younger children, especially in the fields of mathematics and science. However, Peel and his associates at Birmingham University focused on the development of adolescent judgment in a wide range of school subjects (Peel, 1971). In one of these studies, Rhys (1972) examined how a sample of 120 pupils, ranging in age from nine to sixteen years, dealt with various problems set within specific geographical contexts – in this case contexts with which they were unlikely to be familiar. The questions which he asked were designed to test pupils' reasoning capabilities in geography, rather than their factual knowledge. His research findings revealed a trend, which correlated with the age of the pupils tested, from very restricted responses, to increasingly full and more adequate descriptions and explanations, and finally to relatively comprehensive judgements based upon hypothetico-deductive reasoning. Rhys concluded that the responses indicated a developmental sequence which was consistent with the Piagetian model and with the general ideas proposed by Peel. Rhys recognised that individual pupils were not always consistent in the quality of their response and that the problems posed by the various case studies differed in their complexity and level of difficulty. However, one of his findings was that, in terms of the tasks set, pupils in the sample did not make effective use of hypothetico-deductive forms of reasoning until tested at the age of fourteen-and-a-half, and even then only a small proportion did so. Such a finding would appear to have significant implications for planning progression in geographical learning, especially in relation to expectations for key stage 3.

The idea of 'stages' of cognitive development has been subject to much criticism. There has been debate as to whether the categories described by Piaget and others are best construed as 'stages' or 'levels'; and, in the case of the latter, how useful or otherwise it is to think in terms of general levels of attainment. Collis and Biggs have suggested five levels which offer a useful way of analysing the quality of response to the type of problem-solving tasks set by Rhys and others (Biggs, 1980).

1. *A response which reveals a general lack of comprehension.* Answers of this type often involve tautology or irrelevant associations or denial of premises. They appear to indicate a failure to appreciate what the question is about and often consist of little more than guesses.

2. *A response which focuses on one relevant point* which is picked out from the information provided. The pupil does not see the complexity of the problem posed and is readily satisfied with a simple, unqualified answer.

3. *A response which recognises that there are several dimensions* to the problem and offers a partial list of relevant points, all derived from the information provided. There is the beginning of a descriptive analysis.

4. *A more comprehensive and coherent response,* which recognises all the relevant dimensions in the information given and appreciates that there are inter-relationships between them. However, the pupil has attempted to reach a satisfactory answer without going beyond the information given.

5. *A response based on hypothetico-deductive reasoning.* The problem posed is tackled by introducing an abstract principle from which possible solutions are derived and tested against the information provided. The answer reveals that the pupil can generalise from a formal statement to situations not previously experienced. There is an attempt to resolve inconsistencies, but where appropriate the answer remains tentative and open to other possibilities.

Biggs emphasises that these levels should not be attached to individual pupils, in the sense of pupil A being categorised as operating at level 3 and pupil B at level 4, but should be restricted to evaluating the quality of responses to specific tasks. The levels which pupils attain may be influenced by such factors as:

■ the difficulty of interpreting the information supplied;

■ the nature of the task set;

■ their familiarity with the sort of situation to which the task relates;

■ their understanding of potentially relevant ideas;

■ the guidance given by the teacher;

■ the time allowed for them to carry out the task.

The challenge for teachers is to help pupils develop progressively more mature forms of reasoning in association with their acquisition of knowledge and development of geographical understanding. Indeed, the understanding of increasingly complex and abstract ideas is dependent on the development of more mature ways of thinking. Reference to relevant research can help teachers to be realistic in their expectations, to set suitable objectives and to design tasks which match pupils' capabilities. It can provide insights which help them to interpret their day-to-day experience of using particular content, activities and learning materials with pupils of different ages and abilities.

Progression in the National Curriculum and beyond

In the *Draft Proposals for Geography in the National Curriculum,* SCAA (1994) explained its conception of progression within the subject in terms of a gradual process, involving a wide range of elements which it identified as characteristic of geography. It asserted that through key stage 3, pupils would increasingly:

- broaden and deepen their knowledge and understanding of places and themes;
- make use of a wide and precise geographical vocabulary;
- analyse, rather than describe, geographical patterns, processes and change;
- appreciate the interactions within and between physical and human processes that operate in any environment;
- appreciate the interdependence of places;
- become proficient at conducting and comparing studies at a widening range of scales and in contrasting places and environments;
- apply their geographical knowledge and understanding to unfamiliar contexts;
- select and make effective use of skills and techniques to support their geographical investigations;
- appreciate the limitations of geographical evidence and the tentative and incomplete nature of some explanations.

It is a fairly ambitious statement, signposting the direction for progression during the phase when pupils are moving towards adolescence. The statement could be regarded as equally applicable to the 11 to 16 age range, and even be extended to include A level courses. As far as the National Curriculum is concerned, quality of attainment is defined in terms of eight Level Descriptions, together with an additional description for an exceptional performance. The equivalent for GCSE are the descriptions for grades A, C and F, included in the *GCSE Subject Criteria for Geography* (SCAA, 1995). It is important to remember that the descriptions of National Curriculum Levels and GCSE grades are for the purpose of summative assessment. They were not intended to support formative assessment nor to assist the planning of progression in learning.

An analysis of the scope for progression in geography in the secondary school curriculum is more easily undertaken under the headings of:

- breadth of geographical knowledge;
- depth of geographical understanding;
- use of geographical skills;
- attitudes and values.

BREADTH OF GEOGRAPHICAL KNOWLEDGE

Pupils' breadth of geographical knowledge is strongly influenced by the content of the curriculum, which in turn reflects external requirements imposed by the National Curriculum and public examinations. Nevertheless, within the frameworks of the National Curriculum and of GCSE and A/AS level syllabuses, teachers have some degree of choice in the topics to include in their schemes of work, and considerable freedom in their choice of specific case studies. Breadth of knowledge is fostered by ensuring that pupils study a variety of places at a range of spatial scales, and a suitable range of environmental and social conditions and processes.

It is useful to keep a check on the balance between breadth and continuity in the curriculum, or at least to interpret the two principles with care. For example, while 'development' may figure as a theme in key stage 3, GCSE and A level courses, it would be severely limiting to focus on the same 'less developed' country, or even the same continent, in successive phases. Similarly, there would be serious weaknesses in always focusing on fluvial systems or coastlines in the study of landforms, or on equatorial rainforests in the study of ecosystems.

There is no single principle for determining the sequence in which specific knowledge should be acquired, as much depends on context and use. The broadening of knowledge is, to a considerable extent, a cumulative process, with the idea of progression becoming more pertinent when we consider how that knowledge can be structured to develop understanding. A broad knowledge base may at times be a prerequisite to the development of understanding. Previously acquired knowledge is reinforced when pupils perceive it to be relevant to new learning, and long-term recall is usually helped by periodic revisiting. When planning the geography curriculum, teachers need to consider which information is intended to be used by pupils primarily as part of the process of learning and which is intended to be memorised so that it can be recalled when required. This distinction has implications for teaching and assessment.

DEPTH OF GEOGRAPHICAL UNDERSTANDING

Progression in pupils' geographical understanding is closely associated with the development of their ability to describe and explain geographical conditions, patterns, relationships and changes. This often depends on pupils developing general geographical ideas (concepts, generalisations and models) and being able to apply these to new situations. It was precisely this sort of ability which Rhys investigated; and this relationship between understanding and intellectual skills lies at the heart of the general theories and models of Piaget and Peel.

While it is possible to explore the nature of progression in understanding within geography as a whole, or within very broad divisions of the discipline, such as physical, human and regional geography, it is probably easier to start with more specific themes. The nine themes specified for key stage 3 are especially relevant for the geography curriculum in secondary schools, as many of them figure again in GCSE and A level syllabuses.

To plan for progression in understanding within a recurrent theme, it is necessary to:

■ identify the key ideas to be introduced;

■ analyse these ideas to clarify the meaning of each, the links between them, and the scope of their application;

■ consider the level of understanding appropriate for the age, ability and experience of the pupils;

■ explore pupils' pre-conceptions which may inhibit their acceptance and development of new ideas;

■ take account of the various dimensions which can create barriers, or at least difficulties, for learning, for example: remoteness from experience; levels of complexity and abstraction; the degree of precision required; and the extent to which values are embedded in an idea or pertinent to a particular situation (HMI, 1978);

■ prepare learning materials and design learning tasks which are suitably matched to the capabilities of the pupils;

■ devise an overall structure for the theme, which enables the pupils progressively to develop their understanding.

A good example of such a theme is **settlement**, which is not only specified in the key stage 2 and key stage 3 Programmes of Study, but is also prominent in virtually all GCSE and A level geography syllabuses. The theme encompasses settlement patterns and urban geography, with the latter containing several sub-themes:

■ the nature and influence of site and location;

■ the morphology of towns;

■ the functioning of towns;

- changing patterns in towns;
- urban issues.

There is conspicuous continuity in the structure of content for the theme of settlement through key stage 3, GCSE and A level. Progression, therefore, is not to be sought in the broad outline of content, but in the richness of the information to which pupils are introduced and the depth of understanding they are expected to develop.

Key stage 2
The requirements of this key stage should ensure that pupils enter secondary schools with some knowledge of the size and characteristics of various settlements, including the different uses made of land, and some experience of having investigated an issue arising from the way in which land is used.

Key stage 3
In this key stage the treatment can be more wide ranging and systematic, leading pupils to an understanding of some of the general factors which affect the characteristics of settlements and how they change. Such understanding should build on pupils' direct experience and the use of case studies which can support their inductive mode of thinking. The outline for a key stage 3 scheme of work, presented in Chapter 5, illustrates one possible selection and sequence of content for Years 7 to 9. In this particular example, pupils examine:

a. the site, location and specific characteristics of several contrasting settlements, e.g. a town in an industrial region, a large commercial city, ports and holiday resorts (units 3, 4, 8 and 9);

b. the internal characteristics and changing patterns of a town (unit 11); and

c. features of the settlement pattern in the pupils' home region, and in contrasting regions in both an economically developed country and an economically developing country (units 7, 12 and 15).

There are opportunities for pupils to develop general ideas about the significance of site and situation; the factors which influence the growth of larger settlements; the functions of towns, including more specialised functions; the patterns of land use; and the movements of people and goods within a town. An investigation of a conflict over the use of land in the town studied in unit 11 would allow pupils to consider the relevance of the personal interests and attitudes of people involved, as well as technical aspects of the problem.

GCSE
The accumulation of knowledge and greater intellectual maturity of pupils studying for GCSE enable many of them to develop a broader geographical perspective. For example, they can study urbanisation as a process operating on a global scale, and analyse the distribution of 'millionaire' cities and the differences between countries in terms of the percentage of the population living in towns. More generally, many pupils aged 15 and 16 are capable of analysing more complex situations, of making sense of more abstract ideas, and of investigating more difficult issues than they could in key stage 3. Studies of suitable complexity might focus on the changing pattern of shopping and service centres in a town; or the types of residential area to be found in different urban locations. Among the ideas which abler pupils might develop and apply are:

- accessibility, distance decay and spatial behaviour;
- hierarchical spatial patterns;

- urbanisation and counter-urbanisation;
- urban redevelopment and urban regeneration.

The sort of issues which they can investigate include:

- the problems of 'the inner city';
- the tension between urban redevelopment and conservation;
- the impact on towns of the increase in road traffic, and different strategies for dealing with the problem;
- population migration and the development of shanty towns and ghettoes.

In seeking explanations, pupils can examine in more depth the processes which bring about changes, including the roles of different types of decision makers, such as entrepreneurs, politicians, planners and the general public.

A level

The strength of continuity in the sub-themes studied in successive key stages presents a challenge. A level students can easily experience a feeling of *déjà vu* unless they are both introduced to new content and intellectually extended. Fortunately, there is plenty of scope to investigate different issues, explore new ideas, and further develop students' capacity to reason. Attention can be given to contrasts between towns in different parts of the world, and the extent to which these reflect different economic systems, cultural factors and the particular histories of individual towns. There can also be greater depth of treatment of the economic, social and political processes which contribute to urban development. This often involves synthesising ideas from different branches of geography. The study of housing or manufacturing industry or services in a town can combine economic geography and urban geography; analysis of the growth of Third World cities cannot be divorced from broader aspects of 'development'. Above all, it is at A level that it is worthwhile considering abstract ideas and conceptual models which incorporate a deductive logic. For example, it is at this stages that it becomes realistic to introduce bid rents, economic models of land use and central place theory.

USE OF GEOGRAPHICAL SKILLS

The term 'skill' is applied to a great variety of types of achievement, ranging from the performance of simple techniques to the use of highly developed intellectual and social competencies. Invariably, the term refers to an ability acquired through learning that relates to a specific type of activity, and its use implies a level of achievement. The phrase 'geographical skills' is perhaps misleading, because what are referred to are often general skills being applied in a geographical context. Some, such as map skills, are particularly associated with the subject. Other categories, which are widely used in lists of learning objectives, are essentially cross-curricular, for example, communication skills, general intellectual skills, study skills, enquiry skills and social skills.

Such is the range of skills used in the subject that progression in learning is usually best planned in relation to different types of activity. However, even examination syllabuses reveal that there are many ways of classifying skills, and that the categories often overlap. It may be useful to distinguish between:

1. **specific techniques** – such as those associated with fieldwork, mapwork, and the use of diagrams, remote sensing, statistical techniques and information technology in geography;

2. **general categories of cognitive activity** – such as describing, interpreting, analysing, explaining and evaluating; and

3. **strategies of enquiry** – ways of structuring and carrying out investigations so as to arrive at valid conclusions which can be substantiated.

Intensive study of details in the landscape, such as the plants in this quadrat, are an important basis for fieldwork

Photo: **R G Jones**

The first category is the easiest within which to plan tight sequences of learning activities to enable pupils to improve the quality of what they can do. The second is intimately linked to the intellectual maturation of pupils and the development of their geographical understanding. The third brings together elements of the other two within a broad framework which helps pupils to carry out geographical investigations successfully. As investigations are now a feature of all stages of the geography curriculum, it is important to plan for progression in such activities and in the quality of what pupils achieve through repeatedly engaging in them.

Progression in skills involves building on previous learning and matching demands to the capabilities of pupils. In all three categories it is reasonable to expect increasing complexity in the activities which the skills entail and increasing precision in their use. The analysis of complex skills in terms of their prerequisites can suggest a suitable sequence for learning, although there are often alternative routes to reach the same goal. In none of the three categories can the application of skills be divorced from context; progression is, therefore, often dependent on the quality of pupils' knowledge and understanding. Map interpretation skills, for example, require understanding of the features and patterns shown on the map, as well as knowledge of map conventions and of techniques for scanning the map in order to identify relevant information. To interpret a weather map of the British Isles, it is necessary to know something about depressions and anticyclones and how, in different seasons, these influence the weather experienced on the ground. The link with knowledge and understanding is equally strong in the development and use of the higher-order skills of analysis, synthesis and evaluation, and in the carrying out of investigations. It is this link which was explored so usefully by Rhys (1972a,b).

ATTITUDES AND VALUES

The situations studied in human geography often require some understanding of the perceptions, attitudes and values of other people. Furthermore, pupils' understanding of other people's behaviour is often influenced by their own feelings. Values are deeply embedded within such topics as conflicts over urban land use, population migration, and inequalities of opportunities for people living in different places; and within such concepts as quality of life, development, resource management, environmental management, sustainability, stewardship and conservation. Pupils need to develop understanding of how people's attitudes and values influence their decisions and behaviour. They also need opportunities to discuss and reflect on such matters, so that they can develop well-informed views of their own.

Silcock, who researched the social judgements of pupils aged between eleven and fourteen by obtaining their views about 'the thoughts, feelings and possible reactions of imaginary characters in eight situations', found that the pattern of their responses supported Peel's general theory (Silcock, 1984). The quality of responses ranged from:

1. those who did not appear to understand the nature of the task, and made little attempt to identify with the person in the specific circumstances of the story;

   via

2. those who relied on a simple justification for their account, and inadequately conceptualised the various possibilities of thought and feeling that the characters could have had;

to

3. a small number of pupils who revealed some appreciation of key principles concerning social norms, behaviour and relationships, and were able to deduce how circumstances could change in diverse ways and that people might react in different ways to changing situations.

When pupils study an environmental or social issue, they need to be well informed, and to be given opportunities to discuss the possible feelings and reactions of those involved in the issue, and the implications of these for any search for solutions.

Differentiation

Differentiation is a relatively recent addition to the vocabulary of curriculum discourse. The current interest in the concept and practice of differentiation may owe more to political concerns and policies than to developments in curriculum theory. That is not to suggest that the interest is misplaced. The first indication that the idea had become important in the thinking of central government was at the beginning of 1984, when Sir Keith Joseph, as Secretary of State for Education and Science, announced in a speech to the North of England Education Conference that the school curriculum needed to accord, more than it did then, to four principles: breadth, relevance, differentiation and balance. He asserted 'there should be differentiation within the curriculum for variations in the abilities and aptitudes of pupils' and that this was a task which had to be tackled within each school and, where it was relevant, between schools. The case for differentiation was elaborated in the Government's White Paper, *Better Schools*, published in 1985. Drawing on the evidence of HMI reports, the document commented, in respect to secondary schools:

> In a large minority of cases, teachers' expectations of what pupils could achieve are clouded by inadequate knowledge and understanding of pupils' individual aptitudes and difficulties; or by the stereotyping which is a consequence of preconceptions about categories of pupil; whether teaching groups are streamed, banded, setted, or deliberately formed from pupils of widely differing ability, teaching is frequently directed towards the middle of the group and there is insufficient differentiation of teaching approaches. This last weakness is less common in practical areas of the curriculum, but elsewhere it is a widespread and very serious problem, particularly when the class contains a wide ability range (HMSO, 1985).

To this can be added the comment made in relation to primary schools:

> It is not easy, even for experienced teachers, to match the widely differing needs and capabilities of individual children with appropriate objectives, methods and materials (HMSO, 1985).

The first extract usefully points out that differentiation is not only relevant for mixed-ability teaching groups, even though the problems may be more immediate and more sharply defined when teaching such classes. The second extract links differentiation to matching, two sides of the same coin; and hints at the complexity of both, in that they involve 'objectives, methods and materials'.

While the general framework for the National Curriculum was intended to take account of the fact that pupils at any given age will vary greatly in their levels of performance, the structure of the original Order for geography made it extremely difficult to make adequate provision for differentiation. This was because so many

Statements of Attainment contained specific content. The replacement of SoAs by Level Descriptions has made it possible to distinguish between qualities of attainment within the Attainment Target, while defining a common entitlement for all pupils within the Programmes of Study. Some degree of common entitlement has also been established at GCSE, through the subject criteria for geography (SCAA, 1995), which defines those aims, assessment objectives and aspects of content required in all GCSE examination syllabuses. Nevertheless, examining groups design and structure their GCSE examinations in a variety of ways to cater for the wide range of attainment of their candidates. While some make use of differentiated papers, others rely on the different levels of demand of individual questions, inclines of difficulty built into structured questions, and the quality of candidates' response to more open-ended tasks. In addition, some syllabuses emphasise that candidates should be 'guided towards tasks appropriate to their individual levels of abilities'. The purposes of these techniques are to ensure that, as far as possible, the examinations are made accessible to all candidates and all candidates are given opportunities to show what they know, understand and can do.

A FRAMEWORK FOR PLANNING DIFFERENTIATION

So far in this chapter, we have seen that differentiation can involve objectives, methods, materials and assessment. However, there is much more to it than this. In an article in *Teaching Geography*, Waters (1995) commented perceptively on many of the relevant issues, and suggested lines of investigation that a geography department can usefully pursue, and strategies that it can adopt, to develop suitable approaches to differentiation. Many of the considerations relevant to differentiation can be brought together within an input–process–output model (Figure 1). In this model, the **inputs** consist of the provision made for the subject, in terms of the organisation of teaching groups, the allocation of various types of resources, and the curriculum which is planned; the **processes** are those of the curriculum as it functions, with its activities, content and complex interactions between teachers and pupils; and the **outputs** are what pupils learn as a result of the curriculum, and how teachers use the findings of assessment to help individual pupils and improve curricular provision and practices.

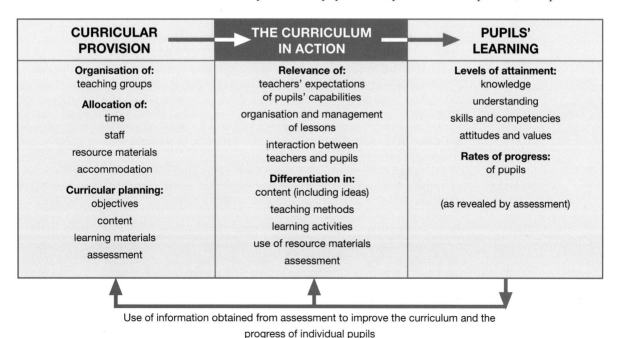

CURRICULAR PROVISION	THE CURRICULUM IN ACTION	PUPILS' LEARNING
Organisation of: teaching groups	**Relevance of:** teachers' expectations of pupils' capabilities	**Levels of attainment:** knowledge
Allocation of: time	organisation and management of lessons	understanding
staff	interaction between teachers and pupils	skills and competencies
resource materials		attitudes and values
accommodation	**Differentiation in:** content (including ideas)	**Rates of progress:** of pupils
Curricular planning: objectives	teaching methods	
content	learning activities	(as revealed by assessment)
learning materials	use of resource materials	
assessment	assessment	

Use of information obtained from assessment to improve the curriculum and the progress of individual pupils

Figure 1: Differentiation within the curriculum

CURRICULAR PROVISION

Some decisions about curricular provision are made at the school level, in particular the overall funding, staffing and accommodation for a subject; the allocation of teaching time; and very often the distribution of pupils between teaching groups. Systems of streaming, banding by ability or mixed-ability grouping, are often applied across whole years. However, heads of departments usually have some choice in distributing the available staff, accommodation and material resources between teaching groups; and, where there is block timetabling, may choose what sort of groups to form. These decisions are relevant to the educational experience which individual pupils receive. Too often, differentiation has negative rather than positive overtones, as when less-able groups are allocated the poorest accommodation or the weakest teachers. Sometimes very difficult decisions must be made, for example, when a department has to make use of non-specialist teachers who lack the knowledge and confidence to teach the subject to examination level.

The greatest scope for constructive differentiation in provision is in planning the curriculum. A department can decide how far it is appropriate, and practical, to have different specific objectives, content, teaching methods, learning activities, learning materials and assessment for different pupils.

One useful strategy, applicable to planning a unit of work, is to identify a 'core' of activities and learning materials, suitable for all pupils; and supplement this with 'extension' work, to encourage and enable pupils to develop understanding and skills at more demanding levels, and 'support' work to help those who are experiencing difficulties in coping with the core. Support materials can be designed to avoid particular difficulties, or may approach some aspect of learning from a different direction. This strategy can accommodate some differentiation in learning objectives, when this is considered to be appropriate.

Another strategy is to make use of a variety of teaching methods and learning activities in order to cater for differences in pupils' preferred styles of learning, and to extend the range of styles which they can use. For example, a department could decide to aim at a balance between whole-class teaching, group work and individual work; and between closely structured activities and more open enquiries.

THE CURRICULUM IN ACTION

What pupils experience is the curriculum as it functions: the implementation of the policies, strategies and plans; and the many unplanned day-to-day events and incidents. Differentiation has to be related to what actually happens inside the classroom and in the field. It impinges upon, and is influenced by, the organisation and management of lessons, the ways in which content is introduced and understanding developed, the use made of resource materials, the effectiveness of teaching methods and learning activities, and the assessment of pupils' progress. Central to most of these is the interaction between teachers and pupils.

The role of the teacher is necessarily complex, and nowhere more so than when teaching a class with a wide range of ability. To get pupils started, care is needed to stimulate their interests and ensure that all appreciate the purposes of activities and understand what they have to do. Whole-class teaching has to be pitched at a suitable level, and not last so long that some pupils are unable to retain their concentration. Group work has particular value in enabling pupils, through discussion, to explore ideas and articulate meanings. But, it is important for teachers to monitor group activities and individual work, and to intervene when necessary to facilitate learning. The pace of work can often be improved by setting realistic time targets. When groups and individuals are engaged on different tasks, it is useful to draw them together periodically, in order to enable them to share their findings and help consolidate their learning.

PUPILS' LEARNING

The 'output' in the model of the curriculum shown in Figure 1 is what pupils learn. It is inevitable that pupils will vary greatly in their rates of progress and in the levels of attainment which they achieve at the end of each stage. Pupils' acquisition of knowledge and their development of understanding, skills and competencies are measured by means of **assessment**. Formative assessment is especially important for the management of differentiation. It can provide relevant information to enable teachers to respond quickly to weaknesses and improvements in pupils' learning. It is, therefore, a working tool to be used as an integral part of the functioning of the curriculum. While summative assessment, especially when it is school-based, can inform teachers' evaluation of their curriculum, formative assessment is more likely to signal which parts of a curriculum should be reviewed, with possible implications for differentiation.

Conclusion

Both progression and differentiation are potentially complex matters which require consideration of the different capabilities of pupils, the ways in which they mature, and the types of learning which the curriculum is intended to promote. Geography teachers have to adopt manageable strategies. These should draw upon their practical experience and, where relevant, on the insights gained from research. The curriculum has to be made accessible to all pupils, and offer all pupils the possibility of making progress, whatever their individual levels of performance.

References

Beard, R.M. (1969) *An Outline of Piaget's Developmental Psychology.* Routledge and Kegan Paul.

Biggs, J.B. (1980) 'The relationship between developmental level and the quality of school learning', in Modgil, S. & Modgil, C. (eds) *Toward a Theory of Psychological Development.* NFER.

Government White Paper (1995) *Better Schools.* HMSO.

HMI (1978) 'The teaching of ideas in geography: some suggestions for the middle and secondary years', *Matters for Discussion, 5.* HMSO.

Joseph, K. (1984) Speech at the North of England Conference, Sheffield, on 6 January.

Peel, E.A. (1971) *The Nature of Adolescent Judgment.* Staples.

Rhys, W.T. (1972a) 'Geography and the adolescent', *Educational Review,* 24, 3.

Rhys, W.T. (1972b) 'The development of logical thinking' in Graves, N. *New Movements in the Study and Teaching of Geography.* Temple Smith.

SCAA (1994) *Geography in the National Curriculum: Draft Proposals.*

SCAA (1995) *GCSE Regulations and Criteria.*

Silcock, P.J. (1984) 'Aspects of adolescent social-cognitive development: a cross-sectional study of social judgment in early adolescence', *Educational Review,* 36, 1.

Turner, J. (1984) *Cognitive Development and Education.* Methuen.

Waters, A. (1995) 'Differentiation and classroom practice', *Teaching Geography,* 20, 2. The Geographical Association.

Chapter 8

Developing skills

EWA SAWICKA

As the basic skills of numeracy, oracy, writing, etc., permeate the whole curriculum, geographers should be aware of the contents of the National Curriculum documents for English and mathematics (DFE 1995a,b). To develop these basic skills in geography without reference to other curriculum areas often means duplication occurs or inappropriate work is given to certain groups. This creates problems in the classroom for both teachers and pupils. Cross-curricular co-operation with English and mathematics colleagues leads to rewarding work which can be assessed in more than one subject. For example; a newspaper article on a recent earthquake can be assessed in both geography and English (see Chapter 2 for a full discussion of geography's place in the whole curriculum).

Talking

Teachers communicate with their pupils at many levels, by providing information; explaining diagrams, maps and concepts; instructing pupils in specific skills; encouraging them by making various comments; or even giving reprimands for lack of application. Similarly, pupils communicate with their peers and teachers, in discussions, answering questions, preparing role-plays, producing written work or through reading. In all classroom activities, language can develop or hinder learning.

In subjects like geography teachers should be aware of the importance of the specialist language in our lessons. How many of us have stopped to think about the language we use in the classroom? Does our everyday use of geographical terminology blind us to how complex and mystifying it is to, say, an eleven-year old, or even a sixth-former? We must, therefore, plan teaching and learning strategies carefully, using a language level that is appropriate to each group. Teachers of geography should also ensure that the techniques and skills to be used are appropriate to the language level of the pupils. In order to achieve this successfully geography teachers should read the National Curriculum Order for English (Figure 1).

The development of language skills depends heavily on teachers who are professional communicators and the main source of information on a particular topic. Teachers decide which particular teaching and learning strategies are to be employed with their pupils. Teachers set the ground rules on oral work: what the topic is, who is to speak, when, and for how long. Teachers must ensure there is a balance between

English National Curriculum key stages 3 and 4 Programme of Study	Key stages 3 and 4 examples from geography lessons (in descending order of difficulty)

SPEAKING AND LISTENING – ASPECTS RELEVANT TO GEOGRAPHY
 	
1. RANGE
a Pupils should be given opportunities to talk for a range of purposes, including:
  ■ explanation, description and narration;
  ■ exploration and hypothesis;
  ■ consideration of ideas, literature and the media;
  ■ argument, debate and persuasion;
  ■ the development of thinking;
  ■ analysis.
	■ Recount a series of related incidents
	  Listen to a television programme on a new topic then discuss it
	  Plan a wall display on a specific topic in a group

b Pupils should be given opportunities to talk in a range of contexts, including those that are more formal. They should be encouraged to adapt their presentation to different audiences and to reflect on how their talk varies.	■ Report on the damaging effects of a particular earthquake
	  Conduct an interview on radio about a local issue
	  Contribute to the planning and implementation of a group activity, e.g. fieldwork in the grounds or the local area

c Pupils should be encouraged to listen attentively, both in situations where they remain mostly silent and where they have the opportunity to respond immediately. They should be taught to distinguish features of presentation where the intention is to be explanatory, persuasive, amusing or argumentative, and should be taught to use this knowledge when preparing and presenting their own oral work.	■ Describe a model which has been designed, indicating the reasons for its design, e.g. the introduction of a one-way road system Produce an eye-witness account of how pollution problems have been addressed in a given area
d Pupils should be given opportunities to participate in a wide range of drama activities, including role-play, and in the performance of scripted and unscripted plays. Pupils should be encouraged to develop both their communication skills and their ability to evaluate language use. In responding to drama, they should be given opportunities to consider significant features of their own and others' performances.	■ Present a newspaper report (desk-top published) on a local issue, e.g. the widening of the M42 motorway in the Midlands Present to the class the results of a group investigation, e.g. interpretation of a particular landscape
2. KEY SKILLS **a** Pupils should be given opportunities to make different types of contributions in discussion, adapting their speech to their listeners and to the activity. They should be encouraged to structure their talk clearly, judging the appropriate level of detail. In discussions, they should be encouraged to take different views to account, sift, summarise and use salient points, cite evidence and construct persuasive arguments. In taking different roles in group discussions, pupils should be introduced to ways of negotiating consensus or agreeing to differ.	■ Decision-making exercise – (in pairs) develop own point of view then present ideas first to small group, then to class Design a model of a New Town centre and explain the decisions for the design to the rest of the class

b In order to develop as effective listeners, pupils should be taught to identify the major elements of what is being said, and to distinguish tone, undertone, implications and other indicators of a speaker's intentions. They should be taught to notice ambiguities, deliberate vagueness, glossing over points, use and abuse of evidence, and unsubstantiated statements. In discussion, pupils should listen and respond. They should be encouraged to make contributions that clarify and synthesise others' ideas, taking them forward and building on them to reach a conclusion. Pupils should be encouraged to ask and answer questions and to modify their ideas in the light of what others say.	■ Debate a contentious issue and summarise the main arguments
	  Explain how human activities can affect the rate of geomorphological processes
	  Take part in a simulated committee meeting discussing plans to develop a new leisure centre

3. STANDARD ENGLISH AND LANGUAGE STUDY **a** Pupils should be taught to be fluent, accurate users of standard English vocabulary and grammar, and to recognise its importance as the language of public communication. They should be taught to adapt their talk to suit the circumstances, and to be confident users of standard English in formal and informal situations. In role-play and drama, the vocabulary, structures and tone appropriate to such contexts should be explored. *(Note: The numbers and letters shown are used in the English National Curriculum Order – Source: DFE, 1995.)*	■ Introduce a researched topic, e.g. on the environment, using slides, OHP transparencies, diagrams, notes Discuss a television programme – recognising and developing various viewpoints, e.g. on tourism in Kenya

	■ Devise and mount a campaign, e.g. on the survival of Amazonian Indians
	  Summarise an argument and help to form a conclusion, e.g. on renewable energy uses in Britain.
	  Appropriate CD-ROMs could be used to research projects.

Figure 1: Developing the skills of speaking and listening through geography

teacher- and pupil-talk. At times teacher-talk is vital, particularly for explaining difficult concepts, techniques or ideas, and it is also important for transmitting enthusiasm for the topic. Too frequently, however, teachers get carried away and talk overmuch. To develop their pupils' language skills teachers should ensure that all their pupils have opportunities to express themselves orally.

There are two ways in which language skills can be developed in a lesson; individually and through group work. In a whole-class discussion there may be limited opportunities for each individual to speak; the main opportunities arise in teacher–pupil and pupil–pupil exchanges, particularly in question–and–answer sessions. The questions may require a low- or high-level response, i.e. simple answers based on information recall (Levels 3 and 4, English National Curriculum) or answers requiring detailed analysis and explanation. One example of the latter is a decision-making exercise on planning a new motorway; pupils are given various possibilities to consider and evaluate (Levels 5 and 6, English National Curriculum).

Language skills can be developed most effectively through pupils working in groups of three or four. In these groups pupils find it less inhibiting to talk and, as they can control discussions and work at their own pace, participation is easier. Group work needs to be well-structured with organisation kept to a minimum and the noise level controlled. During group work pupil motivation increases which often leads to lively debate.

There are ample opportunities in geography lessons for group work to enhance oral language skills; some of the activities which can be used to help pupils are:

Ordering or ranking
Pupils are presented with specific information in random order (possibly on cards or a computer) which they discuss and put in what they perceive is the correct rank or order (a word processor could be used for this task).

Analysing photographs or a video
Photographs are distributed amongst a group and pupils either write speech bubbles for the people in the photograph or devise a series of questions to accompany the image. Pupils watch a video of a television programme then discuss it in structured ways. They could also edit a television programme and write or tape their own commentary.

Role-play
A series of role cards are distributed amongst members of a group, and pupils present the reactions of their role to a proposal – for example, to the development of the Channel Tunnel link railway. The same cards can be used as roles which the pupils assume to take part in a public enquiry or meeting (as in the 'Quarry simulation' in Chapter 12).

Designing
Geography is ideal for design or computer-based work. For example, pupils design a New Town at the end of an unit of work on the subject. They may present their design (perhaps as a newspaper article or leaflet produced using a computer) to the whole class who will use pre-determined criteria to assess each proposal.

Developing a method of investigation

Fieldwork is particularly well-suited to this kind of group work because it enables pupils to devise methods of investigating specific aspects of a topic, and usually involves some type of measurement or recording. Using this approach creates much excitement and makes use of a wide range of personal knowledge and ideas.

Well-resourced debates are a powerful aid to learning

Photo: **Margaret Roberts**

Decision-making exercise

A wealth of information is presented to pupils, including photographs, maps and statistics, from which they must make decisions. Decision-making exercises can be as simple as deciding what development to put on a piece of derelict land close to the school, to the development of an earthquake manage-ment programme in Japan or California.

Debates

Individuals or small groups prepare cases for and against a contemporary issue, other members of the class discuss the type of questions to ask of the two sides. Debating usually works best with older pupils as they tend to have greater general knowledge and powers of argument.

Devising a marking scheme

Groups of pupils prepare a newspaper or poster on a particular topic. A criteria for marking (e.g. 'What particular points would you expect a newspaper to cover?') is devised; the groups then mark each others' newspapers. This involves much productive discussion and careful thought before marks are allocated (see also Chapters 16-18).

Reading

In primary schools reading is given significance with time specifically allocated to it. However, on moving to secondary school, pupils experience new approaches to reading which are not always systematically presented. Most subject specialists in secondary schools assume that reading is a skill each pupil has already acquired. This is not always true, children bring to the classroom only those reading abilities they have developed in primary school. Therefore, the question which we must answer is 'What can I do as a geographer to enhance reading in my subject, year by year, topic by topic?'.

Reading is a skill required in almost every geography lesson, whether as instructions, on worksheets, on computer printouts, in textbooks or for finding information in reference books or on a CD-ROM. It is important, therefore, that the language in which information is presented is of the appropriate level. Figure 2 provides examples of how the development of reading skills can be enhanced in geography at different levels. Figure 2 also shows that as pupils' reading skills develop, they move on to independent learning, whereby they can select, recall and use a variety of materials from different sources in an effective and sustained manner.

English National Curriculum key stages 3 and 4 Programme of Study	Key stages 3 and 4 examples from geography lessons (in descending order of difficulty)

READING – ASPECTS RELEVANT TO GEOGRAPHY

1. RANGE

a   Pupils should be given opportunities to read a wide variety of literature, and to respond to the substance and style of texts. They should also be encouraged to read widely and independently solely for enjoyment.

b   The literature read should be drawn from a variety of genres, including plays, novels, short stories and poetry.

   Plays selected should include works that:
   - extend pupils' ideas and their moral and emotional understanding
   - use language in rich, diverse ways.

   Novels and short stories selected should include works that:
   - extend pupils' ideas and their moral and emotional understanding:
   - offer perspectives on society and community and their impact on the lives of individuals;

   Poetry should include poems that:
   - extend pupils' ideas and their moral and emotional understanding;
   - use language in imaginative, precise and original ways.

c   Pupils should read texts from other cultures and traditions that represent their distinctive voices and forms, and offer varied perspectives and subject matter.

d   Pupils should be introduced to major works of literature from the English literary heritage in previous centuries. They should also read literature by major writers from earlier in the twentieth century and works of high quality by contemporary writers.

e   Pupils should be introduced to a wide range of non-fiction texts, *e.g. autobiographies, biographies, journals, diaries, letters, travel writing, leaflets.* They should be given opportunities to read texts that show quality in language use, and portray information, issues and events relating to contemporary life or past experience in ways that are interesting and challenging.

f   Pupils should be introduced to a wide range of media, *e.g. magazines, newspapers, radio, television, film.* They should be given opportunities to analyse and evaluate such material, which should be of high quality and represent a range of forms and purposes, and different structural and presentational devices.

2. KEY SKILLS

a   Pupils should be taught to:
   - extract meaning beyond the literal, explaining how choice of language and style affects implied and explicit meanings;
   - analyse and discuss unfamiliar vocabulary meanings;
   - analyse and engage with the ideas, themes and language in fiction, non-fiction, drama and poetry.

b   Pupils should be given opportunities to talk and write about a wide range of reading, learning to articulate informed personal opinions. They should be encouraged to respond, both imaginatively and intellectually, to what they read. Within a broad programme of reading, they should be given opportunities to:
   - reflect on the writer's presentation of ideas and the overall impact of a text;
   - distinguish between the attitudes and assumptions displayed by characters and those of the author.

c   Pupils should be given opportunities to read factual and informative texts in order to:
   - select information;
   - compare and synthesise information drawn from different texts, *e.g. IT-based sources and printed articles*;
   - make effective use of information in their own work;
   - evaluate how information is presented.

   In using information sources, pupils should be taught to sift the relevant from the irrelevant and to distinguish between fact and opinion, bias and objectivity.

3. STANDARD ENGLISH AND LANGUAGE STUDY

a   to analyse and evaluate the use of language in a variety of media, making comparisons where appropriate, *e.g. a comparison of a television news bulletin with a report on the same event in a newspaper.*

(Note: The numbers and letters shown are used in the English National Curriculum Order.)

Key stages 3 and 4 examples from geography lessons (in descending order of difficulty)

- Reading of textbook and comprehending it
  Providing pupils with a set of questions and a number of different sources of information which pupils need to use in order to answer the question

- Send pupils to library to research particular topics, e.g. Life in the Amazon. (Check beforehand that the library has a suitable range and quantity of material available and that it is appropriate for the pupils concerned.)

- Provide pupils with a text asking them to summarise the main points, e.g. the Shetland oil-spill disaster

- Pupils to use a variety of reference materials: OHP transparencies, videos, CD-ROMs, the Internet etc. to prepare a lesson on a specific topic, e.g. the decline of industry in South Wales

- Pupils to analyse and evaluate two or three different reports of the same event, e.g. from television, radio and newspapers, and describe evidence of bias

Figure 2: Developing reading skills through geography

WRITING – ASPECTS RELEVANT TO GEOGRAPHY

1. RANGE

a   Pupils should be encouraged to extend their confidence in writing for a variety of purposes and to develop their own distinctive and original styles, recognising the importance of commitment and vitality in what they write.

b   Pupils should be given opportunities to write for specific readers, for a large, unknown readership, and for themselves. They should be encouraged to write:
- for aesthetic and imaginative purposes;
- to inform others through instruction, explanation, argument, narration, reportage, description, persuasion and paraphrase;
- to develop thinking through review, analysis, hypothesis, recollection and summary.

c   The range of forms in which they write should be extensive, *e.g. notes, diaries, personal letters, formal letters, chronological accounts, reports, pamphlets, reviews, essays, advertisements, newspaper articles, biography, autobiography, poems, stories, playscripts, screenplays.*

2. KEY SKILLS

a   Pupils should be taught to improve and sustain their writing, developing their competence in planning, drafting, redrafting and proofreading their work on paper and on screen. They should be encouraged to judge the extent to which any or all of these processes are needed in specific pieces of work. Pupils should be given opportunities to analyse critically their own and others' writing. They should be taught to write with fluency and, when required, speed. In presenting final polished work, pupils should be taught to ensure that it is neat and legible, and makes full use of presentational devices where appropriate.

b   To develop their ability to write **narrative**, pupils should be encouraged to:
- draw on their experience of good fiction;
- develop their use of techniques.

To develop their ability to write **poetry**, pupils should be encouraged to:
- draw upon their experience of a range of poetic forms;
- develop their use of poetic devices;
- write poetry closely related to the poems they read, in their own distinctive style, and also poetry based on their own experience.

To develop their ability to write **scripts and dialogue**, pupils should be encouraged to:
- use their experience of reading, performing and watching plays;
- develop their use of dialogue to convey character.

To develop their ability to write **non-fiction**, pupils should be encouraged to:
- use their experience of reading a wide range of non-fiction texts;
- use their knowledge of the distinctive ways of organising and expressing ideas and information in discursive, argumentative, persuasive and other types of non-fiction writing;
- take notes from written and oral sources, summarise carefully and report accurately.

c   In spelling, pupils should be helped to increase their knowledge of regular patterns of spelling, word families, roots of words and their derivations. They should be taught to spell increasingly complex polysyllabic words that do not conform to regular patterns, and to proofread their writing carefully to check for errors, using dictionaries where appropriate. Pupils should be given opportunities to develop discrimination in relation to other complexities in spelling, including heteronyms, *e.g. minute, lead, wind,* and sight rhymes, *e.g. tough, dough.*

d   Pupils should be taught to use neat, legible **handwriting**.

3. STANDARD ENGLISH AND LANGUAGE STUDY

a   Pupils should be encouraged to be confident in the use of formal and informal written standard English, using the grammatical, lexical and orthographic features of standard English, except where non-standard forms are required for effect or technical reasons. Pupils should be given a range of opportunities to use the syntax and vocabulary characteristic of English in formal writing, *e.g. business letter, critical review, informative article*, and to distinguish varying degrees of formality, selecting appropriately for a task.

b   Pupils should be encouraged to consider apt and imaginative choices of vocabulary and the precise use of words, including consideration of synonyms and double meanings. Pupils should be given opportunities to use dictionaries and thesauruses to explore derivations and alternative meanings.

(Note: The numbers and letters shown are used in the English National Curriculum Order.)

The following tasks can be done using a computer.

- Drawing plan and diagrams of a farm and farmer's year
  Making notes for a fieldwork activity

- Set out a piece of work using titles, paragraphs, etc.
  Write instructions, accounts or explanation of a fieldwork activity, e.g. weather
  Make posters on a given theme, e.g., geographical features of a specific area
  Write letters about the development of a particular road or the construction of a supermarket or housing estate

- Write notes, letters, instructions to plan, inform, explain, etc. a specific topic
  Draft a report in writing or on a computer

- Write a second draft of an account of a group activitiy, following the group's discussion of the first draft

- Write letters, instructions, newspaper articles, radio and TV scripts on a given topic, e.g. migration: causes and effects; the effect of the tourism industry
  Develop a news broadcast of topical interest, e.g. how the level of development affects the quality of life of different people
  Restructure information on a computer or in written form from a factual report to a role-play

- Present an investigative report about a contentious issue, showing different points of view
  Class could be divided into groups and each group asked to present a topic in a variety of written forms – letters, reports, newspaper articles, etc.

- Write a report for a specific audience, using a variety of techniques of presentation including accounts of interviews, analyses of tabulated data and summary conclusions

---

Figure 3: Developing writing skills through geography

The most common resource used in geography lessons, apart from the teacher, is the textbook (chosen for a particular group or level by the specialist). Often the choice of textbook is made mainly on the basis of its content rather than the suitability of its language.

As some pupils have difficulty reading textbooks teachers should be careful not to create extra barriers to learning by using inappropriate textbooks (see Chapter 21). One way of checking the suitability of a textbook is to work out its reading level by using a variety of formulae (not discussed here but fully explained in some of the books listed at the end of this chapter).

Technical and subject-specific language can hinder reading and comprehension, therefore, teachers should define the meaning of a 'new' word, either at the beginning of a lesson or the first time it appears in the text. Pupils will find it useful to write specialist/technical terms in a geography dictionary at the back of their exercise books.

All kinds of printed and electronic materials can be used to supplement the information in geography textbooks. Newspaper articles, magazines, photographs with annotations, travel brochures, maps, CD-ROMs, etc., provide pupils with first-hand information and extend the amount of material available for a lesson. Difficulties which arise with their use are that: they are written mainly for an adult audience and so will assume a high reading age, or they may be written for a specific audience (e.g. a planning committee) and be biased towards a particular viewpoint.

Modern technology has not absolved us from the need to teach young people to write clearly and concisely

Photo: **Margaret Roberts**

Writing

Research suggests that most writing in geography classrooms is transactional, in that it is used most frequently to convey information. This is not surprising because geography frequently deals with situations outside the direct experience of pupils and is, therefore, required to convey a great deal of factual information. If pupils are to learn to question, discuss and express values and judgements about specific topics, transactional writing alone is inadequate. It is important for us to develop a variety of opportunities for different types of writing as part of our strategies for teaching and learning.

The types of writing expected of pupils at key stages 3 and 4 are set out briefly in Figure 3, together with some related ideas for geography lessons. These can form a framework around which different types of writing can be developed in geography.

Experience shows that pupils will most readily learn to question, discuss, formulate hypotheses, make judgements and suggest alternatives if they are asked to undertake a variety of written work. In geography this can include:

- completing sentences or texts;
- re-ordering given information;
- constructing tables or flow diagrams;
- writing letters and reports;
- designing posters and pamphlets;

- writing newspaper articles;
- formulating campaigns;
- writing role-plays and television mini-scripts.

This variety in writing (which can be done using a computer) helps motivate individual pupils and enables them to write in different styles and for different audiences. This in itself is challenging; such audiences may include their teacher, their peers, younger pupils, their parents, and the public.

MARKING

What happens to written work is also an important part of the learning process. Every written assignment will be assessed, either by a friend, the class, or (more likely) the teacher. The form assessment takes will have an effect on the learning process (and perhaps the future performance of the pupil), involving as it does a mark, level or grade, plus a comment. In geography marking involves an evaluation of whether or not the pupil understands the idea, concept or knowledge or has grasped a geographical skill. Geography teachers should check grammar, spelling and punctuation but concentrate primarily on the spelling of subject-specific and technical words. Concentrate on a few of these each time and monitor the pupil's progress. Try to avoid presenting pupils with a page full of corrections as this can be discouraging. Whatever form the mark takes, its meaning should be clear to the pupil.

Marking should always be constructive and this is achieved by making comments which enable pupils to take their learning forward. It is better to mark less often but more thoroughly than to try and mark everything and do it sketchily. (See Chapters 16-18 for more detailed discussions of assessment and marking.)

Number

Number work in a geography lesson can produce mixed reactions. Those pupils who are confident with mathematics will find it relatively easy, others will panic as soon as numbers, calculations or graphs are mentioned. It is important that geography teachers are aware of the difficulties faced by some pupils and take steps to deal with them.

Discussions with the mathematics department can help geography teachers to decide how best to approach concepts and skills needed in geography. Whether it be observing, recording, representing, analysing information, using simple statistical data or selecting and communicating information. Consistent practice is important in this area and a common approach to working out statistics and presenting information may be adopted.

Co-operation with the mathematics department can also help in making decisions about which mathematical skills and techniques are appropriate for key stages 3 and 4 geography (see Figure 4). This will help prevent duplication and avoid valuable time being wasted.

Mathematical work involves pupils in a whole complex of cognitive skills where pupils have to read and also to follow instructions, interpret diagrams, perform calculations and manipulate and analyse information. Thus, it is necessary to return to certain mathematical techniques and skills in successive geography lessons. Teachers must create an atmosphere which encourages pupils to ask openly for help where it is required. Teaching mathematical skills and techniques through geography enables pupils to see the relevance of number work to everyday life. I wonder how many of us have had sixth-formers return, having gone to University to study politics, economics or business studies, and report that they use geographical/mathematical skills for many of the new tasks they face in their university subjects?

Mathematical work in geography involves pupils in performing calculations and analysing information

Photo: **Helen Sail**

MATHEMATICS NATIONAL CURRICULUM
KEY STAGES 3 AND 4 PROGRAMME OF STUDY

Key areas
(Aspects relevant to geography)

Attainment Target 1: Using and applying mathematics

1. Pupils should be given opportunities to:
a. use and apply mathematics in practical tasks, in real-life problems;
b. work on problems that pose a challenge.

2. Pupils should be taught to:
c. find ways of overcoming difficulties that arise; develop and use their own strategies;
b. select, trial and evaluate a variety of possible approaches, identify what further information may be required in order to pursue a particular line of enquiry; break complex problems into a series of tasks.

3. Pupils should be taught to:
b. use mathematical forms of communication, including diagrams, tables, graphs and computer printouts;
c. present work clearly, using diagrams, graphs and symbols appropriately, to convey meaning;
d. interpret mathematics presented in a variety of forms; evaluate forms of presentation;
e. examine critically, improve and justify their choice of mathematical presentation.

4. Pupils should be taught to:
a. explain and justify how they arrived at a conclusion or a solution to a problem;
b. make conjectures and hypotheses, designing methods to test them and analysing results to see whether they are valid;
e. use mathematical reasoning, initially when explaining and then when following a line of argument, recognising inconsistencies.

Attainment Target 2: Number

1. Pupils should be given opportunities to:
a. use calculators and computer software, e.g. spreadsheets;
b. develop and use flexibly a range of methods of computation and apply these to a range of problems.

2. Pupils should be taught to:
a. understand and use the concept of place value in whole numbers and decimals;
b. understand and use decimals, ratios, fractions and percentages and the inter-relationships between them; understand and use negative numbers.

Attainment Target 3: Algebra

1. Pupils should be given opportunities to:
a. explore a variety of situations that lead to the expression of relationships.

2. Pupils should be taught to:
b. explore number patterns arising from a variety of situations, using computers where appropriate; interpret, generalise and use simple relationships;
c. interpret graphs that describe real-life situations.

Attainment Target 4: Shape, space and measures

3. Pupils should be taught to:
a. use co-ordinate systems to specify location, initially using rectangular cartesian co-ordinates in the first quadrant;
d. develop an understanding of scale, including using and interpreting maps and drawings and enlarging shapes by different scale factors.

Examples from geography lessons

■ Development of a derelict area: recognising what information is needed in order to plan a redevelopment (KS3)

■ Change in my local area: looking at changes in shops, roads, transport and buildings – including houses (KS3)

■ River study: tasks to be set – pupils to decide how to complete the various tasks, what equipment to use and to ensure that all data collected is relevant – local river – double lesson (KS3)

■ Village study: use information collected during fieldwork to produce a poster showing the site and functions of a village – to include diagrams and a variety of graphs with a written account which is to include a section on changes in the village (KS3)

■ Decision making exercise: traffic problem in an area, possible solutions. Keep a record of weather over a period of time including negative numbers if possible. Know how to use a computer to do this (KS3)

■ Survey of how pupils travel to school and how long it takes. Relationships explored (KS3)

■ Find information from a railway or bus timetable and plan a journey (KS3). Interpretation of graphs showing flood levels in an area (KS3)

■ Use co-ordinates to locate people in a class (KS3)

■ Four-figure and six-figure grid references – mapwork (KS3). Locate features on an OS map. Use OS map computer software to test knowledge of grid references (KS3)

■ Drawing rooms to scale (KS3)

■ Using different OS maps to work out different scales (KS3)

■ Using instruments to measure various aspects of weather: maximum and minimum thermometer, wet and dry bulb thermometer, rain gauge, etc. (KS3)

■ Use hand-held 'weather computer' to contrast the differences in temperature and humidity on different sides of the school building (KS3)

■ Planning of an environmental area in the school (KS3)

■ Use 'Autosketch' software to draw a plan of the school to scale (KS3). Use OS digital data (or Scamp CD-ROM) to select and plot a map of local parks. Shade all the parks in green (KS4)

■ Working out percentage of people involved in primary, secondary and tertiary industries for a given place/for a given time (KS3). Use Scamp CD-ROM to find the information (KS4)

■ Local fieldwork and collection and processing of data using a computer (KS3/4)

■ Use a spreadsheet to see if travel times by train are quicker or slower than those in the early twentieth century (KS3/4)

■ Mapwork – maps of different scales: e.g. 1:50 000 ; 1:25 000 ; 1:10 000 (KS3). Use a graphics package to increase/reduce the scale of a plan (KS3/4)

4. Pupils should be taught to:
a. choose appropriate instruments and standard units of length, mass, capacity and time and make sensible estimates in everyday situations, extending to less familiar contexts; develop an understanding of the relationship between units, converting one metric unit to another; know Imperial units in daily use and their approximate metric equivalents;
b. read and interpret scales, including decimal scales;
d. find perimeters, areas and volumes of common shapes.

Attainment Target 5: Handling data

1. Pupils should be given opportunities to:
a. formulate questions that can be considered using statistical methods;
b. undertake purposeful enquiries based on data analysis;
c. use computers as a source of large samples, a tool for exploring graphical representations, and as a means to simulate events;
e. look critically at some of the ways in which representations of data can be misleading and conclusions can be uncertain.

2. Pupils should be taught to:
a. design and use data collection sheets, access required information from tables, lists and computer databases;
b. design a questionnaire or an experiment to capture the data needed to follow lines of enquiry and to test hypotheses, taking possible bias into account;
c. construct appropriate diagrams and graphs to present discrete and continuous data, including bar charts, line graphs, pie charts, scatter diagrams and cumulative frequency diagrams;
d. calculate or estimate and use appropriate measures of central tendency i.e. mode, median and mean, initially with discrete data, progressing to grouped and continuous data;
e. select and calculate or estimate appropriate measures of spread, including the range and interquartile range applied to discrete, grouped and continuous data;
f. interpret a wide range of graphs and diagrams, draw inferences based on shapes of graphs and simple statistics for a single distribution, the comparative distribution of sets of data and the relationships between two sets of data, including correlation and ones of best fit;
g. evaluate results critically, and develop an understanding of the reliability of results;
h. recognise that inferences drawn from data analysis of an experiment or enquiry may suggest further questions for investigation.

Key stage 4: Further material

1. Pupils should be given opportunities to:
a. apply their knowledge, understanding and skills to solving problems of increasing complexity in a wider range of contexts.

2. Using and applying mathematics
Pupils should be taught to:
a. explain and evaluate their choice of approach to solving problems set in contexts that are new to them;
c. understand the necessary and sufficient conditions under which generalisations, inferences and solutions to problems remain valid.

6. Handling data
a. use sampling methods, considering their reliability;
b. extend skills in handling data into constructing and interpreting histograms;
c. describe the dispersion of a set of data; find and interpret the standard deviation of a set of data.

(Note: The numbers and letters shown are used in the mathematics National Curriculum Order.)

■ Simulation of coastal erosion or deposition – computer program (KS3/4)

■ Use a computer database such as Pinpoint to write a questionnaire and to process the results (KS3/4)

■ Levels of development: assessing the best methods to use for measuring the level of development of a country (KS4)

■ Use Scamp CD-ROM to print out Census information for the selected village (KS4)

■ Individual project work: geographical enquiry (KS4), e.g. designing and using a questionnaire with multiple responses; collating and analysing results to test hypothesis. Use of computer database package such as Pinpoint

■ Using scattergraph to analyse groups of data to prove or disprove information. Able to explain anomalies (spreadsheets or graphics packages can be used to do this) (KS4)

■ Forming a database on a variety of developing and developed countries. Using the database to find correlations between variables (KS4)

■ Use Scamp CD-ROM to find out which map best illustrates the employment structure in a given area (KS4)

■ Use OS digital data (or Scamp CD-ROM) to calculate the area of parks as a proportion of the land use in the local area. Compare this with another area (KS4)

■ Hypothesis testing, e.g. speed of river; discharge (KS4)

■ Using data on the demands made in a National Park, analyse and evaluate the information and suggest possible solutions (KS4)

■ Individual enquiry piece of fieldwork (KS4) for example:

   i. comparison of two leisure centres - supply/demand basis;

   ii. comparison of shopping patterns in two centres;

   iii. analysis of a traffic problem in a particular area;

   iv. a study of the position and use of allotments in given areas of a city;

   v. a study of the impact of a superstore on an area.

■ Any number of tasks could be set to develop the skills in this section: e.g. consideration of the effects in various countries of the melting of polar ice caps and a consideration of the possible solutions

■ Problem-solving exercise: design, plan and carry through an investigation to a successful conclusion

The examples from geography lessons have not been linked directly to the Level Descriptions in mathematics in the National Curriculum because the Programme of Study in the mathematics document can be interpreted at a variety of levels depending on the complexity of the task set.

Figure 4: Developing numeracy skills through geography

References and further reading

Boardman, D. (ed) (1986) *Handbook for Geography Teachers.* The Geographical Association.

Careers and Occupational Information Centre (1988) *Working on Number: A Practical Approach to the Teaching of Numeracy.*

Chillier, P. and Gold, G. (1984) *Learning and Language in the Classroom.* Pergamon Press.

DES/WO (1990) *English in the National Curriculum.* HMSO.

DFE (1995a) *English in the National Curriculum.* HMSO.

DFE (1995b) *Mathematics in the National Curriculum.* HMSO.

Gillham, B. (ed) (1986) *The Language of School Subjects.* Heinemann Educational Books.

Hills, P.J. (1988) *GCSE Study Skills.* Pan Study Aids.

Lee, V. (1990) *Children's Learning in School.* Hodder and Stoughton.

Wiegand, P. (ed) (1989) *Managing the Geography Department.* The Geographical Association.

SOURCES OF SOFTWARE MENTIONED IN TEXT

Autosketch (1992) *Microsoft for Windows*, Autodesk Inc. (SKWINIGS-02-01).

OS Digital Data available from Ordnance Survey Digital Data Department, Romsey Road, Maybush, Southampton SO9 4DH.

Pinpoint (1991) Logotron Ltd, 124 Cambridge Science Park, Milton Road, Cambridge CB4 4ZS. ISBN 0 582 08393 1).

Scamp (1991 Census CD-ROM) (1993) Claymore Services Ltd., Station House, Whimple, Exeter EX5 2QH).

Section Three

Teaching and learning

SUMMARY OF CHAPTERS

'When...geography is made vivid by pictures, it has the merit of giving food for the imagination. It is good to know that there are hot countries and cold countries, flat countries and mountainous countries, black men, yellow men and red men as well as white men. This kind of knowledge diminishes the tyranny of familiar surroundings over the imagination and makes it possible in later life to *feel* that distant countries really exist, which otherwise would be very difficult except by travelling.'

Bertrand Russell (1926) *On Education*.

Geographical teaching and learning lend themselves to a very wide variety of approaches in the classroom and in the field. Some of the more important approaches are discussed here, with examples.

Because maps remain the most distinctive means of geographical communication, this section opens with chapters on the many and varied uses of maps, including maps in atlases, both printed and electronic. Subsequent chapters deal with simulation and role-play, the effective uses of statistics, the aims and methods of fieldwork and ways of making distant places 'come alive' to pupils.

Chapter 9

Teaching and learning with maps

PATRICK BAILEY AND PETER FOX

Introduction

Maps are the most effective way of presenting spatial information and, as such, are the geographer's most important tool. Teaching with and about maps is an essential part of a geography teacher's work; they need to be incorporated into every part of a geography course and their use developed systematically, with suitable adaptation and progression, as the course proceeds.

Chapters 10 and 11 are concerned with two types of map – Ordnance Survey and atlas maps, respectively – which are used most frequently in geography lessons. This chapter addresses some general issues relating to maps and their use, and focuses in particular on sketch maps and the role these can play in developing map appreciation.

Pupils should be given opportunities to study as many types of map as possible, ranging from simple sketch maps through to complex Geographical Information Systems (GIS) maps (showing, for example, utilities/services under a road or street) to maps which show the distribution of anything and everything from unemployment to earthquake zones. A useful exercise is to help pupils to collect different types of map and to incorporate them into displays dealing with the theme of 'different uses of maps'.

Motivating pupils to use and learn about maps

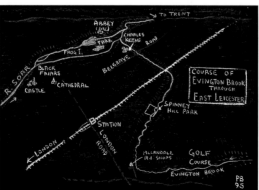

Sketch mapping is one way for pupils to observe and record the details in a landscape

Photo: **Des Bowden**

Tracing a stream through a built-up area Photo: **Patrick Bailey**

All maps have particular properties and limitations and only by using them can pupils begin to appreciate what these are. But how can pupils be motivated to use and learn about maps? One way is to ask them to map their own activities, for example plotting the best route for their paper round, or the route from home to the local sports centre. Incorporating maps into simulations which are part of a larger decision-making exercise is also motivating to pupils as it helps them to see the value of maps as 'natural' tools.

Another approach is to use maps, including sketch maps produced by the pupils, as the basis for local geography detective work. In the context of physical geography, this could involve tracing and mapping the course of a local stream through a built-up area (if this is possible and safe) and relating this to local relief. The results of one such 'stream trail' are illustrated on the previous page. The trail demonstrates the significant variations in slope angle and altitude which can be found even in a closely built-up area and which are important in local flood-control arrangements. Ordnance Survey (OS) 1:50 000 and 1:25 000 maps were used to locate the course of the stream and to plan a feasible route for the trail.

Coming nearer to reality

When first confronted with maps, many young children have difficulty recognising what a 'map view' is, and how this relates to reality. Even at key stage 4 many pupils have problems with drawing two-dimensional views from above.

A typical starting point is large-scale plans of familiar places such as the classroom, school, playground or sports field. The development of a map direct from fieldwork is also a good starting point because pupils begin to ask such questions as, Why can't I get this the correct shape? How do I represent that hill? What sort of symbols should I use to represent a bus stop or a lamp post? In asking such questions, pupils begin to understand the need for map conventions such as scale (which may be in distance, time or cost, etc.) and a direction indicator, and also the need for symbols to represent everything from settlements of varying size to bus stations, roads and relief features. Getting pupils to understand why these conventions are used and to recognise and use them is a central aim in any geography course, as is helping them to appreciate that a map is always selective; what it includes or omits depends upon its purpose. No map can ever be a complete representation of reality.

Sketch maps and their properties

Most of the essential aspects of all maps can be taught very effectively by using sketch maps; remember, though, that even very simple sketch maps involve sophisticated assumptions and conventions which some pupils find difficult. By analysing these assumptions and conventions it is possible to clarify the properties of all maps, and so to work towards a departmental scheme for map drawing and map use which will avoid most of the potential learning difficulties associated with maps. The analysis which follows will be familiar to experienced geography teachers, but may help non-specialists who perhaps do not yet appreciate the crucial importance of maps, or the learning difficulties associated with their use.

THE PROPERTIES OF MAPS

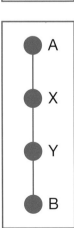

Sketch maps have many of the most important properties of sophisticated maps such as OS and atlas maps and they can be used for numerous purposes and at different levels of complexity (e.g. to show population movements within and into the European Union, or 'migration' of manufacturing industry – car-makers and sports equipment manufacturing, for instance – from the developed to the developing world. At its very simplest level, a sketch map might show where we are (A), where we wish to go (B) and the link between the two. Such a map usually consists of two dots joined by a line.

Scale

If the map is to be of practical use it has to follow certain rules. First, it must tell the user roughly how far it is from A to B. This information may be expressed in terms of distance or of time taken to make the journey. Information may also be included about the cost of the journey and the method of travel used. In summary, the map needs to be drawn to scale, and the scale has to be shown.

Direction

The map must show the general direction from A to B. The user has to know which way up the map is drawn, how it fits into the wider context of the district, town, country and, if air travel is involved, the globe. Does the traveller turn left or right at the end of the street to begin the journey? To enable these questions to be answered, a map needs to show its orientation and this is generally done using a compass rose or north sign. Many users think of maps as having 'tops' and 'bottoms', with north at the top, but this is a false concept and young map users should be dissuaded from thinking of maps in this way. The point must also be made that no area of the earth's surface is flat, so all maps must be drawn on a projection (see Chapter 11).

How Londoners are supposed to 'see' the north; a celebrated 'mental map' devised by Beatrice Urquhart of Notre Dame Grammar School

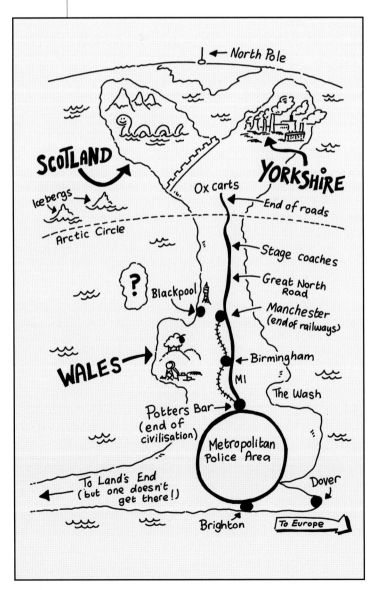

Symbols

The nature of dots A and B has to be made clear. What do they represent? No dots are to be seen on the ground, so they must be symbols; they must show, for example, a house, a school, an airport, New York city. The map must therefore include a key to explain the meaning of all symbols used.

Strictly speaking, this two-dots-and-a-line sketch map is a topological map, or graph. The only visual information it includes is the ordering of points A and B. Were intermediate points to be inserted, showing that the route from A to B passed through X and Y, then we would have a simple form of the topological map invented by Henry Beck in the early 1930s for the London Underground Railway. Beck's brilliant simplification has been copied all over the world by transport companies and is now a standard item in most diaries, filofaxes and their computerised equivalent (see Figure 1).

Colour

If the sketch map is drawn in colour, what colours should be used? Colours are conventions, just like symbols, and it is helpful to have a consistent departmental policy on their use, as well as on all other conventions. The policy which results in least confusion for the pupils is one which adopts, as far as possible, the colour conventions used by the OS and atlas maps, since it is to familiarise pupils with these maps that the use of sketch maps is particularly valuable.

Using sketch maps in class

Ideally, sketch maps should be built up during a lesson, each addition summarising a stage in the explanation. This method allows pupils to see how maps are drawn. Complete, finely-drawn sketch maps presented on an overhead projector or flip chart will not teach pupils how to draw maps for themselves; they need to see maps evolve.

Sketch maps have a myriad uses and space will not allow more than a few to be discussed here. Generally speaking, sketch mapping starts by representing what is familiar and local: maps that show locations, distributions, areal variations and barriers to movement, etc. Using sketch maps to demonstrate change is important; for example, they can show how a settlement has grown in relation to its physical site. They can also summarise reasons for change, as when a port develops because of new international opportunities, and they can help to make comparisons between, say, a village, a street or a market in the UK and in Africa. They can be combined with flow diagrams to show the throughput of materials into a farm or factory, the sequence of processes carried out and the outward flow of products.

It is possible for a department to devise a programme of different kinds of sketch map as part of its course planning and to link this with other forms of information visualisation. Such a programme has to take account of possibly wide variations in map understanding, so it is necessary to ask pupils frequently what a given map means for them. Almost every aspect of geography can and should be mapped at some stage in its teaching.

BLANK SPACES

Referring back to the original sketch map of two dots and a line, it may be noted that most of the area taken up by such a map is blank. Nothing else is included because it is irrelevant to the map's purpose, which is to show someone how to get from A to B. All maps have blank spaces and these can puzzle the inexperienced user. What do the spaces not show? If we were to land by parachute in a particular blank space, what would we find? Most of the space on the OS 1:50 000 sheets (unless heavily built-up areas are shown) is taken up by plain white paper. Experienced map users familiar with, say, lowland England, will know that most of this whiteness represents a landscape of hedged fields; they may be less certain about what it indicates in, say, Orkney or Shetland. Young map readers who may have no direct experience of the countryside will almost certainly not 'see' hedged landscapes when they look at an OS map. How do we help them to 'see' what maps do not show?

In order to tackle this issue, it is advisable to refer repeatedly to the blank spaces on all kinds of maps and to ask, What do you think we might find there? In addition, 'white paper' features should be illustrated. During fieldwork, when the ground is being compared with the map, pupils can be asked to identify what the map does not show and attempt to justify such omissions.

Teachers who believe that plain white paper presents no problems are invited to test themselves by trying to describe a landscape which they have never seen using evidence taken exclusively from the 1:50 000 map. What is the ground like at the end of that parachute drop in Iceland, Tanzania or even the Isle of Mull?

EXAGGERATION AND PROJECTION

These are two other aspects of mapping which need to be dealt with by continual reference, illustration and use. If, say, a main road is to be shown on a 1:50 000 map by a line thicker than the finest hair, its width must be exaggerated. A few measurements of familiar features, such as a local road or the area of the school grounds, will demonstrate that such exaggeration is necessary. Without it, a magnifying glass would be needed to read the map.

All maps are distortions of reality, because the earth is a sphere and maps are flat. The simple idea has to be grasped that flat paper can never accurately represent a spherical surface. Over the years, map makers have tried several well-known geometrical and mathematical systems, but they have only reduced the problem, not eliminated it.

Cognitive/mental/mind maps

Cognitive mapping is just as important as, or maybe more important than, any other type of mapping. We are probably more influenced by the world as we believe it to be than by the world as it really is; and we certainly need to know how maps can be used to manipulate our perceptions of 'real space' as, for example, in the case of maps which are used to persuade investors that a particular location is 'central' and therefore unmatched in its attributes as a potential site for a new factory or office. Many of the maps we use are not necessarily of places or fixed layouts where things happen or where people live, or related to first-hand experiences we have about places. Time and cost, for example, are often more important to us than the measured distance between places, or information about the traffic densities on selected routes.

Suppose, for example, that point A on the sketch map shows where we are, while point B shows the location of a supposed threat, such as might be the case for a refugee. The line between the two points may now seem terrifyingly short and point B large and menacing. The supposed threat may not materialise, but those at point A who believe it will are likely to take action on the basis of that belief. Another example is house buyers at A who may wish to move to B because they believe there are jobs nearby. They may perceive the move as unachievable because of house-price differentials, so in their minds the length of the line will be exaggerated and no attempt will be made to move. In fact, there may be cheap houses near B which have not been advertised in area A's newspapers; imperfect information continually produces faulty mental maps in the real world.

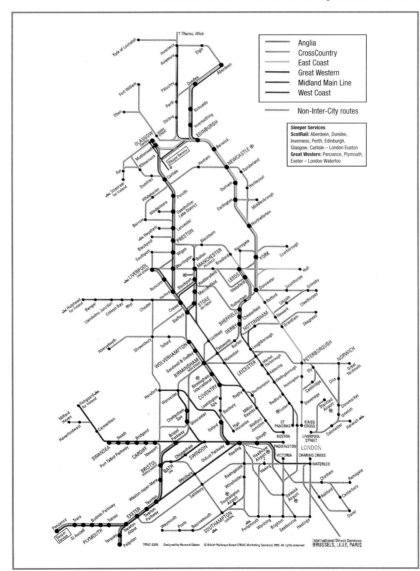

Figure 1: British Rail topological map, 1995. Courtesy British Rail

Mental mapping is a huge topic about which much has been written. It is introduced here simply to make the point that mental maps are simple in concept and that they can be introduced very early in a geography course through sketch mapping. All of us have in our minds a mosaic of mental maps, private and shared. Our pupils' mental maps are rich resources for learning and arguably are the only secure foundations for map learning. Our task is to discover what their maps are like, so we have to devise ways of asking them at every stage in our courses, and to use what we learn to extend our and their understanding of the world.

Devising a scheme for map understanding and use

There is no one way of setting out the objectives of map learning, to be achieved stage by stage in a course. Learning is seldom linear; the learning process is more akin to ink spreading out on blotting paper than to a stepladder of targets reached. What can be done, however, is to identify aspects of map understanding and use which need to be developed, and to keep these continually in mind, looking for opportunities to introduce them.

The matrix in Figure 2 opposite can be a useful planning tool. The examples it suggests are not in any order of difficulty, since no such order exists.

TOPICS	Examples of map skills including uses of maps with air photos, satellite images etc.	Examples of uses of large-scale maps including foreign sheets	Examples of atlas use	Examples of uses of thematic maps, other representational methods
A	Measure distances	Local OS Maps 1:25 000 OS Maps 1:50 000 OS Maps	Use of index, latitude and longitude	Compare relief, climatic and population maps
A	Follow routes			
A	Describe routes	Street plan		
B	Orientate map using compass	Foreign street plan	Grasp significance of colour conventions	Describe relationships, between two thematic maps
B	Draw to scale			
B		Causes of local traffic problem 'location' game 'search' game	Identify differences between projections	
C	Extract information from a general map			Time and movement diagrams
C	Draw own maps: paper-round, routes to school, holiday maps, maps of the week	Learn, use conventions, invent own conventions	Compare maps with pictures, videos	
etc.	etc.	etc.	etc.	etc.

Figure 2: A matrix for map understanding and use

Conclusion

The skills needed to convert geographical ideas and information into maps have to be developed as a language, to be used by teachers and their pupils together. This language will be developed in progressively more precise and subtle ways; effective mapping of complex relationships is a high-level intellectual exercise which will stretch the ability and ingenuity of the most able pupils.

This chapter has been highly selective in its coverage of a huge topic, increasingly influenced by computer technology. As other chapters demonstrate, the continuing development of CD-ROMs will help pupils to develop their knowledge of symbols, scales, direction, etc. and visualise landscapes. Computer mapping programs, however, can only be used to their full potential by pupils who are already familiar with map conventions and their limitations, and able to make maps express particular features or ideas. Ultimately there is no substitute for working in the field, translating three-dimensional or perceived reality into a two-dimensional sketch map by the pupils themselves.

Further reading

Barber, P. & Board, C. (1993) *Tales from the Map Room.* BBC Books.

Downs, R.M. & Stea, D. (1977) *Maps in Minds.* Harper Row.

Robinson, A, Morrison, J., Muehrcke, P., Kimerling, A. & Guptill, S. (1995) *Elements of Cartography.* Wiley.

Whitfield, P. (1994) *The Image of the World: 20 Centuries of World Maps.* The British Library.

Wood, D. (1992) *The Power of Maps.* Routledge.

Chapter 10

Learning with Ordnance Survey maps

DAVID BOARDMAN

In secondary school geography, pupils are required to use and interpret maps and plans at a variety of scales, including Ordnance Survey maps. This chapter focuses on the essential skills which pupils need to develop in order to read and use OS maps, so that they can make full use of them in relation to their work on places and themes.

Comparing maps at different scales

The storage of Ordnance Survey digital map data on computers enables schools to obtain large-scale plans of their locality. The Superplan system allows a plan to be printed out according to a specification centred on any six-figure grid reference. Urban areas are mapped at the 1:1 250 scale (1cm to 12.5m) and rural areas at the 1:2 500 scale (1cm to 25m). Such large-scale maps are useful when detailed information about a small area is needed: buildings, walls, kerb lines, street names and house numbers are shown, and height is given by spot heights and bench marks (see Table 1).

Geography departments should also have a set of topographical maps of the local area showing relief of the land. Ordnance Survey maps on the 1:10 000 scale (1cm to 100m) are the largest-scale maps to show contours, which are drawn at a 5m vertical interval. As the maps cover a ground area of 5 x 5km, they are particularly useful for studying the detailed topography of the area around the school. Other information is derived from the 1:1 250 and 1:2 500 maps of urban and rural areas, so that all the buildings are shown and roads are named.

Pathfinder maps at the 1:25 000 scale (4cm to 1km) cover a ground area 20 x 10km and are widely used by walkers and ramblers because they show footpaths and public rights of way. Contours are drawn at a 5m vertical interval and field boundaries are shown, together with some information about vegetation, such as coniferous and deciduous woodland, bracken and rough grassland. In popular areas Pathfinder maps are replaced by Outdoor Leisure maps which cover larger areas and include information such as viewpoints, youth hostels and camping sites.

Landranger maps at the 1:50 000 scale (2cm to 1km) cover a ground area 40 x 40km and are the most widely used Ordnance Survey maps. The large area covered and the distinctive colouring of the roads make these maps popular and useful for motoring and cycling as well as for walking and rambling. Contours drawn at a 10m vertical interval are a prominent feature of the maps, which are essential documents for interpreting topography and studying relationships between physical and human features.

For comparative purposes, it is useful to display a set of Ordnance Survey maps of the local area at the scales of 1:1 250 or 1:2 500, 1:10 000, 1:25 000 and 1:50 000 on the

Maps are spatial documents, as vital to geography work as written and visual resources

Photo: **Margaret Roberts**

classroom wall. If the same one kilometre square is highlighted on the last three maps, pupils will be able to compare them and see the reduction in detail and greater generalisation as the scale becomes smaller. They will also realise that a map is selective in the features which it shows. The map maker provides information which is considered to be useful for the map reader. Parts of the surface of most maps consist of plain white paper where there is no indication of the surface features. For this reason the local Land Utilisation Survey map, published separately at the 1:25 000 scale by King's College, London, will form a valuable addition to a wall display because it shows the use of the land over the whole area at the time of mapping.

A Travelmaster map at the scale 1:250 000 scale (1cm to 2.5km) is another useful map for a wall display because it locates a place in relation to its wider region. Maps at this scale are used in road atlases and provide a link between medium-scale topographical maps and small-scale atlas maps. Main roads are shown prominently, with their width greatly exaggerated, so these maps are particularly useful for planning motoring routes. Relief is realistically depicted by means of a combination of layer tinting and hill shading in addition to contours.

Maps of the local area will have been printed in different years, so there will inevitably be some disparity between them. Indeed, a department can usefully display early editions of Ordnance Survey maps and subsequent revisions. A set of local historical maps enables pupils to discover the changes which have taken place in their area over a period of a hundred years or more. New features may have been added, such as a housing estate or bypass, while other features may have been removed, such as a factory or railway line.

Ordnance Survey maps on the 1:25 000 and 1:50 000 scales are probably the most complex documents that pupils will study during geography lessons. These maps present a complicated array of conventional signs and symbols which may be classified as **points** (e.g. churches and railway stations), **lines** (e.g. roads and rivers), and **areas** (e.g. woodlands and settlements). Most signs and symbols represent features which can be found on the ground but some are inserted to assist the map reader and do not exist in reality (e.g. contour and grid lines). When learning to read a map, pupils have to perform two distinct tasks. They have to *perceive* the signs, and they have to understand the *concepts* for which they stand. The nature of cartographic communication, and some of the difficulties which topographical maps present for pupils, is beyond the scope of this chapter but is available elsewhere (e.g. Boardman, 1985; 1989).

Title	Scale	Equivalent	Feature
Superplan	1:1 250	1cm to 12.5m or 50in to 1mile	Site-centred plots in urban areas
Superplan	1:2 500	1cm to 25m or 25in to 1mile	Site-centred plots in rural areas
	1:10 000	1cm to 100m or 6in to 1mile	Contours at 5m vertical interval (10m in mountain and moorland areas)
Pathfinder Explorer Outdoor Leisure	1:25 000	4cm to 1km or 2.5in to 1mile	Maps for walking: contours at 5m vertical interval
Landranger	1:50 000	2cm to 1km or 1.25in to 1mile	Maps for motoring and walking: contours at 10m vertical interval
Travelmaster	1:250 000	1cm to 2.5km or 1in to 4miles	Maps for motoring: contours with hill shading

Table 1: Comparison of Ordnance Survey maps at different scales

Locating points

Before pupils learn to locate points on maps by means of grid references, they should learn how to draw and read graphs in mathematics, a core subject which is allocated more curricular time than geography. Just as the starting point for numbering a graph is the lower left-hand corner, so the starting point for numbering grid lines on a map is the south-west corner. The numbers on the map increase from this point to the right and upwards in the same way as the numbers on the axes of graphs. Just as on a graph the value of the x axis is always given before the value of the y axis, so on a map the easting (east of the point of origin) is always given before the northing (north of the point of origin).

It may be necessary to revise co-ordinates and four-figure grid references before teaching pupils to use six-figure grid references. They should be reminded that the intersection of an easting and northing gives the four-figure grid reference of the one kilometre square to the east and north of it. When learning to locate a point to within 100 metres by means of a six-figure grid reference, pupils may find it helpful to superimpose on the one-kilometre square a 10 by 10 grid of small squares printed on tracing paper. It is strongly recommended that pupils should be taught the clearly explained method of giving grid references printed on OS maps.

Following routes

Pupils can attempt route-following exercises when they have practised using grid references. They can be given the starting and finishing points for a road journey and decide on the best route. Alternatively, they can be given the grid references for a number of points along a walk or cycle ride, then be asked to follow the route on their maps and describe what they would see at specific points. They can also work out the distance they would cover by breaking the route into short sections and measuring each one along the edge of a sheet of paper.

Route following is one of the purposes for which maps are designed and should be practised by relating the map to the ground. Opportunities are provided by most kinds of fieldwork, whether to the local shopping centre using a 1:1 250 map or to a more distant locality using a 1:25 000 map. If pupils are transported to a fieldwork location by bus, they should study the route on a map before beginning the journey.

Scouts, guides and youth clubs all provide opportunities for young people to follow routes on maps. Tourist information centres and shops sell leaflets or books containing maps of recommended walks and places to visit. The maps are often sketch maps which have to be carefully followed in conjunction with a commentary describing distinctive features along the route. For some regions recommended cycle routes are highlighted on separately published 1:50 000 maps with directions alongside.

Understanding contours

The interpretation of topographical maps depends on the ability to identify and understand contour patterns. The contour is formally defined as 'a line drawn on a map through all points which are at the same height above, or depth below, sea level'. When teaching the concept to pupils it is easier to explain that the 100 metre contour runs along a line of land that is 100 metres above sea level; so land on one side of the line must be lower, and on the other side higher, than 100 metres. Pupils often experience difficulty with the representation of height, slope and relief by means of contours, and teaching this aspect of map reading requires visual aids.

Even simple aids are useful in teaching the concept of contours. A potato can be cut in half and then into a series of horizontal slices. Each slice is then drawn around on a sheet of paper to form a set of roughly concentric circles and the slices are rebuilt. A piece of clay or plasticine can be moulded into the shape of a hill with a valley and similarly cut into layers which are drawn around and reassembled.

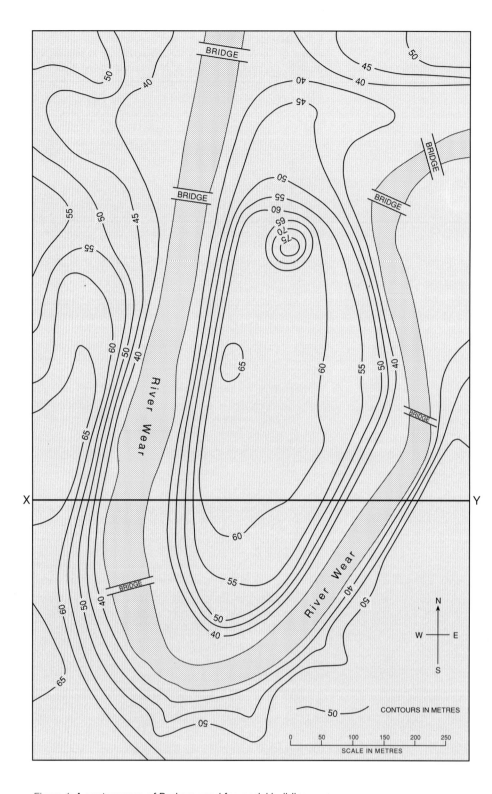

Figure 1: A contour map of Durham used for model building
Based upon the Ordnance Survey map with the permission of the Controller of Her Majesty's Stationery Office © Crown copyright

BUILDING MODELS

Although there is probably insufficient time at secondary level for pupils to build relief models of specific areas, it is recommended that the department should have a permanent model on display and use it for demonstration purposes. An accurate model of a real area can be constructed by using layers of polystyrene ceiling tiles, which are easily cut with sharp scissors. An area of gentle but contrasting relief should be selected from a 1:10 000 map, the largest scale on which contours are shown. This can be enlarged if necessary by projecting an overhead transparency of part of the map on to a sheet of paper pinned to the wall, on to which the contours are drawn (Figure 1). Each contour is then transferred to a large polystyrene ceiling tile by pressing a sharp pencil or ball point pen through the paper at frequent intervals. A row of small, closely spaced holes is thus punched directly onto the tile, making the use of tracing paper unnecessary. Each contour pattern is cut out from the tile and marks are made on it to indicate the correct position of the next-highest contour. All of the shaped tiles are then secured in position with adhesive to build up a layer model.

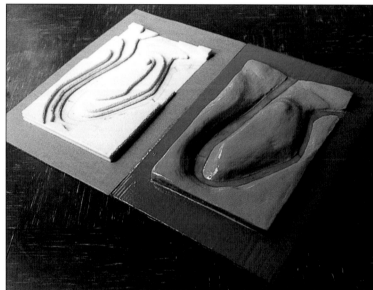

Models made from a contour map of Durham

Photo: **David Boardman**

At this stage of construction the edges of the tiles represent the contours. The stepped or terraced appearance of the model, however, does not resemble the real landscape. Whilst it is useful to leave part of the model in this form to show the method of construction, the spaces between the layers over most of the model should be filled in with plaster or filler and smoothed out, thus being made to resemble reality. Alternatively, two models can be built, one showing the edges during construction, and the other with the spaces between the steps filled in, as recommended by Rhodes (1994) (see photograph). When dry the relief model can be painted green and selected features added to it in different colours, such as a river in blue and a road in red.

Identifying relief

When pupils are looking at a topographical map for the first time, it is useful to begin by forming a general impression of the relief of the area shown. This can be done by looking for the highest points, often indicated by spot heights near to closely spaced contours, and the lowest points, usually found in valleys occupied by rivers, streams or lakes.

These are some of the key features that pupils need to be taught when studying relief:

- when contours are close together, the land is steeply sloping;
- when contours are widely spaced, the land is gently sloping;
- when contours cross a river, they bend upstream;
- every fifth contour is printed as a heavier line than the rest;
- the tops of the height numbers are always printed on the higher side of the contour line.

Pupils need to identify some of the common contour patterns and the landforms which they represent. They should learn to recognise the pervasive V-shaped re-entrants of contours in valleys and the parallel contours on each side of flat-bottomed valleys. They should distinguish valley contour patterns from those of the intervening spurs, in which the highest land is at the centre of the re-entrants. Pupils should also be taught to identify hills, ridges and plains from their characteristic contour patterns before learning how to recognise some of the larger landscape features such as escarpments and plateaus, and the landforms found in glaciated highland areas.

Drawing cross-sections

The side of a relief model is in effect a cross-section, illustrating in two dimensions what the model shows in three dimensions. After pupils have learnt to draw line graphs in mathematics, they should be able to transform contours on a map into a section across the landscape. Placing the straight edge of a piece of paper along the line of the section, they can make a mark on the paper each time a contour crosses the section line and write its height below (Figure 2). When two adjacent contours have the same height, they should insert a plus or minus sign between the marks to indicate whether the land rises or falls.

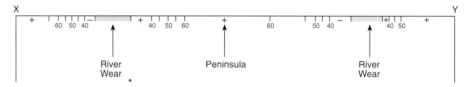

Figure 2: Heights along section line X-Y of Figure 1

To avoid excessive vertical exaggeration, the horizontal and proposed vertical scales should be expressed as ratios and compared. A horizontal scale of 1:10 000, for example, means that 1cm on the map represents 10 000cm on the ground. If a vertical scale of 1cm to 20 metres is proposed, then 1cm on the graph will represent 2 000cm on the ground giving a ratio of 1:2 000. The vertical scale will thus be five times the horizontal scale. This is generally regarded as the maximum permissible exaggeration. Anything greater will tend to distort the relief and even transform a gently rolling hill and vale landscape into one which resembles high mountains and deep gorges.

Using graph paper, the pupils should place their marked piece of paper along the base line of the section and plot the heights they have recorded as a series of dots on the graph. They can then join the dots with continuous smooth curves and insert labelled vertical arrows to indicate the positions of hills, rivers and other prominent features in the landscape (Figure 3).

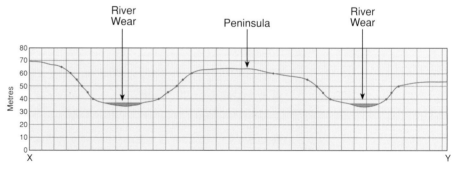

Figure 3: Cross-section along line X-Y of Figure 1 (vertical exaggeration x2)

Maps as records of decisions and change

All maps are records of decisions which people have made. In many cases, these decisions are strongly influenced by relief, as pupils will find if they examine lines of communication. They will see, for example, that canals follow the contours in order to minimise the number of locks, and cuttings and embankments are constructed to reduce gradients on railway lines. Comparisons can be made between the steady gradients on motorways and main roads with the steeper climbs on secondary roads.

The use of maps is central to any discussion about change, both past and present. Maps provide essential documentary evidence which pupils need to help them decide on possible solutions to issues which have spatial implications. For example, if a bypass is to be built round a village, they need a map to help them select a suitable route and assess its impact on the environment. Maps alone are not, of course, capable of supplying all the information that is needed in relation to the social, economic and political implications of developments of this kind. Such implications, and the ways of debating them in class, are discussed by Gossman (1995) in relation to a proposed relief road round north Manchester, abandoned after a public enquiry.

Vertical and oblique aerial photographs, and maps showing an area at different times in the past, can be used in conjunction with current maps to aid discussions about changes in an area, and again, it is useful if these can be displayed in the classroom. Other valuable resources can be gathered as a result of co-operation between teachers and planners, as Dodsworth (1995) has shown in relation to the regeneration of a South Yorkshire valley. Using these materials, pupils can formulate their own plans for the redevelopment of a small area and actively participate in the decision-making process.

Practising skills

Input from the geography teacher is essential when pupils are *learning* new map skills. The widespread availability of computer software, however, does enable pupils to *practise* their skills at the computer. Several programs provide drill and practice routines for such skills as using grid references and following routes (see Table 2). Some also draw cross-sections and convert contour patterns into three-dimensional representations of relief features.

Technological advances, and the further development and refinement of software, have made it possible to store and manipulate large quantities of map data. For example, a CD-ROM of York enables pupils to scroll around the city studying maps and aerial photographs. They can select part of the city and zoom in from 1:50 000 to 1:10 000 and 1:1 250 scales. They are encouraged to attempt a variety of activities, ranging from practising grid references and following a route to devising a tourist trail and measuring the distance covered.

Sophisticated software has been developed to raise the contours from a digitised 1:50 000 map and produce a three-dimensional representation of the relief over the whole of the map. Digital terrain modelling is probably the most striking development in mapping software, but the extent to which it helps pupils to recognise and interpret landscape features remains to be seen. Accurate evaluation of this type of software will be crucial to the development of appropriate resources in the future.

References

Boardman, D. (1985) 'Cartographic communication with topographical maps' in Boardman, D. (ed) *New Directions in Geographical Education*. Falmer Press.

Boardman, D. (1989) 'The development of graphicacy: children's understanding of maps' *Geography*, 74, 4, pp. 321-331.

Dodsworth, T. (1995) 'Co-operation with planners: the Lower Dearne Valley', *Teaching Geography*, 20, 1, pp. 10-16.

Gossman, P. (1995) 'Do we need another urban motorway?', *Teaching Geography*, 20, 1, pp. 4-9.

Rhodes, B. (1994) 'Learning curves...and map contours', *Teaching Geography*, 19, 3, pp. 111-115.

Software
Introducing Map Skills 1 and 2 *Publisher:* Cambridge Micro Software Tel 01291 625439
Micro Map 1 and 2 *Publisher:* Longman Logotron Tel 01223 425558
Micromapping *Publisher:* Nelcal Tel 01985 840329
General Map Reading Coastal Map Reading *Publisher:* Soft Teach Educational Tel 01985 840329
Maps and Landscapes 1 and 2 *Publisher:* Chalksoft Tel 01775 769518
Mapping Skills *Publisher:* ESM Tel 01223 357788
Map Skills *Publisher:* Cumana Tel 01483 503121 Koch Media Tel 01252 714340
Discover York CD-ROM *Publisher:* Ordnance Survey Tel 01703 792795 NRSC Tel 01455 844513

Table 2: Examples of software for practising map skills

Chapter **11**

Learning with atlases and globes

PATRICK WIEGAND

Introduction

Atlases vary considerably in character and content – indeed, what is today called an atlas can often be similar to a textbook, and vice-versa. In this chapter, however, we are concerned only with the small-scale maps that characterise both the 'traditional' atlas and the globe, and with the ways in which teachers can support and enhance pupils' learning by using these endlessly fascinating, though complex, media. The chapter also includes references to electronic atlases. The potential of maps and atlases in CD-ROM or disk form, or accessed through the Internet, is already clear, particularly the possibilities they offer for manipulating and combining data cartographically. The boundaries between atlases and Geographical Information Systems (GIS) are likely to become increasingly blurred and will require teachers and pupils to learn new skills. Nevertheless, given hardware and organisational constraints in most school contexts, a future for the conventional desk atlas seems assured for the foreseeable future.

Reading atlas maps

The information shown on any map is highly selective, but on maps at small scales it is very selective indeed, and its interpretation may require a good deal of abstract thinking. The following are some atlas map features or map types which can present problems of interpretation:

- Complex patterns of colours and symbols
- A wide variety of type faces and type styles
- High density of information – this can create 'noise' which inhibits easy reading
- The intercutting of map labels and labels with lines and colour
- Foreign place names – these may be difficult to spell and to pronounce
- The use of colours with ambiguous meanings (e.g. green areas on topographic maps are often read as 'grassy' or 'fertile' when the colour actually indicates the height of the land)
- Choropleth and isopleth maps – these can mislead pupils into believing that sudden changes occur at the zone boundaries when in reality there is likely to be a smooth gradation from one zone to another

Atlas work helps place detailed studies into a wider perspective
Photo: **Margaret Roberts**

■ Standard world map projections, when used in isolation from alternatives, or a globe, can distort understanding of spatial relationships

As well as the above, there are the problems associated with dating. The information which is plotted on atlas maps is constantly changing so few are ever completely up-to-date. Added to this is the fact that schools cannot afford to replace their stock of atlases more than once every five or more years, so what pupils will be using may often by seriously outdated.

Finally, there is the issue of 'bias'. Atlases are reference works and, like other such works, have an air of authority. This can be dangerous when, however well edited, the content actually presents a partial and selective view of the world rather than one which is balanced or 'neutral' (if such is ever possible).

Map projections for world maps and globes

Globes are the only medium by which land masses on the surface of the earth can be shown accurately. They are, however, awkward to carry and use because of their shape and size – a large globe is needed for really useful detail to be shown. Despite a number of ingenious attempts to solve the problem (such as folding and inflatable globes) as well as advances in Information Technology, it seems likely that the school desk atlas will remain a standard classroom tool for a considerable time.

It is important for pupils to understand the inter-relationship between globe and world map. Curriculum changes in the 1990s have resurrected this central aspect of geography but decades of neglect have meant that there is still much muddle about map projections. Transforming a spherical surface into a flat map inevitably involves distortion of one type or another. You can get the shape of the land masses right and their relative areas wrong; or you can get relative areas right and shape wrong; or you can get them both wrong. What you cannot have is a map that faithfully reproduces both shape and area. Cartographers generally attempt to confine the inevitable error to where it is least noticeable. School pupils need to be familiar with these general principles and with a variety of exemplar projections. They need to see that one projection is not necessarily better than another; the issue is suitability for the purposes to which the map will be put. The following selection of projections provides a basis for comparison and discussion.

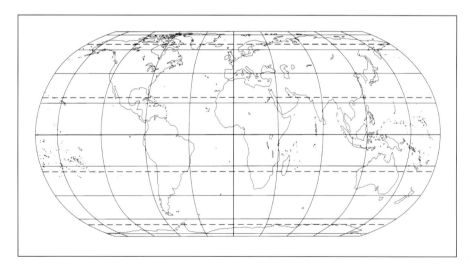

Figure 1: Eckert IV projection

Equal area projection – where the correct relative areas of landmasses are maintained, but at the expense of shape (Figure 1). These maps are used principally for world distributions, such as types of environment. The National Curriculum uses an Eckert IV projection (i.e. the fourth projection devised by Max Eckert, 1868-1938) but pupils could just as well see and use those by Mollweide, Bonne or Hammer. As a teaching point, it would be useful to show an 'interrupted' projection (where the graticule is scooped around the oceans, to better preserve the shape of the land masses). The so-called Peters' projection is also equal area. It attracted much publicity in the 1980s and is included here because copies of world maps based on this projection are readily available. The projection was devised in 1967 by Arno Peters but is essentially identical to that produced by James Gall in 1885. It was espoused by several aid and development agencies who used it as part of their promotional material, and was also reproduced in many textbooks. It has no particular merit other than to demonstrate the extreme distortion of shape that can occur in an attempt to preserve relative area.

Cylindrical projection – such as the map devised by Gerardus Mercator (1512-1594). The special property of the Mercator map (Figure 2) is that straight lines are lines of constant compass bearing and thus the map has been, and remains, indispensable for navigation. The particular use of cylindrical projections in atlases is to show climate and time zones, as all points at the same distance from the equator on the globe are shown at the same perpendicular distance on the map.

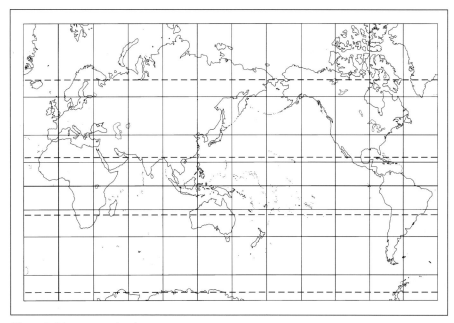

Figure 2: Mercator projection

Polar projection – shows the polar areas as circles (Figure 3). Most atlases have a page or section devoted to the poles and explicit reference to these in the context of projections allows pupils to see, for example, the true shape of Antarctica or the disposition of the land masses around the Arctic Ocean. As a rule of thumb, Antarctica is about the same size as the United States. Pupils may like to speculate that if the world were ruled by polar bears and penguins then this might be the standard wall map of the world!

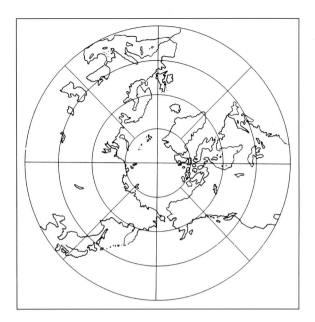
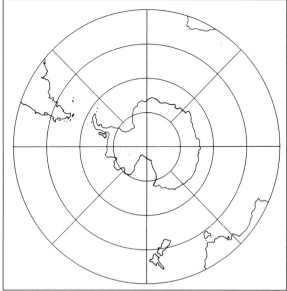

Figure 3: Arctic polar projection (left) and Antarctic polar projection (right)

Transverse projection – 'wraps the map around the world' at right angles to the more usual world map (Figure 4). The principal teaching point here is that it is only because of a convention based on the distribution of human activity that the equator is in the 'centre' of most world maps. With this in mind, it is also helpful for pupils in the British Isles to see projections that are centred on the Pacific Ocean as well as those centred on the Atlantic (Figure 5). An important lesson to learn that is that on the latter, New Zealand is usually represented as two small islands 'on the edge of the map' whilst the British Isles are 'in the centre of the map'. With the Pacific-centred projection the situation is of course reversed.

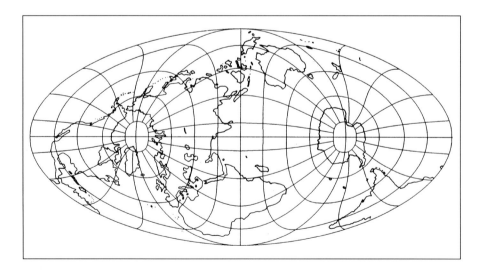

Figure 4: Transverse projection

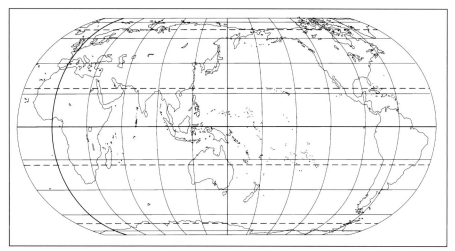

Figure 5: *Pacific-centred Eckert IV projection*

Getting to grips with projections

A number of useful activities can reinforce pupils' understanding of relationships between the globe and world maps. One of the simplest is to colour in Greenland, Africa, Australia and Antarctica on outline world maps of different projections. As these land masses usually show the greatest size and shape distortions, making comparisons between them usually brings out the principal features of each projection and its relative advantages and disadvantages. Another interesting experiment is to stretch a piece of string across a globe to represent the shortest distance between two places. This is the 'great circle' route, such as might be taken by an aeroplane. Pupils note the places crossed and compare this direct route with a straight line drawn on a world map. They then try to draw the direct route on the world map and point to the line of the route suggested by the map on the globe. Without doing this it is difficult to understand why flights from London to Canada head north-west over the Hebrides and then pass near the North Pole; or why a flight from the UK to Australia appears to make a substantial detour via Tashkent in central Asia.

A further useful approach is to ask pupils to select the most appropriate projection for a specific purpose. Which of the projections shown in Figures 1-5, for example, would be most suited to mapping the ring of volcanoes around the Pacific Ocean, or the location and extent of the world's tropical rainforests, or changes in the extent of the ice sheets as a result of global warming?

A world atlas map, with its inevitable distortions of shape and/or area, is more easily fixed in people's minds than a globe because you can only see part of the globe at a time; it has to be rotated to show relative location. This is why is it important for pupils to make comparisons between globes and maps at all stages to avoid distorted images becoming permanent.

Latitude and longitude

When the concepts of latitude and longitude are first introduced, the frequent use of a globe is to be recommended. It may be best to use one that shows land and sea outlines only, rather than a political globe, as the latter often has too much distracting detail for the meridians and parallels to be clearly seen. Plastic globes that show only the outline of land masses and that can take felt tip markers are especially useful. In comparing atlases and globes it is appropriate to use small globes at approximately the same scale as the world maps in the atlas (see photograph, page 130).

Below is a suggestion for a progressive teaching sequence for developing understanding of lines of latitude (parallels) and longitude (meridians):

1   The earth has two poles

2   There are two sets of imaginary lines circling the earth

3   Meridians join at the poles. They are all 'great circles' (lines that go round the earth at its maximum extent)

4   Parallels don't join and only one of them (the equator) is a 'great circle'

5   Meridians and parallels are numbered in degrees

6   Some parallels have special names – the equator, the tropics and the polar circles

7   Meridians are numbered east and west from the prime meridian

8   The prime meridian is not 'natural'. It is only fixed by international agreement

9   Parallels are numbered north and south from the equator

10 The equator divides the world into north and south hemispheres

Comparing atlases and globes.

Photo: **Patrick Wiegand**

Once these principles have been taught using a globe, pupils might use an outline map of the world with an un-named and un-numbered graticule. The lines of longitude and latitude can then be numbered on the map (remembering to add N and S, E and W) and 'special' meridians and parallels can be named. The northern and southern hemispheres can be coloured as well as other regions of the world, such as tropical and polar areas.

Atlas map skills

Topographic maps in atlases are used principally to find out where places are in relation to each other. Typically, pupils in school will use them in conjunction with, or to make sense of, other information derived perhaps from text or illustrations. Movements of raw materials and finished products described in a book make better sense once you see on the map where the places concerned are located.

Thematic maps in atlases are principally used as stores of information. The data they contain may be retrieved, compared, contrasted and used as evidence for the nature of places in order to solve problems. For example, pupils may understand more about the distribution of farming types by looking at maps which show, respectively, temperature, rainfall and relief.

Competent atlas use requires a number of inter-related skills. These are considered in turn in order to focus on progression in teaching and learning but in practice, of course, such skills cannot be taught one after the other. You can no more teach symbols one week, scale the next and location the week after than you can teach someone to drive by giving them successive lessons on the use of the accelerator, gears and the brakes.

As stated earlier in this chapter, atlases have limitations, and pupils must be made aware of them. They do not present an 'objective' view of the world; they are simply a selection of maps whose balance and content have been determined by the perceived needs of the users. A simple exercise in assessing the reliability of data is to ask pupils to check the date of publication. What has happened since the atlas was printed? There is a considerable time lag in many common data sets in atlases. UK population figures, for example, in an atlas published in 1992 will still be based on the 1981 census.

GAZETTEER AND CO-ORDINATE SKILLS

When first confronted with a new atlas most pupils will probably need some browsing time. Developing familiarity with the Contents page is a good way to achieve an overview of the structure of the book; knowing, for example, that for each of the continents thematic maps are followed by topographic maps.

Being able to use the index or gazetteer is a key skill which includes the sub-skills of applying alphabetical order and using a system of co-ordinates. Alphabetical order skills may need to be built slowly for some pupils; exercises in which the order is determined by the first letter are followed by those relying on the second letter, and so on, finally involving more complex examples such as double words and hyphens.

A typical teaching sequence, showing progression, might go like this:

> Write these places in alphabetical order:
>
> 1 Leeds, Manchester, Birmingham, Dublin, Edinburgh
>
> 2 Huddersfield, Hastings, Hounslow, Hyde, Hinckley
>
> 3 Southampton, South Downs, Southern Uplands, Southend-on-Sea, South Shields, Southport

Most pupils are likely to start work on co-ordinates by learning to use a simple alpha-numeric grid code, as on the Irish National Grid. Many teachers provide simple gridded sheets with marginal numbers and letters and pupils have to colour squares, given a series of references. The resultant pattern could be an easily recognisable shape. This exercise can be developed by referring to a particular atlas page and listing names of particular features in, for example, square C3 or D2. A further step is to focus attention on the lines that form the grid rather than the spaces between them by asking pupils to identify the square bounded by particular lines of latitude and longitude. The final step is to deal with the imaginary subdividing of the space between the lines on the map in the same way as the 'tenths' in grid references on large-scale maps. This is usually more complex in atlases as it may involve estimating sixtieths, i.e. minutes between degrees.

Consolidation of all these skills could be achieved by a task such as:

> Use the atlas index to find each of the following places. Name the river on which each city stands.
>
> Tours   Lyons   Amiens   Metz   Bergerac

Co-ordinate skills are likely to get more important, given the recent rapid growth of Global Positioning Systems (GPS) and hand-held devices using satellite signals to give users their exact location on earth. The application of GPS technology to many occupations (aviation, surveying, navigation, building, telecommunications, etc.) may make co-ordinate skills one of the principal geography-related pre-vocational skills of the future. Other locational skills include the correct use of 'global location' terms such as tropical, equatorial and polar, as well as being able to relate compass directions to maps.

SYMBOL SKILLS

Symbols on atlas maps can be thought of as being points, lines or patches expressed in various ways. Colour is one of the most widely used symbols in atlases, and has many uses, some of which are described below. By learning about the different uses of colour, pupils will become aware of the limitations of maps.

Colour may be used:

■ for showing where one country ends and another begins, e.g. on political maps. The use of colour is arbitrary so no key in needed. If France and Portugal are both shown in red, this is simply because the cartographer has a limited palette – no similarity between the two countries is intended.

■ for showing areas with a particular property, e.g. on environmental maps. Areas which are shown in the same colour share the same property (e.g. all green areas are tropical rainforests), so a legend is needed.

■ for showing quantities, i.e. where one colour stands for 'more than' another colour. Land height or layer-coloured relief maps are examples.

The small scale of atlas maps means that they are characterised more by what is *not* shown on the map than by what is. A useful exercise is to compare an aerial photograph or satellite image with an atlas map extract in order to appreciate that the vast and complex patchwork of an urban area, including buildings and communications, is condensed on an atlas map to perhaps just a small black dot and a red line. It is important to stress that there are many settlements that are not shown at all because the map maker has established a threshold population size below which settlements are not included.

A map that uses **point symbols** to show the location of economic activity (such as that in Figure 6) has involved the cartographer in making a generalisation from a complex pattern. Pupils would understand a great deal more about the limitations of atlas maps if they had opportunities to make similar decisions. This 'constructivist' approach, learning by 'being a cartographer', is illustrated in Figure 7. A simple classroom technique for teaching this principle is to create a pattern of dots on an OHP

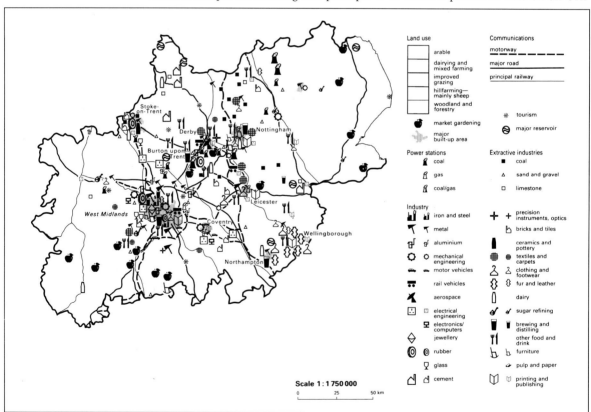

Figure 6: The economic map which tries to show everything is often hard to read

transparency. Each dot stands for a factory. One or more symbols drawn on small pieces of acetate can then be laid on the dots to contrast alternative possible solutions to the problem of locating a small number of symbols on a particular point distribution; only the major centres of activity are shown with a symbol. It is this property of atlas maps to make coarse generalisations that is often imperfectly understood by pupils. So too is the nature of the symbols themselves. The coat hanger symbol may be used to represent 'clothing and footwear', not coat hanger manufacture or the location of dry cleaning establishments. By critically examining common everyday symbols and designing their own for use on maps, pupils come to see that symbology can be quite subtle. You need a clear image, visible when reduced in size, that represents the concept accurately and unambiguously. A collaborative project with the art and design department in which pupils create symbols of a predetermined size for, say, a car or toy factory, a supermarket, a video tape factory, etc., can be instructive.

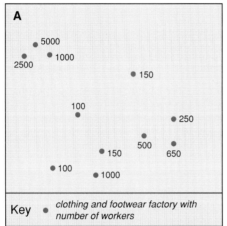

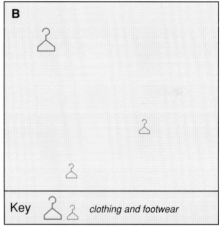

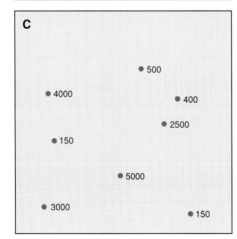

Maps A and B above show some of the problems of deciding where to put symbols. Map A shows the location of every clothing factory in part of Britain and the number by the side of each factory shows how many people work there. There are too many factories to show them all and so the cartographer has put three coat hanger symbols on map B to show where the most important clothing areas are.

Trace map C and decide where to place coat hanger symbols on your tracing. Compare where you decided to put your symbols with a few other people. Did you all have the same solution?

Figure 7: Making economic maps. Source: The Oxford Schools Atlas Skills Book, 1996

Symbols on maps are interpreted through use of the **key** or legend, but this may not be enough to clarify what the symbols really mean. There has to be a connection between the pupil's own experience of the real world and its representation on the map. It is of little use pupils correctly identifying a colour patch on a map as a UK National Park if they believe that the term indicates national ownership and a park-like appearance. This implies that atlas work has to be strongly linked to discussion, the use of pictures, and fieldwork.

It is not always understood that text on a map is part of the symbology; the use of contrasting typefaces holds meaning for the map reader. Common conventions include capital letters for administrative and political units, upper and lower case for settlements, italics for physical features and condensed type for mountain peaks. Type size usually conveys the relative importance or size of features. Type, therefore, is a code which helps to locate place names when scanning the map. It is a useful exercise simply to ask pupils to list all the information they can deduce about a place from the way its name is written. Place-names also provide opportunities for language learning: pupils who can decode the following will be better able to understand a map of Spain or South America than those who cannot: Sierra, Cordillera, Rio, Isla, Bahia, Cerro, Costa, Laguna, Puerto, Pico.

DEALING WITH SCALE

Perhaps the best starting point for dealing with small-scale maps is to establish as clearly as possible the scale of the British Isles or Britain and then make frequent use of a 'comparitor' map to contrast the size of Britain with other parts of the world. How big is Britain? The straight line distance from John O'Groats to Land's End is a little less than 1000km – a useful figure to remember. A medium-range jet would probably take two hours to fly the distance. How long would this take by car? Two days? And to walk? Charity walks have taken something like 40 days. The precise figures don't really matter. The important thing is to involve pupils in the calculations and establish the round figure. Additional activities would include pupils marking their home town and some places they have visited on a map of the British Isles. They use straight lines to join each place and home and construct a table to show travel time, which will vary according to the transport used. Tables and maps are compared so that predictions can be made about the time taken to reach other destinations. Pupils should then be ready to compare the size of Britain with other parts of the world. How many times bigger or smaller than Britain is the USA, or Japan or X? Round figures are also useful for establishing the size of the earth. The circumference is near enough 40 000km or 25 000 miles. How many times 'round the earth' has the school minibus been?

Estimating distances and areas on atlas maps is probably more useful than being able to make precise measurements, not least because the scale on most world maps is only true for the equator, not for other directions across the map.

Selecting a school atlas

All atlases are expensive to produce and the purchase of an atlas set is a major expense for a school geography department. Adopting an atlas for school use therefore requires careful thought. The suggestions which follow are intended to provide a check-list of considerations:

COST

Cost does not equal value. Divide the cost by the number of pages for a more meaningful comparison between alternatives. Check for special deals on multiple copies ordered.

DURABILITY AND FORMAT

Hardback books will be more expensive but will probably last longer. How strong is the book physically? On a 'flick test' through the pages, does the book look lively – the sort of product that might encourage pupils to spend time browsing through it?

BALANCE OF CONTENT

Assess the balance between topographic and thematic coverage and the proportions of British Isles, continental and world pages. Some atlases provide good overall coverage of the world at a reasonable scale; others provide detailed coverage of some parts of the world at the expense of others. Remember that large-scale 'case study' material that looks attractive now, might be rendered obsolete by curriculum or examination syllabus changes. It may be better to buy for the longer term by providing good overall coverage and supplementing this with other materials for teaching the current selection of case studies.

Check the scales of the maps across a number of areas. It may be crucial for the department's teaching programme to have maps of several parts of the world at the same scale so that comparisons can be made. Check especially the provision of UK topographic material. Coverage at 1:1 million is a good standard for all secondary school work. For lower secondary pupils, it is best if all thematic maps of, say, the British Isles are at the same scale, for easier comparison. Check the provision of maps of parts of the world that are likely to be in the news for the foreseeable future. These might include the Balkans, the Middle East and the Caucasus region.

Before choosing an atlas, it is also worth checking what supporting material is available (e.g. on projections, on using the maps and understanding their origins and conventions) as well as other related material such as satellite imagery and town plans.

CLARITY

The more information there is on a map the more difficult it is to read. Paradoxically, the less information the more abstract the map is and the more difficult to interpret. Check the legibility of the typeface. This should be clear black and be visible even where it has to cut coastlines or darker colours. As much type as possible should be ranged left to right (rather than angled) for pupils who are not fluent readers. The density of place-names on maps can sometimes be deceptive. Count the number of place-names on alternative atlases to see which one has most, then decide whether you need all the names.

CO-ORDINATE SYSTEM

Does the atlas have a simple grid code system or rely on latitude and longitude references? Still better, does it have both? The grid code should be clearly visible and the letters and numbers should be as near as possible in straight lines around the map, not snaking in and out of keys and scale information.

LOCATORS AND COMPARITORS

Good atlas maps should have a clear locator (a small map or globe, usually inset, showing the global location of the main map). Comparitors show how big the area of the main map is compared to the British Isles. Both are essential aids for understanding the maps.

KEYS AND SCALE INFORMATION

It is desirable (essential for younger pupils and those with learning difficulties) to have a scale and key on every page. Look for keys that are prominent (but not at the expense of map area) and avoid atlases where the key is located only at the beginning of a section. Every map should have a statement of scale, preferably expressed in several ways.

INDEX

Try looking up some of the places in the index. How easy is the system to operate? Gazetteer entries are generally more readable if the grid references are printed close to the place-names.

ERRORS AND DATING

Editors and publishers do their best to make sure that their publications are as good as they can be and are constantly seeking to improve their products. They do sometimes receive letters from purchasers (my favourite was: 'I've looked up Sidney in the index and it isn't there…') but overall the amount of feedback is disappointingly small, perhaps one letter for every five or ten thousand copies sold. A thoughtful letter pointing out what is helpful, and what is not, will always receive a reply and may help to improve the quality of this central teaching resource.

Always check the date of publication of an atlas and be sure to buy the most recent available. A quick look at maps of 'Russia' will reveal immediately how recently the maps were produced!

Selecting an electronic atlas

COST
Atlases on CD-ROM and disk are becoming cheaper all the time. Indeed, some useful material, such as the *Encarta* CD-ROM encyclopedia which includes a large number of basic maps, often comes free when you buy a personal computer. Check to see whether the software you wish to purchase is subject to a discount – some very expensive materials can be half-price if they are for educational use. Find out whether you have an opportunity to examine the materials before purchase. Philips' *CD-ROM World Atlas*, for example, is available on 30 days approval. The resources exhibition at the Geographical Association's Annual Conference provides a crucial opportunity to assess software that is not available on approval.

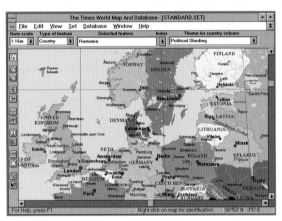
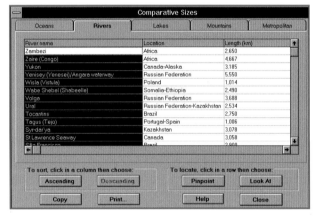

Figure 8: Times Electronic World Map and Database

FORMAT
Although there are several atlases at present available on disk which can be loaded onto a PC hard disk, it would seem at the time of writing that the future for electronic atlases is in CD-ROM. This allows a quicker, more flexible and interactive product that can link pictures and moving images with the maps. Check to see that what you intend to buy will work on your equipment.

LICENCES AND NETWORKING
Software is often subject to a legal agreement between the manufacturer and the user which comes into force when you open the sealed envelope containing the disk or CD-ROM, or when you first install it on your computer. Typically this restricts the use of the software to a single computer on a single screen (to prevent you, for example, doing a deal with the school next door). You do not want to be prosecuted, so if you intend to network the materials and use them on several computers at the same time, buy the network version.

CONTENT
Issues of clarity, legibility and colour contrast are as important with electronic atlases as with the printed version. But what does an electronic atlas offer that a conventional atlas does not? *The Times World Map and Database* allows you to zoom in on a map, customise

the appearance of symbols and text, sort and compare sets of statistics and draw your own thematic maps. A new atlas product from Microsoft is also becoming available which will enable the user to access photographs, text, statistical data, sound tracks and moving images direct from the maps. An infinite number of multimedia routes can thus be taken in a desk-top exploration of the world, offering substantial opportunities for supporting pupils with learning difficulties and extending those of high ability.

GETTING STARTED

How easy is the atlas to use? Is it run with Windows? If so, are the 'point and click' icons or buttons large enough? Are the symbols on them self-explanatory? Are there **Help** menus which explain how each part works? Can you access maps by theme as well as by area? How easy is the index to use? Can you, for example, scroll down a list of place-names as well as type in the name of the place you are looking for?

SCALE

Most electronic atlases have a zoom facility which enlarges the scale of the map on the screen, but the quality of the enlargement generally depends on the scale at which the original map was 'captured' when the software was produced. Try enlarging the map as far as it will go and assess the quality of the mapping at this scale.

PRINTING

Can you print maps for class use from the atlas? Do the coloured maps on screen print satisfactorily on a black and white printer? Can you print charts and graphs from the database as well as cut and paste maps for your own handouts?

SUPPORT MATERIAL

Are the disks or CD-ROMs all you get? *Distant Places*, the interactive atlas from The Advisory Unit, Computers in Education, comes with a substantial folder containing pupil help cards, a teacher's guide, photocopiable worksheets and a large reference section.

Atlas material on the Internet

The Internet takes us further. There is already the possibility of browsing fairly effortlessly through the world's great map libraries and then downloading images and text. I have, for example, just examined Gough's (1360) map of Britain and Sir John Evelyn's plan for rebuilding London after the Great Fire, both from the Bodleian Library in Oxford, without moving from my desk. I also notice that the John Borchert Map Library in the University of Minnesota provides a very helpful cartographic glossary that would be useful for GCSE or A level students and that the University of Texas has an excellent interactive tutorial program on GIS. Maps on the Internet are growing all the time. A useful starting point for surfers is the cartography 'virtual library' at: **http://geog.gmu.edu/gess/jwc/cartogrefs/html.**

A shopping list

The following electronic atlases offer good features for school use:

Distant Places Interactive Atlas
Details from: The Advisory Unit, Computers in Education, 126 Great North Road, Hatfield, Herts AL9 5JZ tel 01707 266714

The Times Electronic World Map and Database
Details from: Bartholomew/Times, Unit 4, Manchester Park, Tewkesbury Road, Cheltenham, Glos GL51 9EJ tel 01242 512748

Philips' CD-ROM World Atlas
Details from: Heinemann Educational Books Ltd, Halley Court, Jordanhill, Oxford OX2 8EJ tel 01865 311366

Chapter 12

The simplicity of simulation

REX WALFORD

The historic origins of simulation

A geography textbook written in 1790 suggested that 'It is a very amufing exercife to children, and, at the fame fime, very inftructive, to let them make an imaginary voyage through all the feas and ftraits of Europe...' Simulation, it seems, exhibiting its twin virtues of enjoyment and enlightenment, was alive and well as a classroom activity in geography lessons at least two hundred years ago. Not quite 'virtual reality' as known by modern technology perhaps, but in recognisably the same tradition.

It has always been customary for children to make voyages of imagination during school lessons (whether bidden to do so or otherwise); and the action of play and taking part in games on school fields and playgrounds is likewise a long and valued tradition (recently given renewed vigour by specific Government action in its support). Simulation as a classroom activity harnesses the essence of both and formalises their potential for educational purposes, hopefully without destroying their attractiveness and enjoyment.

But the acceptance of such activity has come relatively recently to most schools. Only in the last twenty years has the technique become accepted and disseminated, valued and taught as a regular part of the armoury of teaching strategies in geography. Asking pupils to 'put themselves in somebody else's shoes' is now no more likely to raise an eyebrow than drawing a sketch map on the black or whiteboard.

How the idea of simulation grew

When Professor John Cole of Nottingham University first published a duplicated pamphlet called *Geographical Games* (Cole, 1966) there was incomprehension and frank scepticism as to how anything so apparently frivolous as a 'game' could be employed for the serious purposes of education. It was not long before the strong winds of change blowing through geography after the Madingley Hall lectures (Chorley and Haggett, 1964; 1966) had picked up the potential of a pedagogy which could use games in the classroom (Walford, 1969; Dalton *et al*, 1972; many issues of *Classroom Geographer* between 1971 and 1979). In this period also a number of notable philosophers (Huizinga, 1974), psychologists (Berne, 1966) and scientists (Calder, 1967) identified the 'game' concept as an important (if often unconscious) aspect of human life.

Simulations often result in presentations to the class by individuals or small groups

Photo: **Margaret Roberts**

Geography at that time was emerging from a period in which it had mostly emphasised the unique, and was now searching for patterns, models and systems; simulations became the classroom replication of models and systems in active terms. They turned out to have the priceless asset of interesting and motivating pupils who became involved with them; indeed, so seductive were they that the greater danger was in the uncritical acceptance of the particular models which were devised.

The development of simulations represented not only a greater interest in system and process but also a chance to escape from an emphasis on factual learning. This gave geography renewed intellectual stimulation – analysing, synthesising and evaluating in making judgements being more demanding to the mind than remembering. Yet it is salutary to remember that one of the early popular simulations (FitzGerald and Stevens' (1973) three-stage role-play on the changing locations of the British iron and steel industry, in which pupils assumed the roles of Boards of Directors at different periods of history) required pupils to undertake a factual test to demonstrate their knowledge and grasp of certain fundamentals before being judged ready to take on responsible Directorial roles.

A third impetus toward games and simulations came from a different direction. They were discovered to be useful ways of raising empathy for other people's situations. It was not so easy for a relatively affluent English urban teenager to regard a Third World farmer as 'stupid, because he was poor' after having tried and failed to make a go of farming in several rounds of a simulation game – the poverty spiral was apt to entrap even the most ingenious and intelligent in the end. There were also found to be spin-offs for teachers using games and simulations in respects quite unconnected with their content. Classroom atmosphere changed: teachers managed, rather than commanded, the activities; general communication and social skills were learnt; and the inter-disciplinary nature of real life emerged. Though geographers were early and consistent users of the simulation technique, it quite frequently led them into considerations of matters and issues beyond the subject.

Practical considerations for the classroom

Simulation in all forms is basically a simple activity and one easily understood by pupils (Greenblat and Duke, 1981; Jones, 1985). But teachers who use it need to consider carefully three major aspects:

1 choosing appropriate material

2 managing the activity effectively and integrating it into other work

3 assessing and evaluating the results

CHOOSING APPROPRIATE MATERIAL

There are many simulation activities published in course-books and teaching journals, as well as those separately published, and plenty of examples from which to choose. They range from those which might involve only a few minutes' informal imaginative work ('Just put yourself in the position of the planner who has got to decide whether to...etc.') to some which may form the framework for several weeks' study ('This term we are going to work towards staging a simulation of a Government enquiry on pollution in Britain...').

Many teachers will wish to develop their own materials, but it is best to acquire familiarity with the technique by using some tried and tested examples. This will make it clear, if initial difficulties are experienced, that it is management rather than material which is at fault. There are some basic structures (see below) which can be adapted by the insertion of new content (e.g. the structure of a game about farming in the Canadian prairies can readily be re-designed to use data from the UK, West Africa or South-East Asia). Simulations can also be adapted to be simpler or more complex than the original idea by adding extra rules or simplifying the decision-making frameworks.

It may be helpful to identify five recognisable branches of the 'simulations' family, though in practice many designed activities straddle the boundaries of these categories.

Role plays

For the most part, these are simulations with little structure beyond the setting up of an initial situation (a village meeting, a money-awarding committee of a charitable organisation, a Government enquiry) and the assignation of particular roles to participants; the end result may not be predictable, nor should it be.

The task here is for pupils to take on and argue particular viewpoints which may not be the ones they hold personally; and to see if debate and discussion can have sufficient focus and quality for an issue to be decided on its merits rather than on preconceived views. If desired, the teacher may give participants a paragraph or two of description to help fill out the role, though it is not helpful to add cartooned caricatures or crude stereotypical names (e.g. Miss Prim, Mr Profitt, John Skimpy: road builder). A question or two to prompt initial thoughts may be usefully added. It is also important to ensure that there is a gender balance in the roles selected and, therefore, in the role players.

To get the best from such role-plays participants need to have time to prepare and, perhaps, to consult with others. (Sometimes it helps to assign two people to each role so that they can discuss the role between themselves and work out attitudes and viewpoints which might be held.) Some common information can be issued, but other pieces of information only given to selected groups. A teacher may wish to have certain 'chance factors' ready to insert (e.g. a press release announcing a change in government policy, or news of an unexpected event) should discussion initially fail to ignite or seem to be losing its way. Some kind of vote may often terminate such occasions, though it is important to recognise that in real life democratic votes are not the way in which many economic and environmental issues are decided.

Operational games

These are usually distinguished by the fact that they have sets of rules and considerable structure which guide participants towards concentrating on a particular set of decisions (e.g. in *Starpower* the game is about who trades with who; in *Railway Pioneers* it is about deciding where routes should be developed westwards in the USA). Pupils often pick up the role-play element within games quite unconsciously in their desire to make the game work, and this can be an advantage where the more conscious ascription and adoption of roles might be viewed with fear or suspicion.

Some games have 'boards' (such as a map of the world or of a country), some use simple artefacts (tokens, badges, trading chips), some work with familiar game-frameworks (dice, playing-cards). In all cases, it is important to realise that the game used for educational purposes may not have the same artificial 'fairness' that the commercially-produced game needs to have, and that sets of rules are there to be amended, simplified or (on occasion) made more complex to fit the needs of the topic under study. Sometimes players themselves perform a valuable function in drawing attention to the way in which they want a known reality to be better replicated within the game situation; the teacher–manager should respond with alacrity to this pleasing identification of the model with the real world. Games perform a valuable role in revealing the way in which particular systems (e.g. the cycle of production in agriculture, fishing or industry, world trade) work. They should bring participants knowledge that simple blueprints for success need to be modified in the light of feedback from events and that the world in which we live is a constantly changing environment.

Individualised simulations

Role-plays and games imply by their nature that pupils will work in whole classes or, at least, groups; but it is also possible to develop simulations on an individual basis. A pupil can be confronted with an 'in-tray of letters' (e.g. of a development-charity director, or a local councillor) or with an 'action-maze' (in which he or she has to work through a sequence of events which requires her/him to choose a particular strategy and then discover its consequences). It is also possible to pose location or development problems on an individual basis as a pencil-and-paper exercise, as is increasingly done in examination questions. The many examples of simulation ideas transferred into computerised form frequently become more individualised as a result (*SimCity* is perhaps the best-known example of the breed).

Mathematical simulations

Some aspects of the world which geographers study are not susceptible to role-adoption. It is difficult (unless the players are brilliantly imaginative) to role-play empathetically a pebble on a beach, or a plant in the soil, and impossible to role-play aggregate decisions or events (e.g. the tide of migration from rural to urban areas, or the spread of a virus). But these can be represented by particular mathematical procedures such as Monte Carlo simulations, aspects of game theory, or the insertion of probability factors into card games. Many laboratories now use such techniques to generate a range of scenarios for what might happen in the future; in classrooms, however, they can be used to replicate past movements such as the growth of an off-shore spit or the reduction of a grassland to desert by overgrazing.

Hardware simulations

Perhaps the most venerable and easily recognisable member of the simulation family is the hardware model. Here, role-adoption is not called for; it is aspects of the physical world which are most frequently modelled. Geography teachers have produced their own simple models for many years (e.g. the splitting of an orange-skin to show the distortion made by a flat world map, the rucking of a tablecloth to show the genesis of fold-mountains) but more recently we have seen the generation of more elaborate physical geographic models of glaciers (Morgan, 1966), estuaries and rainforests (Job and Buck, 1994). It is also possible, however, to use simple 'hardware' (card, paper, wire, plastic tubing) to simulate industrial processes or built environments of the future.

MANAGING AND INTEGRATING SIMULATIONS

In organising simulations, the teacher has to act variously as **administrator, manager** and **educator**. Administrative skills are involved in preparing the materials, the opportunity and the environment for the simulation; good management is needed to make the actual playing of the simulation successful; the educating comes in drawing out the essence, the correspondence with aspects of reality and the implications of the simulation during and after the activity.

Choosing the time and the place is an important initial decision. Simulations are best used linked to other activities, rather than brandished as isolated novelties. Their capacity to motivate and involve pupils should not lead them to be saved up as fill-ups for Friday afternoons or the end of term when 'serious work' is deemed to be winding down.

Some teachers like to use simulations near the start of a unit in order to open up the topic and stimulate interest; others prefer to leave them till later, as a summarising and synthesising activity. One view is that it is beneficial for pupils to play some simulations through twice in order that they have the opportunity to improve their contributions with the benefit of hindsight. Whichever course of action is taken, it is important that the simulation is properly briefed and debriefed – that is to say, introduced and discussed afterwards with pupils. In many simulations it is helpful to introduce the idea to pupils in one lesson and then give some time (say, through a homework assignment) for them to consider materials and the roles they will assume and decisions they will have to make; this will improve the quality of the exercise itself. Similarly, it is a good idea to arrange to finish a game or role-play in mid-lesson so that there can be immediate discussion and reflection while memory is fresh. Pupils may also be primed to write reflectively about their experiences in an associated following piece of written work; they often produce vivid accounts and unsuspected insights and attitudes to what has been going on.

Good de-briefing, led by the teacher, should include some element of action-replay (to recognise key moments and interventions in retrospect), consideration of the views of participants when they are out of role, and a highlighting and summary of the general concepts and ideas which are illuminated through the experience of the modelling of the particular.

The teacher also needs to be sure to manage the simulation effectively during its actual progress. This does not necessarily mean prominent and frequent intervention, but it should be recognised that often hearts as well as minds are involved, and that the benefits of rational discussion may need to be explained or emphasised to those comparatively unskilled in it. Too much teacher-talk gives too little chance for pupils to explore situations and exercise their own judgements. Pupils should not be protected from the consequences of their own poor argument or performance since this is usually effectively self-monitored, but sometimes the teacher will need to intervene judiciously here and there – guiding thought or argument away from blind alleys, helping a team understand the deeper implications of an issue that they are discussing, or enlivening a declining discussion with fresh insights or information at an appropriate moment. The teacher mixes administration, management and education for the most part, but the latter may be more effective for not being presented in an obvious expositional mode.

ASSESSING AND EVALUATING

'We all know that simulation is the answer,' said Alice Kaplan Gordon (Gordon, 1970) 'and now we just have to find out the question...'. This paradox sharply illuminated a recurring problem for early simulation developers and users in school classrooms. It was obvious that the activity was popular, motivating and stimulating – but was its value confined to the experience itself, or did it teach anything? Traditional evaluation methods proved ineffective for activities in which teachers were unable (and unwilling) to pre-specify objectives and outcomes. A generation later we know a little more, though it is still difficult to untangle cognitive and affective outcomes, short-term and long-term gains. Twenty-five years of experience have enabled research studies to be conducted using a variety of evaluation methods. The fruits of many of these have been distilled through two major journals – *Simulation Games for Learning* (UK) and *Simulation and Gaming* (USA) – and latterly through the yearbooks of the Society for the Advancement of Gaming and Simulation in Education and Training (SAGSET), (published by Kogan Page). One early summary of research studies (Pate and Mateja, 1979) concluded that simulations were clearly effective and superior to other approaches in developing the capacity for pupils to retain knowledge over long periods of time. (The reason may be that in most simulations important issues embedded in the structure of the activity have to be thoroughly understood if participants are to act and interact effectively with others).

But the essence of many simulations involves feelings as well as minds. Thus some simulations (e.g. *Starpower* and *Outsider*) have, as their major objective, the revelation of a particular process in order to have participants re-assess their attitudes towards it. The evaluation of such possible changes does not lend itself easily to orthodox pencil-and-paper testing, particularly if carried out in the immediate post-simulation period.

More recently, with the development of more ethnographic approaches to classroom research, it has become more acceptable to rely on the results of observation (especially when 'triangulated' by teacher, pupil and independent observer) and on participant-evaluation. If teachers step back from the duties of management during simulations, they will observe the individuals in their classes revealing a surprising amount of their own knowledge, attitudes and communication skills. Those who do well in formalised tests may be challenged in simulation contexts, when it comes to showing talent in the appreciation of a situation, persuasion of others, and judgement leading to key decisions. Simulations are helpful complementary activities to more formal aspects of schooling.

Simulations and the National Curriculum

In the consideration of topics such as overseas development, the location of new industries, farming, environmental and planning issues there is much potential to use simulations – as long as chronic overload does not push teachers into a depressing chain of note-dictation. Even so, it is a myth that simulations are time-consuming; research suggests that they can teach just as much knowledge as didactic methods in equivalent time.

The potential of simulations as devices for teacher-assessment should not be overlooked. The teacher acting as observer has a good chance of assessing the individual contributions of pupils in the midst of motivating simulation discussions and decision-making; and simulations can be satisfying summary activities which give the opportunity for pupils to show their overall grasp of material previously presented.

NATIONAL CURRICULUM KEY STAGE 3 TOPICS WHERE SIMULATIONS CAN BE USED

National Curriculum themes	Type of simulation	Examples
TECTONIC PROCESSES 'human responses to the earthquake/volcanic hazard'	Role-plays	
GEOMORPHOLOGICAL PROCESSES 'about coastal landforms and the processes that form them and about the role or rock type and weathering in landform development'	Mathematical simulations (e.g. of spits, waves	
ECOSYSTEMS 'how physical and human processes influence the character of vegetation'	Mathematical simulations (e.g. of plant successions, desertification)	*Grasslands*
SETTLEMENT 'the reasons for the location, growth and nature of individual settlements'	Role-plays about choosing sites	*First landfall* *Spring Green Motorway*
'about types and patterns of urban land use, how conflicts can arise over the use of land, and how they can be addressed'	Games about land use: role-plays on conflict issues (e.g. building a bypass)	*Consejo* *Quarry*
ECONOMIC ACTIVITIES 'about the geographical distribution of one activity; how the distribution of this activity has changed, and is changing, and the effects of such changes'	Games about farming fishing, industrial location	*Sand Harvest* *Caribbean Fisherman*
DEVELOPMENT 'about differences in development and their effect on the quality of life of different groups of people'	Role-plays and games about development	*World Feast Game* *St Philip* *A Fair Deal* *The Paper Bag Game* *The Trading Game*
ENVIRONMENTAL ISSUES 'how conflicting demands on areas of great scenic attraction can arise'	Role-plays about quarrying in National Parks, etc.	*The Greater Carajas Programme* *Quarry*

SOURCES OF SIMULATIONS

(Note: in addition to the simulations listed opposite, there are many examples of simulation activities in school geography textbooks, and in *Teaching Geography*, the secondary school journal published by the Geographical Association.)

A Fair Deal: (computer simulation) Christian Aid, PO Box 100, London SE1 7RT

Caribbean Fisherman: CPS PO Box 62, Cambridge CB3 9NA

Consejo: Oxfam, 274 Banbury Road, Oxford OX2 7DZ

Grasslands: CPS (address above)

Quarry: see pages 158-161

St Philip: CPS (address above)

Sand Harvest: (computer simulation) Worldaware, 1 Catton Street, London WC1R 4AB

SimCity: (computer simulation) Maxis Software, 230-2 Theatre Square, Orinda, California 94563-3041, USA

Spring Green Motorway: CSV, 237 Pentonville Road, London N1 9NG

The Greater Carajas Programme: ActionAid, Hamlyn House, Archway, London N19 5PS

The Paper Bag Game: Christian Aid (address above)

The Trading Game: Worldaware (address above)

World Feast Game: Worldaware (address above)

References

Berne, E. (1966) *Games People Play.* Andre Deutsch.

Calder, N. (1967) *The Environment Game.* Panther.

Chorley, R.J. & Haggett, P. (1964) *Frontiers in Geographical Teaching.* Methuen.

Chorley, R.J. & Haggett, P. (1966) *Models in Geography.* Methuen.

Cole, J. P. (1966) 'Geographical games' in *Bulletins of Quantitative Data* 6, University of Nottingham, Dept. of Geography.

Dalton, T. *et al* (1972) *Simulation Games in Geography.* Macmillan.

FitzGerald, B.P. & Stevens, G. (1973) 'The iron & steel game' in Walford, R. (ed) *New Directions in Geography Teaching,* Longman. pp. 9-18.

Gordon, A.K. (1970) *Games for Growth.* SRA.

Greenblat, C.S. & Duke, R.D. (1981) *Principles and Practices of Gaming-simulation.* Sage.

Huizinga, J. (1974) *Homo Ludens.* Paladin.

Job, D. & Buck, A. (1994) 'Learning through models in the laboratory' in *Teaching Geography,* 19, 3, pp. 106-110.

Jones, K. (1985) *Designing Your Own Simulation.* Methuen.

Morgan, M.A. (1966) 'Hardware models in geography' in Chorley, R.J. & Haggett, P. (eds) *Models in Geography,* pp. 727-774. Methuen.

Pate, G.S. & Mateja, J.A. (1979) 'Retention: the real power of simulation gaming' in *Journal of Experiential Learning,* 1, 1 pp. 195-202. Elsevier.

Walford, R. (1969) *Games in Geography.* Longman.

Walford, R. (1991) *Role-play and the environment.* English Nature.

JOURNALS MENTIONED

Classroom Geographer, published monthly between 1970 and 1986. Neil Sealy.

Simulation and Gaming, published quarterly from 1975. Sage.

Simulation Games for Learning, published quarterly between 1970 and 1993. Kogan Page (replaced by yearbooks from the Society for the Advancement of Games and Simulation in Education and Training (SAGSET).

Teaching Geography, published quarterly since 1975. The Geographical Association.

Quarry: a sample simulation

PATRICK BAILEY

Charndon Quarry as it is now and how it could look

Photos: **Patrick Bailey**

Introduction

This role-play was designed for use with a GCSE group of around 20 students who were looking at the question of conflicts within the environment. Each pupil was given a general briefing sheet and a map (see page 149), and separate role-cards were given to pairs of students, who could thus discuss the role-brief together, with one speaking for it and the other advising. The teacher chaired the 'Public Enquiry'.

The names in the simulation were disguised but it was based on an actual situation – a proposal for a quarry in Charnwood Forest. At the end of the simulation, the teacher revealed this to the class and in the de-briefing discussed with them the outcome of the quarry proposal.

The class prepared a report on the Public Enquiry as a subsequent piece of written work.

General briefing sheet

CHARNDON QUARRY

Charndon Quarry is one of several granite quarries near the Midshire town of Upton which have supplied road metal for roads in the Midlands for more than half a century. Ten years ago the quarry was closed, mainly because its further extension would have produced an ugly gap in the skyline in an area noted for its natural beauty. Since its closure, bushes, trees and small animals and insects have established themselves in the quarry and it has become an informal playground for children from neighbouring estates. It is now regarded by some as an unofficial nature reserve. Moves are afoot among botanists and others to have it declared a Site of Special Scientific Interest (SSSI).

GROWING TOWN – NEW BYPASS

Upton is growing and there is a New Town development to the east called Upton Leys. Council estates (such as Waterlees) and private housing (such as Stonehill Heights) also lie to the east. Stonehill Heights has detached houses in large gardens and extensive scenic views of the woods, heaths and rocky outcrops of Charndon Heath.

As Upton has grown, so have its traffic problems. At long last it has been decided to build a bypass east and north of the town, following the Till Valley. This bypass will require large amounts of road metal. Other quarries in the area are already producing to capacity and a new site needs to be found. Could Charndon Quarry be re-opened in order to provide the necessary materials for the bypass?

THE PROBLEM OF REFUSE

As Upton grows, it becomes harder and harder to find enough space to dispose of its rubbish. Most available holes within 8km (5 miles) of the town are filled up and the nearest one now available is Charndon Quarry. The town council would like to use it, though it realises that nearby residents might object.

THE FARMING COMMUNITY

There is good arable land on the lower ground surrounding Upton but the higher ground of Charndon Heath is of lower quality. Farms in the area have a mixture of both types. The tenants of Spring House Farm have begun to develop a permanent caravan site on their land, believing it more profitable to 'grow caravans' than graze sheep. Their neighbours continue with mixed arable and sheep farming, but times are difficult for them. The small country roads around the farms could scarcely take, in their present state, heavy quarry traffic.

WYNSLADE HALL

Within sight of Charndon Quarry and less than 3km to the west stands Wynslade Hall, a Victorian mansion recently bought by the county for use as a Teacher Education Centre. A lot of money has been spent modernising it, as it is also intended to attract business courses. Part of the surrounding parkland is intended to be used as a camp-site for schools.

A NATURE RESERVE?

The county council would like to establish a proper Nature Reserve and a Visitors' Countryside Centre somewhere near Upton. Charndon Quarry is an ideal location, but another possibility is the flooded gravel workings along the Till Valley, where there are many different species of birds.

WHAT SHOULD BE DONE?

There are at least four possibilities:

1   leave it as it is, as a quiet spot and an informal playground for children

2   re-open it as a quarry (with a crushing and grading plant)

3   develop it as a refuse tip for Upton (it would solve the refuse problem for 20 years)

4   develop it as a Nature Reserve, with a Visitors' Centre and a part-time Warden

A Public Enquiry has been convened to arrive at a decision.

Role cards

ALEC MORETTI, OBE
(AIDED BY HIS PERSONAL ASSISTANT)
You are Managing Director of the Charndon Stone and Gravel Company, part of a large national group currently interested in opening large new quarries in Scotland. Your company owns all the quarries and gravel pits in the Upton area but a rival company owns quarries to the north. You naturally wish to excavate the biggest and cheapest quarries you can and move the excavated materials the shortest possible distance. You are very keen for this proposal to go through, because your company has not been doing too well lately and you are worried by possible competition from your rivals to the north for the contract to supply material for the proposed bypass (… but should you let this be known in public? …)

JOHN AND LUCY GARNET-CLARKE
You are residents of Stonehill Heights. You recently took out an expensive mortgage in order to buy your house. You were attracted to Stonehill, after living in the town of Upton, because of its peace and quiet. What effect will a quarry or a council tip have on your environment – and on the value of your house?

JACK AND MARY LUKER
You began your married life in a rented council house. It has long been a dream for you to own your own house and you have just been able to purchase the council house on the Waterlees Estate in which you have been living for ten years. But Jack has just lost his job, and finances are difficult at the moment. You have a son who has recently been made redundant by the farm machinery sales and servicing firm where he worked after leaving school, a daughter who is a primary teacher and another daughter who is still at school.

PETER AND JEAN GEAR
You live on the Waterlees Estate in a council house and you both work in Upton. You are keen walkers in the local countryside. You have two teenage children, who enjoyed playing in Charndon Quarry as they grew up. They will shortly be leaving school and looking for jobs, but there aren't too many jobs around here at the moment.

INDERJIT SINGH (AND HER PERSONAL ASSISTANT)
You are in charge of the County Roads Department and want to buy the necessary material for the new bypass as cheaply as possible. A quarry close to the route of the bypass would be ideal and would save thousands of pounds for the county. You live in the centre of Upton.

THELMA DIXON (AND HER PERSONAL ASSISTANT)
You are Head of Upton Refuse Department and responsible for finding somewhere to dump and bury Upton's increasing tonnage of rubbish. You want to find a new site for a rubbish tip as near as possible to Upton, to save transport costs. You live on the western side of Upton. Would you mind if the rubbish tip was near your home?

ALAN AND SUE WARD
You are tenants of Spring House Farm. You have recently borrowed money to develop a caravan site for summer visitors. The site is on the part of your farm nearest to the proposed quarry site. Your neighbouring farmers at Coop and Stonehill Farms (whose families have both owned their farms for generations) have discovered that all three farms could be taken by compulsory purchase orders to provide land for the quarry. Even if the land was left in your hands, would the farms be habitable if they were very close to the quarry operations?

DENIS AND DORIS BURNSIDE
You own Stonehill Farm and it has been in your family for generations, but economically, things are not too good for small farms at present. You also have shares in the Charndon Stone and Gravel Company and are worried about its prospects in the light of competition. If the quarry is re-opened your farm might be subject to compulsory purchase; if the price was right would you mind leaving the farm? What would you do if you left?

PAT ALLEN AND CHRIS HILLMAN
You represent Midshire Education Committee. Your Committee has recently invested a large sum of ratepayers' money in creating a Centre for Teacher Education at Wynslade Hall. The county has waited fifty years for such a development, and if the Centre is to pay its way it may need further development into a regional centre and/or a centre for business courses. A camp-site for schools is planned in the grounds. What effect will a huge quarry have, if it is just outside the gates?

PAT GREEN AND KIM FINCHAM
You are President and Secretary respectively of the Midshire Field Club and often speak and write on behalf of those interested in the natural history and landscape of the county. One aim of your Club is to have an East Midshire Nature Reserve created, but you are not sure whether Charndon Quarry or the flooded River Till gravel pits would be the better site. Botanists and insect enthusiasts favour Charndon, but there are more bird species to be found at the Till gravel pits. Many of your members spent the summer voluntarily clearing rubbish out of Charndon Quarry.

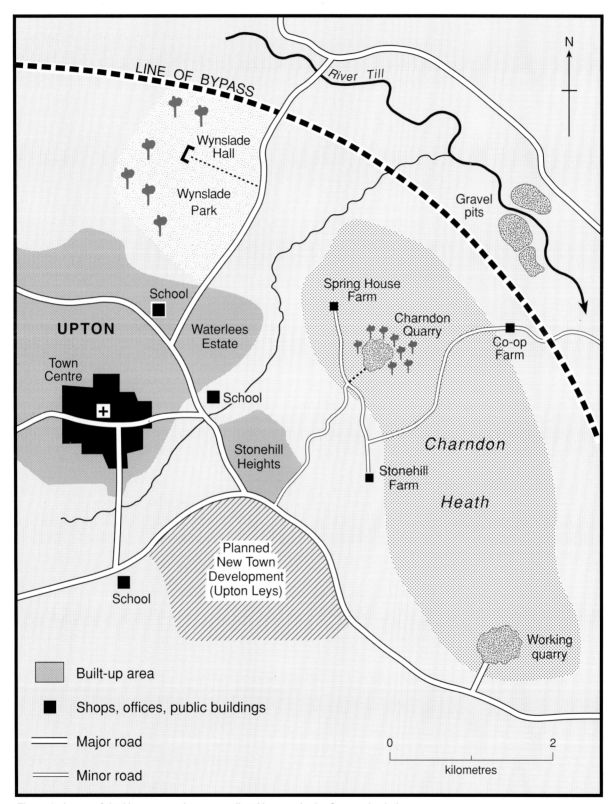

Figure 1: A map of the Upton area given to pupils taking part in the Quarry simulation

Chapter 13

Using statistics

DAVE RICHARDSON

Introduction

In the last chapter, Rex Walford refers to the emergence in the early 1960s of a 'new' geography, characterised by a shift of emphasis away from the descriptive approach towards a more rigorous 'scientific' approach. At that time, geographers became preoccupied with the search for patterns, models and systems which required a new methodology in which statistical techniques were employed in the analysis of data. This 'quantitative revolution' undoubtedly changed the image of the subject: as J.A. Matthews put it:

> Nothing is wrong with a qualitative statement but it will carry more weight if it is possible to make a statement quantitatively, that is in mathematical language rather than words (Matthews, 1979).

The use of 'mathematical language' in geography is, of course, no longer 'new', but for many aspiring geographers it may still be regarded as a potential barrier rather than as an aid to their understanding of the subject. This chapter, written by a self-confessed non-mathematician, offers some guidance on the application of statistical methods to geographical learning.

What is statistical analysis and why use it?

A useful starting point is to think of statistics as raw material, and statistical analysis as a means of manipulating such material which helps us to make informed and objective geographical judgements. The type of data selected and the means of handling the data will vary with the age and ability of the user. A key task for the geography teacher is to plan carefully what data and methods of analysis to use, when to use them, how to use them, and for what purpose.

By collecting, presenting and analysing statistics, pupils will be better able to describe, draw inferences from, predict and even model geographical phenomena (see Figure 1). Maps, graphs, diagrams or tables are ways of summarising information; they enable patterns and trends to emerge in ways that may not be possible from written descriptions. Let us look at this in the context of an example, often found in examination syllabuses. Pupils may be required to study the development of an urban

The uses and limitations of statistics are learned through practical application

Photo: **Helen Sail**

environment and to describe and explain its characteristics. A typical starting point for such a study might be to refer to maps, photographs and videos. These provide information which help pupils to form initial impressions and to draw some basic conclusions. Please note it is only when relevant raw data are introduced that informed assessments can be made.

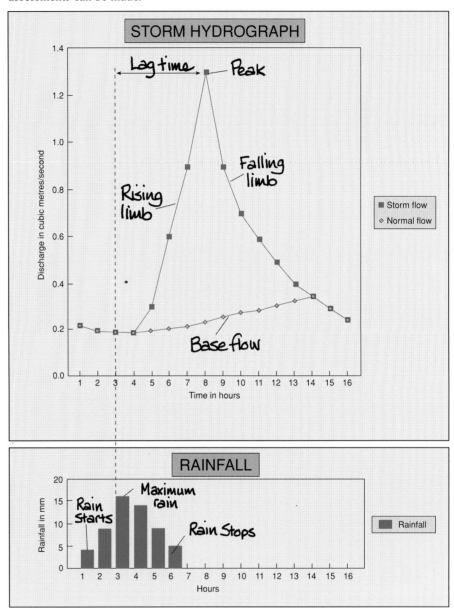

Figure 1: Pupil-produced model of 'storm hydrograph'

Raw data may be collected in the field by the pupils themselves; for example, they might conduct land use surveys and record levels of noise and/or litter pollution – this is called primary data. Alternatively, data may be taken from sources such as Census returns and crime records – this is called secondary data. The collection and subsequent analysis of 'real' data is motivating for pupils; they tend to retain ideas and concepts more readily when involved in this type of experiential learning.

Even more important is that pupils are learning that assumptions can and should be tested fairly. They are living in a media-dominated world where sound bites and superficial or partial news coverage are facts of life, but also one in which advances in IT have vastly increased the range and amount of data available, for example, the rapid introduction of the Internet. Clearly, young people need all the processing and analytical skills that we can give them!

Using statistics: some problems and bonuses

The use of data and data-handling techniques may not always make life easier, and may make it harder, but if managed properly should make the learning process more objective as well as more worthwhile.

ACCURACY

As W.M. Harper stated in 1977 'A statistical conclusion can never be better than the original figure on which it is based.' Geography is a dynamic subject and the data that geographers need is constantly changing. We must be sure that the information we use is both accurate and up-to-date. A conclusion about shopping patterns in a modern suburb may be based on accurate data, but may be inaccurate if based on data collected some time ago.

When a set of data is collected by pupils for use in class, we must ask two questions: Is it accurate? and, Was the sample size large enough to enable valid conclusions to be drawn? It must be stressed that precision (exactness) does not always imply accuracy (correctness) – a distinction which is illustrated in Figure 2.

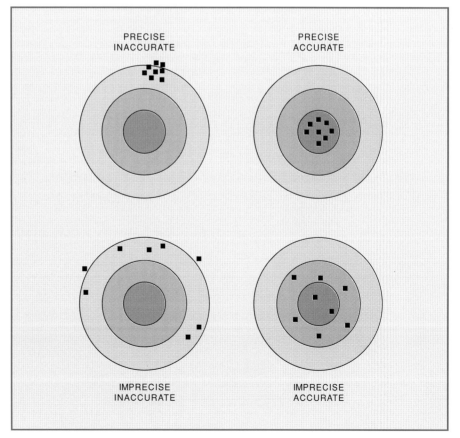

Figure 2: *Precision and accuracy (after Griffiths, 1967)*

VALIDITY

In addition to the point made above, we must also consider how valid a particular set of data will be as a means of illustrating and explaining complex ideas. For example, how do we contrast and explain the land utilisation of two different rural areas (A and B) in the UK? How do we select the data we want to use? Obviously, a comparison between land use types and their percentage frequency in each area would be a good start, but different types of data are needed to explain these differing patterns (see Figure 3). We must ask if we are providing the most appropriate information for the tasks we set.

LAND USE CATEGORY	AREA – A (percentage frequency)	AREA – B (percentage frequency)
Arable	60	6
Pasture	17	22
Rough grazing	1	51
Woodland	11	14
Setaside	8	0
Other	3	7

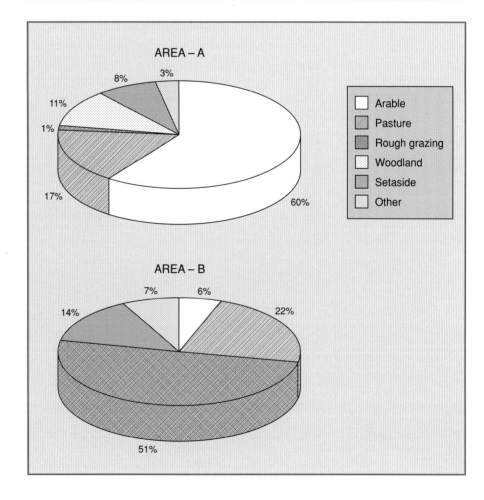

CLIMATIC DATA	J	F	M	A	My	J	Jy	A	S	O	N	D	TOTAL
TOTAL RAINFALL in mm													
AREA A	60	45	48	47	47	65	52	50	60	62	65	63	664
AREA B	163	102	73	74	78	75	93	143	149	170	163	162	1445
MEAN TEMPERATURE in °C													
AREA A	2.1	2.8	5.8	9.4	11.3	18.5	21.6	19.8	15.6	11.1	6.2	3.4	
AREA B	4.2	3.9	7.2	9.1	10.2	16.7	18.6	17.5	13.2	10.3	6.3	4.9	

TYPICAL FARM	AREA A	AREA B
Size of farm (hectares)	53	178
Animals kept	22 pigs	290 sheep & 21 beef cattle
Typical soil type	silts & chalky boulder clay	podsols & hill peat
Altitude range (metres)	15 - 19	162 - 790
Mean slope angle range	1° - 9°	2° - 31°
Distance to market (km)	11	75
Mean annual potential evaporation (mm)	512	452
Mean annual soil moisture deficit (mm)	149	14

1981 EMPLOYMENT STRUCTURE	AREA A	AREA B
Primary	4.7	7
Manufacturing	34.5	26.2
Construction	6.8	6.4
Services	54.1	60.3

Figure 3: *Land use and other data for two rural areas (Area A – East Anglia and Area B – Lake District)*

SUITABILITY OF DATA FOR A PARTICULAR AUDIENCE

In deciding what information to provide, and the form it takes, you will need to take account of the age and ability of the pupils who will be using it. If working with mixed-ability groups, you need to be able to provide information of a kind, and in a form, which pupils working at different levels can grasp. It is also worth noting here that we can use statistics and data-handling exercises as a way of differentiating pupils.

It is important to be aware that certain techniques may be difficult to construct but straightforward to interpret, e.g. isolines, flow lines and 3D surface graphs (see Figures 4, 5 and 6). This does not preclude their use, especially since modern computer software can carry out the complex operations involved in representing given data quickly and easily.

Some techniques may be straightforward to apply and an end result produced by pupils following basic instructions. But are we sure that they fully understand what they have produced? It is easy to apply a Spearman Rank formula, or Nearest Neighbour test, but is the pupil able to fully understand the results, or the limitations involved?

CONTROL

It is easy to dictate what your pupils learn, or the conclusions that they are likely to make, by controlling the information you give them. Indeed, such control is vital if pupils are to be presented with techniques which are appropriate to their level of ability.

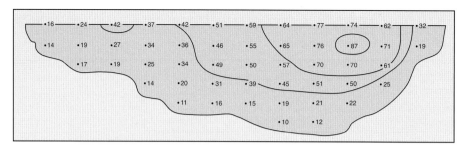

Figure 4: An example of an isoline map. This shows isovels joining points of equal velocity in a river meander. The velocity readings (in metres per second) were taken at regular intervals and depths across the meander then plotted onto an accurate cross-section of the meander. Source: St John and Richardson (1989)

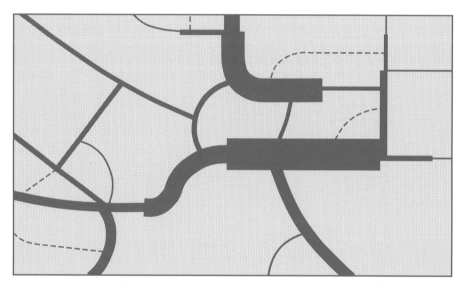

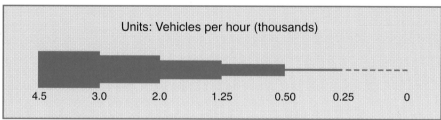

Figure 5: A flow diagram showing traffic flow using a graduated scale. Source: as figure 4

If a complex technique is introduced before a pupil is ready for it, the pupil can be put off for ever.

Much of the data you will want to use may not always produce cut and dried conclusions – e.g. fieldwork data. It is important to be aware that not all pupils, for various reasons, are able to cope with this, many are happier with black and white situations than with varying shades of grey. For the less able pupils, for example, it may be desirable to provide 'simple statistics' that produce the desired conclusion.

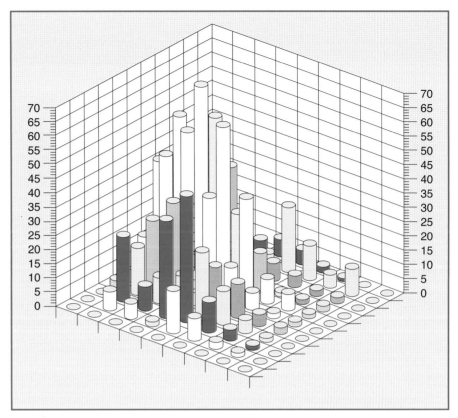

*Figure 6: A 3D surface graph to show the results of a pedestrian count in a town centre
(Note: this graph was constructed using a basic computer graphing program
(DeltaGraph Professional) and is a good example of how such software may be
used to represent complex data in a visually attractive and accessible format.)*

ACCESS TO AND MANIPULATION OF DATA

With advances in computer technology and the advent of the Internet, CD-ROMs, etc., the process of acquiring data has been transformed and there has been an enormous increase in the types and quantity of information available. Though few schools have access to the wide range of systems and data available, many pupils will be aware of it so it is important for teachers to be informed of it too (see Chapter 22 for a discussion of the use of IT in geography). Many of the 'traditional' sources of secondary data (see end of chapter) are also now available in easily accessible computerised form (see Chapter 22).

Powerful spreadsheets (e.g. Excel) are already widely used in schools and most pupils are capable of using such content-free software to manipulate data in order to produce high quality maps and graphs. The great value of such software is that it reduces the laborious number crunching tasks thus enabling more time to be spent on the important question: What does our end result tell us? Fieldwork, in particular, can benefit from the use of computers. Without their assistance, pupils might spend hours collecting and manipulating data manually for, e.g. a river survey – a boring task involving the repetition of set procedures. By the time the task is complete, pupils have often lost sight of their original aim. By using computers to log and analyse the data, pupils are not only more motivated, but are also free to spend much more time on analysis and on reaching useful conclusions.

TYPE OF INFORMATION (Data)	POSSIBLE TECHNIQUE	POSSIBLE EXAMPLE(S)
1. Introducing the reader to the subject matter of the study	Field Sketches	Illustrating geographical features and study areas
	Tabulation	Fieldwork results, Census data, class exercises
	Base maps	Defining a field study area, initiating the study of a region
	Flow diagrams	Geographical processes (limestone succession)
2. The organisation of raw data into a manageable form	Tabulation	Preparation for statistical testing (Chi Square, Spearman Rank)
	Dispersal diagrams	Preparation for choropleth mapping, graphing (working out scales)
	Use of logarithmic graph paper	When a range of values is too great for normal scales or the purpose is to compare rates of growth
3. Where the data shows a sequential change over time	Line graphs	Climatic data, river flows, industrial output, etc. over set time period
	Circular graphs	Continuous data over a yearly cycle (rainfall, mean temperatures)
	Pictograms	Any data that needs to be 'eye catching'; can be shown as a picture but only where exact precision is not vital
4. Where observed data is at specific sites or locations. The data will have distinct component categories	Bar charts	One qualitative scale (type of plant, shop type, etc.) ...
	important differences between these and...	and a quantitative scale (frequency, size, etc.) not ...
	Histograms	Two quantitative scales (pebble size, class & frequency)
	Multiple and/or Composite graphs	Land use for three different farming practices at two or more sites
	Mirror graphs	Population pyramids - male/female (back-to-back histogram)
	Reverse bars	Population changes between 1981-1991 by age categories
	Pyramid graphs	Population pyramid for a food webb in an ecosystem
	Pie graphs	Land use types, traffic counts, age of housing, etc.
5. Where data is used to show correlations between two variables	Scattergraphs (correlation graphs)	Altitude v temperature; wind speed, etc. Many examples possible.
	Mirror graphs	Plant species, land use, etc. at two sites (back-to-back bar graph)
6. Where data is used to show correlations between more than two variables	Constellation diagrams	Plant associations along a sand dune succession (complex, may need computer)
7. Where data displays orientation	Rose diagrams and azimuths	Wind directions, corrie orientation, till fabric orientation
	Polar co-ordinate	Corrie orientation v altitude; till orientation v angle of dip
8. Where data has component categories expressed as percentages and total 100%	Triangular (Ternary) graphs	Need three categories - employment structure (primary, secondary, tertiary)
	Composite bar graphs	Percentage of cars sold in Preston 1990-1994 categorised by make
	Block graphs	Land use changes with increased altitude up a slope
9. Where data showing side views need to be displayed	Profiles	Slope and soil profile across a limestone escarpment
	Cross-sections	River channel cross-sections drawn at various stages downstream
10. Where data has been collected along a transect either continuously or at regular intervals	Scattergraphs	Housing variables (density, quality, etc.) v distance from CBD
	Profiles/Cross-sections	Vegetation change or land use change up a hillside
	Mapping and divided bars	Land use change with distance from a town centre
	Kite diagrams	Vegetation changes away from the centre of an eroded footpath
	Block graphs	CBD transect showing changes in retail type away from the PLVI
11. Where the data to be displayed is to show spatial variation	Base maps using the following: Dot maps	Limestone pavement distribution in the UK
	Symbols and proportional symbols	Markets for different coal types by UK region (proportional pie charts)
	Choropleth maps	Population changes between 1981 and 1991
	Isopleth maps	Pedestrian counts in a CBD, Isovels around a meander
	3D surface, area, column or ribbon	Values collected on a network or grid; land values; pedestrians. Displayed as 3D surfaces, columns, etc. Difficult to draw - use a computer.
	Location quotients	Rented accommodation in given area
12. Where the data to be displayed shows spatial variation of flows and/or movements	Composite bars	Traffic flow by category (car, lorries, etc.) at a crossroad
	Flow lines	Total traffic or pedestrian flow network around a town centre
	Desire lines	Shoppers using a town centre - identification of its sphere of influence

Each of the above techniques is described in St John & Richardson, 1989. All techniques are fully illustrated with worked examples

Figure 7: Graphs and maps. A guide to choosing the appropriate technique for varying sets of information

Fieldwork produces statistical data for 'real'

Photo: **NCET**

LIAISON
The use of quantitative techniques is not exclusive to the geography department, of course, but the way in which they are used may vary from one subject department to another. This can cause confusion for some pupils, so it is highly desirable to liaise with colleagues in order to co-ordinate your teaching strategies. For example, much confusion can be avoided if terms are standardised (scattergraph or correlation graph, bar graph or block graph). It may also be helpful to agree on a common method for constructing graphs, etc., and on the age and level at which certain techniques are introduced.

Data handling and statistical tests

The presentation and analysis of results or data can be a crucial part of any exercise, or fieldwork project. Graphs, tables and diagrams are used to summarise data and as illustrations; they help pupils to grasp the meaning of numerical data more easily and quickly. In some cases, they can have a predictive value, and can be extrapolated from to produce a projected result set against an observed trend.

Much of the work that we do as geographers is concerned with identifying patterns. Maps, graphs and other devices are vital tools in helping to identify and to analyse these. Patterns can be more apparent than real, however, and statistical tests enable us to establish a valid picture, as well as enabling us to assign numerical values to observed phenomena.

Statistical techniques are the means whereby we make sense of numerical information. As geographers, we may not necessarily be interested in how a technique operates mathematically, only in what it can do to advance our understanding. Statistics cannot magically make valid data that is inaccurate, or create meaning where none exists – 'rubbish in, rubbish out'!

Which methods should we choose?

It is not the purpose of this chapter to examine individual techniques in detail (see references and further reading at the end of the chapter for some texts which do this), but rather to offer guidance on the best choice of technique for a given purpose. The choice that faces us as geographers is enormous, as is the variety of data available. Figure 7 is intended to offer some help in finding your way through the maze by providing a key to most of the graphing/mapping techniques available. It also suggests under what circumstances each could be used.

Figures 8, 9 and 10 illustrate some of the methods described in Figure 7. They were compiled using the same sets of raw land use data which were collected along various transects radiating from a town centre and categorised in order to observe any resulting patterns in land use. The information was then plotted against distance from the town centre as defined by the Peak Land Value Index. You will notice that Figure 10 only uses three of the land use categories up to a distance of 700m from the town centre. How might this graph look if the complete data set is used?

The purpose of any graph or map is to present a 'picture'; to do so effectively it must be visually attractive as well as easily understood. With this in mind, you may wish to consider which of the three graphs (Figures 8-10) is most effective.

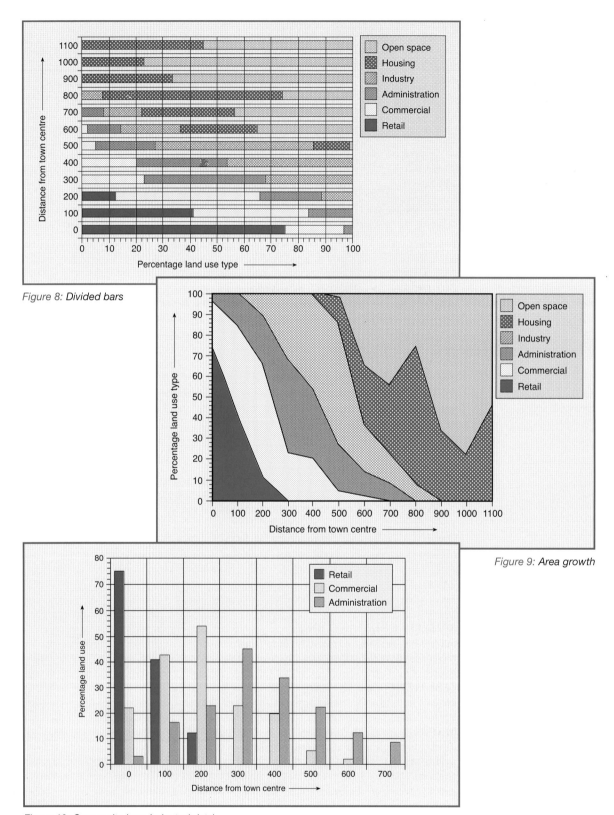

Figure 8: Divided bars

Figure 9: Area growth

Figure 10: Composite bars (selected data)

Choosing the right technique for a given audience

This is the hard part and little guidance is available, the usual reason given being 'when and with whom you introduce the various techniques will depend on the age, experience and ability of your pupils and only you as the professional at the 'chalk face' can make that decision'. For this reason, the information contained in Figure 11 should be viewed within the context of the readers' experiences. It outlines a sequence for the introduction of the techniques and tests suggested in Figure 7, starting with key stage 3 and ending with A level.

These are only suggestions, which, if nothing else, can be used as a basis for discussion between colleagues in the mathematics and other departments at the course and lesson planning stage.

Secondary sources of information

The following list suggests some sources of secondary data which provide information which may be used both in class and field investigation exercises.

CENTRAL GOVERNMENT SOURCES

Census returns: provide a whole range of information at enumeration, ward, district and national level. A full Census is carried out every ten years (the last being in 1991) so is also an invaluable historical resource.

HMSO publications: cover a wide range of subjects and include annual estimates of population, census migration tables, passenger transport statistics for the UK, annual agricultural statistics, surface-water year books, employment/productivity gazettes, economic activity tables, and many more.

LOCAL GOVERNMENT SOURCES

It should be possible to obtain most HMSO publications through your local authority which can also supply local statistics. Many local authorities publish their own local data (e.g. the Lancashire Planning Department publishes a quarterly up-date of local data called *Monitor* and many Lancashire schools are on the mailing list).

Examples of information you should be able to obtain through your local authority are: up-dated census figures (population, unemployment rates, housing stock), planning documents, electoral registers, business rates and community charges, transport studies, maps of the local area, structure plans, and many more.

PARISH REGISTERS

These contain records of births, deaths and marriages within the Parish.

SPECIFIC ORGANISATIONS

Specialised information is available from various sources. For example, climate and meteorological data from the Meteorological Office (raw data and synoptic charts); hydrological and water quality data from local river authorities; yearbooks and demographic yearbooks from the UN; UNESCO's statistical yearbook; the British Road Federation's basic road statistics for the UK.

MAPS

These are a fundamental resource for geographers and there are numerous types available. Large-scale plans are particularly useful for urban studies since they show the shop premises for most major towns and cities. Studies of 'change in urban areas' can be greatly enhanced by using large-scale plans for successive years.

TECHNIQUES	KEY STAGE 3			KEY STAGE 4 GCSE COURSE	SPECIFIC CASES AT THIS LEVEL	A LEVEL COURSE	SPECIFIC CASES AT THIS LEVEL	COMMENTS (disclaimers)
	Yr 7	8	9					
Field sketching								The suggestions for graphing/
Tabulation								mapping techniques at the various
Flow diagrams								age levels assume that they are
Dispersal diagrams								introduced at a basic level and
GRAPHS								later case studies/examples
Line graphs								become increasingly complex
Bar (block) graphs								with student progress.
Mirror graphs and reverse bars								This chart assumes that all
Pyramid graphs								operations are carried out
Pictographs								manually and do not include
Composite bars								the use of IT
Histograms								(calculators may be used)
Scattergraphs								
Profiles and cross-sections								For some of the techniques it
Circular graphs								may be advisable to provide
Kite diagrams & block graphs								starting points such as
Ternary graphs								base maps, scales, etc.,
Polar co-ordinates								either for encouragement or for
Rose diagrams & Azimuths								saving time.
Log - semi-log graphs								
Constellation diagrams								
MAPPING								
Base maps								
Choropleth maps								
Simple symbol maps								
Simple proportional symbols								
Dot maps								
Desire lines								
Complex proportional symbols								
Flow lines								
Isopleth maps								Simple contour patterns
Location quotients								
3D surface maps								
STATISTICS								
Mean (average)								'Statistics' is an area in which
Median, Mode								there is great diversity in terms
Standard Deviation								of student ability and teacher
Quartiles & Inter-Quartiles								expectation. Yes, some Year 7
Spearman Rank Correlation								pupils can perform Spearman
Chi Squared test								Rank but . . .
Pearson Product Moment								It is also an area in which the use
Regression analysis								of IT will greatly reduce the hours
Comparison of two means								of tedious number crunching.
Student t Test								However, students should first
Mann Whitney U test								attempt the tests manually. It is
Nearest Neighbour Index								only by doing this that they will
Inter-Quartile area								be able fully to understand the
Lorenz Curve & Gini Coefficient								true meaning of the end result;
Diversity Indices								merely inserting data into a
Zingg diagrams & shape indices								machine does not lead to a full
Vector analysis								understanding.

Figure 11: When should I teach the various techniques?

GEOGRAPHY TEACHERS' HANDBOOK

OTHERS

Many of the publications, such as newspapers and journals, which are listed elsewhere (see Chapter 21), are valuable sources of statistical data. *Kelly's Directories* are particularly useful and have been published since 1840; these list the residents within settlements. Bus, train, airline and ferry timetables are, of course, rich sources, as are telephone directories, Ceefax, etc. The list is endless! And do not forget to 'surf' the Internet!

References and further reading

Chalmers, N. & Parker, P. (1986) *Fieldwork and Statistics for Ecological Projects.* Open University.

Hammond, R. & McCullagh, P.S. (1978) *Quantitative Techniques in Geography.* Oxford University Press.

Lenon, B.J. & Cleves, P.G. (1984) *Techniques and Fieldwork in Geography.* University Tutorial Press.

Matthews, J.A. (1981) *Quantitative and Statistical Approaches in Geography.* Pergamon Press.

St John, P.R. & Richardson, D.A. (1989) *Methods of Presenting Fieldwork Data.* The Geographical Association.

St John, P.R. & Richardson, D.A. (1990) *Methods of Statistical Analysis of Fieldwork Data.* The Geographical Association.

Various authors (1986) *Sources and Methods in Geography* (set of six). Arnold Wheaton.

Chapter 14

Fieldwork

KEN BLAND, BILL CHAMBERS, KARL DONERT
AND TONY THOMAS

Geography without fieldwork is like science without experiments; the 'field' is the geographer's laboratory where young people experience at first hand landscapes, places, people and issues, and where they can learn and practice geographical skills in a real environment. Above all, fieldwork is enjoyable. A field trip is a working holiday: a refreshing change from the predictable routines of the school and the 'virtual' or 'simulated' reality of the book, slide and video. It provides an opportunity for pupils to relate in new ways to each other and to their teachers, and so to break some of the patterns of behaviour that become fixed in the school environment. It is an adventure, and like all adventures, can be alarming as well as fun!

Planning the field trip

When planning a field trip, there are many choices to be made by the teacher in terms of the distance travelled, the environment chosen, and the approach adopted for study in the field, as shown in Figure 1.

PLANNING CHECKLISTS

For fieldwork to be both successful and safe, it is essential that it is thoroughly planned. The choice of the activity to be undertaken and the amount of preparation needed for pupils, staff, school and parents will depend on a number of variables including:

- the nature of the location/environment
- the distance from the school
- the duration of the activity
- past experience of staff
- past experience of the pupils/group
- the age and size of the group
- the number of staff involved

When planning a field trip, there are several key questions that the geography teacher must ask (see Figure 2).

All geography begins with somebody, somewhere, going out and finding out

Photo: **Helen Sail**

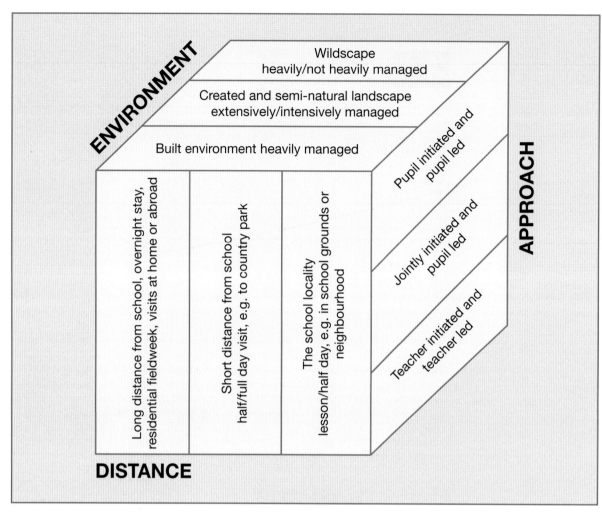

Figure 1: *Fieldwork planning requires teachers to consider many options*

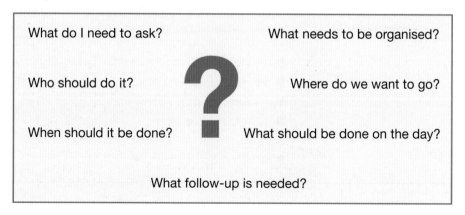

Figure 2: *Key planning questions*

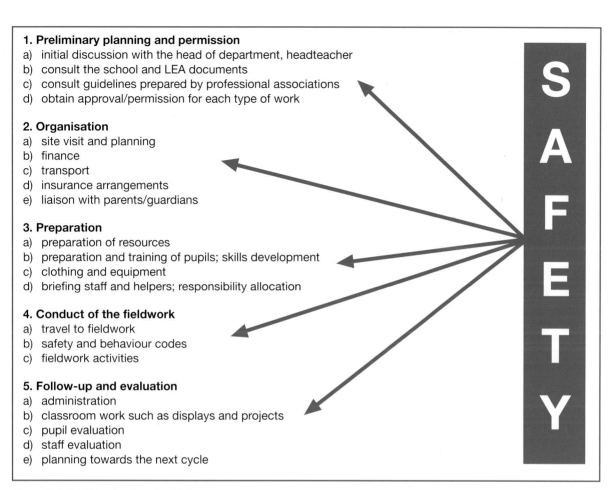

1. Preliminary planning and permission
a) initial discussion with the head of department, headteacher
b) consult the school and LEA documents
c) consult guidelines prepared by professional associations
d) obtain approval/permission for each type of work

2. Organisation
a) site visit and planning
b) finance
c) transport
d) insurance arrangements
e) liaison with parents/guardians

3. Preparation
a) preparation of resources
b) preparation and training of pupils; skills development
c) clothing and equipment
d) briefing staff and helpers; responsibility allocation

4. Conduct of the fieldwork
a) travel to fieldwork
b) safety and behaviour codes
c) fieldwork activities

5. Follow-up and evaluation
a) administration
b) classroom work such as displays and projects
c) pupil evaluation
d) staff evaluation
e) planning towards the next cycle

S A F E T Y

Figure 3: A field trip planning checklist

Geomorphological processes operate most effectively under extreme conditions, such as snow melt!

Photo: **Helen Sail**

An essential part of the planning process is making a detailed checklist (see Figure 3). From this checklist, four items have been selected for more detailed consideration:

Letter of consent When requesting parental or guardian consent for a pupil to make a particular visit or journey, it is imperative that the educational objectives of the visit are set out clearly and that a clear itinerary is provided, with the statement that the leader has the option to change the programme where deemed necessary. The school or group leader may also request confirmation of information about a pupil by using a 'Health Questionnaire' (Figure 4) which is sent to parents or guardians along with the consent form (Figure 5).

Health Questionnaire

The following information will assist the party leaders in caring for your child/children on the proposed field excursion:

1. Special dietary needs ---

2. Does your child suffer from:

   Asthma ---------------------------- Hayfever ----------------------------

   Diabetes--------------------------- Epilepsy ----------------------------

   Any allergies --

   Other --

3. Blood Group ---

4. Date of last tetanus injection --

5. National Health No.---

6. Name, Address of Family Practitioner ---

   Telephone No. ---

7. Home Address --

   Telephone No. ---

8. Emergency contact Telephone No. --

Figure 4: Possible format for a health questionnaire

The site visit and risk assessment A visit to the proposed fieldwork site is essential if the field visit is to be properly planned. It is also vital in that it enables all potential hazards to be assessed so that appropriate measures can be taken in advance and/or at the time of the visit. In making a 'risk assessment', lists should be drawn up under the following headings:

- potential risks to those taking part
- point of contact (telephones, shops, hotels, etc.)
- places to contact in an emergency

Risk assessment will need to take account of:

- hazards peculiar to the environment (rural or urban)
- the weather conditions likely to be encountered
- the age of the group
- pupils with special educational needs

Parental/Guardian Consent Form

---School

An educational visit to -- [place]

from ---------------------------------- [date] to ---------------------------. [date]

I agree to my son/daughter --- [name of child] taking part in the above-mentioned visit and, having read the information sheet, agree to his/her participating in any or all of the activities described. I declare that to the best of my knowledge, my son/daughter is in good health and will not be travelling contrary to medical advice.

Signature of parent/guardian ---.

Date ---

If your child has any medical condition which may need to be taken into account, please give details including blood group (if known), allergies or whether the child suffers from diabetes.

Are there any reasons (e.g. religion/customs) why your child may require special treatment on an educational visit/journey? If there are, please give details.

Figure 5: A sample parental/guardian consent form

Clothing and equipment for fieldwork Pupils and their parents must be told about the specific requirements for the field trip, such as clothing (Figure 6), personal equipment, pocket money and expected behaviour. It is important to identify what can be provided by the school and what must be provided by the pupils and parents/guardians.

Groups away from permanent supervision (GAPS) Special care needs to be taken when pupils are working in groups which are not continuously supervised by adults. These pupils will need special briefing, with clear instructions concerning the conditions and likely hazards involved in their fieldwork. The names of points of contact, an instruction sheet on what to do in an emergency, a first aid kit and proof of identity will also normally be necessary.

Progression in fieldwork

When framing departmental field policy, a key consideration must be the provision of opportunities for pupils to progress in relation to:

- the skills and techniques used
- the level of difficulty of tasks performed
- the level of supervision needed
- place and theme studies undertaken

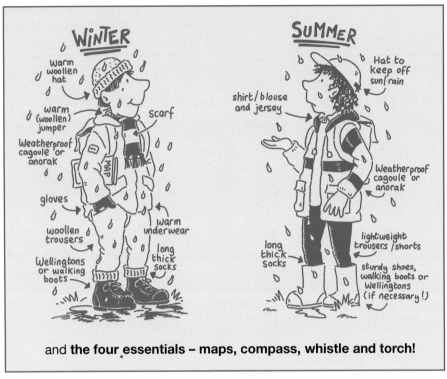

Figure 6: A clothing checklist

- geographical ideas and concepts studied
- issues and problems investigated

For example, in planning for greater progression in skills and techniques, you may expect older pupils to use more sophisticated methods of collecting data, to demonstrate greater precision in recording and presenting data, and to need less help with the interpretation and analysis of data. It is also likely that older pupils will have more autonomy over the structure and methodology of their fieldwork enquiry (Figure 7).

Teaching and learning styles

There are many teaching and learning approaches to fieldwork. The approach chosen will reflect and depend on:

- the knowledge, experience and intuition of the teacher;
- the commitment, personality and experience of the pupils;
- the syllabus of the relevant Examination Board;
- the nature of the fieldwork location;
- the aims and balance of the fieldwork;
- the educational philosophy of the individual teacher and the school.

Looking and seeing under instruction is an excellent method of learning in the field

Photo: **Helen Sail**

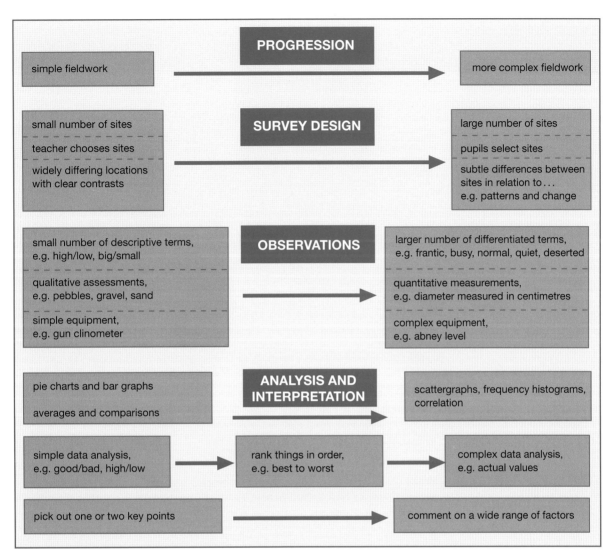

Figure 7: *Progression in fieldwork*

In choosing the most appropriate approach, the teacher is generally faced with two extremes: at one extreme is the pupil who is dependent on the teacher for the choice of ideas, techniques, site, group structure and roles; at the other extreme is the pupil who is fully autonomous – choosing the topic to investigate, the location of the study, the other group members, the techniques and equipment to be used, and even the transport arrangements.

From the wide range of fieldwork styles that can be adopted, the three most commonly used are the 'look and see', the 'investigative' and the 'enquiry-based' approaches (see Figure 8). These approaches are illustrated in Figure 9 using a street as an example of geographical theme which might be studied.

The fieldwork audit and policy

In order to maximise the benefits of fieldwork, an overview of its provision in the department is important. This is best achieved by auditing the existing provision, then formulating a departmental policy.

Fieldwork Activities	LOOK AND SEE 'Out of the window you can see...'	INVESTIGATIVE 'If it moves, measure it.'	ENQUIRY-BASED 'There's no simple answer'
type of activity	eye-balling Cooks' tour talk and look guided tour field teaching	field study field testing investigating process studies model testing pure	field discovery hypothesis testing issues problem-solving applied
characteristics	passive transmission teacher-centred factual knowledge prescriptive specific qualitative observation-orientated non-participatory information-based	active finding out teacher-led, pupil-centred methodological systematic scientific qualitative and quantitative measurement-orientated participatory activity-based	interactive evaluating pupil-centred, pupil-led interpretative open-ended scientific and humanistic qualitative and quantitative outcome-orientated fully participatory discovery-based

Figure 8: *Three commonly used approaches to fieldwork*

THE AUDIT

Fieldwork should be planned as an integral part of a scheme of work. The audit can be used to compare the existing fieldwork provision with additional opportunities and then with the demands of the National Curriculum and exam syllabuses. The audit can be carried out chronologically, year by year and term by term, or by locality from year to year (Figure 10).

YOUR FIELDWORK POLICY

This might include statements about, or descriptions of the following:

- the importance of fieldwork in geography
- the aims and objectives of fieldwork
- the teaching and learning styles to be used
- the suggested entitlement for each pupil per year, including duration of fieldwork undertaken
- how fieldwork opportunities fit into the units of work planned for each year group – this involves you in determining at what stage during the unit of work the fieldwork is undertaken
- suggestions of possible locations and activities for each proposed visit
- how progression in fieldwork might be achieved
- links with out-of-school policies for other subjects and cross-curricular elements such as Personal and Social Education and Environmental Education
- a planning checklist, including preparation and follow-up to the visit
- links with school and LEA policies
- equipment and resources available
- cost and charges to parents/guardians
- number of staff and adult helpers required
- copies of letters sent to parents/guardians
- health, safety and behaviour statement
- Country Code and other conservation codes
- an assessment of fieldwork with regard to pupil achievement, suitability of location and activities

LOOK AND SEE – STREET

Process	Quotes	Themes
teacher has knowledge show listen write observe draw photograph demonstrate guided tour follow trail meet the mayor or a planner	**teacher** In 1863… Note the shape of the… Look at the architectural… Can you see the…? This is the oldest… This postcard shows… Ms Snape will tell you about… Keep together! There are three solutions… **pupils** I'd never noticed that… Can you repeat that Sir? What do you want us to do now? Can we go up that street?	old and new continuity and change building function land use transport services shops conservation areas architecture

INVESTIGATION – STREET

Process	Quotes	Themes

teacher provides equipment and theme
measure
count
survey
sample
sense
question
list
display
	teacher
	Imagine you're a real researcher…
	You should measure…
	To find this out you will need to…
	Make sure you've got enough information.
	Are there any trends or patterns?
	What can you conclude?
	
	pupils
	So that's how it's done!
	How many shall we interview/count?
	Where shall we…?
	How often…?
		land use
		shopping patterns
		shop frontages
		building heights
		traffic counts
		pedestrian census
		spatial patterns
		questionnaire
		streetometer
		shop clustering
		pedestrian movements
		relationships between:
		    land value and distance
		    traffic flow and time
		    floor space and trade
		    land use and shopping hierarchy

ENQUIRY – STREET

Process	Quotes	Themes
teacher provides sources of information and resources guided discovery enquiry questions/brainstorm formulating hypotheses testing hypotheses role-play purposeful data collection identifying an issue problem solving empathy presentations of findings	**teacher** What do you think…? What would you feel like…? How could you begin to…? How would you solve the…? What view does each group take The planners… **pupils** Different people think differently. There's no easy solution. Now I know what it feels like. I've looked at all the evidence and… We could do with the answer to… This is real! This is an important issue. Our results could be used by…	locate the new zebra crossing the waste ground on the corner the litter problem traffic safety and congestion a new superstore closing the market pedestrianising the High Street access for disabled more green space changing land use

Figure 9: Three styles of fieldwork illustrated by the theme of 'street'

Year	Term	lesson	length of fieldwork				location		themes and topics	teaching/learning activities	skills
			one lesson	half day	day trip	residential	local area	contrasting region			
7	1	Local Services ✓	✓				✓		Jobs in the local area	Use of 1:10,000 map of localares formula-ting questionnaires	Surveying, Mapping
	2										
	3										
8	1										
	2										
	3										
9	1										
	2										
	3										

Figure 10: Auditing fieldwork

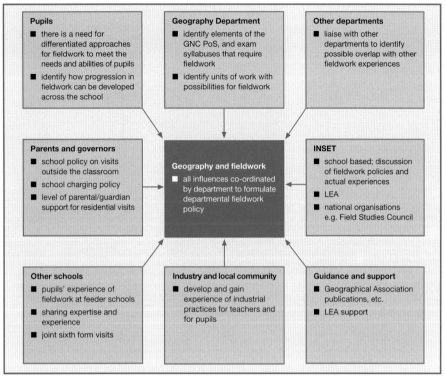

Figure 11: *Factors associated with the formulation of a school policy for fieldwork*

SUMMARY

Figure 11 is a summary of the factors associated with the formulation of a school policy for fieldwork. The starting point must be a judgement of the value of fieldwork in the teaching and learning associated with individual units of work. We all have to make a judgement about the most effective use of the limited fieldwork opportunities available and this will obviously be linked to the location and duration of those opportunities. Of equal importance is the need to ensure a progression in fieldwork across the geography department, and to meet the needs and abilities of all pupils. We all teach in the real world, so the school policy on charging for visits outside the classroom, and the likely level of parental/guardian support, will influence our decisions.

Some of the factors are external to the department – for example, liaison with science colleagues over the possibility of joint field visits. Some influences will be external to the school – for example, the possibility in the local area for visits to industries, etc., and the availability of in-service support.

Further reading

Booth, R., Chambers, W. & Thomas, A.D. (1992) *Reaching Out*. Living Earth.

May, S., Richardson, P. & Banks, V. (1993) *Fieldwork in Action 1: Planning Fieldwork.* The Geographical Association.

May, S. & Cook, J. (1993) *Fieldwork in Action 2: An Enquiry Approach.* The Geographical Association.

St John, P.R. & Richardson, D.A. (1989) *Methods of Presenting Fieldwork Data.* The Geographical Association.

St John, P.R. & Richardson, D.A. (1990) *Methods of Statistical Analysis of Fieldwork Data.* The Geographical Association.

Thomas, T. & May, S. (1994) *Fieldwork in Action 3: Managing Out-of-Classroom Activities.* The Geographical Association.

Chapter 15

Teaching about distant places

TONY BINNS

People, places and geography

Probably more than any other subject in our education system, geography has traditionally been responsible for promoting awareness, interest and understanding of the diversity of the world's peoples and places. Vital educational objectives such as global awareness and international understanding have long been the domain of geography in schools and in institutions of further and higher education. Furthermore, in the general absence below sixth form level of the formal study of economics, sociology, anthropology and development studies, it is geography which lays the foundations for these and other disciplines and fires concern and enthusiasm in young people at an early and impressionable stage. This is a heavy responsibility for the subject and its teachers; but because such concerns lie at the heart of geography, the subject is immediate, interesting, exciting, topical and relevant.

This chapter focuses specifically on teaching about distant places, whatever 'distant' might mean. Twenty years ago the term 'distant' might have referred to most of the world outside Europe, which at that time relatively few people from Britain had visited. But since then the spectacular increase in air travel has brought the world's peoples and places much closer together. Family visits to Florida or Australia, for example, are now commonplace, and those seeking greater adventure can, and many do, go trekking in the Himalayas or white-water rafting down the Zambezi. The 'global village' is rapidly becoming a reality for those who can afford to fly. All the more reason, therefore, that our pupils should gain more knowledge and understanding (and empathy) of the world's different peoples and places and should learn, insofar as this is possible, what it is like to be Spanish or Polish or Australian or Chinese.

Definitions, perceptions and stereotypes

Even the youngest children are fascinated by distant places. Where once stories, films and television programmes provided the only images of such places, it is now increasingly likely that at least one child in each class will have encountered environments and peoples that are very different from those of the home area. Whether it is a trip to Disneyland, a safari and beach holiday in tropical Africa, or a visit to relatives in India or East Africa, the young people of today are incomparably better travelled than previous generations. Also, our classes often include children from ethnic

The study of a blacksmith in Tanzania reveals many principles of large-scale modern steelmaking

Photo: **Patrick Bailey**

minority groups, who perhaps visit the family 'home country' regularly with their parents and who have much valuable knowledge of far-off peoples and places which they can share with their classmates. Teachers should build upon such experience and enthusiasm wherever possible.

Young people must learn to appreciate the diversity of the world's environments and societies, to empathise wherever possible and to realise that because someone or something is unfamiliar to us they are not necessarily inferior or 'funny'. To break down some of the many myths and stereotypes which exist about distant places and their peoples, as well as myths about Britain itself, pupils must be encouraged to examine them critically. Overcoming such myths and stereotypes is a major problem in teaching about distant places and one which has been addressed on many occasions in books and articles (see for example Binns, 1979; Development Education Centre, 1987, 1992; Pike and Selby, 1988). Concepts such as 'Third World', 'North-South', 'development', 'underdeveloped' and numerous others are complicated and potentially confusing and require careful and sensitive explanation. For example, the term 'economically developing', used in the first geography National Curriculum Order, was particularly problematic because there are many cases of countries with rapidly rising Gross National Product (GNP), but where true development, in terms of a reduction in poverty and inequality, has not occurred (the UK and USA being prime examples). Increased wealth, rather than 'trickling down' to the poorest and remotest communities, often gravitates towards already wealthy urban-based elites, thus increasing inequality. Such inequality is reflected in various key development indicators, for example, life expectancy and infant mortality.

Another matter of concern is that the concept of 'development' is rarely considered in the context of the home region, UK or the European Community (Bailey, 1981). 'Development', some would argue, is entirely concerned with solving the many problems of Third World countries. But why should a concept which is about social and economic well-being be so often restricted to poor, developing countries? Within the European Union there are parts of western Ireland, Scotland, Wales, north-east England, southern Italy, Greece, Spain, Portugal, and the former East Germany with social and economic conditions similar to many so-called Third World countries. Is this a case of double standards – of applying one set of criteria for one part of the world and a different set of criteria for the other? Pupils should appreciate that 'development' studies begin at home, perhaps even in their own street or village. Variations in poverty, inequality and unemployment, which are often cited as key elements in definitions of development, can be examined nationally in a UK context, but perhaps more usefully at a regional and even local level.

Distant places in the geography curriculum

Secondary school geography teachers should be aware that since the implementation of the geography National Curriculum in September 1991, much progress has been made in teaching and learning about distant places in many, though sadly not all, primary schools. It is in key stages 1 and 2 that the impact and benefits have probably been most strongly felt. Primary teachers, and particularly the great majority who are not specialist geographers, have had to work hard in seeking out and developing appropriate resources and formulating programmes of work (see Chapter 1). This has often not been easy, not least because primary teachers are usually expected to deliver all the core and foundation subjects. As a result of this progress in the primary school sector, it is now quite likely that children will enter secondary school having studied, for example, the West African kingdom of Benin or the Caribbean island of St Lucia, or indeed other distant 'localities'. If this is the case, children will probably also have been introduced to a range of excellent and innovative resources which have been developed to support the teaching of 'localities' (see, for example; Bunce *et al.*, 1992; Morgan, 1994; Hughes *et al*, 1992; Weldon, 1994a, 1994b). Many of these resources can be adapted easily for use in secondary schools.

Whereas the first geography Order prescribed places to be studied, the 1995 Order gives much greater, and very welcome, flexibility. Good geography teaching should be able to make use of issues and events which are in the news. For example, an earthquake in California or Japan, famine in Ethiopia, and ethnic clashes in the Middle East or South Africa, are the sorts of issues which need to be examined at the time of their occurrence.

The 1995 geography Order contains explicit statements relating to distant places, and implicit references in the 'thematic studies', for which teachers could, if they desire, draw case study material from such locations. For example, for the 'Ecosystems' theme at key stage 3, pupils are to be taught:

> '…the characteristics and distribution of one type of vegetation, e.g. savanna grassland, tropical rain forest'.

In the thematic section headed 'Economic activities', pupils are required to be taught:

> '…about the geographical distribution of one economic activity, e.g. a type of farming, the car industry, a form of transport'.

Teachers choosing to focus on the car industry, for example, might draw their case studies from Brazil, China or South Africa, as well as from countries closer to home.

Also at key stage 3, for the theme of 'Development', pupils must be taught to understand:

> '…ways of identifying differences in development…, the effect of differences in development…on the quality of life of different groups of people', and '…how the interdependence of countries influences development'.

In the first two, case study material might be usefully drawn from the UK and Europe, as well as from more distant and developing countries, thus avoiding the stereotype that development issues are entirely a Third World concern.

Explicit reference in key stage 3 to distant places comes under the section headed 'Places'. Teachers must select two countries (other than those in the UK) for study, one from List A, and one from List B.

List A	List B
Australia and New Zealand	Africa
Europe	Asia (excluding Japan)
Japan	South and Central America (including the Caribbean)
North America	
Russian Federation	

Thus, there are ample opportunities for teachers to introduce case study material from distant places, and places which are 'in significantly different states of development'.

Resourcing the teaching of distant places

Geography is fortunate in that over the years teachers, publishers, the BBC and others involved in geographical education have generated a range of printed, visual and field-based resource materials relating to distant places which are the envy of many other school subjects. Many textbooks contain useful case study material which can be used to 'bring to life' particular issues (see, for example, Binns 1994; Bunce 1994; Lambert 1993). Photo packs, simulations, CD-ROMs, videos and slide sets are now produced by various commercial and charitable bodies, such as development education centres, non-governmental organisations (NGOs) and the Geographical Association. Catalogues are produced by all these organisations, most of whom also exhibit their products at the GA's Annual Conference.

There are many other ways to bring distant places into the classroom. Music, prose, poems and film all have great potential, and both the variety and availability of these resources have improved considerably in recent years. Exciting cross-curricular work is possible through drama, and the use of indigenous literature and music can do much to enhance 'a sense of place'. Such teaching strategies are often a good way to deal with political and controversial issues, such as the role of transnational companies, trade and aid, the arms trade, poverty and inequality. Rainforest destruction and conservation, for example, is a topic which lends itself to the acting out of various roles and viewpoints, with pupils considering many different elements of the debate ranging from the effects of global warming to the perceptions of local peoples who need jobs.

The same principles of site choice apply in African markets and European shopping malls

Photo: **Patrick Bailey**

For those able to visit London, much can be gained from a day-visit to the Commonwealth Institute or the Museum of Mankind. Kew Gardens provides an excellent location to study tropical and subtropical plants and environments. Courses and workshops for teachers and pupils are provided by all three institutions. Better still, why not take your pupils on an overseas field course? I have taken many sixth-form groups on fieldwork to southern Morocco and The Gambia. Several tour companies now have specialist 'schools sections' to help plan such expeditions and if you pick your time and place carefully, overseas field courses can sometimes be cheaper than those at home.

Overseas visitors and school links can also help develop empathy and foster international understanding. The GA's International Committee has done much in recent years to encourage links between schools in the UK and overseas, as well as strengthening links with teachers in particular regions. The 'West Africa Link', for example, between 1993 and 1996, established valuable contact between teachers in West Africa and the UK and involved the regular publication and distribution to West Africa of a news and curriculum broadsheet, *Palaver*.

Teaching about distant places has always been one of the most exciting and challenging aspects of geography. There is great potential and a vast array of resources to support such work. With the impressive development of 'distant places teaching' in primary schools since the introduction of the National Curriculum, children entering secondary schools now have a more systematic base upon which secondary teachers can build. Furthermore, as advances in technology bring peoples and places in different parts of the world even closer together, there is a greater need than ever for mutual understanding and respect.

Some practical suggestions

Each of the ideas below could be adapted to the age and ability of the group.

1 GETTING TO GRIPS WITH PERCEPTIONS, MYTHS AND STEREOTYPES

■ Divide the class into groups of three or four pupils, and ask them to list as many words and ideas as possible which they associate with the Third World, Africa, or the specific country or region being studied.

■ Ask the groups to try to answer the following questions:

Do you know anyone who has visited Africa, etc?

Do you know anybody who has come to Britain from Africa?

How does Britain help Africa?

How does Africa help Britain?

■ Ask each group to give feedback and develop a class discussion on some of the common and the more unusual points raised.

■ Has any pupil visited Africa etc., and/or is there someone in the group who was born there or has relatives living there or coming from there? What images do they have of these places, and how do their own images compare with those produced in the group 'brainstorming' session?

■ Examine some other media images of Africa etc. There are now many excellent photo packs available which can be used to promote debate about images and stereotypes. Particularly useful, accessible and inexpensive resources are travel brochures. How do the images in these differ from those discussed and/or directly experienced? Ask the small groups to make two lists; one of their own images and the other of the travel brochure images.

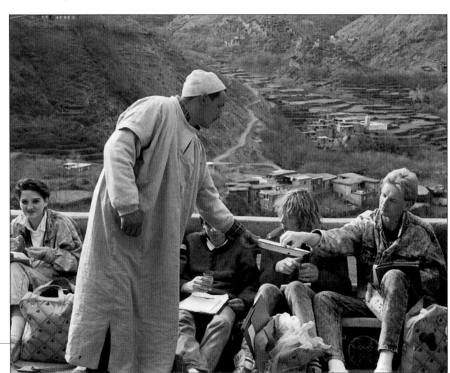

Writing up in the High Atlas Mountains, with local sweets

Photo: **Tony Binns**

2   WHAT IS DEVELOPMENT AND HOW CAN IT BE MEASURED?

Working in small 'brainstorming' groups, ask the pupils to try to answer the question:

What shows that one country is more 'developed' than another?

Rearrange the list of countries below so that what you think is the most developed country is at the top of the list and the least developed is at the bottom:

China

Brazil

United Kingdom

India

Saudi Arabia

Greece

Jamaica

Bangladesh

USA

Kenya

Nigeria

With the whole class, discuss the order of the countries and try to agree on a series of variables or indicators of development. After an initial listing, each indicator would have to be explained carefully. For example:

Gross National Product per capita

Infant mortality and life expectancy

Proportion of people who are employed in agriculture

Proportion of people who are literate and/or are receiving full-time education in primary schools

The size of the national debt

Population size and density

The values of each variable for each country could be tabulated and then discussed afterwards. (Up-to-date statistics can be obtained from the World Bank's *World Development Report* and the United Nations Development Programme's (UNDP) *Human Development Report*, both published annually by Oxford University Press – essential for every school library!)

Pupils might then be asked to produce, either individually or in groups, a poster which summarises what they think should be the most important goals of development. They might be asked to consider two broad headings and sets of objectives:

a   Meeting the needs of individuals

b   Improving society and the economy.

Development might then be considered in the UK context – national, regional and local. Issues such as poverty, inequality and unemployment might be considered, as well as housing quality, number of free school meals, etc. Try to obtain statistics on these, and after tabulating and/or plotting on maps, pupils might attempt to identify patterns and possible underlying processes. Assess the possible impact of, and the arguments for and against, a major local development project such as the construction of a reservoir or bypass (see Chapter 12), or the opening of a new quarry. Who will benefit and suffer most from this development?

3 UNDERSTANDING CULTURE AND SOCIETY

In studying a particular country or region, try to encourage pupils to empathise with the people who live there; understanding their way of life and appreciating that they may be 'different, but equal'.

This can be done in a number of ways, for example:

Role-plays and simulation exercises (see Chapter 12).

Artefacts and food The Commonwealth Institute and Museum of Mankind in London have excellent collections of artefacts. A number of provincial museums also have good ethnographic collections. Many tropical foods are available in UK supermarkets and can be shown to pupils, for example: mango, paw paw, sweet potato, yam and cassava. International recipe books are widely available, for example Oxfam's *Recipes from Around the World*. The large supermarkets are increasingly selling ready-made 'ethnic' meals. In my local supermarket recently, to my great surprise I discovered, and subsequently enjoyed, 'Jollof Rice', a popular dish from The Gambia. As more people visit other countries on holiday, so they are attracted to trying 'ethnic' dishes back home.

Video, slides and photographs

Poetry and books from important Indian, Caribbean and African writers, such as Chinua Achebe's *Things Fall Apart, No Longer at Ease* and *Anthills of the Savannah*.

Music Specialists such as Andy Kershaw on BBC radio have done much to popularise world music. We might ask pupils, 'What do the lyrics of Bob Marley's songs tell us about Caribbean life?' or 'What does Youssou N'Dour's music tell us about Senegal in West Africa?' As music critic Rick Glanvill writes in the notes to accompany N'Dour's album, *Hey You!* (Music Club, 1993), 'N'Dour, always an observer of the broader picture, simultaneously used his music as a news medium back home and an ambassadorial tool abroad'. The track 'Shakin' The Tree', for example, is about the emancipation of women, in a country where polygamy is routine and literacy rates among women are well below those of men. The track 'Toxiques', on the same album, is a protest about transnationals that dump toxic waste in the poor developing countries. These are important social and development issues.

School links Many schools have established links with schools overseas and pupils have often acquired 'pen-pals' who can give a useful personal insight into local and family life. Such links established by primary schools might be continued and developed further in secondary schools. Exchange visits for teachers and pupils are also becoming increasingly popular. The Geographical Association's International Committee can advise on such links and exchanges.

4   UNDERSTANDING DISTANT ENVIRONMENTS

Many UK cities, such as Sheffield and Edinburgh, have botanical gardens where plants from different environments can be studied. The next best thing to visiting the African savanna or the Brazilian rainforest is to organise a day visit to one of these. Kew Gardens, in south-west London (contact the Education Department at Kew for details), has particularly fine examples: the Palm House there houses a wide range of 'economic' trees and plants from tropical regions, such as banana, cacao, rubber and cotton, and the new Tropical Conservatory provides an exciting and unrivalled opportunity to walk through a series of simulated environments with closely controlled temperatures and humidity.

Resources

Useful material for teaching about the Third World may be obtained from the following sources:

Action Aid, Hamlyn House, Archway, London N19 5PG

Birmingham Development Education Centre, Selly Oak College, Bristol Road, Birmingham B29 6LE

Christian Aid, Inter-church House, 35 Lower Marsh, London SE1 7RL

Commonwealth Institute, Kensington High Street, London W8 6NQ

Development Education Association, 29-31 Cowper Street, London EC2A 4AP

Earthscan Publications Ltd, 120 Pentonville Road, London N1 9JN

Geofile published by Stanley Thornes, Ellenborough House, Wellington Street, Cheltenham GL50 1YD

The Geographical Magazine published by the Royal Geographical Society (available from: Subscriptions, PO Box 425, Woking GU21 1GP)

Geography Review published by Philip Allan Publishers Ltd, Market Place, Deddington, Oxford OX5 4SE

International Broadcasting Trust, 2 Ferdinand Place, London NW1 8EE

Leeds Development Education Centre, 151-153 Cardigan Road, Leeds LS6 1LJ

Oxfam, 274 Banbury Road, Oxford OX2 7DZ

Teaching Geography and *Geography* published by the Geographical Association, 343 Fulwood Road, Sheffield S10 3BP

Worldaware, 1 Catton Street, London WC1R 4AB

References

Bailey, P. (1981) 'The Northamptonshire Development Education Project: a mainly geographical initiative', *Teaching Geography*, 7, 1, pp. 4-5.

Binns, J.A. (1979) 'How "we" see "them": some thoughts on Third World Teaching'. *Teaching Geography*, 4, 4, pp. 176-177.

Binns, J.A. (1993) 'The international dimension in the Geography National Curriculum', in Speak, C. & Wiegand P. (eds), *International Understanding through Geography*, The Geographical Association.

Binns, J.A. (1994) *Tropical Africa.* Routledge.

Bunce, V., Foley, J., Morgan, W. & Scoble, S. (1992) *Focus on Castries: St Lucia photopack.* The Geographical Association.

Bunce, V. (ed) (1994) *World Geography: Case Studies.* Cambridge University Press.

DFE (1993) Geography in the National Curriculum. HMSO.

Development Education Centre (1987) *Whose Development? Geographical Issues in West Africa from The Gambia and Senegal.* DEC, Birmingham.

Development Education Centre (1992) *Developing Geography: A Development Education Approach at key stage 3.* DEC, Birmingham.

Hughes, J. Paterson, K. & Rafferty, P. (1992) *Ladakh Photopack: An Activity-based Pack Focused on the Life of a Tibetan Community*. The Geographical Association.

Lambert, D. (ed) (1993) *Society Pieces.* Cambridge University Press.

Morgan, W. (1994) *Lessons on Castries: St Lucia.* The Geographical Association.

Pike, G. & Selby, D. (1988) *Global Teacher, Global Learner.* Hodder and Stoughton.

Weldon, M. (1994a) *Kaptalamwa: A Village in Kenya.* The Geographical Association.

Weldon, M. (1994b) *Discovering Distant Places.* The Geographical Association.

Section Four

Assessing and examining

SUMMARY OF CHAPTERS

'We…find that examinations in geography are capable of testing much more than the memory; they give evidence of clear apprehension and power of statement, of breadth of view, and of style of composition.'
H C Rawlinson, President of the Royal Geographical Society,
in a letter to the Vice Chancellors of Oxford and Cambridge Universities, 1871.

This section considers the nature of achievement in geography and its assessment. It outlines different types of assessment and indicates how achievement may be measured and recorded. Examinations and assessment at key stage 3, GCSE and higher levels are discussed.

Chapter 16

Issues in assessment

DAVID LAMBERT

Introduction

There are two distinctive cultures in educational assessment. On the one hand, we have what is sometimes referred to as the assessment industry, dominated by public examinations such as GCSE, A level and, increasingly, GNVQs, and externally set and marked key stage tests which have been introduced for the core subjects of the National Curriculum (English, mathematics and science). On the other hand, there is the kind of assessment which is integral to teachers' day-to-day professional lives, forming an essential element of teacher-pupil relationships and which includes 'marking'. The advent of National Curriculum assessment arrangements has blurred the boundary between these two cultures because, in geography, teachers are now responsible for making key stage assessments of their pupils (see Daugherty and Lambert, 1994; Lambert, 1995). This is done on the basis of 'teacher assessment', a process which, though not subject to strict central control (unlike public examinations), is required to provide reliable data from which comparisons between schools can be made.

This chapter is concerned with the second of the two cultures: that is assessment that is designed to inform teachers about individual pupils' progress and help identify their next steps (see also Chapters 17 and 18). The evolving meaning and role of teacher assessment is considered in this professional context and suggestions are made to develop teacher assessment in practice. One important distinction is that between 'marking' and 'teacher assessment'. Although marking contributes to the process of making teacher assessments, it cannot, exclusively, fully perform the function of teacher assessment which requires an overall 'synoptic judgement' of each pupil's progress in relation to broad, multi-faceted criteria.

What is assessment?

...the process of gathering, interpreting, recording and using information about pupils' responses to an educational task' (Harlen *et al.*, 1992, pp. 217-218).

Assessment in education involves both:

- more formal contexts and procedures including written, timed tests marked under strict conditions; and

- less formal settings including reading pupils' work and listening to what they have to say.

Assessment should always be an integral part of the teaching and learning process

Photo: **Sally and Richard Greenhill**

Thus assessment encompasses responses to regular work as well as to specially devised tasks (Harlen *et al*, 1992, pp. 217-218).

Assessment in education requires teachers to make judgements about pupils' responses measured against some standard of expectation. This is either,

- norm-referenced – set by the average performance of the age group,

or

- criterion-referenced – set by the interpretation (and statement) of the progression of skills, knowledge and understanding which form the objectives of learning for the subject.

The generally agreed roles of assessment in education are:

- providing feedback to teachers and pupils' about progress in order to support future learning – **the formative role**

- providing information about the level of pupils' achievements at points during and at the end of their school career – **the summative role**

- providing the means for selection by qualification – **the certification role**

- contributing to the information on which judgements are made concerning the effectiveness or quality of individuals and institutions in the system as a whole – **the evaluative role**.

Listening to what students have to say is a vital element of assessment

Photo: **Margaret Roberts**

A key idea in considering assessment is **fitness for purpose**. It is the purpose to which an assessment is to be put that exerts the greatest influence on the principles which govern the assessment processes in practice. Thus, public examinations adopt certain features, such as externally set papers and rigorously moderated mark schemes, in order that they gain an adequate level of public confidence for their primary role; certification. Assessment which has a formative purpose does not have to face this level of external scrutiny. Indeed, it can adopt a rationale which is entirely *ipsative*, that is seeking to measure a child's progress purely in terms of that individual's unique circumstances and characteristics.

One conclusion we may draw from this is that it is difficult to imagine a single assessment system being able to perform adequately to meet simultaneously the requirements of all four roles identified in the above list. However, most educational assessment has to serve more than one function at the same time.

Marking

In educational assessment it is vital, therefore, constantly to keep in mind the question 'What am I doing this for?' Coming to an answer to this question helps departments to refine marking policies, and to clarify how 'marking' and 'teacher assessment' are both complementary and distinctive. Marking is a form of assessment which gives teachers the chance to respond immediately to an individual's work. It helps both teachers and pupils to develop a shorthand language which facilitates efficient and clear communication. Figure 1 shows an example of one department's policy (see also Chapter 17).

Margin mark	Meaning	Mark in writing
np.	new paragraph needed	⌐ around first word of new paragraph
run on	no new paragraph needed	⟩ between paragraphs
⋏	something is missed out	⋏ Where something should be put in
⋏.	full stop missing	
Sp.	spelling mistake	underline word. Print correct spelling in margin if needed. Maximum of four on each occasion
⋏" ⋏"	quotation marks needed	
lc	change from capitals to lower case (small letters)	circle the letters to be changed
?	doesn't make sense	
X	wrong	
✓	good point	
✓✓	very good point	

Figure 1: One department's marking conventions

Given the prominence of marking in teachers' lives (all teachers do a lot of marking, and, if they do not, it is seen as a serious deficiency) it is remarkable how little emphasis was given to it during training in the past. Read what this experienced geography teacher, reflecting on his marking practice at the beginning of his career, had to say:

We had very little training in assessment and marking. Everyone knew you had to do it but it was something like a 'black box' – difficult to penetrate and almost impossible to find anyone to give you advice about it. So how did I mark? Well, I could draw from my experience as a pupil: marking seemed simply to be a process which resulted in a number out-of-ten accompanied sometimes with a comment. The number was important: it enabled you to compare your work, but I remember feeling that the comment was potentially even more valuable. I resolved, therefore, to write lengthy comments on pupils' work before returning it to them. But the problem remained of what mark to give. In the end the solution (which survived for some years) was simple. I gave seven-out-of-ten for work I deemed to be satisfactory, eight if it was better than satisfactory and six for deficient work. Occasionally I strayed beyond these limits for outstanding or particularly shoddy work but basically I had invented for myself a three-level assessment system. It was easy to operate, gave me rough information about my pupils, and seemed to satisfy their desire for me to give them marks.

The above passage can be used to illustrate what is deficient about an assessment strategy which is ill-defined or unfocused. The marks were awarded on the basis of a norm which was implicit. Such **norm referenced** assessment essentially sorts the pupils' work into three piles: average, below average and above average. The norm, or standard, may remain hidden – even from the teacher – until the work itself is received for marking; it is on the basis of the overall quality of the work that the norm (7/10) is set. It is quite possible that different definitions of 'quality' are applied to different pupils and it is likely that this is reflected in the teacher's comments, or descriptive assessment of the work, addressed to the pupil. This can be a strength, providing an ipsative perspective, whereby the pupil sees the assessment purely in terms of his/her previous performance. It can also be a weakness if learning goals are not clarified, because pupils are left with no clear idea of the teacher's expectations let alone what they have to do in order to achieve a better performance.

There is a powerful case, therefore, supporting **criteria referenced** assessment, even in the context of day-to-day marking. The advantage of moving from an essentially norm-referenced assessment strategy to one guided by criteria lies principally in the act of formulating or agreeing the criteria with colleagues. This helps the teacher to specify what she/he wants to achieve with a group of pupils, and to articulate these expectations or targets, to them. Figure 2 shows a simple matrix designed to be used in this way with undergraduate students. Figure 3 shows an early example of how the same principle has been used with Year 7 pupils. The aim would be to work, over a period of time, toward a common understanding of the criteria. The list is addressed to the pupils, but it would be unlikely to have the desired impact on them without careful mediation by the teacher.

A The criteria

- A willingness to argue for a particular viewpoint
- An ability to support an argument with reference to relevant literature and examples
- An ability to evaluate and weigh up different kinds of evidence
- An ability to answer a specific question
- An ability to think independently

B The criteria translated into a marking matrix

	Knowledge/ content	Citation of literature	Structure/ organisation	Response to specific questions	Critical argument
Excellent					
Good					
Average					
Poor					
Unacceptable					

Before marking the essays, decide what criteria are important (A). These criteria can then become one axis of a marking matrix (B). Examining boards add sophistication to this process by giving different weightings to the criteria. These are shown on the 'specification grids' which form part of the syllabus documentation.

Figure 2: Broad criteria for marking essays   Source: Lambert, 1990

Another benefit arising from using criteria in marking is that it generates the content base for conversations between teachers and their pupils. The following extract is from the Report of the National Commission on Education, entitled *Learning to Succeed:*

Your work will be marked for one of the following skills:

- ■ Finding out information, i.e. reference skills
- ■ Showing information, i.e. communication skills
- ■ Understanding information, i.e. interpretative skills
- ■ Making decisions, i.e. evaluative skills

Your work will receive a mark 0-5. This is what it means:

Finding out information

0 I am unable to assess your ability

1 You have failed to select the information required (you are wrong)

2 You have managed to select and express only one or two points

3 You have selected the important points but expressed them poorly

4 You have selected and expressed most of the important points

5 You have selected and expressed all relevant information – your work is excellent

Showing information

0 I am unable to assess your ability

1 Your presentation of the information is wrong

2 You have presented some of the information in an accurate way or you have understood some of the information but the production is poor

3 Your presentation of the information is mostly correct and reasonably clear

4 You have presented the information given in a clear and accurate way

5 You have presented the information given in a very clear and accurate way – your work is excellent

Understanding information

0 I am unable to assess your ability

1 You have misunderstood the information given

2 You have understood part of the information

3 You have understood the information

4 You have shown a clear understanding of the information and attempted to use it

5 You have shown a clear understanding of the information and used it well – your work is excellent

Making decisions

0 I am unable to assess your ability

1 Your work is muddled. You have made no decisions

2 Your decisions are vague with few reasons given

3 Your decisions are clear but not well reasoned

4 Your decisions are clear and you have attempted to present your opinions in a convincing way

5 Your decisions are very well reasoned – your work is excellent

Figure 3: Marking criteria for use with 11 year olds   Source: Collarbone, 1983

'We commissioned a survey of the views of pupils in the early years of secondary school. It found that 44% of Year 7 pupils and 45% of Year 9 pupils indicated that they never talked individually to their class teachers about their work, and 42% of Year 7 pupils and 41% of Year 9 pupils indicated that they never talked individually to other teachers about their work. Only 55% of Year 7 pupils and 50% of Year 9 pupils indicated that all or most of their teachers praised them when they did their work well' (NCE, 1993, p. 205).

It seems that the teaching force as a whole could identify subject-based conversation with individual pupils as a goal for improvement. 'Well done' or 'could do better' can, on occasion, be replaced by diagnosis which is detailed and analytical, based upon the guiding assessment criteria. Of course, there are challenging classroom management issues for teachers to overcome, which may explain why many pupils do not feel individually catered for in their lessons. These are addressed later in this chapter under 'Pupil portfolios' (page 198).

Diagnostic assessment

'Diagnosis' has a medical ring to it; doctors diagnose illness on the basis of evidence which they observe or have brought to their attention. The quality of the diagnosis depends largely on the professional skills of the doctor: his or her knowledge and training, and the various aids (including past records) which can be brought into play. Above all it depends on how well 'tuned in' the doctor is to the patient.

There are ways in which this analogy is useful to teachers. Consider the pupils who think of themselves as 'no good at mathematics'. There is no doubt that some people have greater gifts in the field of 'logical-mathematical intelligence' than others (Gardner, 1988), but the apparent finality of this self-judgement could be deeply worrying. It should be of some concern to the teacher, either simply to understand more fully (make a better diagnosis) or to correct (make better).

The origin of the pupil's negative self image in mathematics could be relatively simple. Consider the contrast in the teacher's practice in the examples below. Both concern just one aspect of mathematics, namely the multiplication of fractions.

Example A
The pupil consistently fails to come to the correct solution in a series of examples set in class and for homework.

The teacher marks them conscientiously and accurately, makes some written comment to encourage the pupil to concentrate harder on the explanation – to try harder – and records in her markbook a series of low marks. This builds a picture of low attainment in mathematics.

Example B
The pupil consistently fails to come to the correct solution in a series of examples set in class and for homework.

The teacher marks them conscientiously and accurately. The teacher decides to have a chat with the pupil during the next lesson. The three minute conversation reveals that the pupil had been using the wrong algorithm for the task. This is corrected (the 'penny drops'), the homework is repeated with more success and the markbook records this improvement.

In Example B, the assessment has more than one facet. It consists of marking the work (a formal and sometimes quite impersonal activity) and the informal conversation with the pupil. The aim of the conversation can be expressed, very simply, as a 'getting to know' activity. In large classes containing a wide range of individual differences this can be an exhausting business, but is vital because it enables the teacher to step beyond the superficial 'diagnosis' of the pupil being 'no good at mathematics' – no more effective a statement than the medical diagnosis that the patient is ill.

Aspects of geography, most notably graphical and cartographic activities, are the source of 'mental blocks' (with pupils of all ages) similar to the mathematics example above: for many pupils, when learning about scale, grid references or contour lines, the 'penny has to drop' in the same sort of way and this can be speeded up with timely and appropriate help from the teacher.

Evidence exists that this kind of problem is widespread, not just confined to spatial or numerical aspects of the subject, but embedded in the dominant medium of geographical education – the English language. Technical terminology, such as 'relief', 'industrial location', 'erosion' (as distinct from 'weathering'), can impede learning in a number of subtle ways. Using language actively and creatively, such as writing for different audiences, can provide the circumstances in which these hindrances can be cleared. Effective diagnostic marking is concerned with teachers learning about such things in relation to the individuals they teach and the work produced.

Discussion points

Assessment is about knowing what questions to ask?

In order to know what questions to ask we need to be sure what we want to find out. How far have we advanced from this scene – recalled by David Hall – from a map extract question in an O level examination?

> Questioned on the distribution of railways around Keswick, statements such as 'they avoid the lakes', 'they go round the hills!' were accepted with additional credit if they were supported by six-figure grid references. Routes avoided flood plains, villages existed at spring lines, towns at route centres. The pupil able to diverge from the stereotype and suggest footloose and dynamic factors disqualified himself (sic) by reference to the mark scheme (p. 55).

We might also add that the pupil unable to 'crack the code' of such an assessment ritual is also disadvantaged.

This may sound a warning to departments who, since the advent of the National Curriculum, have grown dependent on regular tests as their main or only source of assessment information on children.

Source: Hall, 1976

Diagnostic assessment, then, is designed to find out how to help pupils in their learning. It is usually multifaceted, as we have seen, and takes a complex view of the human mind which resists the tendency to reduce pupils' potential to a single dimension such as 'ability', a deeply problematic and ill-defined concept which carries predictive, sometimes deterministic and harmful, connotations. When we mark a pupil's work, or test script, we are judging a *performance* undertaken at a particular point in time, under particular conditions and circumstances. We have to assume that the performance is related to that pupil's geographic attainment, which in turn may well be a product, or an indirect measure, of his/her 'ability'. The way we respond *directly* to the performance depends on knowledge of the pupil, the work set and the criteria identified to help guide our judgement. Marking, in this formulation, is interpretative or analytical and must involve the learner.

Food for thought

Consequential validity

Teacher talking:

> After years of marking books I have now come to the conclusion that I need to use my time more carefully. Don't get me wrong – I haven't given up on marking. But I only ever want to do any more marking when I am confident that it'll make a difference. Will it help the pupil improve?

Educators increasingly talk about formative assessment. This does not just mean 'feeding back' to the children. It means that the assessment should have *consequences*. Hence, *consequential validity,* as the above teacher described.

Trying to avoid bias

It is a well known fact that certain forms of assessment practice do not work with equal effect for all groups of pupils. For example, multiple-choice testing techniques tend to favour boys over girls (EOC, 1987). Some standard IQ tests have been strongly criticised for their cultural bias, apparently recognising and rewarding only certain kinds of 'intelligence'. Certain groups of the population are, therefore, not so well prepared to answer the questions set as others, resulting in disadvantage.

Take, for example, the following question from a reading test (Hannon and McNally, 1986). Over half the children who had English as their second language did not select what was judged to be the correct response. Researchers who examined this case concluded that this was a significantly atypical performance by this group of children which could be explained by their lack of knowledge of the colloquialism 'jump' rather than their lack of reading ability. Unless the word jump is known in its colloquial sense then 'on' makes no more, or less, sense than 'by' or 'at'.

An example from a reading test:

The man was very late and just managed to jump _____ the bus as it was pulling away from the stop.

1 at

2 up

3 on

4 by

It is possible to identify potential traps in geography which are similar to that illustrated above. Testing pupils on population pyramids or footloose industries regularly results in entries on the exam howlers page. But what do we as teachers learn from inappropriate pupil responses? How better to present ideas to pupils? How to help pupils assimilate such abstractions as real knowledge?

There is considerable potential in assessment for reinforcing assumptions or prejudices about, say, girls' achievement in physical geography or mapwork. Bias can work in other ways too but it is difficult to draw firm conclusions as to what the root cause of the problem may be, or what action teachers can, or should, take. For example, does the tendency for girls to outperform boys in the GCSE coursework indicate something significant is being measured which improves the fairness and balance of the examination as a whole, or does it demonstrate a bias based upon (as has been suggested) the coursework being a softer option distorting the more objective written examination performance?

Multifaceted diagnostic assessment of the type being proposed in this chapter puts assessment on an individualistic basis, in which differences can be recognised through the use of a variety of assessment strategies: Figure 4 provides a glimpse of the range of potential evidence which geography lessons can generate. Exploiting this provides a strong foundation for reducing bias – at least most forms of group bias – in the assessment process.

Oral evidence	Written evidence	Graphic evidence	Products
Questioning	Questionnaires	Diagrams	Models
Listening	Diaries	Sketches	Artefacts
Discussing	Reports	Drawings	Games
Presentations	Essays	Graphs	Photographs
Interviewing	Notes	Printouts	
Debates	Stories	Overlays	
Audio recording	Newspaper articles		
Video recording	Scripts		
Role-play	Short answers to questions		
Simulation	Lists		
	Poems		
	Descriptions		

Consider:

- Which of these are produced frequently in your geographical classrooms?
- Which are produced infrequently?
- Why?
- Are any of the above underused in your geography classrooms?

Figure 4: Evidence generated in geography classrooms

Validity and reliability in educational assessment

An important distinction to make in considering any educational assessment is that between its validity and reliability. At its most straightforward, **validity** is the question of whether or not the assessment is testing what it claims to be testing. It is debatable, for example, whether a short-answer or multiple-choice test format can measure, with validity, pupils' problem-solving or decision-making skills. **Reliability**, on the other hand, concerns the effects of external variables on the test outcome: different markers, different amounts of help, different completion times – all can affect the test results. Reliable tests are those for which these effects are reduced to a minimum, the ultimate expression of this being the multiple-choice examination.

Ways sometimes have to be found of assessing students' contributions to collaborative work

These facets, validity and reliability, exist in some tension with one another. Maximise one and we have to compromise on the other. One of the original aims of National Curriculum assessment was to maximise both. This was to be done through the combination of external tests and internal assessments made by teachers based upon the same criteria, the so-called Statements of Attainment (SoA). So difficult was this to bring to meaningful and manageable fruition that, in geography, attempts to pursue these goals further were abandoned and the 1991 National Curriculum, cumbersome in structure and overloaded with content to assess, was reformulated. The Level Descriptions in the revised Order now form the standards for making so-called 'Teacher Assessment' (TA).

Teacher Assessment

Firstly, although marking should feed into TA, as should a whole range of additional assessment data, it is not the same as TA. Perhaps this point is best made simply by contrasting Figure 1, one department's marking 'policy' or conventions, with the statutory Level Descriptions. Secondly, though marking contributes to the synoptic assessment required by the National Curriculum (the overview of the pupils' achievements) its main purpose is to communicate the detailed and immediate response to pupils' work. As teachers gain greater confidence and understanding of the Levels so they will help guide teacher judgement of geographical attainment. However, teachers will also be concerned to include other considerations in their responses. Figure 5 may help in this context, acting as an *aide-memoire* to wider aspects of achievement than those denoted by the National Curriculum.

We offer these four aspects (of achievement) in order to clarify our own and our readers' thinking about achievement and we believe that such a scheme is appropriate to the educational aims of comprehensive schools and secondary school teachers. The categories are neither watertight nor beyond criticism, but they provide a useful framework.

Aspect 1
The aspect most strongly represented in GCSE: written expression, capacity to retain propositional knowledge and select from it in order to answer questions. Examinations tend to emphasise knowledge more than skills; memory more than problem solving or investigation; writing more than other forms of communication; speed more than reflection; and individual more than group achievement.

Aspect 2
The capacity to apply knowledge. The emphasis here is practical rather than theoretical; oral rather than written; investigation and problem solving rather then recall. This aspect forms an element, but rarely an important part, of public examinations. It is more time consuming and expensive to assess than Aspect 1.

Aspect 3
Personal and social skills. The capacity to communicate with others face-to-face; to work co-operatively in the interests of a wider group; initiative, self-reliance and skills of leadership. This is not an element assessed directly by traditional public examinations, including GCSE.

Aspect 4
Motivation and commitment; the willingness to accept failure without destructive consequences; readiness to persevere and the self-confidence to learn despite the difficulty of the task. This is often seen as a prerequisite of achievement rather than achievement in its own right, and yet motivation can be seen as an achievement in most walks of life. It is in many ways the most important Aspect as it can affect outcomes in the other three.

Figure 5: Aspects of achievement   Source: Hargreaves, 1984

THE SUMMATIVE FUNCTION OF TA

Another way in which TA is different from marking is that it contains a clear summative function in addition to its formative purpose. The central purpose of Level Descriptions is to generate end-of-key stage judgements of pupils' attainment in geography. The Level Descriptions are not designed to apply to individual pieces of work (in the way it was assumed that the detailed 1991 SoA were to be used). What they are, according to the official documentation (SCAA, 1994), are 'best-fit' statements against which teachers attempt to match a range of a pupil's work. This implies that this *synoptic* assessment is undertaken at a stage well into a course of study, possibly at intervals during the course, as well as at the end. On this basis teachers can report level attainment in geography at or near the end of the academic year and of course at the end of a key stage, at seven, eleven and fourteen years old.

A major cause for concern in this process, notwithstanding its considerable attractions in comparison with the 1991 arrangements, is the question of reliability, particularly if, as seems likely, data generated by TA are to be used to compare schools, departments and, ultimately, teacher effectiveness. In the absence of national tests, or an enormously expensive national moderation exercise, the system has to rely on the professionalism of teachers and their ability to make honest and dependable judgements of pupil attainment (see Lambert, 1995). Regular inspections by OFSTED will provide, over time, some measure of national standards; as will non-mandatory test material to be produced by SCAA, but how, apart from the guidance from SCAA or the GA (see Butt *et al*, 1995), can teachers inform themselves of the expectations set out by the geography Level Descriptions?

In pondering this question, it appears that there is no ready-made or easy answer. The most exciting and productive response lies in the creation of **portfolios**, either (as some have tried) in the form of individual pupil portfolios or as departmental 'level' portfolios. The former has the advantage of including the pupil in the process of selecting work and assessing its quality. Both, however, fulfil the eventual requirement that the geography National Curriculum levels are 'negotiated' and 'brought alive' by pupils' work.

Pupil portfolios: Most secondary school pupils' work is collected in their exercise book or file. This constitutes an important document representing the accumulation of much of the pupil's achievements. It is relatively indiscriminate in the sense that it contains a totality of written work; good and bad, finished and unfinished, refined and unrefined. It is therefore somewhat indigestible on inspection, say, by other teachers or parents. The *portfolio* is an abstraction from this. Pupils, with some guidance, can select a small number of pieces once a term or twice a year to transfer into their portfolio. Leaving aside entirely superable practical issues (how is the work copied or cut?) and assuming that pupils select their best work, the portfolio becomes a digestible representation of what the pupil can do. It is important that the portfolio does not become unwieldy, and after a certain point (five or six pieces of work has been suggested) it should grow no more: thus each new selection of work requires an existing item to be discarded. Nevertheless, the portfolio will represent the pupil's 'best shot' and the progress being made (see also Chapter 17).

The portfolio, in the form briefly described here, becomes an important part of the evidential base for TA. Moreover, it becomes the crucial tool in a geography department's internal discussions on standards and a very useful document to have at hand at parents' consultation meetings. Conceivably the portfolio's main potential lies in its ability to encourage pupils to *engage meaningfully* in the assessment process – the sign of a truly formative assessment regime. The lessons designated as 'portfolio periods' naturally link with school profiling and Record of Achievement activities, providing a sound context for pupils to identify their own strengths, weaknesses and targets.

Departmental portfolios: The management of individual pupil portfolios is difficult, particularly during the early stages of such a regime when the pupils themselves are not clear about what to do or need convincing of its purpose. As an alternative teachers may compile a departmental portfolio. This could be a compilation of examples of pupils' work across a range of topics sorted according to what the members of the department consider to be different levels. It could result in three volumes of extracts of pupils' work of, say, levels 3, 5 and 7. Each volume should contain just enough work to be indicative of the *basis for teachers' 'level' judgements* and should be refined and revised annually as experience grows and as opportunities to share 'level judgements' with colleagues arise.

The departmental portfolio could become the most important piece of departmental documentation in exemplifying schemes of work, standards of attainment and departmental 'level' judgements. It can become an induction tool for new teachers, the basis of departmental INSET and evidence to use at parent evenings.

INSET ideas

1. Departmental marking policy

a. Carry out an audit of the formal and informal assessment methods which have been used with, say, a particular teaching group over the years.

b. To what extent does one form of assessment dominate? To what use are the results from each assessment opportunity put?

c. To what extent are assessments communicated effectively to pupils?

d. To what extent is assessment practice (including marking) 'legible', (i.e. commonly understood) across the department?

e. What implications arise from discussing points a-e for departmental assessment policy?

2. Understanding Level Descriptions

Teachers need a shared understanding of Level Descriptions before they can be used effectively. In order to reach this shared understanding and exercise their professional judgement, the following method of analysis may provide a useful starting point. However, it must be realised that this dissection is just a starting point – we need to be clear that Level Descriptions should not be broken down into tick lists against which the daily performance of children is monitored. This exercise is an aid to initial understanding, not a method by which Level Descriptions will be used for assessment purposes in the classroom.

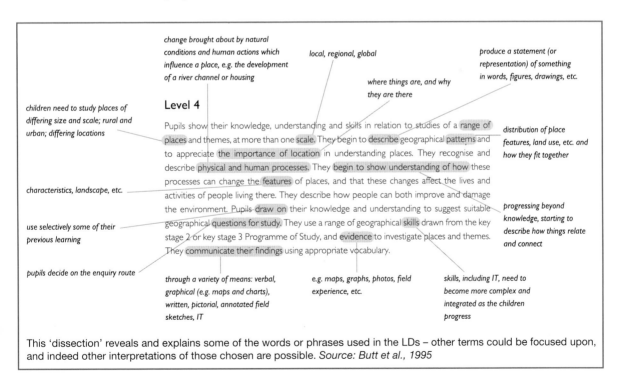

change brought about by natural conditions and human actions which influence a place, e.g. the development of a river channel or housing

local, regional, global

produce a statement (or representation) of something in words, figures, drawings, etc.

children need to study places of differing size and scale; rural and urban; differing locations

where things are, and why they are there

Level 4

Pupils show their knowledge, understanding and skills in relation to studies of a range of places and themes, at more than one scale. They begin to describe geographical patterns and to appreciate the importance of location in understanding places. They recognise and describe physical and human processes. They begin to show understanding of how these processes can change the features of places, and that these changes affect the lives and activities of people living there. They describe how people can both improve and damage the environment. Pupils draw on their knowledge and understanding to suggest suitable geographical questions for study. They use a range of geographical skills drawn from the key stage 2 or key stage 3 Programme of Study, and evidence to investigate places and themes. They communicate their findings using appropriate vocabulary.

distribution of place features, land use, etc. and how they fit together

characteristics, landscape, etc.

use selectively some of their previous learning

progressing beyond knowledge, starting to describe how things relate and connect

pupils decide on the enquiry route

through a variety of means: verbal, graphical (e.g. maps and charts), written, pictorial, annotated field sketches, IT

e.g. maps, graphs, photos, field experience, etc.

skills, including IT, need to become more complex and integrated as the children progress

This 'dissection' reveals and explains some of the words or phrases used in the LDs – other terms could be focused upon, and indeed other interpretations of those chosen are possible. *Source: Butt et al., 1995*

a. Try the above activity with the descriptions for Levels 3 and 5.

b. Identify, in your own terms, progression between the Levels.

3. Teacher assessment in the planning cycle

Examine the diagram below:

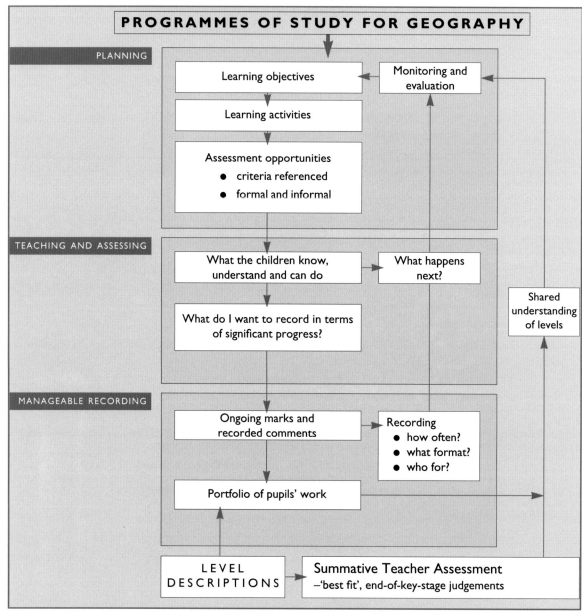

PROGRAMMES OF STUDY FOR GEOGRAPHY

PLANNING

Learning objectives

Monitoring and evaluation

Learning activities

Assessment opportunities
- criteria referenced
- formal and informal

TEACHING AND ASSESSING

What the children know, understand and can do

What happens next?

What do I want to record in terms of significant progress?

Shared understanding of levels

MANAGEABLE RECORDING

Ongoing marks and recorded comments

Recording
- how often?
- what format?
- who for?

Portfolio of pupils' work

LEVEL DESCRIPTIONS

Summative Teacher Assessment
–'best fit', end-of-key-stage judgements

Source: Butt et al, 1995

a. Discuss how closely the process depicted on the diagram represents practices in your department.

b. List and justify any divergences from the 'ideal' shown in the diagram.

c. Can you identify ways of using Level Descriptions in the teaching and learning process without some form of portfolio development?

d. Identify the potential benefits and costs of introducing and/or administering a system of either (i) pupil portfolios, or (ii) departmental portfolios, as part of your department's assessment practice.

References

Balderstone, D. & Lambert, D. (1992) *Assessment Matters.*
The Geographical Association.

Butt, G., Lambert, D. & Telfer, S. (1995) *Assessment Works.*
The Geographical Association.

Collarbone, P. (1983) 'What do your marks mean?', *ILEA Geography Bulletin,* 17.

Daugherty, R. (1995) *National Curriculum Assessment: A Review of Policy 1987-1994.*
Falmer Press.

Daugherty, R. & Lambert, D. (1994) 'Teacher assessment and geography in the
National Curriculum', *Geography,* 79, 4, pp. 339-349.

Equal Opportunities Commission (1987) 'National testing and equal opportunities',
Appendix F in *Task Group on Assessment and Testing: A Report.* DES/WO.

Gardner, H. (1983) *Frames of Mind.* Basic Books.

Gipps, C. (1995) *Beyond Testing: Towards a Theory of Educational Assessment.*
Falmer Press.

Hall, D. (1976) *Geography and the Geography Teacher.* George Allen and Unwin.

Hannon, P. & McNally, J. (1986) 'Children's understanding and cultural factors
in reading test performance', *Educational Review,* 38, 3, pp. 237-246.

Hargreaves, D. (1984) *Improving Secondary Schools.* ILEA.

Harlen, W., Gipps, C., Broadfoot, P. & Nuttall, D. (1992) 'Assessment and the
improvement of education', in Moon, B. and Shelton Mayes, A. (eds)
Teaching and Learning in the Secondary School, Routledge, pp. 273-286.

Lambert, D. (1990) *Geography Assessment.* Cambridge University Press.

Lambert, D. (1995) 'Assessing pupil attainment', in Kent, A., Lambert, D., Naish, M.
& Slater, F. (eds) *Geography in Education: Viewpoints on Teaching and Learning.*
Cambridge University Press.

National Commission on Education (1993) *Learning to Succeed: A Radical Look at
Education Today and a Strategy for the Future.* Heinemann.

SCAA (1995) *Consistency in Teacher Assessment: Guidance in Schools.*

Slater, F. (1989) *Language and Learning in Geography.* Routledge.

Chapter 17

Practical approaches to assessment, record-keeping and reporting

KEITH GRIMWADE

Introduction

Assessment, recording and reporting are different but related activities. In essence, assessment is *collecting* evidence about pupils' progress; recording is setting out that evidence so that it is easy to interpret; and reporting is communicating that evidence to one of a number of potential audiences (Figure 1). This chapter considers practical approaches to each of these activities, and the links between them.

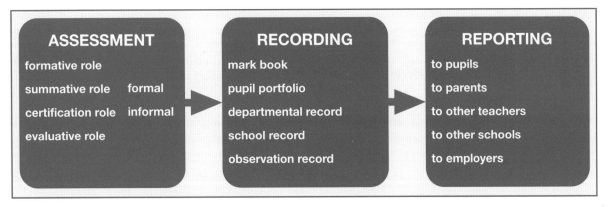

Figure 1: *Assessment, recording and reporting*

Assessment

General assessment issues and formal assessment strategies are considered in Chapter 16 of this book, so the emphasis here is on the less formal day-to-day assessment of classwork and homework.

MARKING

With regard to written work, the importance of marking cannot be underestimated. Marking is direct communication with the pupil and in a large class, where individual attention is inevitably difficult to give, it may be the only guaranteed feedback the pupil has. It is worth thinking back to your own school days and to how the marks/comments

Assessment styles must match teaching styles; practical work in class needs practical assessment

Photo: **John Freeman**

your teachers gave you affected your perceptions of your ability, the subject and the teacher. I suspect that, from time to time, we were elated, or disappointed, or relieved; but that we were always interested!

There are, of course, many ways in which a pupil's work can be marked but the most important consideration is that the pupils understand the mark they have been given. '7 out of 10', 'B', or 'good work' are of limited value unless the pupils know what they could have done to achieve '10 out of 10', 'A', or 'very good work'. This presents geography teachers with a challenge because many of us teach 200 or more pupils a week and it is simply not possible to provide them all with a detailed analysis of their work and individual targets for improvement on a monthly, let alone a weekly basis. More informal methods of grading using faces can be very effective with younger pupils!

A school marking policy, or at the very least a departmental marking policy, helps because pupils only have to understand one marking system. They also get a more consistent message from subject to subject and teacher to teacher: these reasons help pupils to get a 'fix' on the standard, and their own progress. Extracts from the department's marking policy could be glued in the back of each pupil's book so that they can check, for example, what an 'A' means.

Some general points to consider in relation to marking policies are:

- **Pupil groupings** Take, for example, a mixed-ability group where the pupils have been set the same task. Marking 'out of ten' against an absolute standard is going to be de-motivating for the less able, especially if the experience is repeated week after week. One way round this is to set pupils different tasks, i.e. strategies for differentiation have a direct impact on strategies for assessment. A second way is to 'sweeten the pill' with an additional comment or grade about effort, as opposed to attainment. A third strategy is to give all pupils the same mark or grade for the first piece of work they do and then to judge their next piece of work against this standard, e.g. if it is better than the first piece they get a higher mark or grade. Their third piece of work is judged against their second, and so on. This is not as cumbersome a procedure as perhaps it sounds; it generates a great deal of pupil interest and it makes the individual's progress very much the focus for assessment.

- **The nature of the task** For example, a 'mark out of ten' is appropriate for questions with right or wrong answers, such as grid references, but not for questions that invite pupils to express their opinions. Marking may have a specific focus for a specific item of work.

- **The reason for marking** Comments may be appropriate for day-to-day marking, for example, but a numerical mark may be required if the piece of classwork/homework is to contribute towards a more formal assessment.

It is also important to assess non-written work, e.g. contributions to discussions or practical activities such as the drawing of a field sketch/use of a piece of equipment. This can be done systematically; by awarding a mark or grade for a class presentation or by assessing a pupil's work outside the classroom against a range of criteria. However, much of your assessment of non-written work is opportunistic, such as when a pupil impresses you with the answer to a question in a class discussion, or when you observe a pupil getting successfully involved with a fieldwork activity. The important thing here is to draw attention to such opportunities in your marking policy and to make sure that there is a system for recording such observations (see 'Recording' below).

Marking is also an opportunity for pupils to communicate with you. It is very important to involve them in the assessment process by talking to them about their marks. Their written work may not be a true reflection of their understanding of a topic.

Some National Record of Achievement (NRA) systems require pupils to write an explanatory statement about the work they are handing in – what they thought of it and how well they have done (see Figure 2). However, it is perfectly adequate, and highly informative, for pupils to write a sentence or two 'to the teacher' in their exercise book before they hand in any piece of work. Such comments can help you to make judgements and generate a meaningful dialogue.

PROJECT REPORT SHEET

Name: _____ Title: _____

Can you please fill in the 'pupil's assessment' column on the sheet below. The letter grade should be from **A** to **E**. **C** would be an average mark, **A** excellent and **E** very poor. Be as honest and realistic as you can.

	PUPIL'S ASSESSMENT		STAFF ASSESSMENT	
	A to E grade	Comment	A to E grade	Comment
CONTENT (written work, maps, diagrams)				
PRESENTATION (neatness and quality of diagrams)				
ORGANISATION (logical sequence of work)				
EFFORT (amount of classwork and homework done)				
FINISHED PRODUCT (overall result)				
ADDITIONAL NOTES				

Figure 2: *Student report sheet*

Recording

Pupil records may be kept in different places, and in different formats; these are considered below.

THE MARK BOOK
The mark book, with a little creativity, can become an important record of pupils' work and progress. It needs to be organised to fit in with the school's system of recording but, as long as it enables departmental and academic records to be completed, and reports to be written, it can be unique to each teacher. Consequently, the example in Figure 3 is no more than an illustration of what could be done: there are as many alternatives as there are teachers.

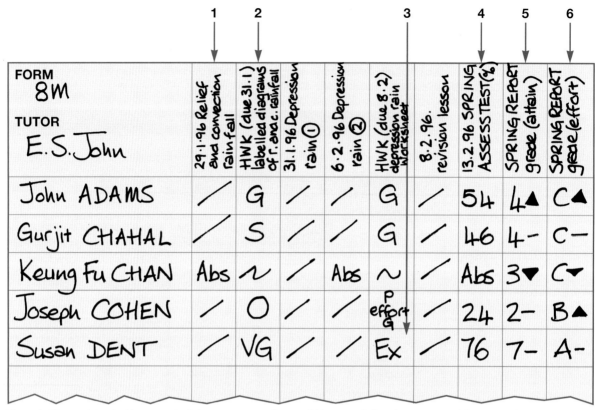

FORM 8M TUTOR E.S.John	29.1.96 Relief and convection rainfall	HWK (due 31.1) labelled diagrams of r. and c. rainfall	31.1.96 Depression rain ①	6.2.96 Depression rain ②	HWK (due 8.2) depression rain worksheet	8.2.96 revision lesson	13.2.96 SPRING ASSESS TEST(%)	SPRING REPORT grade (attain)	SPRING REPORT grade (effort)
John ADAMS	✓	G	✓	✓	G	✓	54	4▲	C▲
Gurjit CHAHAL	✓	S	✓	✓	G	✓	46	4–	C–
Keung Fu CHAN	Abs	∿	✓	Abs	∿	✓	Abs	3▼	C▼
Joseph COHEN	✓	O	✓	✓	P effort G	✓	24	2–	B▲
Susan DENT	✓	VG	✓	✓	Ex	✓	76	7–	A–

Figure 3: The mark book. Note: much of the assessment data could be stored directly on a spreadsheet as well as in the mark book.

The main points to be made about Figure 3 are as follows (the numbers referred to are those shown on the figure):

1. The mark book is the record of work experienced by the pupils. At a glance you can see who has missed what, and if they subsequently catch up this can be noted.

2. This column makes it easy to keep track of homework. A set of symbols has been used: the letters here refer to the absolute quality of the work (VG = very good, G = good, S = satisfactory; a circle indicates that the homework was not handed in on time (when it is it can be completed and dated); and the wavy line indicates that the pupil was absent when the homework was set.

3. Sometimes a pupil makes a good effort but the absolute standard of their work is poor. Here, symbols have been used to record this fact.

4. This column has been used to record the results of a formal assessment test, but these could be recorded on a different page.

5-6. These columns record attainment and effort grades for the spring term report, using the school's reporting system. The annotations are for the teacher's benefit, indicating whether each pupil's grade has gone up (▲), down (▼) or stayed the same (–).

The system can be extended to indicate pupil weaknesses, e.g. in spelling, use of map scales and directions, use of sentences, use of headings and titles.

THE PUPIL PORTFOLIO

The pupil portfolio is, most importantly, the place where exemplar pieces of work are kept. It is also where formal assessment tasks/tests, pupil self-evaluation sheets, copies of reports and *ad hoc* notes (e.g. to record a good contribution to a class discussion), can be filed. In this way the portfolio becomes an in-depth record of pupil achievement. The pupil should be in charge of the portfolio and should take the lead in selecting work for it. One way of solving the dilemma of how to get their best work from their exercise book into the portfolio is for them to record the title, date, mark/grade and teacher comment on a proforma; there is then no need to remove or photocopy the work at all (it is in their exercise book for reference, if necessary). The pupil could explain the reasons for their selection(s) and this is an easy and successful way of involving them in the assessment process (see also Chapter 16).

DEPARTMENTAL AND SCHOOL RECORDS

It may be useful for quick reference and other purposes (such as setting and discussing estimated grades) to keep a separate departmental record of key data such as test percentages and attainment and effort grades. This data can be stored in a workbook then, periodically, put into a database or spreadsheet, depending on the purpose and complexity of the record.

It is almost certain that the school will keep a central record of key data and, if this is computerised, it may be possible to access this source instead of keeping a separate departmental record. The pupil's school file will also contain information about progress in geography, even if it is only a copy of the school report. The school file is where any confidential information should be stored; there are strict guidelines for the recording of such information and it is very important that the school's policy is adhered to.

OBSERVATION RECORD

This is your impression of the pupils as they are at work inside as well as outside the classroom, and it includes the instances discussed above of pupils performing well in discussion work or fieldwork activities. Much of this information is inevitably going to be stored in your head and it is very much in the spirit of the National Curriculum that such knowledge can be used to help judge pupils against the Level Descriptions at the end of key stage 3. However, pupils rarely have the same teacher for the whole of their secondary school career – and many of them attend more than one school – so it seems sensible to record some of these observations in the pupil portfolio, as has already been suggested. If the note is addressed to the pupil, e.g. 'Anwar, you made a really good contribution to today's debate and showed an excellent understanding of the locational requirements of out-of-town superstores – well done!', they will be delighted to file it themselves! All geography teachers should perhaps set themselves the target of giving all pupils this sort of feedback once every half term.

Reporting

You are often required to report on pupils to a number of different audiences (Figure 1). Indeed, on most occasions you find yourself reporting to more than one audience simultaneously and this is just one of the reasons why reporting is such a challenging part of your role. For example:

- At key stage 3, although NRA-style reporting is increasingly common, most reports are still written to parents – but you want to get to the pupil as well.
- At GCSE the NRA is the main method of reporting. The logging sheet, the on-going record of pupil progress (Figure 3), is invariably written to the pupil but it usually goes home to the parent as the school report.
- At A level reports tend to be longer and contain more subject-specific information but they are also used by sixth-form tutors to compile references for Higher Education and employment.

Geographers inevitably find themselves operating within the framework of the school's reporting system. However, certain general points are applicable to all report writing:

- If possible print the details of the course on the back of the report.
- **Avoid specialist vocabulary** – both geographical and educational. Reports must be intelligible to everyone likely to read them: it is easy to forget that very few will understand the terms that are part of our professional language.
- However, do **include references to important aspects of geography** that are part of everyday language and experience, e.g. skills such as map work and atlas work; the use of IT; details of any fieldwork done; themes/issues such as rivers and the environment; and places such as the countries selected for study. These details will give a geographical flavour to the report and will help to establish the subject's identity in the eyes of the parents.
- **Consider the whole child** – are they enthusiastic? reliable? helpful? Commenting on qualities such as these shows that you know who you are talking about; as well as being important qualities in their own right.
- **Praise achievement/progress** There are few pupils about whom nothing positive can be said and commenting on the good creates a sense of fairness which means that comments on the bad – if applicable – are likely to be taken more seriously.
- **Do not avoid criticism** but make it constructive, i.e. as well as reporting on what has gone wrong, make suggestions as to how things can be put right.
- **Indicate future prospects** and, if there is space, refer to specific targets.
- **Be tactful;** never write anything that you would not say to the pupil's/parent's face.
- Use a colleague (preferably from another department) as a **quality control check**. They will be able to judge the balance you have achieved between subject-specific and pupil-specific comments, and whether or not the report is appropriate for its intended audience.

Figure 4 is a transcript of a Year 10 National Record of Achievement logging sheet which illustrates many of the above points. It has been addressed to the pupil and written with the parent(s) in mind – it forms part of the pupil's mid-year report which they take home.

It is worth emphasising the contribution geographers can make to references for post-16 education, Higher Education and employment. Occasionally you may be asked by a student to write direct to an employer but usually you will supply information to a member of the pastoral team who compiles the reference – either way there is much that you can say. For example, GCSE and A level geographers have to be numerate and literate; they will have interpreted and presented a wide range of statistical data; they will have carried out investigations and written reports; they will have worked as part of a team on fieldwork tasks; and they will probably have had experience of IT in an applied context. Also, they will have learnt about industry, both in this country and abroad, with examples ranging from how a single factory is organised to the structure of transnational corporations; you should not underestimate the interest employers have in such knowledge.

Conclusion

The main purpose of assessment, recording and reporting is to support the learning process. It is vital, therefore, that the links between each of these activities are carefully thought out. For example, for a report to have a geographical flavour it is necessary to record information about important aspects of the subject such as map work and place study, and so they must be assessed. The best way to plan for assessment, recording and reporting is to ask yourself five key questions:

- Why am I assessing?
- What am I assessing?

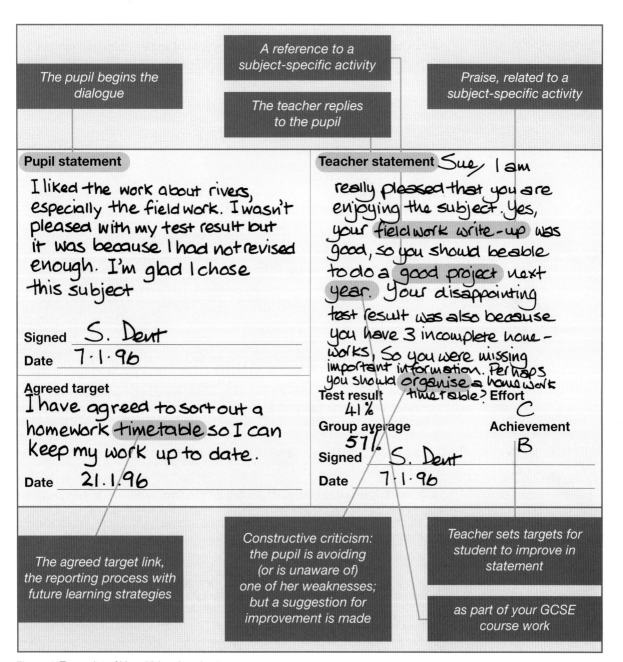

Figure 4: *Transcript of Year 10 logging sheet*

- Have I chosen an appropriate way of recording the results of my assessment?
- How can I best communicate these results?
- Is there a clear link between my assessment, and my recording and reporting of that assessment?

This approach will ensure that judgements – whether formative or summative – are based on reliable and clear evidence and this will benefit all who have an interest in the assessment, recording and reporting process; principally it will benefit your pupils.

Chapter 18

Assessment at key stage 3

KEITH GRIMWADE

Introduction

This chapter is about assessment tasks and tests at key stage 3, as distinct from the day-to-day assessment of classwork and homework. The purpose of such tasks and tests has traditionally been formative and, to a lesser extent, summative (see Chapter 17). However, statutory teacher assessment at the end of the key stage against the eight Level Descriptions in the geography National Curriculum has enhanced the summative role and added an evaluative role. This presents the geography teacher with a new and significant responsibility. However, as long as the principles of good assessment are followed throughout the key stage there should be sufficient evidence for informed and accurate judgements at the end of Year 9. It is these principles which are discussed below.

There are many different types of assessment and which to choose depends on your aims and objectives (i.e. *why* you are assessing and *what* you are assessing). For example, if you want to check pupils' knowledge of geographical vocabulary, a factual recall test is an appropriate strategy, e.g. ten questions read out at the start of a lesson to do with river features, such as 'What is a meander?' and 'What name is given to the place where a river begins?'. If you want to assess pupils' understanding of concepts, a data-response task is appropriate, for example, you could provide them with a map showing the distribution of nuclear power stations in the UK and ask them to explain it. If you want to assess map drawing skills, for which a time constraint is inappropriate, pupils could complete a task over the course of two or three lessons, e.g. constructing a choropleth (shading) map to show population density.

An assessment can combine different aims and meet different objectives. For example, an end-of-year test could be formative in that it points the way forward for the following year, and summative in that it records the pupil's achievement to date; and it could test knowledge, understanding and skills. However, as a general rule, do not ask too much of your assessment. For example, you cannot assess a whole year's work in a one-hour test. You could set a single question about most of the topics studied but it would be better to set five or six questions about a limited number of topics so that the pupil has more than one chance to demonstrate what he/she knows and can do, and so that you can judge the depth of his/her knowledge, understanding or ability.

Carefully graded in-school assessments help to prepare students for public examinations

Photo: **George Turnbull, AEB**

Preparation of assessments

All assessments require careful preparation, they serve an important purpose and are rightly perceived by pupils as being a special type of activity. Although we often wish that our pupils would take assessments more seriously, we must remember that many pupils become anxious about even the shortest of tests. Also, a poorly written assessment test/task can demoralise pupils unnecessarily, leaving the teacher with a difficult problem. Of course, at key stage 3 there are no 'past papers' put together by the examination boards to help with preparation and even published materials usually have to be selected and adapted to the scheme of work you are following. It is very important, therefore, that a range of issues (in addition to the ones about aims and objectives discussed above) is considered before an assessment is given:

- **Will it allow all pupils to show what they can do?** An assessment must enable weaker pupils to demonstrate their achievements and, at the same time, allow the more-able to show how they have progressed. Various strategies can be adopted. The most common is 'stepped tasks', i.e. tasks with an incline of difficulty so that all pupils can answer some of the questions but only the most able can attempt all of them (Figure 1).

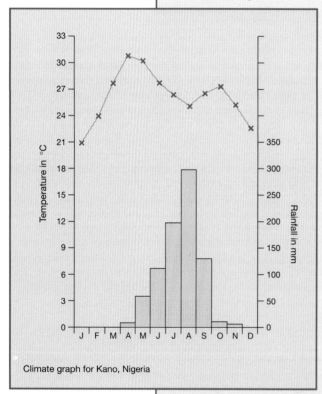

Focus

The savanna ecosystem, unit 10 of the key stage 3 Programme of Study

Climate graph for Kano, Nigeria

Question

Look at the climate graph for the Nigerian town of Kano, which is in the African savanna.

a) What is the temperature in April? (1 mark)
b) What is the rainfall in August? (1 mark)
c) What is the main type of vegetation in the African savanna? (1 mark)
d) Which of these savanna animals are carnivores: lion, wildebeest, hyena, elephant? (2 marks)
e) Describe, with examples, two ways in which trees in the savanna cope with the dry season. (4 marks)
f) Describe and explain why fires, started naturally by lightning, are important to the savanna ecosystem. (6 marks)

Commentary

- Parts a) and b) are simple data-response questions which most, if not all, pupils should be able to answer.
- Parts c) and d) are testing basic knowledge of the African savanna.
- Part e) requires a more detailed knowledge of the savanna ecosystem and, to an extent, a degree of understanding.
- Part f) can be answered at different levels of response (see Figure 3) but for full marks a detailed knowledge and understanding of the savanna ecosystem is required.

Figure 1: A climate graph and related stepped tasks

An alternative strategy is 'tiered papers', i.e. setting a harder and an easier assessment on the same topic. It is less common because so much geography at key stage 3 is taught in mixed ability groups and there is an understandable inclination to set the same assessment for all pupils. However, different assessments could be used in the same classroom and, as departments gain experience of 'differentiation by resource' as a teaching strategy (and of tiered papers at GCSE), such an approach may become more common and is certainly worth considering.

Another approach is to set a common task which allows differentiation by outcome (Figure 2).

Introduction

As part of a unit of work about farming (our chosen economic activity, unit 13 of the key stage 3 PoS) pupils visited an arable farm for a morning. They had a worksheet to complete while they were being taken round by the farmer and they had prepared questions to ask him. Back at school the main facts about the farm were summarised on the blackboard so that those who had problems writing down all that the farmer said had enough information with which to tackle the assessment task. Pupils were given one 60-minute lesson and a homework to complete the assessment.

The task

Pupils were given the following instructions:

'Your task is to design a poster about Worlick Farm. You can use words, pictures, maps, tables and graphs. Include information about:

- where the farm is;
- what the land is like;
- what the farmer grows, and why;
- who works there;
- farm machinery;
- inputs, outputs and processes;
- how the farm has changed in the last 50 years.

Make your poster as attractive as possible.'

The outcome

The two posters presented here are a very good effort on the part of two pupils, who were evidently motivated by the visit. However, the posters also demonstrate different levels of achievement. For example, pupil one has located the farm and has tried to explain why the crops were grown, whereas pupil two has not attempted these parts of the task. Also pupil one has presented crop acreage as a bar chart whereas pupil two has simply listed this information in a table.

Pupil 1

Pupil 2

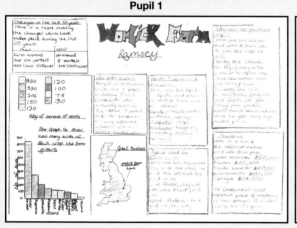

This task could be used for formative and summative assessment. With regard to formative assessment, pupil one could be praised for a high standard of work but also given opportunities to explore appropriate scales of map for showing different locations/distributions. Pupil two can also be praised (it is interesting to note that this pupil has included a sketch of the reservoir – his own observation – which reflects, perhaps, a personal interest) but could be given opportunities to present information on maps and as graphs, and to attempt explanations. With regard to summative assessment, a portfolio of pieces of work like these, together with more formal assessment tests, should provide sufficient evidence for pupils to be judged against the end-of-key-stage Level Descriptions.

Figure 2: Worlick Farm assessment task

■ **Will it be easy and reliable to mark?** This is important for a variety of reasons, not least of which is that assessments have to be marked very carefully and you do not want to make a rod for your own back! More significantly, it is important that you can judge an answer accurately and that the pupils can understand their mark – and why their friend got more or less than they did! Some questions lend themselves to 'point marking' while for others 'levels marking' makes it easier to identify a range of achievement and to reward good, but different, answers (Figure 3). Whatever type of mark scheme is used, it must be put together in advance: only by doing so will you discover any shortcomings.

---

a) 31 degrees Celsius: allow +/- 1 (1 mark)
b) 300 mm: allow +/- 10 (1 mark)
c) Grasses (1 mark)
d) Lion, hyena (1 mark each)
e) For example, storing water in their trunks, e.g. baobab (1 + 1), protecting their leaves with thorns, e.g. acacia (1 + 1)
f) **Level 3, 5 – 6 marks.** A very full, clear, description/explanation which mentions a range of relevant factors and the ways in which they are related, e.g. fire gets rid of dead vegetation which allows new shoots to grow through; many plants have adapted so that their seeds will only germinate if they are heated; ash from the burnt vegetation fertilises the soil which helps new growth. The frequency of fires (on average, once every four years) could also be mentioned.
Level 2, 3 – 4 marks. A full description mentioning most, but not all, of the factors listed above. Some understanding of the relationship between the various factors.
Level 1, 1 – 2 marks. A brief description which does little more than list one or two of the factors mentioned above.
0 marks. Nothing to credit.

Commentary
■ Parts a) – d) are appropriate for 'point marking' because the answers are either right or wrong.
■ Part e) lends itself to 'point marking' but a range of points are equally valid: credit can therefore be given up to the question maximum.
■ A good answer to part f) depends on a number of things, e.g. the pupil's knowledge and understanding; recognition of the ways in which the various factors are related; and the clarity of the description/explanation. 'Levels marking' allows an overall judgement to be made so that a range of achievement can be identified and so that good, but different, answers can be equally rewarded.

Figure 3: Mark scheme for the questions in Figure 1

■ Will it allow for successful recording and/or reporting? An assessment is wasted if the result is difficult to record and/or yields little information for reporting to pupils, parents and other teachers. Giving the assessment a clear structure helps. For example, if the question in Figure 1 was part of a longer test about ecosystems, parts a and b of all questions could be skills-based; parts c, d and e could be knowledge-based and part f could always require understanding/explanation. The test would, of course, give an overall mark but it would also be easy to work out sub-totals for skills, knowledge and understanding. This would draw attention to a pupil with a low overall mark but a good total for, say, knowledge; or to a pupil with a high overall mark but a bad total for, say, skills.

Interpreting assessment results

The interpretation of any assessment result is very important. Even a quick 'ten question test' at the start of a lesson raises the issue of what is a good mark, both in an absolute sense, and for the individual pupil. What you say about the result will affect the pupils' perception of their progress and you do not want them to get the wrong message. 'Seven out of ten' can be good for some and bad for others, and they should know! Some comment is therefore necessary if the assessment is to be of value. A summative assessment requires even more careful interpretation. Ideally, such assessments should be common to a whole department. The tasks should be agreed in advance and a mark scheme provided. The head of department should check a sample of scripts to make sure that everyone is marking to the same standard. The results for all classes should be put together and there must be discussion about what represents achievement at different levels. The result then needs to be communicated to the pupil, perhaps as part of the record of achievement process. It also needs to be put into context because no single assessment can define a pupils' level of achievement; however, it can be an important piece of evidence to put alongside other work in a portfolio, the sum total of which can be judged against the Level Descriptions at the end of key stage.

Frequency of assessment

A further consideration is how often the types of assessment described above should be carried out. I would argue that frequent, formal testing is undesirable and unnecessary: it could demotivate pupils and there are plenty of alternative types of assessment that can be built more naturally into a scheme of work. However, formal testing has an important summative role and it is also good practice for 16+ examinations: one, or perhaps two, such tests a year is about right. Other types of assessment can be used more frequently. However, if they are to get the attention they deserve from both teacher and pupil alike, no more than two or three per term seems appropriate. A unit of study presents many opportunities for assessment so it is necessary to select which of these opportunities is/are to be given a formal treatment. For example, a sequence of lessons about earthquakes presents assessment opportunities such as cartoon illustrations of the Richter/Mercalli scales; newspaper-style reports about a real earthquake; and disaster plans to cope with imaginary earthquakes: one of these could be selected and developed into a formal task/test.

It is important to plan for a variety of different types of assessment. This variety will contribute towards an interesting key stage 3 course; will help to ensure that the full range of geographical abilities is being assessed; and will give pupils who find a particular type of assessment (e.g. timed tests) difficult, but who can cope better with other types of assessment (e.g. a newspaper-style report), the opportunity to demonstrate what they know, understand and can do.

The original National Curriculum Order, with its 183 Statements of Attainment and its attendant tick-lists, made assessment a burden for teacher and pupil alike. The introduction of Level Descriptions in the revised Order means that this should no longer be the case. As long as the process is tackled methodically and seriously it is possible to incorporate into a scheme of work meaningful assessments which enhance the learning process, meet the statutory requirements and avoid 'death by a thousand tests'.

Chapter 19

GCSE syllabuses

KEITH ORRELL AND PAT WILSON

Introduction

Until the introduction of a National Curriculum, the very nature of geography in secondary schools was influenced, if not defined by, syllabuses for public examinations such as the General Certificate of Secondary Education (GCSE) which, after 1988, replaced the old GCE Ordinary Level and the Certificate of Secondary Education with a single examination for all 16 year olds. Now, with a National Curriculum for geography, the geography Order sets the style and content of geography for all pupils up to 14 years of age. The current geography Order is a product of the Dearing Review, a pragmatic attempt to make an earlier Order manageable rather than a defining statement.

The GCSE Subject Criteria for Geography, published by SCAA and distributed officially in March 1995, replaced earlier criteria from which the syllabuses launched in 1986 were developed. Syllabuses introduced in January 1996 for the 1996-98 examination cycle are based on these new criteria which now effectively define the goals of geographical education for students in key stage 4, and for that matter others wishing to gain a GCSE qualification. The eleven syllabuses available from the examining groups in England and Wales were finally approved in late 1995. In meeting the requirements, the groups have managed to produce syllabuses with some distinctive features and with varying degrees of imagination.

The subject criteria give clear directives on syllabus aims, assessment objectives, content, schemes of assessment and grade descriptions. The subject criteria document is worthy of attention in itself as a general description of what all 16 year olds with a qualification in the subject should share. It also spells out how they should be assessed, but some requirements are derived from two documents introduced in March 1995, namely the Regulations for The General Certificate of Secondary Education and the Mandatory Code of Practice which all examining groups have to follow. This chapter reviews the GCSE syllabuses which were launched in January 1996 in terms of how they reflect these various constraints. A complete summary of all eleven syllabuses appeared in *Teaching Geography*, April 1996.

Syllabus content

The criteria require that syllabuses include a balanced coverage of physical, human and environmental aspects of the subject. This should be taken to mean that there should be a balance in amounts of content to be studied, and, by implication, in the marks and

Increased standardisation between examination syllabuses has brought greater comparability to GCSE, AS and A level papers

Photo: **Sally and Richard Greenhill**

assessment time allocated to the three aspects. The inclusion of environmental geography, which is a strand running through the National Curriculum Programmes of Study, represents an added emphasis from the old criteria. However, no definition of what it involves is provided; this must be inferred from other detail.

Candidates must also study a range of themes at a variety of scales from local to global in different parts of the world and in different environments. The contexts for these studies must include the United Kingdom (with, for syllabuses developed for use in Wales, a focus on Wales) as well as the European Union and countries in various states of development. Add to this the need to study a variety of places and it becomes clear that the emphasis on places at GCSE level is similar to that at key stage 3.

Processes which influence spatial patterns and the character of places, the inter-dependence of places, and people/environment relationships are also prominent. Attention is drawn to the need to study the geographical aspects of issues, and of values and attitudes, but the stress is still on the role of values in a geographical context rather than on geography as a vehicle for values education.

A range of geographical enquiry skills are demanded which include, most significantly, the ability to identify geographical questions and issues and to establish appropriate sequences of enquiry. These are higher order abilities which are not easily developed or assessed. They require students to be responsible for making decisions about their work both in the classroom and the field.

The schemes of assessment, which are discussed more fully later, must give each of knowledge, understanding and skills a 30-40% weighting and include a geographical investigation supported by fieldwork There must also be opportunities for extended writing, graphic and practical work. These requirements have implications both for what is taught and how it is delivered in the classroom.

Clearly, the criteria document placed heavy demands on syllabus developers, despite its brevity. In essence, they had to deliver a geography based on the study of places and themes using enquiry- and issues-based approaches which at the same time provided a balanced coverage of physical, human and environmental aspects of the subject. How did they tackle this considerable challenge?

THEMES

All the syllabuses have a content based on a number of themes or topics which could be seen as teaching units, especially in the case of syllabuses with five themes which could fit nicely into the available five teaching terms. However, some of the syllabuses point out that there are other ways in which the content could be taught; for instance, a places or regional framework could be adopted into which the syllabus themes or topics are woven.

The number and content of themes varies enormously. SEG's Syllabus A has thirteen topics, although the choices available in the examination mean that candidates need only study and answer questions on six of them. Most of the syllabuses have four, five or six themes but there are considerable differences between them. For instance NEAB's Syllabus B has five systematic themes with an apparent overall emphasis on human geography:

**Physical geography   Economic activity   Transport and trade
Population and settlement   Environmental issues**

At first sight this structure contrasts with that of the MEG A Syllabus with its four themes suggesting a more integrated approach:

**People and the physical world   People and places to live
People and their needs   People and the environment**

However, close reading of the content of the syllabuses reveals that, in general terms, they cover the same ground but with differences in emphasis and format.

Other examples are the SEG Syllabus B which has Leisure, Recreation and Tourism as a major theme, and the WJEC syllabus in which the two themes – The Fragile World and The Interdependent World – suggest an interesting approach to physical, human and environmental aspects.

Some syllabuses make it possible to be selective in the coverage of key topics either by offering a choice of questions in the terminal examination or by rigorous pruning to the minimum required by the criteria.

The themes and unit titles in some syllabuses suggest a strong emphasis on an issues approach although it is questionable whether this is encouraged in the classroom by the style of coursework and examination questions.

PLACES

How have the examining groups dealt with the place demands of the criteria? Their responses range from a specification of the places to be studied (NEAB B) through to suggestions for appropriate case studies (as in ULEAC B), and the provision of a matrix to assist in the selection of places to be studied at different scales (MEG C, Bristol Project). This matrix (see Figure 1) serves a more general purpose in that it shows the range of place and scale requirements that all syllabuses from all examining groups have to meet.

Places \ Scale	Local	Regional	National	International	Global
UK	Case studies as appropriate to illustrate themes	Chosen region for coursework	Selected aspects of the UK or any of the four countries of the Union		
More economically developed country (not EU)	Case studies as appropriate to illustrate themes	Two contrasting regions in a MEDC	One MEDC		
Less economically developed country	Case studies as appropriate to illustrate themes	Two contrasting regions in a LEDC	One LEDC		
EU	Case studies as appropriate to illustrate themes	Two contrasting regions in the EU		Selected aspects	
World	Case studies as appropriate to illustrate themes				Selected patterns and issues

Figure 1: *Minimum place and scale requirements (Midland Examining Group)*

Schemes of assessment

The GCSE geography syllabuses developed to meet the 1985 geography criteria were very different from the 1996 suite mainly because the original criteria permitted a wide range of assessment strategies. They allowed, for instance, any number of common or differentiated papers. Coursework, too, could range from a single geographical enquiry covering a narrow spectrum of skills (worth 20%), to several pieces testing many assessment objectives and, in the case of one syllabus, worth 60% of the marks.

TIERED PAPERS

So what significant changes were introduced in 1996? The most obvious is the requirements for tiered (i.e. differentiated) papers and the restricted coursework weighting of 20-25%. This happened because, unlike the previous syllabuses, the 1996 suite had to conform to the regulatory documents referred to earlier as well as to the revised geography criteria.

Probably the most sweeping change was the introduction of two tiered papers covering grades G-C and D-A* and the ruling that a candidate can only be awarded a grade within the range prescribed for the papers taken. This means that examiners now have to write questions which match candidates' abilities and stretch the more able while providing for positive achievement by the less able.

All the syllabuses have two terminal examinations except MEG's Syllabus C which has one terminal paper worth 50% and a Decision Making Exercise (DME) completed earlier in the course. However, there are considerable variations in the way in which the examining groups have structured the terminal examinations. For example, some syllabuses have different amounts of time allocated to the tiers. In the case of NEAB's Syllabus C, there is a half-hour difference between the Foundation and Higher tier Paper 2, justified on the grounds that the abler candidates need more time to show their ability through extended writing. In several syllabuses, the Foundation tier paper employs an answer booklet which helps candidates to organise their responses. The allocation of time to individual papers, as well as the two together, also varies from WJEC's 3 hours for 80% of the marks to 3¾ hours on MEG/WJEC's Syllabus B (Avery Hill Project) Higher tier papers for 75% of the marks. MEG's modular Syllabus C also has 3¾ hours examining time but the DME is taken two months before the terminal examination.

THE STRUCTURE OF PAPERS

It is in the structure of the papers that variations between syllabuses are most apparent, the most obvious distinction being between those in which all the questions are compulsory and those which allow choice. There is a noticeable trend towards restricting the choice of questions within papers, probably in the cause of greater comparability and to ensure that the subject criteria are met. Indeed, in some syllabuses, like NEAB B, all questions are compulsory on both papers; others, such as ULEAC B, have only one compulsory paper, while in MEG A only the Foundation tier in Paper 1 has no choice of questions. Where choice is available it has been structured in such a way that all candidates must answer questions on physical, human and environmental geography.

THE STRUCTURE OF QUESTIONS

The sample assessment materials suggest that most examiners have chosen to write questions with built in inclines of difficulty while keeping in mind the need to cover the assessment objectives. Typically, questions begin with sub-questions requiring a brief response and lead up to a longer task requiring some extended writing. Resources and stimulus materials which are common to both tiers are also a feature. Clearly there are advantages in having as many similarities as possible between tiered papers, for instance in the rubric, in the question structure, focus and sequence, as well as in the data provided. Such common approaches to tiered paper design will assist teachers working with mixed ability groups. The task of setting sufficiently differentiated questions is a much bigger one, the scale of which is highlighted by the inclusion for the first time in the subject criteria of a grade description for the award of an A (see Figure 2). A comparison between this and the now familiar requirements for the award of an F soon shows how unrealistic common papers have become.

Candidates recall accurately detailed information about places and themes, across all scales, as required by the syllabus, and show detailed knowledge of location and geographical terminology.

Candidates understand thoroughly geographical ideas as specified in the syllabus and apply their understanding to analyses of unfamiliar contexts. They understand thoroughly the way in which a wide range of physical and human processes interact to influence the development of geographical patterns, the geographical characteristics of particular places, and the interdependence between places. They understand complex inter-relationships between people and the environment. They evaluate the significance and effects of attitudes and values of those involved in geographical issues and in decision-making about the use and management of environments.

Candidates undertake geographical enquiry, identifying relevant geographical questions, implementing an effective sequence of enquiry, collecting a range of appropriate evidence from a variety of primary and secondary sources, using effectively appropriate techniques, drawing selectively on geographical ideas to interpret the evidence, reaching substantiated conclusions, communicating clearly and effectively the outcomes, and evaluating the validity and limitations of the evidence and conclusions.

Figure 2: Grade description for an A award at GCSE (from GCSE Subject Criteria for Geography, SCAA, 1995)

DECISION MAKING EXERCISES

One of the most interesting developments is the appearance of a decision making exercise (DME) in several syllabuses. There is variation in approach but all involve DMEs either on an announced theme or issue from the syllabus. ULEAC B, MEG C and NEAB C include DMEs based on material sent out to centres in advance of the examination. Only MEG (syllabus C) announces the actual title of the DME in the first term of the examination cycle and tests it, under the modular rules, in the March preceding the terminal examination. All the other examining groups treat the DME as part of the terminal papers.

ASSESSING 'PLACE' KNOWLEDGE

In the revised criteria, building on the key stage 3 threads of skills, places and themes, 'place' in particular is given more emphasis now than it was before. Approaches to assessing knowledge of places differ widely. For example, the NEAB Syllabus B Paper 1 tests only the UK whereas for SEG's Syllabus A and B places are chosen by the centres and used as illustration within thematic questions. The MEG Syllabus C terminal paper is divided into two sections, one of which specifically examines knowledge of the EU, Less Economically Developed Countries (LEDCs) and More Economically Developed Countries (LEDCs) while the other assesses the syllabus themes.

Finally, it is noticeable that many syllabuses not only provide detailed skill requirements but also state which resource items, such as OS maps and satellite images, will appear in particular questions on the papers – a practice reminiscent of GCE Ordinary level papers set in the 1960s.

Coursework

Ten syllabuses have coursework components with the maximum weighting of 25%; only the WJEC syllabus uses the minimum weighting of 20%. The coursework packages vary from syllabus to syllabus; ULEAC's Syllabus A requires a single geographical enquiry, MEG's Syllabus C requires a mixture of enquiry plus a coursework unit or portfolio of items, and NEAB's Syllabus C requires a decision making enquiry to be completed either as a separate item or included in the fieldwork investigation.

The MEG/WJEC Syllabus B includes a fieldwork-based investigative study and a cross-unit task which is a synthesising and research exercise based on both physical and human aspects of the content. This approach exploits the opportunities provided by coursework to develop a variety of study skills.

All GCSE coursework is internally assessed and externally moderated. Section 4 of the *GCSE Code of Practice* sets out the arrangements for coursework assessment and moderation. When a syllabus is introduced or significantly changed, examining groups are expected to provide training on the setting and conduct of coursework and to take steps to ensure that any work not derived from exemplars produced by examining groups is acceptable There are significant differences in the ways in which the GCSE groups have interpreted these requirements. MEG, NEAB, ULEAC and WJEC all need prior approval of coursework tasks by board-appointed consultative or advisory moderators, while in addition NEAB requires, in 1997 only, a compulsory attendance by all centres at an introductory meeting followed by annual standardising meetings. SEG provides a support booklet of exemplar material, as do the other groups, but access to advisory moderators on request only.

Support from the groups

All GCSE groups provide a variety of reports, guidance booklets and feedback meetings. WJEC is actively involved in exam related research and produces research reports derived from the two syllabuses it is involved with, while MEG is committed to regular meetings between teachers and examiners and a supportive relationship between its consultative moderators and centres. For the syllabuses linked to the Avery Hill Project and the Bristol Project, support is also available to teachers through newsletters, annual conferences, INSET, advisory committees and local consortia activities.

Choosing a syllabus

In spite of the common criteria to which all of the GCSE syllabuses conform, there is enough variation between them for a genuine choice to be made, and that choice will have a crucial bearing on what students learn and how they are assessed. For these reasons, it is worth comparing all the syllabuses on offer before making a choice, and one way of doing this constructively is to look at them in relation to a set of questions, such as the following:

- Is the support provided by the examining group sufficient and useful?
- What guidance is provided on the conduct of coursework?
- What are the content requirements for coursework, if any?
- Is there a mechanism for coursework approval?
- What help is given on the choice of places to be studied?
- What is the policy on the use of OS maps, photographs and satellite images?
- How do the tiered papers differ in terms of their design and structure?
- How do the demands of the tiered papers differ?
- Are the stated goals or aims of the syllabus delivered by the content and the scheme of assessment?
- Is there scope in the syllabus for emerging issues to be built into the teaching programme?

And most important of all,

■ Will the syllabus lead to an interesting geographical experience and appropriate grades for the students?

Many schools and colleges tend to stay with one examining group if they are satisfied with both the service and the results they have received in the past. However, it is well worth looking at the opportunities available from all the examining groups, especially when new syllabuses are coming on stream. As mentioned earlier, there are significant variations between syllabuses so some may be more suitable than others for your particular needs, or those of your students.

Chapter 20

Assessment post-16

DAVID BURTENSHAW

Introduction

The changes to assessment at the post-16 level over the last decade have been on an unprecedented scale. This chapter focuses on the reformed exams for A and AS levels; the pre-vocational strand of post-16 is considered in Chapter 28. Starting with a brief look at the background to the reforms, this chapter then presents an outline of the common core, and moves on to examine two ways in which a tutor might prepare students for the A and AS level exams. The chapter concludes with a study of the impact of modular assessment with reference to a specific A level syllabus.

Reforming assessment at A and AS level

The introduction of AS levels in the 1980s was heralded as an innovative means of diversifying the traditional A level diet of three subjects, but, in assessment terms, it was a return to the past. The Government, through the agency of SEAC, imposed a very tight timetable on the examination boards for the development and approval of AS level syllabuses in 1987. It was decided that an AS level should be equivalent to half an A level, though experience has shown that in practice an AS level is closer to 60% of an A level. The twin pressures of a tight schedule and the need to deliver AS alongside A level forced the syllabus developers into a conservative framework (Burtenshaw, 1988a). The outcome was a series of syllabuses, including that for geography, which were conventional in both content and method of assessment. All too often AS exams were assessed as miniature A levels. Projects became guided field studies; two papers were collapsed into one.

In the 1990s, under pressure to redevelop the post-16 curriculum, the Government again allowed only a very short period for development, possibly to stifle more radical initiatives. The rules were also tightened: all syllabuses had to conform to a subject core of knowledge and ideas, and the proportions of different types of assessment to be used were clearly prescribed. The National Curriculum Council (NCC) and the Schools Examination and Assessment Council (SEAC), the two quangos which managed the curriculum and assessment, were merged to oversee other developments such as the revision of the National Curriculum, but the School Curriculum and Assessment Authority (SCAA), the new body, continued to manage the development of a subject core for A and AS level geography and also developed a Code of Practice which governs the assessment practices of all examination boards in England and Wales.

In addition the Dearing Review of the 16-19 Curriculum, due to report in April 1996, has introduced fresh uncertainties about the future of A levels into a wider debate over the nature and content of post-16 education. The merging of the Departments for Education and Employment into one reinforces some of the Dearing preliminary findings, which appeared to be searching for a merging of education and training, and is a further signal about the future role of education in our society. The examining boards are reacting in various ways; for instance, ULEAC's merger with BTEC announced in 1995. (One suggested name for the new Department, rejected when the acronym was realised, was Department for Education and Training!)

Not satisfied with a single policy initiative, the government has requested that SCAA's current (late 1995) tasks include the following:

1. To investigate ways of recognising the achievements of the most able, which could be the use of an A* or common S level paper based upon the common core.

2. To investigate standards over the past 20 years through an analysis of performance and grades, or through the administration of a standard test each year (did I hear General Studies?!), or a compendium of results over time.

3. To improve the use of Board Scrutinies as a measure of quality assurance.

4. To reduce the number of syllabuses.

5. To see if the demands of current modular examinations are the same as in the past and to look at the timetables and structures for modular syllabuses.

6. To address the concerns of those who want A levels to have more specific outcomes, akin to those of GNVQs.

7. To look at the issues surrounding the comparability of awarding when there are several options in one syllabus; the use of archive scripts in awarding procedures; changes in the grade review process; and the introduction of a synoptic assessment to all traditional syllabuses.

8. To monitor the Code of Practice.

The A/AS subject core for geography

The new A and AS level examinations will be assessing the subject core, although each examination board may choose to interpret the core differently and indeed assess it in a different manner. However, the rules devised for the exercise and the sheer speed of development will ensure that the different patterns of assessment have much more in common in future.

The **core** is common to A and AS levels and demands a range of knowledge, understanding and skills through the integrative study of:

(a) a theme which emphasises the interaction between people and their environment at different spatial scales and focuses on the relevant systems and responses, their outcomes, changes through time and consequent issues, responses and strategies;

(b) a chosen physical environment – its characteristics, processes (terrestrial, atmosphere, biotic and human), their interaction, consequent spatial outcomes and changes over time;

(c) a chosen human environment - its characteristics, processes (economic, social, political, cultural and physical), their interaction, consequent spatial outcomes and changes over time. (Common Core, 1993)

The fourth requirement is not common to both levels. A level students should:

undertake personal investigative work. This must be based on first-hand and secondary data.

AS students are *not* required to undertake this work as a part of the core, although they may do so as part of the non-core work. All geography syllabuses have to conform to the assessment objectives which are related to the four/three elements of the core. With regard to **Knowledge and Understanding**, students must be able to demonstrate an ability to select and recall accurately information about:

(i)   the location and geographical characteristics of the chosen environments, their external relationships and how they are changing;

(ii)   the physical and human processes responsible for the development of those characteristics, the interaction and relative importance of these processes;

(iii)   relevant concepts, principles and theories

(iv)   the complex interaction of people and their environments in space and over time.

Students must also be able to:

(v)   use a range of methods/techniques for the analysis and understanding of places and environments;

(vi)   select and apply geographical concepts, principles, theories and methods;

(vii)   identify, analyse and evaluate the relative importance of interrelationships, spatial outcomes and processes influencing both physical and human environments;

(viii) appreciate and analyse the role of values, perceptions and decision-making processes in geographical contexts;

(ix)   demonstrate a critical awareness of the potential and limitations of different forms of data and of the concepts and theories used by geographers.

In terms of **Skills** the student should show an ability in a geographical context to:

(i)   collect, record and interpret a variety of evidence from a range of first-hand (A level only) and/or secondary sources;

(ii)   select from a range of enquiry methodologies and apply them appropriately;

(iii)   organise, present and communicate information and data in a coherent manner;

(iv)   demonstrate skills of analysis, synthesis and critical evaluation;

(v)   produce a complete enquiry;

(vi)   use quantitative and qualitative investigative techniques (common core, 1993)

Obviously, assessment patterns will have to meet these objectives, but those already familiar with them will have noted that there cannot be many changes in terms of assessment methods as a result of these objectives. For some, particularly those teaching the pre-1996 Geography 16-19 Project, there are many familiar phrases in the core. However, the universal restriction to 20% of the proportion of an award to be gained from coursework will powerfully affect the nature of assessment of this same syllabus. In other cases it will be the compulsory nature of a project which will cause concern. Therefore the next part of this chapter will look at ways in which the tutor may focus upon assessment and assist students to obtain their desired grades.

Preparing for the project

Now that project work comprises 20% of an A level it is important to ensure that students are well prepared for this part of the assessment. Fortunately, it is rare today to find a tutor who behaves in the cavalier fashion of a decade or so ago, when it was almost de rigueur to state that 'no help has been given'. Report-writing skills are now part of all post-16 education and they have to be taught and encouraged. Table 1 attempts to outline the types of support demanded of an effective project tutor.

RESOURCE NEEDS	SUPPORT ROLE	STUDENT STAGE
Obtain the marks scheme from the Board	Field exercises Classroom activities Course breadth	Awareness of project demand
Textbook studies Examples of previous studies *Geographical Review* *Geographical Magazine* *Geography*	Consultant	Topic selection
Recipe books (with health warning)	Subject group consultant **Approval forms to Board**	Background reading Final decision **Prepare approval form**
	Confirm go ahead	Methodology
Library resources Census Other data sources	Check pilots of questionnaires Letters of authorisation	Information and data gathering Fieldwork
Recipe books Laboratory needs Calculators	Group consultations	Graphing, Mapping Laboratory work Data processing
Word processors (if permitted)	Consultant	First draft
		Revision and correction
	Despatch and/or assess	**Final draft/report**

Table 1: *Supporting project development – the tutor's tasks*

The prime role for the modern tutor is that of consultant – not an easy role to perform, given the pressure on staff time and the increasing numbers of students in any cohort. Obviously the tutoring needs to be shared by all the staff in the department, including part-timers, and it needs to be structured. Consultations are time-consuming, but the following ground rules may help:

1 have an appointments system. This encourages the student to prepare for the consultation.

2 consider holding group consultations with those undertaking similar topics or with similar problems. These can be arranged in normal class time.

3 consider establishing a voucher system; this system has been successfully used for assignments in higher education. It gives all students the same opportunities to 'purchase' access to a tutor and means the tutor has a record of visits.

The second role for the tutor is as a provider of resource backup at each stage in a project's development. Table 1 outlines some of these needs; the resources to fulfil them are already present in most geographical areas. However, there need to be 'health warnings' about the over-use of field technique manuals, which can stifle student initiative. From 1996 most examination boards will be operating a system of project approval so that no project can be submitted without prior signed approval. This represents a formalisation of the role which tutors already perform: that of ensuring that a candidate has a viable topic. The role of the tutor in reviewing student proposals

STAGE	QUESTIONS TO BE ASKED
TOPIC SELECTION	1. What am I interested in? 2. What classwork, reading, fieldwork has interested me? 3. Is this an issue, a problem or a question? 4. Does my home area offer the chance to study the issues, problem or question? 5. Is the topic too large? 6. Is it geographical?
APPROVAL FORM COMPLETION	1. Is the title correct? 2. Are my aims achievable? 3. Is my route to enquiry or method possible in the time? 4. Do I have any ideas about the primary and secondary date to be collected?
METHODOLOGY	1. What information is needed? 2. How will I gain information and where will I collect it? 3. What sampling methods will I use? 4. How will I process and analyse the data? 5. What recipe books should I consult?
DATA COLLECTION	1. What equipment do I need? 2. Have I piloted the questionnaire? 3. Where will data be collected? Are there sufficient sites? 4. When will the data be collected? Is the sample size correct? 5. Have I got permission to collect the data? Have I got a letter of support? 6. Have I obtained the secondary data?
DATA ANALYSIS	1. Have I tallied all the data? 2. Can the data be graphed? What do the graphs show? 3. Have I mapped the data? 4. What statistical techniques can be used to analyse the data? 5. Have I carried out the correct laboratory procedures?

Table 2: Questions to guide the student (after Burtenshaw (1988) and Hacking (1991))

is crucial to their success, but unapproved proposals are not uncommon, and tutors must be prepared to fulfil a counselling role when ideas are rejected.

Table 2 provides a 'project countdown' for the student together with a list of questions which should be answered as part of the preparation process. Experience at several centres has shown that requiring students to answer these questions, in either group or single consultation, does help them to obtain higher grades on project papers. No time scale is shown in the table because the timetable for each examination board varies. Nevertheless it is possible to work backwards from the submission date, allowing one month for writing up and a month for each of the activities shown in the five boxes of the table. Experience shows that from initial gestation, the best-prepared projects will take ten months, not including vacation time, to complete.

A further strategy is beginning to emerge in response to the role of projects in modular syllabuses. If a student is disappointed with the grade of a paper, it is possible to revisit the module with a view to improving the mark. Extending this strategy to the project advances submission of the project to the New Year examinations, so unsatisfactory grades may be revisited before the final, summer examination. This strategy has both strengths and weaknesses. The very able, and those who respond well to such pressure, will dispose of the work effectively. However, it must be approached with caution. Will the earlier start mean a narrower scope for projects, because students will not have studied a broad enough curriculum when they make a choice? Will a poor result become self-fulfilling, as many repeat A levels became in the past? Will repeating and upgrading a study take time away from preparation for the final modules, including the synoptic assessment?

Essay skills

The 1996 syllabus revisions, by assessing quality of English as part of the overall examination, will place even greater emphasis upon traditional essay-writing skills. While it is outside the scope of this chapter to discuss the merits and demerits of this policy, it is fair to point out that communication skills have always featured in post-16 assessment. The mark scheme being developed by one board for its project paper already contains 5% for communication skills. Under *Quality of language* the same board states 'In papers 1, 3, 4 and 5, continuous prose answers are required and the marks awarded will take into account the quality of language used by candidates' (AEB 1995). The new London Syllabus B (9211/8211), successor to the 16-19 Project, states

'Candidates will be assessed on their ability to organise and present information, data, ideas and arguments clearly and logically. Continuous prose answers are required in all end-of-module tests... the mark schemes will be written to include the assessment of the quality of language. In the essays on People and Environment Perspectives and the research-based essay on Global Futures, marks will be specifically designated for quality of language' (ULEAC, 1995).

Analyse	Provide a detailed description and explanation of a phenomenon or event. Often used with diagrams and photographs.
Assess	An evaluative command which implies that there are several explanations which need ranking in your own answer.
Briefly describe	Do just that – do not explain but make sure that the description is complete. Be concise and straightforward.
Classify	Place the facts, explanations or theories in groups which are obvious to the reader. Summarise the classification in the conclusion.
Compare	Find the common elements. Sometimes contrast is implied.
Contrast	What are the differences? Can be linked with compare as 'compare and contrast' so keep the two separate in an answer. Summarise both in a conclusion.
Consider the view that	Another evaluative request which can ask you to uphold a particular viewpoint. It may expect you to refute the opinion as well.
Discuss	Outline and explain a range of factors. There might be an element of evaluation in the question.
Describe	Do just that – do not explain.
Explain (or Account for)	Make sure that you give reasons or explanations. Do not merely describe.
How do	Another form of explanation.
How far	Evaluation again. Expect to agree or disagree giving your reasons.
Illustrate	Describe and explain with the use of examples.
Justify	Make sure that you give geographical reasons which may be based upon your values and attitudes.
To what extent	The classic evaluative command expecting several potential explanations to be assessed. You are expected to say which explanation you favour.
Why is it	A logical explanation is required.
With reference to	Make sure that the examples are real and convincing and not 'as in London' or 'as on the Northumberland coast'.
Annotate	Normally used in conjunction with stimulus material that needs completion. Make sure that there are labels to explain process or theory.

Table 3: Key command words and statements

The ULEAC statement highlights the importance of this issue by pointing out that the regulation applies to modules: with more A levels becoming modular, the time available for delivering language skills is now more constrained then ever.

To write sound geographical essays under examination conditions, students need to fulfil two conditions. First, they must *understand the subject matter*. Second, they must be able to *interpret the command words* used on the question papers: these do give the candidate guidance, and tutors can do much to improve their candidates' examination performance by making constant reference to them (see Table 3).

Modular syllabuses

The third, more difficult issue for the tutor is how to meet the demands placed upon candidates as a result of the current tidal wave of modular syllabuses. Until the recent revision there were two experimental modular syllabuses: Ridgeway, a modular version of London 210; and Wessex, a TVEI-led approach managed by AEB. More recently both Cambridge and NEAB have introduced modular syllabuses which are being modified

MODULE	UNIT	% OF MARK	EXAM LENGTH
AL1 The Challenge of Natural Environments 6211	1.1 Managing Landform Systems 1.2 People, Weather & Climate	15%	1.5 hours
AS1 Introducing Physical and Human Environments 6212	1.1 Managing Landform Systems 2.1 The Challenge of Urbanisation	40%	1.5 hours
AL2 Managing Human Environments 6213	2.1 The Challenge of Urbanisation 2.2 The Impact of Changing Economic Activities	15%	1.5 hours
AS2 People and Environment Perspectives 6214	3.1 Ecosystems & Human Activity	40%	1.75 hours
AL3 People-Environment Perspectives 6215	Either 3.1 Ecosystems & Human Activity or 3.2 Resource Management and *one* of 3.3 Pollution of Natural Environments 3.4 Managing Rural Environments 3.5 Managing Wilderness Areas 3.6 Sustainability and Growth	15%	1.5 hours
AS3 Individual Investigation 6218		20%	–
AL4 Global Futures 6216	One from 4.1 Hazard Management 4.2 Recreation & Tourism 4.3 Alternative Approaches to Development 4.4 Global & Regional Disparities 4.5 Health & Welfare 4.6 Environments & Political Systems	15%	1.5 hours
AL5 Synoptic Assessment: Decision Making Exercise 6217		20%	2.25 hours
AL6 Individual Study 6219		20%	–

Table 4: London 9211 Advanced and Advanced Supplementary level modular assessment structure

in the current round of submissions. Modular syllabuses have certainly become the norm now that the London board has embraced the concept for 9211, the inheritor of the 16-19 Project mantle.

If we examine the London 9211 syllabus we can see some of the issues which will have to be faced in preparing candidates for the new pattern of assessment. One rule common to all boards is that 30% of the externally assessed work must be part of the final, terminal assessment. Candidates may offer to be assessed in any manner. Some centres might prefer one terminal assessment, as at present, while others could opt for AL1 and AL2 in June of year 1, AL3 in January of year 2 and AL4 plus 5 in June of year 2 (see Table 4 for the total structure). It is also possible for students to be entered at the end of each year: this might be a preferred format to take account of maturation which is always greatest in the early part of the A level course, a factor noted on the Wessex syllabus.

It is up to the tutor to decide the ideal format for local circumstances and the pattern may vary from cohort to cohort to take account of group strengths and weaknesses. Do not necessarily follow the first advice heard from a guru; let your own department's pattern evolve. Flexibility is the keynote for the tutor as much as for the system of assessment. Flexibility should extend to the choice of extension units (options). Large departments may be able to offer choice by dividing a group or, in an ideal world, by giving the students some say in the choice of units; the latter pattern would be a better preparation for higher education.

Conclusion

At this time (late 1995), with syllabuses still awaiting approval, it is difficult to be certain of the nature of assessment at the 16-19 level after 1997. Much will depend on how Chief Examiners interpret the code of practice and the syllabuses. There are unlikely to be many surprises because a major benefit of the developments of the eighties – namely the route to enquiry – has survived unscathed. Examination boards will be producing their marks schemes, which will be increasingly sophisticated, and many will follow the lead provided by AEB in 1984 when it introduced component grading. There is no longer any excuse for not comprehending the system. I and my fellow Chief Examiners expect interaction with our clients!

On the debit side, the ideas being discussed by both the Dearing Committee reviewing the system, and the Flowers Committee on university entrance, might reduce the time for assessment and thus place new stresses on a system which already demands much of examiners in terms of their time and energies at the end of an increasingly crowded academic year.

References

AEB (1995) *Syllabuses for A and AS Geography.*

Burtenshaw, D. (1988a) 'Redefining the Core at 16-18: The British experience' in Gerber, R. & Lidstone, J. (eds) *Skills in Geographical Education Symposium '88* Proceedings, 2, pp. 477-86.

Burtenshaw, D. (1988b) 'Preparing for the Field Project Paper' in *Geography Review,* 1, 3, pp. 23-4.

Burtenshaw, D. (1991) 'Answering structured and open-ended essays' in *Geography Review Exam Special* March, pp. 18-19.

Burtenshaw, D. (1994) *Longman Revise Guide,* A level and AS level Geography, Longman (6th impression).

Hacking, E. (1991) 'Carrying out an Individual Project' in *Geography Review,* 4, 3, pp. 16-22.

SCAA (1995) *Code of Practice for GCE A and AS Examinations.*

ULEAC (1995) *Geography Syllabuses Advanced Supplementary and Advanced level.*

Section Five

Resources and their uses

SUMMARY OF CHAPTERS

This section looks at the wide range of resources, including IT and televisual resources, on offer to geography teachers and outlines how these resources may be evaluated and managed.

Resources are defined here as materials that are used for information, ideas and activities in the classroom and at home. Many would rightly argue that the teacher is often the best resource of all; this, however, is not the present focus!

Chapter 21

Evaluating and using resources

FRED MARTIN AND PATRICK BAILEY

Introduction

Geography is a resource-rich subject. Few if any other subjects taught in schools command and demand the use of such a rich variety of resources, in terms of both type of resource and range of geographical content. Failing to make full use of this range is to fail to take advantage of one of the key attractions that the subject has to offer. The aim of this chapter is to outline the range and sources of geographical resources, but also to raise issues relating to how these resources can be evaluated and used. Examples of resources are provided as illustration; they are not intended to form a definitive list of what is available.

National Curriculum background

Ideas about resources must be set in the context of the current geography National Curriculum Order. Although this now relates only to key stages 1-3, key stage 4 and more advanced courses should be seen as a continuum in terms of ideas, content, skills and the deployment of resources being used.

The present Order has removed much of the element of compulsion in terms of factual content and minutiae of other detail that was characteristic of the original Order. There are broad guidelines as to what must be taught as a minimum, though even within the Programmes of Study, there are options with regard to the choice of topics and places. The separation of Level Descriptions from Programmes of Study has created a situation in which any topic, skill and place can be taught in any order to any level. Syllabus decisions can now be made based on criteria devised by teachers. This is a responsibility and a freedom to be welcomed. Resources are a key to enabling these choices to be real.

Textbooks and their uses

Before the National Curriculum, there was a good deal of variety in what and how geography was taught up to key stage 4 – a variety reflected in the range of publications available. In response to the National Curriculum books became much more uniform in terms of content, and whilst the present Order enables the use of a diversity of resources, the cost of major new purchases means that the impact of the pre-Dearing Order on textbook resources is likely to remain in schools for some time.

Computers are a potentially valuable resource but require a high level of support

Photo: **Sally and Richard Greenhill**

Textbooks are likely to remain a core resource in most schools, but each school must decide about the role a textbook is to play. Broadly speaking, teachers stand somewhere between two methodological extremes. Some teachers tend towards the view that education is mainly a process of handing down knowledge and therefore adopt a predominantly didactic style. Other teachers believe that the way in which the learner acquires knowledge is all-important; the style they adopt is therefore mainly that of a manager of learning, rather than an instructor. Generally speaking, the former will rely heavily upon a good class text while the latter will regard it as one of a range of resources, particularly valuable for homework.

When choosing books for a department, it is important to remember that not all teachers of geography are specialists in the subject. Books which provide plenty of examples and exercises for pupis can help to maintain a high standard of geographical teaching in departments where there are several non-specialists.

The frequency of lessons might also affect the choice of textbook; if there is only one geography lesson a week, a text comprising self-contained blocks of work will be necessary. Student profile in a class might also affect the choice of textbooks, for example, if there is a high absentee rate, it can be useful to choose textbooks in which the content is divided into short sections which can be used in several different sequences (though beware that brevity does not equal superficiality).

LANGUAGE, LAYOUT AND ILLUSTRATION

It is obviously important to choose books which students will be able to read easily and which help to improve their use of clear, direct English. The use of simple words and basic phrasing to convey complex ideas need not disadvantage more able students. Teachers learn by experience what level of language suits their students, but sometimes it is difficult to assess the level of a new book. You could run a sample piece of text through the 'readability check' facility offered by many word processing packages, or make a rough assessment by means of Gunning's FOG (1952) Test. There are also several useful books on the subject (e.g. *Readability in the Classroom*, by Colin Harrison, 1980).

In this context, topicality and 'relevance' present problems for the geography textbook author. Extracts from newspapers or other secondary sources lend authenticity to a textbook and provide ready-made resources, but many are written for an audience with a higher reading age than the readers of the textbook in which they appear. Again, teachers need to be aware of this, and be prepared to produce simplified versions of such resources if necessary.

Accessibility of content is clearly related to the book's layout. Books which have an open layout, an attractive design, short line lengths and plenty of sub-sections are more accessible than those with dense, overcrowded pages and few sub-headings. Larger print can be an advantage to students with special reading problems, though there is a danger that this can appear patronising. It must also be possible for the reader to follow the flow of content on a page – this can be difficult where a two-column layout is used, or where the text is broken up by numerous illustrations.

Books rich in photographs and other visual resources may *seem* more accessible than books which have more text than visuals, but this is not necessarily the case. Photographs and maps, for example, may contain far more information than is required or can be identified or absorbed and students need as much skill to obtain information from illustrations as from text. Few 12-15 year olds can be expected to possess the sophistication to interpret a seven-colour flow diagram of dairy farm economics, or a whole-page perspective drawing which shows twenty ways in which the UK environment is being polluted – to name two examples from otherwise useful publications.

ACCURACY AND BALANCE

Geography books often deal with topics that are ethically and politically sensitive, and in recent years publishers have paid much attention to what some call 'political correctness'. In selecting photographs, cartoons and text authors and editors are sensitive to issues such as gender and race stereotyping and other forms of bias. Questions of the suitability of a resource in this regard are now mainly a matter for teachers to decide and each will have their own ideas of the degree of balance which they find acceptable. (See Chapter 3 for a fuller discussion of balance in geography textbooks.)

Resources produced by such 'hidden persuaders' as transnational corporations, national embassies and pressure groups are open to accusations of bias and are often supplied to textbook authors free of charge in generous quantities. It is therefore important to check all potential book purchases for bias of various kinds. Clearly, students need to be made aware of bias and to learn to defend themselves from prejudice and hidden persuasion, so 'biased' resources can be valuable when used carefully by a confident teacher. The fact that a book is pro-Israel in its stance, or shows very few black people in South Africa, or is clearly in favour of the dumping of nuclear waste in the North Atlantic, does not automatically mean that it is unsuitable for school use.

DEALING WITH DIFFERENTIATION

In their promotional material, educational publishers will often describe their publications as being suitable for all students in a particular year, or, even more implausibly, throughout a key stage. Such claims need to be treated with caution; a textbook suitable for students in a potentially high-achieving class can surely not be suitable for all students in the same year; the same must be true for lower-ability students. A textbook designed for use in a mixed-ability class presents an even greater challenge.

The amount of factual material in a textbook, and the way it is presented, ought ideally to be different for different audiences. The nature of student activities and the amount of structured guidance given ought also to vary. Differentiation by outcome is sometimes, but not always, the most appropriate technique. Apart from other considerations, a single textbook does not usually have the space to cater for the range of ability of its readers (see Chapter 7 for a full discussion of differentiation), though some authors and publishers have attempted to deal with this problem in a variety of ways. One way has been to produce sets of photocopiable worksheets or supplementary material pitched at different ability groups; another has been to provide core and supplementary texts.

As a consequence of some of these inevitable imperfections, teachers need to be prepared to write additional materials to make textbooks more usable in their own classes. The need to do this should be built in to any time and cost equation relating to choosing a textbook. Extra material means more flexibility, but it also means more work, so a balance has to be struck between the two.

COST EFFECTIVENESS

Books are bought to be used, not held in stock cupboards, so it is important before buying them to consider their likely frequency of use. How many students will use a book in a given year and for how many weeks in that year, for example? Cost, of course, is an important factor: a salutary exercise is to calculate the cost of each page that you expect to use (which may be less than half a complete textbook) before making a commitment to buy a particular quantity.

When ordering books it is vital to consider the needs of the whole department. A set of books which cover sixth-form topics in depth, for example, would clearly be a bad buy if it meant twenty-eight 14 year olds going without a set of new books which would last them for two or three terms (see Chapter 26 for more detail on the management of resources).

Finally, there is the question of durability. If books are likely to be used intensively, they must be printed on good quality paper and strongly bound.

Choosing and generating resources for courses

One of the features of the revised National Curriculum is the wide range of options it offers. At key stage 3, for example, all students do not need to study the same country from either List A or List B; they can choose rivers or coasts for their study of geomorphological processes; they can select one of many types of ecosystem and economic activity, etc. This has bonuses and disadvantages. When assessing students' work, for example, apart from data-response questions, tasks need to be virtually content free, though students will still require factual content to illustrate their ideas. This should not be too problematic given that the essence of good geography is that it should be more concerned with ideas than transitory examples. Some GCSE examining groups have been setting tasks of this nature for years.

It may not be feasible to provide resources which enable students to choose any topic or place for their scheme of work, but it should be possible to provide enough of a range for them to make at least some choices. Some choice was always possible using reference books in the school library and single copies of other resources, and these should still be available. Now, however, access to computer databases on a network or on stand-alone multi-media machines make the concept of choice more of a practical reality.

Sources of information

Information sources for school geography courses are vast and varied. There are specialist geography textbooks, dictionaries, journals and software etc.; resources for a wider audience, such as maps, census returns, photographs, satellite images, newspapers and television programmes; and resources produced for specific audiences which may have relevance to geographers, such as company reports, aid agency and charity magazines and publicity material from industry. Most geography teachers will be familiar with much of what is available, but for those who are new to the subject or to teaching it, the brief summaries below, and the information given at the end of this chapter, may be helpful.

AID AND DEVELOPMENT ORGANISATIONS

Although not always produced to a high standard, and sometimes too full and detailed, such sources are a rich seam for geographers. Some of the most useful are detailed case studies of specific issues or localities, mostly set in developing world locations. The resources include posters, photo packs and CD-ROMs, and often involve students in a variety of active teaching and learning styles that are lacking in standard textbooks.

ORIGINAL DATA

All major industries, organisations and public bodies produce public relations material, and some is packaged with educational use in mind; much of this includes raw data. Sources include electricity and water companies, tourist boards, National Park authorities and oil companies. Foreign embassies and local government departments involved in attracting industry are variable but often exceptional sources of information. Much of this is very well produced, much of it is in English and is generally contained in public relations material (see above regarding issues of bias, etc.)

Figure 1: A newspaper resource. This article appeared in a Nottinghamshire newspaper in 1995. It provided a one-off lesson on a topic of current interest. It is, however, an example of a resource that could be used in a variety of ways with students. For example:

■ Construct a flow diagram to show the effects of the period of thunderstorms.

■ Imagine that a similar thunderstorm affected the area around your home. Write a newspaper article with illustrations on computer to describe what its effects might have been.

Freezer lightning strike stuns mum

TERRIFIED Wollaton mother-of-two Carole Sculthorpe was today recovering at home after being struck by lightning when she reached inside her freezer.

Her near-miss came as freak storms left a trail of mayhem throughout Notts, stretching police and fire services to the limit.

By ALEXANDER COHEN

Firemen battled through the night to contain a fire started by lightning at Clipstone Forest and another at Langwith, near Warsop.

Around 25 hectares of land was affected in the two incidents.

Traffic throughout much of the county was gridlocked.

Chaos on the roads was caused by a combination of heavy rain and the rush hour.

Mrs Sculthorpe, 41, of Calderdale, was hit by lightning after it ran through her house, into the electricity system.

Cousin Susan Lylak said: "She was shocked and terrified.

"Flames jumped out and spread up her arms."

Mrs Sculthorpe was treated at the Queen's Medical Centre in Nottingham.

Aerial

Lightning also struck a house in Aston Green, Toton.

It travelled down the TV aerial and blew out the house's electrics.

No one was hurt.

The rain caused major problems too.

The Royal Mail sorting office in Beeston was forced to shut for five hours when the roof started leaking.

Firemen from Ripley and Belper battled to keep flood water away from the electrics at Budget Fabrics, Eagle Street, Heage.

And Asda in Front Street, Arnold was closed for 90 minutes after flood water came up through manholes.

The freak weather was also blamed for the death of hundreds of fish.

National Rivers Authority staff are working flat out to rescue distressed fish and re-oxygenate the water.

Flushed

Affected stretches include the River Erewash between Sandiacre and its confluence with the River Trent, which is also hit.

The storms flushed oil and dirt off roads, into drains and into the rivers, causing contamination.

At the same time, the thundery, oppressive conditions drew the oxygen from the water.

Fish are being moved to emergency holding pools.

The spokesman said: "It is a natural phenomenon but it has happened on an enormous scale this time."

EVALUATING AND USING RESOURCES

NEWSPAPERS AND OTHER MEDIA

One of the delights of teaching geography is that it is such a topical subject. Events that were covered in yesterday's newspapers, or last night's television or radio, can be discussed in the classroom the next day and incorporated into the curriculum, thus bringing immediacy and relevance to the subject. Indeed, the National Curriculum now encourages the use of secondary sources of this kind and states that thematic studies at key stage 3 'should have topical significance'. Examination syllabuses, too, encourage students to investigate topical issues at a range of scales, from local to global.

This emphasis on topicality places a responsibility on the teacher not only to be aware of current events and to be prepared to discuss them, but also to ensure that up-to-date resource material is available, catalogued and stored in such a way that it is accessible to all members of the department (see Chapter 26). It also requires students to be aware of world events and to build up their own knowledge base.

Newspapers are excellent sources of topical, local and international material (see Figure 1). At the tabloid end of the spectrum, the text tends to be less dense and has a lower reading age than the quality broadsheets, though reliability is questionable and brevity may mean over-simplicity. Back issues of some national newspapers are available on CD-ROM and with a relatively basic network capability can be used by many students simultaneously.

AUDIO-VISUAL RESOURCES

TV and radio programmes provide another useful resource, though there are copyright issues involved in recording non-educational broadcasts (see Chapter 23). Films, likewise, are a popular resource and can be exploited by a geography teacher. One example, though dated, is *Crocodile Dundee* which includes scenes of the Australian landscape that are hard to match in the classroom. Similarly, *The Piano* vividly illustrates the problems of penetrating the New Zealand rainforest.

TEACHER GROUPS

The education departments of many local authorities often produce resources related to their own area. They are usually produced by teams of teachers and serve to encourage teachers to develop their own skills in writing and producing resources.

COMPUTERS

The volume of information available on some CD-ROMs far exceeds the capacity of any textbook. Maps and statistical data for any country can be researched using a CD-ROM atlas (Figure 2), including such detailed information as a street map of New York, and satellite images can now be studied on a computer screen. Encyclopedias are also available on CD-ROM and include photographs as well as text.

The number of schools with access to the Internet and e-mail is growing enormously, permitting contacts with schools in other countries as well as providing access to a world-wide information system of almost unlimited capacity. As the use of such systems increases, however, teachers will be faced with the problem of information overload and how to manage it effectively; students need to be encouraged to discriminate between relevant and irrelevant (though interesting) information.

Information on CD-ROM can be displayed on a large screen in the classroom by using an LCD panel on an overhead projector and operating the CD-ROM by a hand-held remote control panel. Photos, text, animation and video clips can all be used either direct from disks, or put together as a pre-set trail. Unfortunately, this equipment is still very costly, so only very few schools can take advantage of it.

Some textbooks are already being translated into interactive format on CD-ROM and it can only be a matter of time before publishers sell their books in both printed and electronic versions, including a CD-ROM option with a range of interactive activities. This could be bought either as a disk, or downloaded via a modem immediately before the student needs to use it.

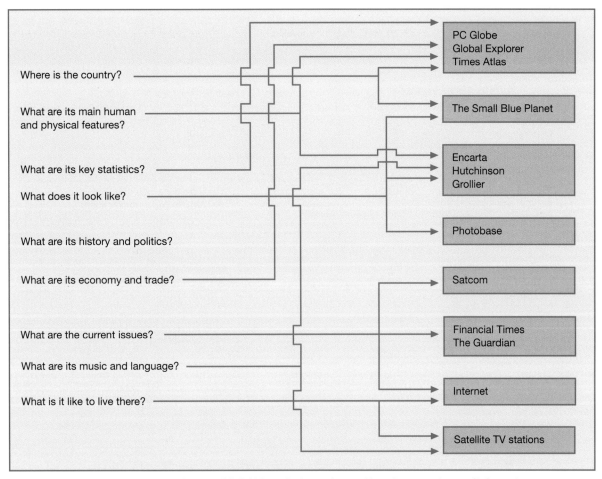

Where is the country?

What are its main human and physical features?

What are its key statistics?

What does it look like?

What are its history and politics?

What are its economy and trade?

What are the current issues?

What are its music and language?

What is it like to live there?

PC Globe
Global Explorer
Times Atlas

The Small Blue Planet

Encarta
Hutchinson
Grollier

Photobase

Satcom

Financial Times
The Guardian

Internet

Satellite TV stations

Figure 2: How to make a country study using CD-ROMs and other software. Note that many items of information are on several CD-ROMs. Only some have been shown here for illustration.

RESOURCES PRODUCED IN SCHOOL

Opportunities to create high quality resources in school are greater now than ever before. This applies to both teachers and students. Word processors with laser printers can be used to write, design and produce resources and worksheets; facilities such as 'cut and paste' make it possible to take text, photographs, and other extracts, then to incorporate them into new documents (Figure 3); video clips from a local field visit can be loaded into a multi-media computer to form part of a program; an ion camera that takes digitised images can be used to create photo banks that students can access on a network (Figure 4). The latter has the advantage over slides that the student takes control of both the selection of images and the time they want to study them. There is also the option for teachers and students to develop their own full multi-media resources.

Doing all this takes time, but the benefits in terms of student interest as well as educational attainment are potentially enormous. Perhaps the time could be found by reducing the hours spent on some of the other initiatives that have visited schools in recent years.

EXISTING RESOURCES

Over time, a department will build up a wealth of resources, and from time to time will face the question of what should be done with them. A good rule for resource

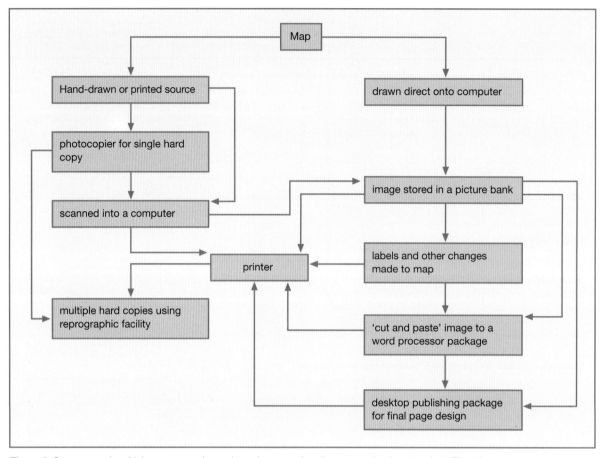

Figure 3: *Some ways in which a resource (a map) can be moved and processed using standard IT packages*

management is not to throw anything away without first considering if it will be useful in five years' time. That way, when you decide to investigate a new topic or issue, many of the resources will already have been collected. The following is an example of how one geography department was able to take advantage of its existing resource bank:

A few years ago, the Aral Sea disaster began to make the news. At first it was only mentioned in journals such as the *Geographical Magazine* and *New Scientist*, then various quality newspapers ran articles on it. Television programmes such as 'Horizon' came later, and then a schools programme followed even later in the year. Over a period of months we gradually filled a file on this issue without ever really setting out to build a resource bank on it. To cap it all, we found some old textbooks in the back of a cupboard, on the Soviet Union, which described the aspirations of the Virgin Lands schemes as they developed. Later, *Geofile* and *Geo-Active* distilled many of these resources into summary articles for students. However, an exercise we have carried out on other topics is to get students to write their own *Geofile* article by giving them selections of the original articles to research. We even produced a fictional letter from the publishers of *Geofile* commissioning an article from the head of department, who in turn enlisted student help on the project.

Unique resources can be created in school using IT capability. The use of an ion camera and scanning are two techniques that can be used. Video and full multi-media productions are also possible using appropriate hardware and software.

Using an ion camera

An ion camera takes pictures in the same way as a camera. The difference is that the images are captured in a way that can be instantly loaded into a computer. Images can then be enhanced to obtain maximum clarity. Pictures of the local area or from field visits, for example, can be stored.

Images once installed can be changed by using a standard graphics package such as 'Paintspa' or 'Paintbrush'. This allows a pupil to add labels to an image, draw on additional lines and details or to remove parts of an image. A set of images, for example, can be produced to show different stages in the development of a sea stack. This technique can also be used to show what a landscape might look like if a proposed development took place.

A program can be created to store the images in a photo bank. These can then be accessed by a simple search facility. Text in the form of notes and pupil activities can be added to the program.

Scanning

Pictures and maps can be scanned into a computer. The quality of the images depends on the quality of the technology available. Line drawings are generally effective with this process.

Once stored in an image bank they can be recalled, analysed and changed in the same way as an ion camera image.

Figure 4: Creating resources using an ion camera and scanning

Enquiry skills and information exchange

Researching material requires enquiry skills; these must be developed before appropriate material can be selected and used to best effect. Research needs key ideas, structure, a knowledge of what resources are available and the ability to search and operate the relevant systems. Selection techniques are needed; more than ever now that students can print out reams of material from a computer simply by clicking a mouse.

Enquiry skills can be developed by asking students to write off to organisations for information and resources as part of their own learning experience through project work. As with textbook evaluation, teacher groups provide a good forum to exchange ideas, contacts etc. Subject panel meetings could be held in different schools in rotation, with the first item on the agenda for each meeting being a briefing from the host departments on some of the resource material that the department has discovered. The local branch of the GA could provide such a forum if none exists in the local authority. Finally, there is the publishers' exhibition at the GA Annual Conference, where not only textbook publishers but numerous other organisations display their products and services.

LONG-TERM PLANNING

A long-term plan is needed to lead students towards the necessary enquiry skills. There are practical skills relating to the use of the department or school computer hardware and software, as well as using the library index system (that is probably also on a database). Students must be able to search for topics then scan for relevant information. Coping with material at a wide range of reading levels is also likely to be involved. Research templates may initially need to be provided, so that students can be taught to think out how best to structure and present their work. Finding out just what new skills are needed and how they can be developed will involve a considerable amount of work.

WHO IS IN CONTROL?

Most teachers are accustomed to being in control of what is taught. A framework of ideas will still be needed, but students now have access to a range of content in a way that is hard to control. Minimal control by the teacher could result in a high level of motivation and the discovery of new relationships between data. Subject boundaries could be seen as irrelevant by the students. An alternative scenario, however, is that the students become 'surfers' of disparate facts that serve no genuinely educative purpose.

Many students are now more familiar than teachers with the skills needed to access computer data. They can create and print out complex graphs and manipulate data on spread sheets, though they may lack judgement as to what is appropriate. New teachers should ensure that they are computer literate; more experienced and slow-learner teachers should make every effort to catch up. The department as a whole must exercise skill, imagination and ingenuity in its use of IT.

Conclusion

Teaching and learning geography is in the process of change; the increasing range of resources is one of the forces that is enabling that change to take place.

The geography National Curriculum offers opportunities to develop courses that are flexible in factual content and therefore flexible in the resources that can be used to support them. A re-written National Curriculum could go even further in this direction by removing some of the remaining vestiges of unnecessary compulsion, and the changing nature of resources will be one pressure amongst many that should demand that this will be done.

Different resources have been considered in this chapter in relative isolation from each other; they should, however, be considered as part of a total package. Textbooks, maps, slides, computer software and all the rest have a part to play in teaching and learning geography (Figure 5) and will enhance its appeal and the effectiveness of teaching it. A balance between different types of resource and a choice of the most appropriate type for each activity needs to be achieved.

There are numerous references to IT throughout this book, and this should need no apology. When its predecessor was published in 1986, IT in schools was in its infancy; now it is gathering momentum at such a rate that hardware is out-of-date as soon as it is purchased, as is much of the software. There is nothing futuristic about this chapter; much of what is described here is already happening in schools – indeed, there are probably even more creative uses for IT that have not been mentioned.

By the time the next edition is made available, probably on a world-wide superhighway, strategies will have been devised to cater for many of the questions that have been raised here. There is a lot to be done by the new entrants to the profession. By then, of course, there will be new issues to raise and new resource issues to explore.

Resources for teaching geography

The following list is not intended to be either definitive or balanced, and provides **examples only** of information sources.

JOURNALS

Geography The Geographical Association, 343 Fulwood Road, Sheffield, South Yorkshire S10 3BP

Teaching Geography The Geographical Association

Geography Review Philip Allan Publishers, Market Place, Deddington, Oxford OX5 4SE

GCSE Geography Review Philip Allan Publishers

Volcanoes can be studied using a range of different resources presented in a variety of different ways. This list is an example of how key questions can be answered by using this range.

Extract from the KS3 Programme of Study
Tectonic processes
a) the global distribution of earthquakes and volcanoes
d) the nature, causes and effects of volcanic eruptions

What is a volcano?
■ Video for a basic introduction to volcanic activity

Where are volcanoes?
■ Slides to show a world map of volcanoes and earthquakes
■ Atlas

What are the different types of volcano?
■ 'Encarta' CD-ROM encyclopaedia for categories of types

What do volcanoes look like?
■ 'Small Blue Planet' CD-ROM for satellite images of volcanoes
■ Textbook for photographs
■ Photobase and 'Encarta' CD-ROMs for ground view photos
■ Library books research

How big are volcanoes?
■ GRASS database of volcanoes

Why do volcanoes erupt?
■ Textbook information
■ 'Encarta' and 'The Physical World' CD-ROMs for information

Why are volcanoes in some places?
■ Atlas map of volcanoes and plate boundaries
■ 'Small Blue Planet' CD-ROM for map of world plates
■ 'Encarta' CD-ROM for cartoon animation

What happens when a volcano erupts?
■ *The Times* and *The Guardian* CD-ROMs to research case studies

What comes out of a volcano?
■ Textbook
■ 'Picturebase' CD-ROM for information

What can be done to plan for an eruption?
■ Decision-making simulation of Mount St Helens
■ Tape and slide presentation of Mount St Helens

Figure 5: Resources for studying volcanoes at key stage 3. A similar inquiry structure and set of resources can be written for earthquakes, and students offered the choice of either volcanoes or earthquakes to study. Considerable extra guidance however, is likely to be required as to how information can be obtained from each type of source.

The Geographical Magazine (subscriptions) PO Box 425, Woking GU21 1GP

Eurogeo European Standing Conference of Geography Teachers' Associations

Scottish Geographical Magazine The Scottish Geographical Society, Graham Hills Building, 40 George Street, Glasgow, Strathclyde G1 1QE

Area The Royal Geographical Society, Institute of British Geographers, 1 Kensington Gore, London SW7 2AR

Transactions of the Institute of British Geographers RGS/IBG

The Geographical Journal RGS/IBG

GENERAL, TOPICAL AND MEDIA RESOURCES

World Magazine Hyde Park Publications Ltd, Hyde Park House, 5 Manfred Road, Putney, London SW15 2RS

National Geographic National Geographic Society, 1145 17th Street NW, Washington DC20036, USA

The New Internationalist New International Publications Ltd, 55 Rectory Road, Oxford OX4 1BW

The New Scientist Specialist Group, Kings Reach Tower, Stamford Street, London SE1 9LS

The Countryside Campaigner Council for the Preservation of Rural England, Warwick House, 25 Buckingham Palace Road, London SW1W 0PP

Friends of the Earth supporters' newspaper Friends of the Earth, 377 City Road, London EC1V 1NA

The Times and *The Guardian* (on CD-ROM)

Local area advertising newspapers

AID AND DEVELOPMENT ORGANISATIONS

OXFAM, 274 Banbury Road, Oxford OX2 7DZ

ActionAid, Hamlyn House, Archway, London N19 5PG

Christian Aid, Inter-church House, 35 Lower Marsh, London SE1 7RL

Catholic Fund for Overseas Development (CAFOD), 2 Romero Close, Stockwell Road, London SW9 9TY

Centre for World Development Agency, 128 Buckingham Palace Road, London SW1W 9SA

Development Education Centre, 998 Bristol Road, Selly Oak, Birmingham B29 6LE

The Commonwealth Institute, Kensington High Street, London W8 6NQ

World Wide Fund for Nature (WWF UK), Panda House, Weyside Park, Cattershall Lane, Godalming, Surrey GU7 1XR

GOVERNMENT AND INTERNATIONAL ORGANISATIONS

- United Nations Environment Programme (UNEP), POB 30552, Nairobi, Kenya (Europe: CP356, 15 chemin des Anemones, 1219 Chatelaine, Geneva, Switzerland)
- World Health Organization (WHO), Avenue Appia, 1211 Geneva 27, Switzerland
- Food and Agriculture Organization (FAO), Viale delle Terme di Caracalla, 00100, Rome, Italy
- United Nations High Commissioner for Refugees (UNHCR), CP 2500, 1211 Geneva 2 depot, Switzerland
- International Labour Organization (ILO), 4 route des Morillons, 1211 Geneva 22, Switzerland

Note: Some UN agencies produce regular newsletters, for example *Refugees* from UNHCR. All produce reports on specific topics and places.

UK MINISTRIES AND OTHER NATIONAL ORGANISATIONS

- The Department of the Environment, 2 Marsham Street, London SW1P 3EB
- Overseas Development Administration, 94 Victoria Street, London SW1E 5JL
- The Countryside Commission, John Dower House, Crescent Place, Cheltenham, Gloucestershire GL50 3RA
- Central Statistical Office (CSO), Great George Street, London SW1P 3AQ
- National Parks Authority and individual National Parks *National Parks Today* (back issues pre-1995 only) (see Countryside Commission)
- The Forestry Commission, 231 Corstorphine Road, Edinburgh EH12 7AT
- The European Union, 20 Kensington Gardens, London W8 4QQ

Note: The EU produces a wide range of occasional papers on every aspect of EU affairs.

FOREIGN EMBASSIES

These are listed in every library; several embassies also house organisations for tourism and economic affairs. Some produce regular newsletters, such as *Invest in France* from the Invest in France Bureau.

SOURCES OF ADDRESSES

The *Europa Year Book* is an annual publication that contains names and addresses of embassies, government ministries and commercial organisations for every country in the world.

There are statistical handbooks and other sources of country data for many countries. As an example, the *Statistical Abstract of the United States* from the US Department of Commerce, Bureau of Census is an annual production.

In 1981, the old DES published *Environmental Education: Sources of Information*, a pretty comprehensive listing of sources for environmental education; and in 1986 the Overseas Development Administration produced *Overseas Development and Aid: A guide to sources of information and material*, which was very useful for sources of development information. Between them, they listed the majority of the main sources of information, but neither has been recently updated.

ORIGINAL SOURCES

The National Rivers Authority, 30-34 Albert Embankment, London SE1 7TL or Rivers House, Waterside Drive, Aztec West, Almondsbury, Bristol BS12 4UD

Electricity companies

Water companies

Meteorological Office, Bracknell, Berkshire RG12 2SZ

The Institute of Hydrology, Maclean Building, Crowmarsh, Gifford, Wallingford, Oxon OX10 8BB

British Tourist Authority, Thames Tower, Black's Road, Hammersmith, London W6 9EL

County Planning Departments

BUSINESSES AND RELATED ORGANISATIONS

Note: Public relations material is available from almost every UK company and the trade organisations that represent them. A few examples are listed below.

BNFL (nuclear energy), Risley, Warrington WA3 6AS

ICI (chemicals), Head Office, 9 Millbank, London SW1P 3JF

Sand and Gravel Association (sand and gravel), 1 Bramber Court, 2 Bramber Road, London W14 9PB

British Petroleum (oil and natural gas), 1 Finsbury Circus, London EC2M 7BA

Rio Tinto Zinc (RTZ) (mining), 6 St James's Square, London SW1Y 4LD

Harland and Woolf Ltd (shipbuilding), Queen's Island, Belfast BT3 9DU

English China Clays, 1015 Arlington Business Park, Theale, Reading RG7 4SA

Note: Sources of information about companies to be found in these and other directories:

Kompass, Company Information: CBI

European Country Information: The London Business School

Chapter 22

Information Technology and the geography department

JOHN DAVIDSON

Geography and Information Technology

Since the introduction of the National Curriculum, Information Technology (IT) has become a part of the curriculum of all secondary schools. As teachers of geography we therefore need to be clear about what IT means; to appreciate why we should be using IT in our classrooms; and be aware of pupils' expectations of IT.

WHAT IS IT?

IT is the use of Information Technology and information sources (such as computer systems and software packages) to support learning in a variety of ways. These can include the processing, analysis and presentation of data, modelling, measurement, and the controlling of equipment or events. The study of IT also includes its implications for people and their work.

WHY DO THOSE WORKING WITHIN THE GEOGRAPHY CURRICULUM NEED TO BE USING IT?

Since the 1995 National Curriculum Order for geography, all teachers of geography at key stage 3 are also teachers of IT. 'Pupils are to be given opportunities, where appropriate, to develop and apply their IT capability in their study of geography'. In the Programme of Study for Information Technology (SCAA, 1995), there is a clear implication that subject areas, including geography, will help deliver IT. The latest GCSE criteria make it clear that the appropriate use of IT is an important area of geographical skills, while at 16 + there is the expectation that the use of IT will be an important part of the delivery of the subject. Teachers of geography may also be involved in the teaching of GNVQs, for which courses on, for example, travel and tourism, will include the use of IT.

Teachers are being encouraged to make use of IT in the teaching of geography because IT can and does make a valuable contribution to pupils' learning. Examples of this have been documented in *Teaching Geography* articles and the regular 'IT Page', and also in many of the publications listed in 'References and further resources' at the end of this chapter. By enabling pupils to handle, process and present data collected by them or from other sources, IT fosters enquiry approaches to learning, and through IT, pupils can pursue 'What if…?' questions, and present results of enquiries in appropriate ways. Consequently, as well as equipping pupils with valuable skills, the incorporation of IT into appropriate geographical schemes of work can also enhance the quality of learning.

Photo: **Richard Greenhill**

A PUPIL'S ENTITLEMENT

In 1994, the leaflet *Geography – a pupils entitlement for IT* (GA/NCET, 1994a) was produced jointly by the GA and NCET. It included the five entitlement statements shown in Table 1. These can be linked to the opportunities detailed for pupils in the Programmes of Study for IT in the National Curriculum (DFE, 1995). Opportunities must be provided for pupils to:

- use a variety of equipment
- use IT to solve problems
- compare their own use of IT with its use in the wider world
- consider the implications of IT and the issues raised by the use of IT in society.

Pupils should also be taught to communicate and handle information, and develop competence in controlling, measuring and modelling using IT.

Pupils studying geography are entitled to use IT to:

- enhance their skills of geographical enquiry;
- gain access to a wide range of geographical knowledge and information sources;
- deepen their understanding of environmental and spatial relationships;
- experience alternative images of people, place and environment; and to consider the wider impact of IT on people, place and environment.

Source: GA/NCET, 1994a

Table 1: Geography entitlement statements

How can you use IT in geography?

Information Technology has been used in geography for over twenty years. For over fifteen years each issue of *Teaching Geography* has included 'IT Pages'. During this time, IT in geography lessons has included the use of:

- data-handling packages, including databases, and spreadsheets for collecting, organising, analysing and presenting data collected by pupils from a variety of sources, including fieldwork enquiries;
- word processing, and desk-top publishing packages for presenting reports on geographical issues;
- data loggers for collecting data electronically, e.g. weather data;
- satellite images, downloaded directly, accessed from disk or used as hard copy;
- simulation programs, which enable pupils to study systems like the hydrological cycle, and the movement of lithospheric plates;
- electronic mail (e-mail) to download data from remote databases, and to exchange data with other schools and institutions.

During the 1990s, many CD-ROMs (Compact Disk-Read Only Memory) have been published with geographical themes which pupils are now making use of when studying geography. There is a growing interest in the use of e-mail to link schools and exchange data (specifically the use of the Internet). Portable computers are used during fieldwork to organise and process data on site as well as in the classroom. Another recent development has been Geographical Information Systems (GIS) specifically intended for school use, where pupils can study variations in distributions over given areas and analyse how two or more such patterns may be related. GIS software has considerable potential for schools, and is already widely used in the commercial world.

Much of the commercially-produced software is now being used by schools is well designed and user-friendly; the real challenge is to develop lessons which combine sound geographical content with appropriate use of IT. The considerable range of options for utilising IT in geography enables departments to develop a variety of uses appropriate to their access to hardware and software and their levels of expertise. All computers used in schools have standard software packages which can handle geographical data and support geography lessons; it is not necessary to use only those software programs that have been written specifically for the subject. Table 2 shows how geography can be enriched and enhanced by IT in the classroom at key stage 3. There is clearly a wealth of ways that IT can be used in geography, and some examples and pointers are provided here. Detailed ideas can be found in some of the references in 'Going further' on page 257.

KEY STAGE 3 THEME	GEOGRAPHY ACTIVITY	IT CONTRIBUTION
Tectonic processes	Enquiry on effects of earthquakes on different parts of the world	Use of newspaper or encyclopaedic CD-ROMs as information sources
Geomorphological processes	Enquiry on how flood risks can be reduced	Use of a spreadsheet to study what size of flood channel is necessary to carry predicted flood discharges
Weather	Enquiry into how microclimates vary around	Use of datalogging equipment to collect data which is then analysed using a data-handling package
Ecosystems	Enquiry into the effects of rainforest removal	Use of a word processing or desk-top publishing package to create a newspaper article on deforestation issues
Population	Enquiry into population changes in a developing country	Data retrieval from a world database. Use of a spreadsheet to model how changes in birth and death rates can affect population totals
Settlement	Investigating the issues associated with possible locations for a new city recycling centre	Use of a spreadsheet to enter environmental impact scores for various sites
Economic activities	Enquiry into how land is used on a farm	Use of a data-handling package to present data obtained from a farmer on a fieldwork visit, or from an e-mail link with a rural school, on field size, crop type and yield in a 5-year period
Development	Enquiry into regional contrasts in Italy	Use of a data-handling package to retrieve, analyse and present data to identify contrasts
Environmental issues	Enquiry into oil in the USA	Use of IT to present data in the form of graphs and diagrams to show how far the USA is dependant on oil as a major fuel and on oil imports

Table 2: *Classroom ideas for enhancing and enriching geography with IT*

Five examples of how IT can be used to support geography at key stage 3 and GCSE

1. AN ENQUIRY ON CHANGES IN A LOCAL SHOPPING CENTRE

The opening of a new store or closure of a well-known local shop can make or break a shopping centre. In an enquiry on the effects of the closure of a local store, there is considerable scope for IT to be used to support the work. Pupils can design a shoppers' questionnaire to investigate where people come from; which shops they visit; whether they use the store that is closing and where else they shop; and use it, in groups, during fieldwork in the local area. Peoples' views on the shopping centre and the effects of store closure can also be recorded, however, if fieldwork is impractical, such information could be sought through school contacts and parents. A data-handling package can be used to organise the responses to the questionnaire and for presenting summaries to see what patterns emerge. The shoppers who come to the centre to use the store that is closing could be identified and their results compared with other shoppers. A word processing package could be used to write an account of the impact of closure using evidence collected from the database; thus encouraging pupils to search the database to identify patterns.

A similar enquiry could look at the effects of opening a new edge-of-town-store in an existing central shopping area. The use of IT would enable a potentially large amount of data to be quickly and efficiently organised and a variety of enquiries into the result to be followed up rapidly.

Further development of the above and other examples of shopping and traffic data can be found in *Geography and IT: Shopping and Traffic Fieldwork* (GA/NCET, 1994b).

2. AN ENQUIRY ON WEATHER DATA

A wide variety of sources of data exist to support enquiries on weather, including pupils' own data collected by using traditional instruments or data loggers; automatic school weather stations; media sources; Metfax and e-mail. An enquiry on weather patterns during one month could use data obtained from data loggers or other sources in a database to enable pupils to investigate questions such as 'How many days did it rain in the month?' and 'What is the most common wind direction?' Spreadsheets can be used to look at relationships between rainfall and pressure or rainfall and wind direction, with charts being used to present results and show patterns. Such charts could be included in a desk-top published report on the month's weather. As IT allows a wide range of data to be accessed and searched effectively this helps patterns to be found and ideas to be proved or disproved. The use of data loggers/automatic weather stations ensures that the data are accurate and topical, and enables links with science to be developed. In one school, the weather records and resulting forecasts were compared with those given on national television and the question of 'accuracy' discussed.

Further ideas on the use of IT in weather enquiries can be found in *Geography and IT: Investigating Weather Data* (GA/NCET, 1994c).

3. LOOKING AT DEVELOPMENT DATA

In an enquiry on ways of identifying differences in development and its effects on quality of life, pupils could use a datafile for selected countries with data on wealth, education levels and health. Examples could include data on GNP, birth and death rates, urban population, percentage of children in secondary education, female literacy and infant mortality. Pupils could make use of either a commercially available datafile, one produced by the teacher, or simply add information to one prepared from secondary sources (thus enabling them to study how the datafile is built up). By sorting the data, pupils can investigate which countries have the highest indicators of wealth. These can be compared with indicators of health and social development. Important points can be raised about the accuracy of the original data. By using scattergraphs pupils can go on to investigate possible relationships, e.g. between infant mortality and GNP, enabling them to look at variations in quality of life and linked factors.

IT allows a wide range of data to be investigated in a number of different ways and fosters enquiry, as a number of alternative investigations can be completed quickly. Work would also involved atlases and possibly mapping of some of the results. The topic could also be studied using world data on CD-ROM.

Further ideas on the use of IT in relation to development data can be found in *Using IT to Enhance Geography: Case Studies at Key Stages 3 and 4* (Hassell & Warner, 1995).

4. MODELLING IN GEOGRAPHY

Pupils can now use IT for modelling possible outcomes of geographical situations. One example of this is the use of prepared spreadsheets to model rainfall intensity and the related response of a river. Pupils can alter rainfall intensity and amounts, and vary land use for a catchment in order to look at whether or not a river will flood. They can also look at the capacity of the river channel, and model what might happen to a flood if the river channel was artificially deepened and widened. In this context the use of IT enables a range of 'What if...?' questions to be asked and a range of options to be studied. Pupils can then assume the role of consultants to write a report of flood risks and possible alleviation measures, using desk-top publishing software.

5. CD-ROM IN THE GEOGRAPHY CLASSROOM

CD-ROMs provide information, pictures, sound, moving images and animations, with the facility for the user to search through the disk for the information they require. A large number of CD-ROMs now have specific geographical information and applications. Types of CD-ROM include:

- newspaper;
- encyclopedia;
- atlas (see Chapter 11);
- database, e.g. Census data;
- resource base, e.g. pictures and images on landscapes/earth sciences/weather;
- simulations;
- electronic books.

CD-ROM systems are frequently sited in library or resource areas, although a growing number of geography departments are acquiring a CD-ROM system for their own departmental work area.

The following example of a pupil enquiry into earthquakes in California provides an illustration of how CD-ROM can be used in a geography class.

> The class was 'role-playing' the staff of a newsroom producing a 20 minute newsround-style report on earthquakes in California, following a recent event. The resource area with two CD-ROM computers was available for the lesson. One group used a newspaper CD-ROM to find out about how many earthquakes California had suffered in recent years, and what the consequences were. A second group used an encyclopedia CD-ROM to collect information on the causes of earthquakes and on major Californian earthquakes in the past. Important information was printed out for use by other groups, and some was saved for use on a word processor as part of the script production.

CD-ROMs have obvious and beguiling qualities but they vary widely in price, content and quality. It is very important, therefore, that before buying one, you evaluate it carefully in terms of its relevance, ease of use, value for money, and how you think your pupils will use it to support their learning.

Further information on CD-ROMs can be found in the leaflet *CD-ROMs for Geography* (GA/NCET, 1995).

CASE STUDY 1: A large comprehensive school	CASE STUDY 2: A small comprehensive school
In this school, two computers are always available in the geography room. Responsibility for development of IT capability has been delegated to departments, with geography covering information handling. The department has four staff with IT expertise and a newly qualified teacher who still needs support.	In this school, there are two central networked rooms of computers, and the geography department has blocks of time allocated for their use. Only one member of the department of three is confident with computers, the others have in-class help from the IT co-ordinator. At key stage 3, IT is used within one complete geographical investigation per year, using the allocated computer room time.
IT is used in geography at key stage 3 as follows:	IT is used in geography at key stage 3 as follows:
In Year 7, pupils draw a graph which summarises methods of transport used by the class to get to school, and use a pre-formed spreadsheet to calculate the best site for a settlement.	**In Year 7**, pupils carry out an enquiry on a local issue, such as the location of a science park, involving collection of data, creation and interrogation of a database, graphical representation and use of a word processing package.
In Year 8, pupils extract information on world economic development from a database and create comparative maps. They use desktop publishing to produce a newspaper report giving one view on the destruction of rainforest in Brazil.	**In Year 8**, pupils undertake an environmental enquiry as part of the school's 'Environment week', for example on siting a waste disposal/recycling plant. This involves collection of data (e.g. on noise levels), with the science department, and the use of a modelling package/spreadsheet to consider alternative locations for the plant.
In Year 9, pupils use Metfax information and data from the school weather station data loggers to construct a database and study local weather patterns.	**In Year 9** pupils undertake an enquiry about a developing country (e.g. 'Brazil – progress for whom'?) involving the use of desktop publishing to present different images and viewpoints, and also the extraction of information from CD-ROMs and computer atlases.
In this department, IT entitlement is being progressively built up throughout key stage 3, and the agreement to deliver aspects of IT capability in information handling has meant that the second computer was funded from the IT budget. The department is keeping careful records of pupil work in IT as part of assessment.	In this department, access to the computer room and the support of the IT co-ordinator in class time has helped the department to strengthen geographical investigations through the use of IT, and to develop IT skills. However, the use of IT is focused on one major piece of work in each year. The development of a school Learning Resources Centre in the future will increase opportunities for IT to be integrated more fully into the geography curriculum.

Table 3: Case studies of two schools using IT in geography, adapted from GA/NCET, 1994a

Managing IT in geography

Table 3 shows how geography departments in two different schools have managed the use of IT in the classroom. There are no 'right' methods for the management of IT within geography and approaches vary widely according to different school situations. The following six items need to be considered in relation to the management of IT in a geography department:

1. GEOGRAPHY AND IT ACROSS THE CURRICULUM – DEPARTMENT AND SCHOOL POLICIES AND LOCATIONS OF HARDWARE

The geography department will need to work within the existing school framework. In some schools the department may have total responsibility for providing hardware and software and organising IT opportunities, while in other schools the department may use IT facilities in a central location, but will have no hardware or software of its own. Many schools lie somewhere between these two situations. As schools develop and revise their whole-school IT policies, geography departments have an opportunity to be involved in decisions over access to hardware and software. They can make a strong case for the use of facilities because geography departments can demonstrate a number of appropriate uses to develop pupil IT awareness and capability. More and more schools are standardising on desk-top publishing, data handling, and spreadsheet software which pupils come across in a number of subject areas. This means that teachers of geography can concentrate on the use of IT to build up good geography, while developing and reinforcing their pupils' IT skills.

2. THE IDEAL GEOGRAPHY ROOM FOR IT – AND THE REALITY

Provision of IT hardware within a geography department varies from no computer at all to a number of computers sited around the room. The ideal room would be one which has enough computers for each group of pupils, plus CD-ROM systems and a satellite system in one corner. However, the reality is that teachers of geography have to make the best of what is available. If access to an IT room or resource area with several computers can be fairly easily arranged then a single computer with a printer may be sufficient for the geography room, particularly if it has the capacity to run CD-ROMs. If IT facilities cannot be easily accessed elsewhere, then a department may have a good case for needing more computers on specific occasions. The best approach is to look for activities in geography where the pupils would gain most from the use of IT and to then consider what resources (hardware and software) are needed to make it possible. This enables a case to be made for either more access to an IT room or extra hardware in the department for appropriate periods of the school year.

3. PLANNING THE USE OF IT IN SCHEMES OF WORK

In planning opportunities to use IT to teach geographical skills, places and themes, the first stage is to review the geography department's contribution to the development of IT capability across the curriculum. For example, the department may have been given the task of developing data handling skills. The next stage is to consider what is feasible, in terms of teacher and pupil expertise and access to hardware/software, and what will help pupils to gain most from their use of IT. It is helpful to remember that, for some topics, an appropriate use of IT may be as a source of data from a data file or CD-ROM which would be possible with a single computer. Other topics may be built around a more extensive use of IT involving entering and organising data, producing charts and writing a report. Most schools start by looking at IT opportunities within existing schemes of work, aiming to ensure that all year groups receive opportunities for the use of IT. Table 2 can be referred to for further ideas.

4. HARDWARE/SOFTWARE PROVISION

The geography department needs to be aware of a number of issues about resourcing and storage of IT equipment, particularly if purchasing and maintenance of software is not organised centrally. Clear rules for the use and care of hardware need to be understood by both pupils and teachers, and maintenance programmes followed. Most software programs are copyright protected with licensing agreements which limit the number of machines a particular piece of software can be used on within the school. Teachers need to be aware of this and ensure that the law is not flouted. Strategies which ensure that only authorised copies of software are made need to be in operation.

To protect computers from 'viruses' ensure that clear rules on the use of personal disks are followed, and regularly use appropriate virus-checking software on all computer systems. Finally, agree on and operate a reliable disk back-up system for the department as a whole; this should ensure that all vital software systems and datafiles are protected. If computers are used for school or departmental administration, a disk back-up system may already be in operation so this can be extended to files relating to individual lessons and pupil work. In many schools, whole-school policies are being developed which cover all of the above issues.

5. PORTABLE COMPUTERS

Portable computers, including laptops, notebooks and palmtops, have attracted the attention of schools and particularly geography departments. They can be moved easily

from one classroom to another without the necessity of a trolley; connected to data-logging equipment for particular pieces of work at a suitable site; and can be taken out of the classroom. In the school grounds or on fieldwork data can be entered directly into a pre-prepared database or spreadsheet and some immediate conclusions drawn while still on site. One example is the collection of data on river channel characteristics, where the velocity and discharge at different points can be calculated and displayed from pupils' own data on site, to begin to explain results. Portables have also helped teachers of geography to develop their own levels of expertise by allowing them to work on a computer in school or at home. Information about the use and issues associated with portables is available from NCET.

6. PURCHASING SOFTWARE AND CD-ROMS

It is clear from the above that purchasing software and CD-ROMs may not always be the responsibility of the geography department, but even if this is the case, the department is often asked to provide recommendations. The following checklist provides information on what teachers of geography should consider before purchasing subject-specific software, and particularly CD-ROMs. Where possible, it is worth seeing software or CD-ROMs in operation. Each issue of *Teaching Geography* includes reviews of software and CD-ROMs and so provides a useful source of information.

> **A checklist for selecting and evaluating subject-specific software and CD-ROMs**
>
> 1. Is it relevant to your current or planned curriculum/schemes of work?
>
> 2. Is it appropriate for your pupils?
>
> 3. Is it easy to use?
>
> 4. Can it be used to support a number of topics or pieces of work?
>
> 5. Does it have sufficient support materials which enable you to make full use of it?
>
> 6. Does it provide value for money?
>
> 7. Does it enable you to do things that other resources cannot?
>
> 8. Can you actually see opportunities to use it with your pupils?

IT and the geography department administration

Many teachers have found that the best introduction to IT has been through using it for administration. This has given them the confidence to use IT in the classroom. There is clearly much value in using word processing/desk-top publishing software for departmental policy statements, set lists, standard letters, resource lists and internal assessments. Such documents require regular updating or amending which can be easily achieved with the help of IT. Documents can also be presented to a high standard. If the departmental computer is compatible with the school administration system, department lists and records can be produced efficiently from the main school databases. This can make the production of set lists for field trips much easier and quicker. However, clear guidance on all aspects of data protection must be provided.

Marks for internal assessments and coursework can be put onto a spreadsheet, saving hours of calculations at the end of term or year. Spreadsheets can also be used for keeping track of departmental budgets and for modelling spending on resources or field trips. Provided that there is quick and easy access to both the computer and a printer, teachers have found that the use of IT can save time and be an effective way of keeping track of this kind of administrative information.

Going further

Table 4 suggests one action plan for looking at IT within a geography department. It is very important to build in a regular **review** of the use of IT within the department, particularly with the National Curriculum requirements in mind, and the school cross-curricular IT policy. From this, departments can **identify needs** on a regular basis, and create appropriate **action plans**. Resourcing and experience in departments vary widely so there is no single correct approach. Table 5 offers a way forward for a department which is just beginning to use IT.

■ **Review what you do already**
How far do your existing geography units make use of IT?

■ **Plan what you could do**
Do you have a successful study unit which could be developed further by the use of IT?
Which new planned study units at key stage 3 could make use of IT?

■ **Identify what you need to do to develop IT in your geography teaching**
Consider what staff training, hardware and software is needed and establish what IT equipment is likely to be available. (It is important here to look at the whole-school IT policy and the geography department's contribution). Look at what software packages are already available in the school.

■ **Create an action plan**
Plan how you can introduce and develop IT in geography over a one- to three-year period, bearing in mind your own school situation. Have clear aims and identify needs for resources and INSET. Work out ways of checking the progress of pupils and evaluating how far units of work are successful in helping to develop IT capability.

■ **Evaluate your success!**
See how the use of IT in geography studies is helping pupils to handle data more efficiently, discover trends, and use a wider range of data sources. Assess also how IT is helping pupils to develop a greater understanding of people, their environments and spatial relationships.

Going further – action plan (Adapted from Davidson, 1995)

TIME	IT IN GEOGRAPHY SCHEME
First year of introducing IT	Use a data-handling package to organise, process and analyse data from a Year 7 fieldwork enquiry on what people think of their local shopping area.
	Pupils in Year 8 use a word processing/desktop publishing package to write accounts of an issue such as pollution of a local river or estuary. Pupils can make use of a range of resources including a database of information.
	Use CD-ROMs and a world database to support a Year 9 pupils' enquiry on a country such as France or Japan.
Second year of introducing IT	Review the outcomes of the first year of using IT and identify how far the use of IT has helped pupils to have access to a wider range of information, to support their enquiries and to investigate geographical patterns and relationships.
	Consider how to develop further the use of IT in the schemes of work used in the first year, and what new applications of IT can be introduced in the second year.
	An example might be to use data from an automatic weather station plus Metfax to support an enquiry on a month's weather patterns.
	Review what INSET needs the geography department has, and what new IT resources may be required.

Table 5: A plan for action for a geography department starting to use IT at key stage 3

Table 6 provides a list of organisations who can help with information about the use of IT in geography and the 'References and further resources' lists publications which may be useful. To achieve both good geography and good IT needs careful planning, and it is important to observe how pupils are progressing by using IT and to evaluate its success. Finally, geography teachers must build upon their pupils'

WITHIN YOUR SCHOOL SITUATION:	AT NATIONAL LEVEL:	
■ Your school IT co-ordinator ■ Your senior management team ■ Your LEA advisory team ■ Your local IT centre ■ Your local ITE establishment	■ ACAC Castle Buildings Womanby Street Cardiff CF1 9SX Telephone: 01222 344946 ■ Geographical Association IT Working Group c/o GA Headquarters Solly Street Sheffield S1 4BF (ITWG members help run INSET activities on IT at conferences) Tel: 0114 267 0666	■ Geography and IT Support Project, GA/NCET ■ NCET Milburn Hill Road Science Park Coventry CV4 7JJ Telephone: 01203 416994 ■ SCAA Newcombe House 45 Notting Hill Gate London W11 3JB Telephone: 0171 299 1234

Table 6: Who can help with information about geography and IT?

experience which may have come from elsewhere in their schooling, e.g. from their primary school, or experiences in IT lessons, or another subject.

Conclusion

In the information age in which we now live, all teachers of geography should be actively looking at the use of IT in their schemes of work; this is an opportunity as well as a challenge. IT can provide ways of handling large amounts of data to make them accessible to pupils; it can foster enquiry approaches; it can allow dynamic 'What if...?' questions to be posed and answered; and it can enrich many topics. In short, IT tools can help the geography teacher to support learning effectively and efficiently.

References and further resources

Barnett, M., Kent, A. & Milton, M. (1995) *Images of Earth: A Teacher's Guide to Remote Sensing in Geography at Key Stage 3 and GCSE.* Support materials for teachers. The Geographical Association (A key stage 2 pack is also available).

Davidson, J. (1995) 'Information Technology opportunities', *Teaching Geography*, 20(2), pp. 85-87.

Davidson, J. & Rudd, M. (eds) (1993) *Geography and IT at Key Stages 3 and 4.* The Geographical Association.

DfE (1995) *Information Technology in the National Curriculum.* HMSO.

GA/NCET (1991) *Geography, IT and the National Curriculum: Teacher's Guide and Case Studies Booklet.* Although written for the original National Curriculum, the first booklet contains useful ideas for planning and INSET, while the second booklet contains a variety of case studies.

GA/NCET (1994a) *Geography – A Pupil's Entitlement for IT.*

GA/NCET (1994b) *Geography and IT: Shopping and Traffic Fieldwork.**

GA/NCET (1994c) *Geography and IT: Investigating Weather Data.**

GA/NCET (1995) *CD-ROMs for Geography.*

GA/NCET (1996) *Geography and IT: Investigating Aspects of Human Geography.**

All of the above GA/NCET leaflets/publications have been produced as part of the Geography and IT Support Project 1994-95.
*Contain software packages designed to support the geography National Curriculum.

Hassell, D. & Warner, H. (1995) *Using IT to Enhance Geography: Case Studies at Key Stages 3 and 4.* A compilation of some of the classroom activities undertaken as part of the Geography and IT Support Project 1994-95. GA/NCET.

NCET (1991) *IT's Geography. The role of IT in PGCE geography courses.* Occasional Paper 3. NCET.

NCET (1995) *Approaches to IT Capabilities, Key Stage 3.*

SCAA (1995b) *Information Technology, Key Stages.* Contains a specific geographic booklet, geography and IT.

Teaching Geography 'IT-Pages' and software reviews (including CD-ROMs) in each issue. The Geographical Association.

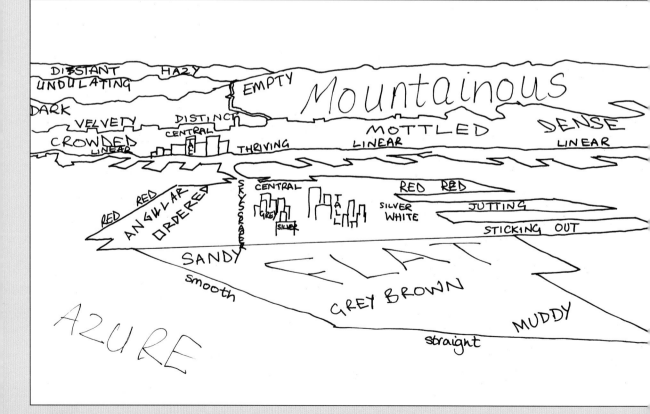

Chapter 23

Teaching geography with televisual resources

CHRIS DURBIN

Once there was chalk and talk; now there is a whole range of multi-media resources. Never has it been so important to ask what are the strengths and weaknesses of each medium for geography teaching and learning. Chapter 21 addresses the question of how to evaluate some of these resources; here the focus is on the medium of televisual resources (that is television programmes, whether live broadcasts, recorded, or bought on video) – how to evaluate them, and how to use them in the classroom.

Research suggests that geography teachers like using television and video because they:

- bring distant places to the classroom;

- enable people's views to be heard, although they are often short sound bites;

- can explain a difficult concept or process using a combination of images, graphics and commentary;

- can relate the location of a place to a wider region or even the world, through a series of 'nested' maps;

- can give a visual impression of change over time in relation to various geographical phenomena.

It is important to recognise that televisual resources have limitations and constraints, which is why support materials are also essential. It is difficult for televisual resources to:

- convey detail on maps and also specific locational knowledge;

- convey complex geographical data;

- give subtle and complex viewpoints about an issue;

- allow enough time for the viewer to absorb complex information.

A pause button allows detailed word-scapes to be constructed from a television 'still'

Photo: **Len Brown**
 BBC Education

In short, television is not a medium which enables the user to dwell on things or to take in large quantities of information; a high quality slide projected onto a screen, or multiple copies of photographs and maps, will often do the job much better. Tempting as it may be, we must not use television as a surrogate teacher; it is only one of several tools which teachers can use as aids to teaching and learning.

How should televisual resources be evaluated?

Every televisual resource is different and we must evaluate each in turn. Making time to do this is important, though more time-consuming than looking at textbooks, for example. A quick tick-list of criteria helps (see Figure 1) and this can be used by all members of the department. Sticking this tick-list to each video cassette box helps others to use it more easily and effectively.

EVALUATING TELEVISUAL RESOURCES

SUMMARY AND TIMINGS OF PROGRAMME:

Curriculum Uses

IMAGES

Clarity	very clear	☐	☐	☐	very unclear ☐
Appropriateness	very appropriate	☐	☐	☐	very inappropriate ☐

NARRATION

Language level	very high	☐	☐	☐	very low ☐
Clarity of speech	very clear	☐	☐	☐	very unclear ☐
Clarity of explanation	very clear	☐	☐	☐	very unclear ☐

GRAPHICS

Explanation of	very clear	☐	☐	☐	not at all clear ☐

CONTENT

Geographical content	very accurate	☐	☐	☐	inaccurate ☐
Value position	biased	☐	☐	☐	unbiased ☐
	represents one view	☐	☐	☐	represents many views ☐

OTHER POINTS OF INTEREST:

Figure 1: An evaluation tick-list for televisual resources

How to make best use of televisual resources for teaching geography

Given the popularity of televisual resources in schools, it is surprising how little research has been done on how children learn from the medium of television. The following experiment conducted by Margaret Roberts (1987) serves to illustrate one aspect of this.

A group of student teachers were shown a television programme and asked to take notes on what they learned from it. The programme was stopped after five minutes and the transcript of the commentary was read out. The students were asked to delete from their notes anything which they had written down during the programme that was in the transcript. Not a single student had anything left! They had made no record of what they had just seen.

This revealed that the students were not interpreting the pictures; they had behaved as if it was a simple dictation exercise. Visual information was not recorded.

The art of interpreting and describing pictures is intellectually demanding, but we as teachers must develop strategies to encourage it; it is important that children learn to develop their vocabulary from what they see on the screen as well as what they hear or read. Given the amount of time and money that television producers invest in selecting pictures for geography teachers, it seems an awful waste if they are not used to full advantage!

Think about the way you have used televisual resources in the past. Was the resource in the unit of work used:

– as a stimulus to a unit of work?

– to explain a process?

– to raise an issue?

– to illustrate an example or case study or a key idea?

– to compare another place with your local area (or another place you have been studying)?

– as a summary at the end of a unit of work?

It is suggested that you could use all these strategies according to the fitness for purpose of each piece. Did you use:

– a whole programme uninterrupted?

– a clip in isolation?

– a series of clips with activities interspersed?

Whole programmes are good for providing a quick overview of a situation or place and are excellent for reinforcing learning. Clips are useful for very specific learning outcomes. Using more of the programme than the specific clip allows pupils a few moments to 'tune in'. A series of clips with activities interspersed enables an enquiry to take place. Often a geography programme follows a line of enquiry and is over before the pupils have assimilated the issue, let alone the case study and the relevant 'stakeholders' involved. It is important, therefore, to identify the breakpoints in a televisual resource which are often indicated by televisual chapter headings. Breakpoints are not always obvious; they may be rhetorical questions, musical 'stings', a switch of scene from ground to aerial shots (or vice versa), a screen of graphics or text. They are simply intended to break up the narrative of a programme. A teacher can use them to pause and allow pupils to 'do' an activity.

> Here are some more questions you might ask.
> ■ Did your pupils take notes?
> ■ Did your pupils watch with no task?
> ■ Did your pupils watch a section and then have a whole-class discussion?
> ■ After watching a section did they move on to a related activity?
> ■ Did you set a variety of tasks for different groups of pupils?

Taking notes on a programme can be a valid activity, but breaks in viewing are important to enable the learner to pause to recall. Allowing pupils to watch without a related written task is often appropriate, but always provide a thinking task and outline what task(s) will follow their viewing. Make time for discussion about particular issues raised by a programme, and intersperse discussion with viewing.

Often teachers attempt to do too many things after one viewing. They expect their pupils to get a visual impression of a country, to understand how it has changed in economic and social terms, to have empathy with the people featured and to understand key issues and processes. Some pupils may be able to achieve all this, but it is best to assume that most will not. Use the class as a team, with each pupil being responsible for a particular task designed to achieve a particular learning outcome.

In an article in *Teaching Geography*, Graham Butt (1991) called for teachers and pupils to be much more investigative in their approach to using televisual resources and listed a range of strategies for investigating the role of the film maker. Media studies is concerned with issues such as these, many of which are very relevant to the teacher of geography.

In summary, there needs to be variety in the teaching strategies adopted when using televisual resources, and each strategy should be appropriate to the purpose. Below are some ideas for different approaches and specific activities for use in geographical enquiries relating to places and themes. While reading about these, it is worth thinking about active watching strategies that you might use to lift the medium from being one of passive entertainment to the powerful educational resource that we know it can be.

Figure 2: **A 'still' from Japan 2000. Photo: Len Brown/BBC Education**

Exploring perceptions

Much of geography is about facts, but much also is about perception. The way that we perceive distant places, for example, will depend to a very great extent on the visual images we are shown. Our pupils may have already encountered some of the places we teach them about, so we must take account of this, and of their perceptions of those places.

A 'brainstorming' session, in which words that pupils associate with the place being studied are listed, is a useful exercise with which to begin. Television programmes about the place can be used as part of this process to make it more interesting, fun and

```
                THE SONG
            THE BURNING SONG
         THE DEMON VULTURES
       THE HAZY TENTS    THE RAW
     HORIZONS   THE DRUGGED SANDS    THE SCREAMING
   THUNDER  THE RATTLING BONES THE DUSTY MOUTHS
  THE INFINITE EYES   THE DREAM POWER   THE CIRCLING
 SKY  THE TREACHEROUS BIRDS  THE SHIFTING TOWNS  THE
 SNARLING GUNS  THE BURNING STORM  THE VAST RIVER THE
 CLAY DANCERS  THE BLACK MASKS  THE RICH SANDS  THE HAZY
 DEMON  THE SCREAMING SKIES  THE VULTURES MOUTHS  THE RAW
 EYES  THE THUNDEROUS SONG  THE SHIFTING TRACKS  THE VAST
 CIRCLE  THE RATTLING BIRDS  THE DUSTY TENTS  THE GUNS SNARL
THE STEAMING HORIZON  THE BONE FOREST  THE BURNING TOWNS  THE
 SAND FLOWERS  THE TREACHEROUS INFINITE  THE BLACK TRACKED THE
 DANCERS SCREAM  THE MASKED GUNS  THE THUNDERS MOUTH  THE FOREST
 TOWN  THE CLAY HUTS  THE STORMS POWER  THE DRUGGED RIVER THE
 SHIFTING SONGS  THE SKYS EYE  THE RATTLING DREAM  THE SNARLING DUST  THE
 SANDS DEMONS  THE BURNING BIRDS  THE CIRCLING HAZE  THE RAW BONES THE
 RICH TENTS  THE SCREAMING FLOWER  THE STEAMING CLAY  THE BLACK SAND
   THE MASKED    DANCE  THE TREACHEROUS HORIZON  THE STORMS TRACK
              THE RIVER THUNDER   THE SHIFTY VULTURES  THE
            FORESTS POWER  THE RAW SKY  THE SCREAMING
           EYES  THE DREAM SONGS  THE DRUGGED HUTS
          THE HAZY TOWNS  THE BURNT CIRCLE  THE
          GUNS MOUTH  THE SNARLING BONES  THE
           INFINITE BIRDS      THE DUSTY FLOWERS
         THE STORMS MASK  THE THUNDERING
        DEMONS   THE TENT DANCERS  THE
         RICH CLAY   THE SHIFTED POWER
         THE SANDY RIVER     THE BURNING
        TREACHERY   THE RATTLING TRACK
        THE BLACK STEAM    THE POWERFUL
       DREAM  THE FLOWERING SONG  THE
     DRUGGED STREAM  THE DANCING EYE          THE
     HORIZONTAL HUT  THE MOUTHLESS           SNARLS
     THE TRACKLESS SKY    THE RAW               FOREST
       THE TENT TOWN    THE HAZY                RIVER
     THE INFINITE SHIFT      THE                 BIRD
     STORM  THE TREACHEROUS                    DEMON
     THE BURNING DRUG    THE                    GUN
       DANCE    THE SINGING
        BONE    THE MASKED
        RICH    THE BLACK
       CIRCLING    THE
       VAST DREAM
        SINGING
```

Figure 3: A word shape (Africa – compiled by Dave Calder)

informed. For example, you could begin by showing a clip from a programme about Japan (Figure 2) without commentary, just music. Pupils can then select adjectives that describe the images they see. These are written on the board or OHP, and then discussed. These words could also be written into a blank outline map (see Figure 3). The results will reveal the diversity of perceptions that pupils have – some will be 'negative' (dense, enclosed, depressing), some 'positive' (exiting, dynamic, rich).

Exercises like these help us to examine the things that influence our perceptions about places. They also help pupils to understand that the study of places is about attitudes and values as well as about facts (Durbin, 1995), and that, when used on their own, visual images (and music) have serious limitations, as well as being capable of manipulating our ideas.

Building descriptions

We all learn new vocabulary by picture and word association and geography teachers share with their colleagues the duty to develop young people's vocabulary. In a study of contrasting regions in the USA the teacher and a class of 35 watched five minutes of a documentary programme about the Colorado river. She paused the programme on a vivid landscape and asked the class to annotate a pre-prepared outline sketch of the Arizona desert. On another occasion, the teacher used an envelope of adjectives and asked the class to select appropriate words to describe the landscape of the river Rhine. The pupils were then asked to create a 'wordscape' where the selected words are inserted, appropriately shaped, into an outline sketch (Durbin, 1995). Figure 4 shows a still from *USA 2000* (BBC Education, 1995) which is typical of the many opportunities that can be found in televisual resources. These can be used for developing geographical vocabulary in interesting ways, such as wordscapes and shape poems (see Figure 5).

Figure 4: Colorado river 'still' from USA 2000
Photo: Len Brown/BBC Education

Me and Amanda meander like rivers that run to the sea We wander at random, we're always in tandem, meandering Mandy and me.

Figure 5: A shape poem: me and Amanda (compiled by Colin West). Source: Wes Magee, 1989

Explaining geographical phenomena

Educational geography programmes usually include graphics, these are designed to explain why things are like they are or why things are located in a particular place. Such programmes are also invaluable for illustrating change (Sharp, 1995). Here are some ways of using television graphics:

Teacher A

Class of 11-12 year old pupils

Task: To explain why there are different climates in different parts of the world.

Method: A television programme on the world's weather (designed for key stage 2 pupils), which included a graphic of a globe showing the sun's rays falling on the earth, was used. The class watched the whole programme once, were then given a list of twenty statements and were asked to decide which statements they thought were true; which not true; which they were unsure about. The class watched the programme again and were asked to write a commentary suitable for use by younger, primary school children.

Teacher B

Class of 11-12 year old pupils

Task: To learn about the stages involved in the formation of an ox-bow lake using differentiated activities.

Method: The class watched a clip from a BBC TV programme, *Le Rhône Sauvage*, showing the formation of an ox-bow lake (see Figure 6). Immediately after the clip was shown four different stages in the process were sequenced by the pupils. Pupils who completed this easily and quickly were given more complex explanations to add to the sequence. The final extension activity was to design a visual explanation for another river feature using a storyboard.

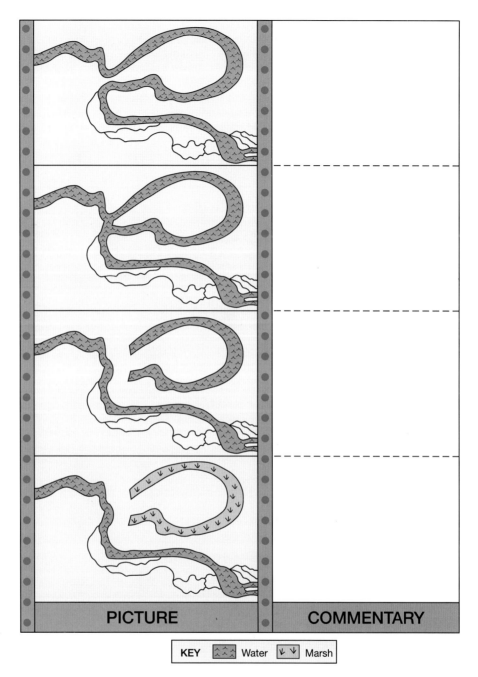

PICTURE   COMMENTARY

KEY [≛≛≛] Water [↓ ↓] Marsh

Figure 6: Storyboard: ox-bow lake formation

Exploring issues

Geography teachers often use devices such as role-play, debate, simulation and so on, to enable pupils to hear and evaluate a range of viewpoints about a particular issue. Pupils can then evaluate further the evidence (however partial/impartial), decide their own (or their character's) stance on the issue and qualify why they hold this viewpoint.

Televisual aids have particular value in this area of teaching. Unlike books they can be topical and show real people expressing personal opinions. They are also useful for providing thought-provoking and catchy sound bites (see Figure 7).

The sound bites shown in Figure 7 come from a Horizon programme called 'After the Flood' shown in 1994. The clip in which these people appeared was used in one class at the start of an enquiry into the impact of people on rivers. The pupils had to discuss the issue and to decide which viewpoint, if any, they agreed with. They then watched the programme in full, and were asked to note down any evidence which supported their view. The pupils went on to look at a range of other resources (books, etc.) to compare what they found with what they had learned from the programme.

Figure 7: Two sound bites – one from a river engineer in the US corps of engineers and one from a representative of Friends of the Earth

Valuing people's views

Research (Sharp, 1995) has shown that reactions to people from 'distant' places can be very confused and that pupils interpret what they see and hear from their own cultural perspective (see Chapter 3). Young people, therefore, need support from teachers when they are listening to people from distant places and must be alerted to listen carefully to the variety of viewpoints. They may need a transcript of what a person says. Profiles will also help pupils to get to know individuals better, and help them to understand and empathise with people in cultures different from their own. This is why it is important to provide some cultural background and to create a climate of empathy with people featured in the programme. Frequently, it is the priorities expressed by people directly involved in local issues which help pupils to understand why a place is changing in a particular way. These are much valued aspects of all geography television programmes and significant efforts are made to set them up and get them right.

Active watching strategies

Television is mainly used passively in the home. Getting the most out of televisual resources in the classroom involves thinking and planning activities very carefully and imaginatively. Ask yourself: Am I trying to explore perceptions, set up a debate, show a sequence of events, give a case study? These are **active watching strategies**. As teachers we have a duty to make the most of its learning opportunities and to develop television into an active learning experience. To enable us to do this we should ensure that we:

- try to appeal to a range of emotions in the pupil;

- give a clear briefing about what to watch for;

- set clear tasks before, during, and/or after clips;

- allow enough time for thinking and responding in discussion, writing, drawing and so on.

Sources for geography teaching with televisual resources

EDUCATIONAL TELEVISION

Both BBC Education *(The Geography Programme)* and Channel 4 Education *(Geographical Eye)* produce geography programmes for schools. These are targeted at the 11-18 curricula for the constituent parts of the UK. Notable highlights from the BBC have been *Japan 2000, USA 2000, Brazil 2000* and *Investigating Britain*, and from Channel 4: *Geographical Eye Over Europe* and *Geographical Eye Over Africa*. Every year a wall chart is produced for heads of department showing repeats and new series. There are also broadcasts at night, usually a series *en bloc*. The BBC in Scotland (S4C), Wales and Northern Ireland also produce programmes to reflect their own geography.

Support materials are available to accompany the series. Built around classroom geographical investigations, *Japan 2000* has an accompanying pack which comprises a set of photograph and map cards, a booklet of activity maps, data files and more in-depth information discovered in the research phase of these programmes. Channel 4 have produced sets of satellite images to accompany the *Geographical Eye* series. Some series are available for purchase on video. There are other commercial or charitable suppliers of educational material on video, but these are rare. This information is mailed directly to schools when it is published. The main sources of information are:

- BBC Education Information Unit, BBC White City, 201 Wood Lane, London W12 7TS. Tel: 0181 746 1111. e-mail bbc.education@bbc.co.uk

- Channel 4 Schools Programme information is available from: Educational Television Company, PO Box 100, Warwick CV34 6TZ.

GENERAL TELEVISION

There is a wide range of geography programmes on non-educational television. *Horizon* has provided a rich vein of physical and environmental geography over the years, some notable examples being 'Dodging Doomsday' (1990) and 'After the Flood' (1994). The Open University carries some excellent series for the study of geography. These are not always appropriate to show in full to school pupils, but are useful in short clips or to update the teacher's own knowledge. Finally, do not forget the news and weather; topicality in geography is very important. The Kobe earthquake in 1995 and the Scarborough cliffs landslip in 1993 are typical examples of topicality. The late-night weather reports are often longer and more detailed than others and also give information about the weather worldwide.

COPYRIGHT

Copyright status is complex; LEAs negotiate licences with, and pay fees to, the Educational Recording Agency on behalf of their maintained schools. For grant-maintained and independent schools a separate fee must be negotiated. Details from:

Educational Recording Agency, 74 New Oxford Street, London WC1A 1EF.

A separate flat-rate licence for schools is also needed for Open University programmes. For further details contact:

Open University Enterprises Limited, 12 Cofferidge Close, Stoney Stratford, Milton Keynes MK11 1BY.

References

Butt, G. (1991) 'Have we got a video today?', *Teaching Geography,* 16, 2, pp. 51-55.

Calder, D. (1981) *Continents.* Leaflet published by the author.

Durbin, C. (1994) *Japan 2000.* BBC Education.

Durbin, C. (1995) 'Using televisual resources in geography', *Teaching Geography,* 20,3, pp. 118-121.

Magee, W. (ed) (1989) *Madtail Mini Whale – And Other Shape Poems.*

Viking Kestrel.

Roberts, M. (1987) 'Using videocassettes', *Teaching Geography,* 12, 3, pp. 114-117.

Sharp, C. (1995) *The Use and Impact of Schools Broadcasts.* NFER.

Section Six

Management matters

SUMMARY OF CHAPTERS

'No institution can possibly survive if it
needs geniuses and supermen to manage it.
It must be organised in such a way as to be
able to get along under a leadership of
average human beings.'

Peter Drucker,
The Practice of Management, 1955.

How should a department organise its work?
How can it be developed and appraised?
How should departmental resources be
acquired, deployed and renewed? How
should the department cope with
inspections? This section looks at the issues
and challenges of departmental
management, many of which arise in limited
forms even when the 'department' consists
of just one person.

Chapter 24

Managing the departmental team

GARY CAMBERS

Heads of geography departments must now accept that their management is open to intrusive public scrutiny as well as internal monitoring and review. Accountability has moved a long way from the opening up of the classroom 'black box' of the 1980s. The Education Acts of the 1990s have devolved to schools the responsibility for spending budgets from public money; they must account for their performance through published test and examination results. Schools must also account for the quality of teaching and learning. In addition to observing colleagues teach as part of in-house appraisal, heads of departments must respond to OFSTED judgements such as 'In some lessons teachers displayed insecure geographical knowledge and set undemanding tasks'. It is clear that a 'New Century' manager will need to be more than 'a good teacher of geography' and must deliver more than 'evidence of working well in a team'.

The National Curriculum also has major implications for the future management of geography teaching. It has been reinforced at key stage 3 as part of a common entitlement for all, while beyond this its importance is demoted to an option, or even may not be on offer for the GCSE and post-16 cohorts. The 14-16 age range (key stage 4) presents heads of geography departments with their biggest challenge; unless a demand for the subject at GCSE level is created by work at key stage 3 and below, there may be no geography department left to manage! Retaining a GCSE curriculum while developing GNVQ Foundation provision will put pressure on geography; its survival will need to be justified not only as an important GCSE subject but also as one which will contribute much to aspects of GNVQ provision. This dual function is likely to determine the standing of the subject within the whole school.

With school budgets dependent on around 80% of formula funding through Age-Weighted Pupil Units, school governors and heads will scrutinise any subject failing to attract sufficient numbers to meet the minimum size of teaching group agreed in a Pupil–Teacher Ratio policy. These numbers will become targets to reach if the subject is not to wither on the vine. Even then, GCSE geography may have to run the gauntlet of a long Option Box where pupils have one or two choices to make from all the other subjects which the school's curriculum designers think are important additions to National Curriculum requirements.

Increased public accountability is also causing parents and pupils to 'shop around' between and within schools. This is less apparent in all-through 11-16 schools but in systems such as the Leicestershire Plan, where pupils attend High School up to age 14 and make their GCSE choices in Year 9 *before* moving to their chosen Upper School,

Departmental meetings may be difficult to arrange but are a valuable part of departmental management

Photo: **Gary Cambers**

comparisons are being made quite overtly. The choice of school and courses is made based on what they hear and perceive about a department and its work at key stage 4 and comparative performance in 'league' tables. The prime responsibility for making sure they like what they see and hear must be with the head of the department. Unless the department consists of only one person, the head will have a number of colleagues to work with and manage. The key to departmental survival and success will depend on how effective the head is in managing the learning of geography through the department's members and communicating a positive image about the quality of teaching and learning to potential pupils.

Marketing the department

With schools increasingly at the whim of market forces through competition for pupil numbers, schools cannot afford to be seen as remote from local parental and community concern. National publicity has ensured that the local community, especially present and potential parents, is well aware that it is paying large sums of money into national education budgets and that this money is being transferred directly into local school budgets through Local Management of Schools arrangements. Parents and pupils, while usually supportive of their school, are beginning to take on the character of 'consumers' with perceptive questions at open evenings, and complaints about any teacher who they feel is not delivering what they are entitled to expect.

Schools and departments risk all if they fail to respond to such external interest. Parental suspicion of complacency and arrogance in a school or department at a time of heightened media interest in education can quickly lead to a poor reputation and the loss of pupils and their friends to another school. Glossy brochures and prospectuses are not enough to improve the school's reputation; it is what existing pupils, parents and the local community say about the school that attracts or repels future intakes. With funding for a dozen pupils being equivalent to one teaching post, a school which allows itself to get into such a downward spiral could quickly find whole subject areas impossible to staff or offer beyond key stage 3.

Geography departments must accept this general context as one of which they are part and within which all their members carry a responsibility. All staff need to develop the habit of celebrating successes and being actively concerned about weaknesses. If the school is to respond to challenges in constructive, confident and positive ways, it will need every unit in it to contribute to the whole of its work. Once a whole-school philosophy and related policies have been agreed, these will provide a sense of direction for departments and they must be supported by all a department's members.

A crucial part of the head of department's role will be to develop an informed awareness of the rapidly changing whole-school context and to convey this to all the department's members. It may be necessary for the successful department to share the secrets of its successes with others. The survival of the school, and consequently each subject within it, will depend on the strong helping the weak. A New Century head of a geography department must strive to engender such a co-operative spirit and sense of corporate responsibility among all the department's staff. Arguably, this is the most important single aspect of a head of department's role today. Perhaps it always was?

WHAT'S IN A NAME?
Recent advertisements for heads of geography departments reveal that the title is changing to one which relates to the style of leader required. *Director* of Geographical Studies, Geography *Team Leader*, Curriculum *Co-ordinator* all suggest an emphasis upon management style. The last two involve bringing people together and sharing responsibility rather than directing their work. Heads of department should consider whether they prefer to be a 'titular head' or whether their style and what they actually do could be more accurately expressed through another title. Time should be set aside for a department to discuss the most effective management style and structure.

The School and Department Development Plan

School Development Plans are a welcome and useful initiative in that they bring together interested and responsible parties to ask such fundamental questions as:

- What is the philosophy and ethos, and what are the values of this school?
- What are the short- and longer-term aims and objectives for future development?
- How will these be achieved?
- When will these be achieved?
- How will progress towards goals be monitored so that everyone knows what progress is being made?
- What are our priorities and what ought we to do next?

Development Plans are important documents at both school and department levels. They form a key part of the requirements for a school inspection (see Chapter 27), and the influence of OFSTED reports must not be under-estimated. Such reports often express scepticism about Development Plans and other paperwork if links to budget setting and planning cannot be demonstrated. Perhaps more importantly from an educational point of view, OFSTED reports are highly critical if evidence from classroom observation does not reflect the stated intentions of the Plan. This is where the head of department has a crucial role to play. Links must be clearly established between the School Development Plan and plans at departmental level. The latter must be set down in written form and their effects must be observable in practice in classrooms and in other areas of the department's activities.

Aim	Priority Activity What is to be done?	Strategy How will it be done?	Cost	Success Criteria How will we measure success?	References to college aims and SDP priority areas		Staff responsible
					Aim	SDP	
To improve the quality of learning in the department by promoting increased self-esteem and confidence in pupils.	A department policy on the assessment and reporting of written work will be produced.	A team of three review existing department practice on marking technique and style. SPAG correction and timing feedback to pupils.	Two half days of INSET for planning and production. £300 for supply cover.	A departmental policy will be produced, agreed and implemented from 1 January. The team will monitor its impact on the quality of learning of pupils by Easter.	1. To promote self-esteem, confidence, self discipline and the development of mature independent minds.	6. To promote self-esteem and confidence by providing positive and constructive responses to pupils' written work	SA/GC

Figure 1: *Example of how to link the aims of a School Development Plan and a Department Development Plan*

Figure 1 illustrates a possible link between a School Plan and a Department Plan. It clearly relates a general aim to an assessment policy review; sets out a time scale for the work; costs the necessary in-service training; and states criteria for success. It also indicates who will carry out the work.

One of the first tasks for a head of department is to draw up, with other members of the departmental team, a manageable and realistic Department Development Plan which shows precisely how the department intends to contribute to whole-school priority areas besides developing specific initiatives at department level. Figure 2 contains several examples of policy areas that could be part of the Plan.

Departmental Statement: A brief statement of the Geography Department's philosophy, ethos and aims and a justification for its existence in the curriculum.

Departmental Context: Description of the department with some historical/futuristic context, e.g. number of staff, teaching rooms, pupil grouping policy, current/future courses.

	Within the classroom	Beyond the classroom
Section 1: Curriculum Management e.g. key stages 3, 4 and post-16 structure and assessment, recording and reporting	Teaching/learning processes Assessment/marking policy Grouping policies	Day/residential fieldwork Group sizes for fieldwork
Section 2: Staff INSET & Development e.g. development of staff skills by activity within the department/school or through external in-service training in subject skills and management	Classroom observation by colleagues Research into GCSE/GNVQ links Internal moderation exercises	External courses developing subject and management skills Paid work as external examiners/moderators
Section 3: Resource Management e.g. managing and developing the resources for use in learning at key stages 3 and 4 and post-16	Recommending/buying books, software Filing/updating of worksheets	Liaison with library, IT centres, reprographics personnel re: planned curriculum activity Booking school minibus and outside visits
Section 4: Community/Public Relations e.g. developing mutually beneficial links with local and other communities and a positive image within and beyond the school e.g. liaison links with feeder primary or high schools in curriculum matters of continuity and progression and transfer issues at the various key stages	Use of local community, e.g. oral archives, opposing views concerning local issues Displays of pupil work in own school	Press coverage through school PR system of geographical events, wildlife activity and achievement in competitions Displays in local schools, banks, shops. Assembly presentations by former pupils. Joint school surveys. Distribution of research activity to local bodies, e.g. traffic count

Figure 2: Possible structure with examples of content and a Department Development Plan

WHY ARE WE HERE?

Any self-respecting department made up of professional geographers should want to produce its own statement of why it feels the subject is worth studying at secondary level; otherwise, the department becomes the servant rather than the master of which knowledge, skills and understanding is to be taught. This departmental philosophy has to be compatible with the school's ethos and provide the overview within which key stage 3 requirements are taught and within which GCSE, A level syllabuses and GNVQ courses are matched. This statement provides the focus for the more detailed management of learning through the Department Development Plan (DDP). Examples of such statements include:

■ to develop a sense of place and an understanding of relative location;

■ to develop a range of communication skills; oral, written and graphical.

WHAT MUST WE AGREE TO DO AS A TEAM THROUGH THE DDP?

Although the drafting of the departmental statement may be carried out by a small number of teachers, it is important that working out the policies involves everybody. Here it will be necessary to break down the work into sections and share these out among the departmental team. These additional tasks or areas of responsibility may not carry any monetary reward; staff who wish to gain managerial experience will need to take on unpaid tasks if they are to enhance their career prospects. A department might divide up its work into:

• Curriculum Management • Staff Development and In-service training
• Resource Management • Community Development and Public Relations

Figure 3 shows a non-hierarchical departmental staffing structure which assigns equal responsibility and equal payment to each section. If a teacher took on two of the Development Plan sections then higher payment would be justifiable. Certainly, in developing a team culture based on equal contribution, the hierarchical system of old ceases to be appropriate. Each task within the sections will provide management experience of liaison with other personnel within and beyond the school, e.g. parents, the community, support staff, senior management.

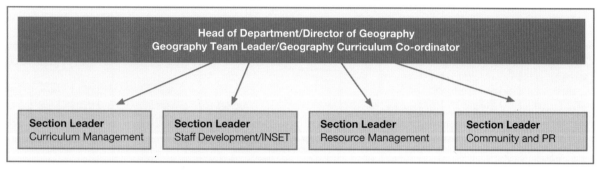

Figure 3: Departmental structure in a team approach to management

Although a number of these tasks would normally be carried out by the head of department, the need for this should always be questioned. The head of department's managerial responsibility is to get things done, not necessarily to do them personally. It is likely that a secondary geography department in a moderately large school will consist of three or four full-time staff, some staff from other subject areas who help with parts of the work, and supply staff. In addition to this teaching team there may be support staff for pupils with special needs, and library and resources staff including reprographics and IT technicians. The whole of this extended team has to be considered when a Department Development Plan is being drawn up, for all are responsible in part for the quality of geographical learning that takes place and need to contribute to the Plan by sharing some tasks.

HOW CAN WE DELIVER THE HIGHEST POSSIBLE QUALITY OF LEARNING?
The major thrust in every aspect of the Geography Department Development Plan is to ensure that the learning it provides is of the highest possible quality. In practice most of this plan will relate to classroom activities and to resources to support those activities. Given the nature of geography it is useful to distinguish between work in class and work outside, as shown in Figure 2. The nature of the subject justifies a separation in order to emphasise the importance of the outside world in geographical education; this is an essential part of geographical education, not an optional add-on.

HOW AS A TEAM CAN WE ACHIEVE MORE?
The forward-looking geography teaching team will wish to review progress regularly, by comparing what is actually taking place with the Development Plan as well as reflecting upon the past year's successes and failures. If nothing else, a Development Plan must in effect be an Action Plan if it is to influence the department's work. *How well have we done?* at secondary level has traditionally been answered by referring to end-of-year examination results; but in fact far more is involved in appraising the quality of a department's work. These wider aspects of departmental appraisal, essentially self-assessment, are discussed in Chapter 25.

Chapter 25

Departmental self-assessment

GARY CAMBERS

> 'Evaluation in geographical education is not restricted to the assessment of student progress. It is concerned with the total process of education and is a vital part of reviewing the effectiveness and quality of teaching, curricula and the learning environment.'
> Geography Teachers Association of Victoria, 1986, p. 10.

Why is self-assessment needed?

Teaching to the best of one's ability and having this recognised by others provides the basis for self-esteem and confidence in attempting more challenging tasks. Never satisfied with existing standards, the professional continually strives to improve and perform more effectively from year to year. Forward-looking and optimistic human beings possess an innate curiosity to know how well they are doing at the job. Teachers who show little concern about the standard of their work are quickly discovering that if the head of department is reluctant to address the issue then vigilant parents and pupils can become quite vociferous, demanding that the head and governors do something about it. Whereas self-assessment has often been based on public examination results and/or a voluntary, reflective, holiday activity pursued for one's own betterment, the severity of the now transparent and competitive school system makes it an urgent and essential strategy for improvement from within.

Increased public accountability, parental choice and the linking of pupil numbers to school budgets have added to the pressure on curriculum managers to assess, formally and informally, how a department and its individual teachers are performing and to make judgements about the quality of learning. Any demoralised teacher demotivated to improve, or at worst cynical and unhelpful about their own need to bring their work up to standard, will find limited sympathy from colleagues. Without a corporate commitment to improvement and excellence, poor reputations will lead to pupil loss and a falling budget with the possible consequence of voluntary or compulsory redundancy. It is in the interests of staff as well as pupils that each department makes a commitment to self-assessment and continual improvement.

The move towards external and public assessment of schools and departments through official inspections has acted as a spur for departments to devote time to self-assessment. Schools and departments have often been disappointed by inspectors' criticisms, believing that the one-week sample of lessons and activity, usually without

Keeping all the balls in the air is a full-time departmental task!

much meaningful dialogue, is not a full and fair context in which to be judged. Irrespective of external interest and official inspection, a conscientious department of professionals will want to improve their work by collecting evidence of present quality through unprompted assessment.

Planning for assessment within the geography department

The importance of a corporate and written **Department Development Plan** is discussed in Chapter 24. It is within this Plan, and especially in the Curriculum Management section, that the team must clearly set out their aims regarding the systematic assessment of their work in the forthcoming academic year. Evaluation and judgement can only be made against a pre-determined set of assessment aims, following which the collection of data and information can take place. For example, unless it is agreed at the outset that a head of department will see every teacher in action in the classroom or on fieldwork at least twice a year, this is unlikely to happen because it will involve arranging supply cover (which will need to be planned before the demands of a busy term make things impossible to arrange) for the observation and follow-up.

It is important that before a department plans a short- and long-term programme of self-assessment, it produces a **departmental handbook** containing its current policy and practice in relation to the Development Plan. This establishes what each teacher should carry out in order to meet the department's aims and objectives.

The implementation of a marking policy serves as a topical illustration. Recent inspection reports have quite fairly pointed out that in larger secondary school departments there remains a tendency for teachers to be left to mark, assess and comment on pupils' work using their own professional judgement *without any internal monitoring*. For example, marking may take place in line with an overall school assessment policy that pupils' routine classwork and homework is seen and marked regularly. However, what is not acceptable is if the pupil feedback varies from a numbered mark, with constructive written and verbal comment on a weekly basis, to the lazy, unprofessional, 'cerebral' marking scheme in the room next door which may involve a cursory one-term, one-line inspection of books during the course.

Despite (or because of?) the fact that large departments have shared workrooms, teachers are often very protective about their own marking policy. This is frequently the consequence of lack of leadership and fear of over-uniformity. In fact it is the pupils who need consistency and uniformity so that they are better able to judge their work against known standards.

The head of department should consider it their duty to discover what practice is being carried out by colleagues and to make a statement about an overall marking policy. The team must agree on certain standards, to apply consistently in all teaching groups, even if these involve some compromise between the above extremes.

The development and retention of coursework at key stage 4 has brought many teachers together to discuss criteria, common standards, mark and assessment schemes, and it has provided valuable experience of internal and external moderation. This now needs to be extended into the routine assessment of pupils across the whole department, thus enabling staff to make sound judgements about how well pupils are doing in geography. A pupil's performance in turn reflects on the quality of the teacher's own work.

As new policies are established, the policy statements in the department handbook should be revised and monitored throughout the year according to the Development Plan.

Pupils need to be involved in departmental self-assessment. They are the 'consumers' and more often than not make their feelings known if they are unhappy with the deal they perceive is being offered in the classroom. If their independence and sense of responsibility are to be developed they need to know exactly what is expected of them. Therefore a **pupil handbook** should be provided for each course offered. It should include details of the relevant course, state clearly how and when pupils will be assessed, and set out the policy for the setting, collection and returning of work. It should also state how pupils can get full benefit from all the departmental resources – including the teachers. The inclusion of such useful things as 'Term Planners' with space in which to write homework, a list of relevant library books, library/resource centre opening hours and available videos and computer software, adds to pupils' ability to access data and information. Resources should be related to courses rather than being placed in a generic index attached to each booklet.

The above will take time and should not be rushed. Ideally the School Development Plan can be ratified early in the summer term once budgets have been agreed and staffing issues resolved. The Department Development Plan then follows in June with departmental handbooks, schemes of work and pupil handbooks being produced in early July (and August!) ready for the start of the new school year. In practice many schools are now working on bi-annual School Development Plans which take account of the dislocated academic and financial years and relieve pressure by using a more pragmatic and realistic pace to achieve progress. What matters is that real progress and planned developments are seen to be taking place, whether it be over a one- or two-year schedule according to what is possible within each school and department.

How are we doing?

Assessing departmental performance should involve more than a mere discussion of policies. It should begin with a clear recognition of the prime task of the department: to generate high quality teaching and learning. Once agreed the department must identify its own criteria for achieving this. The best criteria are grounded in the experience of the classroom with teachers sharing thoughts on the lessons that really worked, why they worked and how they judged that high quality learning was achieved.

On the basis of this review, general departmental policies such as staff development, consistent marking styles and standards, strategies to achieve differentiation, methods of pupil grouping and pupil–teacher ratios, can then be reconsidered. General discussions about policies often lead to interesting educational debates but rarely produce an immediate impact upon classroom practice; whereas starting with a classroom focus allows a department to get real information on the impact of policies and makes it possible to effect changes.

Assessing and improving teaching and learning

Although the bulk of teaching time is in the classroom, a good deal of less defined activity also has a large influence on learning, especially in a subject which includes fieldwork and coursework at key stage 4. Ideally a professional team should meet at least once per term for a two-session (full day/two half-days) **Teaching Review Workshop** if the school's INSET budget will allow.

This important meeting should take the form of an honest review of the department's quality of teaching, both inside and outside the classroom, with individuals sharing the strategies and resources that have/have not worked. This discussion should feed into a revision of established Departmental **Schemes of Work**, which can present a co-ordinated plan for organising the learning for each term or module, and also list successful choices of process. The content to be covered can be noted, with an indication of where the resources are kept and advice on their use. The latter is vital; too often a successful set of resources is shared with a second teacher who finds, to their and the pupils' cost, that the input of the first teacher between and through the tasks made them work. If resources are to be shared within a team, the advice on how to get the best from them must also be shared.

Assessing teaching quality must involve judgement about preparation and input to the lesson or fieldwork. The most effective way to do this is to involve a colleague from the outset. In a department with a 'flat' (non-hierarchical) structure, this colleague need not be the head of department. For an objective, non-specialist view, a colleague from another curriculum subject could focus on aspects of a lesson, for example, an English teacher might be useful in observing or helping with oral assessments.

It seems realistic for a department to review the teaching of one particular course each year. There is a logic in sharing responsibility between the department team not only, as is often the case, for producing resources, activities and schemes of work, but also for monitoring and assessing the quality of teaching for each item.

A fieldwork expert, a coursework expert and a number of module planners would be needed; in smaller departments more will be required from each individual. Sharing in such self-assessment helps give every teacher a sense of ownership and responsibility for the successful implementation of part of the course; also an equal share of the often sensitive task of seeing colleagues' prepared materials, as well as their teaching. This approach offers potential for rotating the responsibilities to achieve staff development.

A DEPARTMENTAL TEACHING REVIEW WORKSHOP (PART ONE)

The first part of a department's **Teaching Review Workshop** can set out to answer a number of questions, with each planner leading the discussion on their respective parts of the course. Initial questions for discussion might include:

1. How well presented were the department's written materials, i.e. worksheets, OHPs, video note sheets? Was the presentation of these consistent across similar teaching groups in terms of style, reading levels, range of skills and tasks?

2. Did the team vary the materials and their style according to the ability of the pupils within each group and between groups in order to achieve differentiation? How were materials varied? With which groups did this differentiation work or fail?

3. How effective were the team's spoken and written inputs in explaining the tasks on the worksheets and in response to queries from pupils?

4. How were the pupils motivated by each teacher's approach, style or strategy?

5. How effective does the team, and individual teachers within it, feel their contribution was?

6. What implications does the review hold for the development of future teaching process and practice, e.g. the location of and access to resources, and consideration of new syllabuses more appropriate to the existing/ desired style of teaching?

Following such discussion it is crucial to consider what action the team is going to take, both immediately and in the longer-term, to improve its teaching. Action points and realistic deadlines are the hallmark of a self-improving department; without such focuses, the recurrent pressure of day-to-day work can overwhelm good intentions.

Using assessment to improve learning

Having established where there is room for improvement in teaching, the second part of each Teaching Review Workshop can focus on an honest assessment of the quality of pupil learning. There is always plenty of evidence of it, but it is a rare department that finds the time to use quality of learning fully, for example to check for consistency across groups. Whether formal or informal, formative or summative, the co-ordination of agreed methods, styles and standards is scarce unless externally prompted by the requirements of an examination board.

Before the introduction of the National Curriculum, the GCSE and A level examinations cycles were the only times that teachers came together to agree mark schemes for internal and trial examinations and criteria for assessing coursework. Consequently it was only in these situations that pupils received detailed reports or progress summaries (see Figure 1) related to agreed objective criteria. A department must establish such criteria so that it has accurate, consistent and known policies that are applied fairly across all teaching groups throughout the secondary age range.

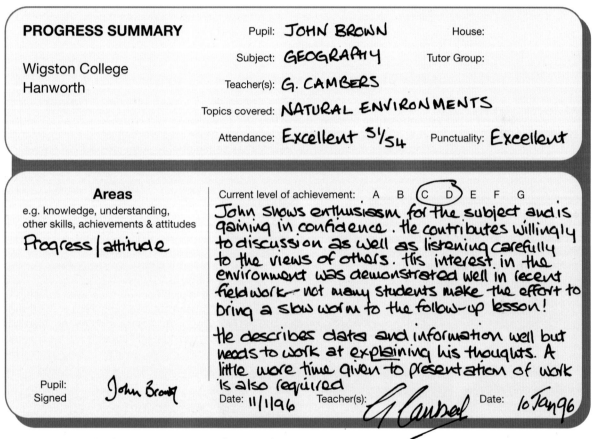

Figure 1: An example of a completed Progress Summary form

With the National Curriculum establishing content and clarifying what is expected of each pupil to reach the levels or GCSE grades, departments must plan their various methods around such levels so that, whenever and however a test is carried out, the pupils and staff know which part of the course is being assessed, how it is being assessed and what is expected from each pupil to reach a certain level. Hence, each expert or planner in the team will include in their schemes of work, fieldwork booklets or coursework items, a set of assessments to be applied with each group.

Assessments can be oral tests, role-plays in groups, assignments, short tests, problem-solving exercises, or previous exam questions relevant to the module. Examples of pupil work at different levels with agreed marks and model mark schemes should also be included. The style of these needs to be consistent, as should the reporting back of spelling, punctuation and grammar.

None of this conformity precludes teachers continuing with their own favoured style of assessment (the occasional quick test or Christmas Geography Quiz still has its place), but there should be a set of objective testing materials relevant to and applied across the whole cohort of pupils so that comparisons are possible. Co-ordinating and moderating such results after initial marking would be part of the role of each module planner who can make recommendations about the performance of each group, the movement of pupils into higher- or lower-ability teaching groups, and give feedback on any concerns about the accuracy and consistency of assessment.

Accurate assessment of pupils' work, especially their written work, which is always likely to count for more in formal examinations, must be the cornerstone of the assessment of learning. Only when this is done can a department know what is being achieved across all its teaching groups and respond accordingly. However, the assessment of learning is not just about achieving consistency through planned and co-ordinated testing arrangements.

What about the learners?

Involving pupils in assessing their own progress is a well-tried and useful motivator for helping them to discover where they are struggling or succeeding as well as to develop a sense of responsibility for putting matters right. Involving pupils in making a formal assessment of the quality of teaching, as an input to departmental self-assessment, is a more sensitive issue. Nevertheless, it is important to involve these 'consumers', however subjective and ill-informed some of their observations may be! This is where

One-to-one tutorials are a particularly valuable kind of assessment

Photo: **Margaret Roberts**

regular classroom dialogue and interviews can be useful in an evaluation of teaching and learning. Evidence from written work and other assignments – such as oral contributions – will help a teacher form a yardstick of successful learning; but it is incumbent on each team member to attend the Teaching Review Workshop with an honest opinion of what the pupils thought about the work in which they were involved. The discussion should not only encourage the production of **Individual Action Plans** for pupils but also contribute towards the Department Plan for reviewing the course and its own wider self-assessment.

Involving parents can also help reinforce the traditional parent–pupil–teacher partnership. Parents' meetings, open workshops and an annual/termly newsletter are all useful in explaining to parents what the department is trying to do and in gauging their support or opinion on a venture. The occasional constructive comment by a perceptive parent, helping out on a fieldwork day, has often been of great use in reviewing the success of such an activity.

A DEPARTMENTAL TEACHING REVIEW WORKSHOP (PART TWO)
The Teaching Review Workshop (part two) could consider a series of questions concentrating on particular aspects of pupil learning such as:

1. In which parts of the work did particular groups of pupils appear to do well or to fail? Why were they successful or otherwise?

2. To what degree did the characteristics of resources (written, visual, tapes, etc.) help or hinder different groups of pupils in learning the work?

3. What did different groups of pupils enjoy most and least? Why?

4. From which strategies/activities did the pupils feel they learnt most? Why? Can they articulate their impressions?

5. Did the variety of tasks set lead to differentiation through tasks or through outcome? Which of these is departmental policy?

6. How effective and forthcoming does the team feel the contribution of pupils has been through their written and spoken inputs to their learning?

7. Were homeworks suitable for, and regularly completed by, all groups of pupils? If any group failed to complete, why was this and what can be done about it?

8. What have parents said about the teaching and learning of this work?

9. Have the pupils learned as much as we feel they should have done, bearing in mind our expectations of their potential based on start-of-course assessment of ability?

10. What implications does the review hold for improving the motivation, commitment and learning of pupils, e.g. increasing organised oral contributions, revising the language used on written resources, increasing understanding through more local fieldwork?

The overview

It is argued that only through detailed and regular review of the teaching and learning process can a department begin self-assessment and progress in development. The head of department should be managing this assessment and using the findings of the Teaching Review Workshop to draft revised plans for future Department Development Plans. Such discussions provide leads to future policy developments, ensuring the department moves forward and improves the quality of its work.

Departmental self-assessment is not a general review of examination results as part of a brief agenda before continuing with the day-to-day business, although value-added work is a useful objective indicator of pupil progress and past performance. It must be an honest debate about what learning is actually happening within and beyond the classrooms. To be successful this requires planned time for team discussion and a willingness on the part of teachers and pupils to want to do better. It also requires a leader committed to improving the quality of teaching and learning within the geography department. Due largely to advances in information technology the management of people can now take precedence over the management of paper. It is a challenge which is difficult and time-consuming, but the rewards are considerable. After all, what head of department would choose to face a form for routine examination entries in preference to talking with a colleague or pupil about an aspect of their work that needs improving or has been successful?

Reference

Geography Teachers Association of Victoria (1986) *The Value of Geography*. GTAV, 402 Smith Street, Collingwood, Victoria, Australia.

Chapter 26

Managing resources

KEVIN LUKER

An important part of a head of department's job?

Ensuring that all classes have access to the relevant textbooks, or that there are enough Ordnance Survey maps to go round, is not a very rewarding aspect of a head of department's job. If these resources are not available, for whatever reason, it will probably be pointed out that it is the head of department's fault. On the other hand, when teachers are well resourced and things run smoothly, heads of department are unlikely to collect any compliments. It is hardly surprising, then, that this aspect of 'managing resources' is seen as a mundane and bread-and-butter task by most heads of department. In my own job description as head of department, 'management of department budget and resources' does not appear until Section C, point (e), half-way down the second of two sides of A4.

The above description of a manager of resources does not do justice to the broader and more important aspects of the role which involve responsibility not only for textbooks, atlases, stationery, etc., but also for the team of teachers that comprise the department and for non-teaching staff and classrooms (including furniture and equipment). In addition, the role includes the management of access to centrally-held school resources such as books in the library or computer facilities. These are all crucial aspects of a head of department's job and vital to the effectiveness of the departmental team as a whole.

Departmental challenges

All departments face different challenges and how these are met will depend upon the department's local and historical circumstances. Here are three examples to illustrate this point:

a. A department of specialist geography teachers will face different resourcing problems from a department which is composed of teachers who teach across the range of the humanities subjects and who therefore see themselves essentially as non-specialists. In the current climate, following the introduction of the National Curriculum, many trained specialist teachers and non-specialist teachers, can feel an acute lack of confidence and inadequacy if the appropriate teaching resources, supported by INSET, are not available. It is, therefore, imperative that sensible planning of where, when and how resources will be used, and what INSET will be provided, becomes as essential part of the head of department's task. Some of the most effective INSET is that mounted within the school in response to specific needs.

b. Another challenge departments have faced recently has been the implementation of, and subsequent changes to, the geography National Curriculum Order. Whether departments find resourcing the Order a major problem or a minor difficulty will obviously depend on the nature of the resources already in use. An important factor in whether teachers feel confident about teaching something new or different often boils down to having the 'right tools for the job'.

c. The allocation of teaching rooms to staff during timetabling can be an important issue in schools where one teacher cannot have exclusive use of a teaching room. Sensitive discussions and a fair policy for all are therefore essential for maintaining departmental morale. As a general rule, the head of department must be prepared to share any inconveniences.

These illustrate the way that mundane tasks (ordering textbooks or allocating rooms) can have a significant knock-on effect to teacher and department effectiveness and morale.

Sources of department income

The most important source of regular income for a department is capitation, which is divided up among departments in a school according to a variety of formulae. It is worthwhile scrutinising the formula used in your school and seeing whether or not it favours 'practical' subjects. Some heads of geography departments have argued successfully for a greater share of the cake by saying that they do in fact operate in a 'practical' way.

Apart from capitation, there are other sources of income, often of a one-off nature or available only for a limited number of years. Unfortunately, in such cases, you will more than likely have to go through the lengthy and detailed procedure of making a bid for the money. Funding through Technical and Vocational Educational Initiative (TVEI) in the Authority where I work (Doncaster) is shared equally amongst the schools. Within my school, however, any interested department or individual can make a bid for the money, providing they fulfil the Authority's criteria. An evaluation progress report and a final evaluation must also be provided. You may feel you are in an endless paperchase, but it can be a lucrative way of enhancing the department's resources or providing INSET for colleagues.

The school's Parent–Teacher Association (or equivalent), and local industries or businesses, may provide funds, often for specific requirements. Again it is important to make your bid and to present a good case at the appropriate time.

Some school departments have recently started to receive money from higher education institutions with which they have 'partnership' links for Initial Teacher Training, a development which looks set to grow.

Spending policies

Decisions on how to use departmental income will depend on whether there are any spending policies. Few departments have a detailed, forward-looking spending policy because, in most cases, spending is essentially needs-driven and dependent on pupil numbers year by year. In recent years, for example, priority has been given to resourcing the National Curriculum as it came on stream with particular year groups. It is prudent to have some idea of what you want to spend money on over the medium term (the next two to three years); for example, to achieve a certain level of textbook provision for a key stage, or to complete the accumulation of certain types of fieldwork equipment. Ironically, saving money from one year to the next for that big purchase, as an aspect of financial planning, is discouraged in many schools because departments have to have spent-up by the end of the financial year.

As a matter of policy, it is sensible for heads of department to consult colleagues about spending plans; involving them in the decision-making process enables them to appreciate the true cost of resources.

Making the most of resources

Looking after the resources that you have is obviously important and staff need a simple and effective system for storing and retrieving textbooks, information sheets, videos, fieldwork equipment, etc. Storage areas need to be secure and staff need to be aware of, and be vigilant about, 'shrinkage' of non-consumables. Textbooks can be protected in storage and transit by using plastic boxes, and heavily used information sheets or pupil enquiry guides can be laminated to prolong their lifespan. Look out for discounts on large book orders from publishers, and take advantage of any 'freebies' that come your way.

Over-use of the photocopying machine is often a drain on a department's finances. In a large department striking a sensible balance between photocopying what is essential, and what is merely convenient, is difficult. It seems that whatever regulatory system you operate, it is never as good as you would want and it will no doubt continue to be the subject of calls for restraint from head of departments to team members in the future.

On 1 January 1995 the Copyright Licensing Agency (CLA) introduced a new copyright licence agreement. The CLA wishes to control the reproduction of copyright material and has set limits on the number of copies to be made by educational institutions. Twenty copies per pupil per year is covered by the educational copyright license paid for by an LEA. Permission to make further copies of copyright material can be obtained, but the licence to do so must be paid for by the school at a rate of 4p per copy. A copy is taken to mean any sheet or part sheet of A4 paper, not the whole article. The CLA provides a log book for recording the number and type of copies made, and information and guidance which, for optimum effect, should be kept beside the photocopier. Of special note to geographers is that maps and newspapers (except the *Independent*) are not included in the educational licence, and therefore cannot be copied without permission from the copyright owners.

Conclusion

An effective head of department sees the role of managing resources in its broadest sense and is aware of the benefit this can have on the effective working of a department. In the final analysis, it is the careful management of human resources within the department that matters most – a well resourced and supported team is more likely to have a positive impact on the learning experience of the pupils than one which lacks proper resource management.

Chapter 27

Managing, and benefiting from, an OFSTED inspection

COLIN HARRIS

This chapter addresses two audiences: those who are planning and preparing for an inspection in their department, and those who have been through the experience and need guidance on how to build on it to improve their performance.

The completion of this chapter was delayed until shortly after the publication of *The OFSTED Handbook* in October 1995. This comprises three volumes covering secondary, primary and special schools. In what follows, we shall be concerned only with *Guidance on the Inspection of Secondary Schools* (HMSO, £9.95) which, together with the *Inspection Resources Pack*, provides school inspectors with the framework and guidance they need for secondary school inspections, as from the summer of 1996. The Guidance document provides insights into the inspection process which will be invaluable to school and departmental managers and staff. It is against the background of that document that this chapter has been written.

Assessing the whole school

The main outcome of the inspection process is the inspectors' report which deals with the following aspects of a school:

- the quality of the education provided;
- the educational standards achieved;
- whether the school's financial resources are managed efficiently;
- the spiritual, moral, social and cultural development of the pupils.

GATHERING EVIDENCE

For sound and fair judgements to be made a substantial evidence base is needed, based on first-hand observations of the work that goes on in the school. This evidence is collected by a team of inspectors, some concerned with general aspects of the school, others with subjects. Evidence is gathered in the following ways:

- reviewing documentary evidence;
- observing lessons and other activities;
- talking with pupils;
- sampling pupils' work;
- discussions with staff, the appropriate authority and others involved in the work of the school.

The inspector's first task is to gather information

Clearly, an inspection involves the examination and evaluation of a large pile of policies, handbooks, schemes of work and records. The school and individual departments need to prepare these carefully, but it cannot be assumed that exemplary and faultless documentation will automatically lead to a favourable report.

It is from the evidence gathered that the inspection team will eventually compile their report. Part II of the Guidance document sets out in detail those aspects of the school which need to be considered and these are summarised briefly below:

1. **Educational standards achieved by pupils in the school**
   Attainment and progress
   Attitudes, behaviour and personal development
   Attendance

2. **Quality of education provided**
   Teaching
   The curriculum and assessment
   Pupils' spiritual, moral, social and cultural development
   Support, guidance and pupils' welfare
   Partnership with parents and the community

3. **The management of the school**
   Leadership and management
   Staffing, accommodation and learning resources
   The efficiency of the school

Clearly, all the above are interlinked and relate to the school as a whole. The OFSTED document gives only very generalised guidance for subject inspectors, but the outcome of their observations will be a critical component of the final report. Thus, geography departments need to be aware that they are contributing to a total school picture and should therefore promote their work in the form of documents, action and interviews.

Preparing for an inspection

The stress experienced by teachers before and during a school inspection is a well documented reality and many argue that the situation is so fraught that it is impossible for 'best practice' to be on show. At best it is a snapshot and no more. But until the rules are changed, however, once every four years an inspection will take place, so it is well worth looking for the opportunities as well as the threats.

One benefit is that it concentrates the mind – rather like facing an execution, some say! You may find yourself doing things that you have wanted to do for ages, such as sorting out the stock cupboard or cataloguing the maps. Contrary to common belief, however, such activities are not essential for a successful inspection and there are more important things to consider than sticking on labels. Nevertheless, such activities are worthwhile – a totally chaotic cupboard clearly suggests that a department is disorganised – and may not otherwise get done.

In a department with more than one member of staff, early collaboration on a programme of preparation will always pay dividends. An imminent inspection is also a useful impetus for general organisation within a department. For example, that last tranche of books may be ordered to complete the range for KS3, and draft documents might at last become finalised. Dates on documents are a real give-away – a startling number post-date the notification of inspection!

Quality and standards

Observation of what goes on in the classroom is crucial to the outcome of the inspection exercise as far as the quality and standards of education are concerned, so it is important to know what aspects of classroom activity come under particular scrutiny. Inspectors must pay close attention to pupils' attainment and progress during lessons and that involves the quality of teaching and its impact on pupils in terms of the responses and progress they are able to make.

Under the stressful conditions of a lesson inspection, teachers naturally become anxious about the quality of their teaching. A surprising number will not have been observed since 'probation' days, in spite of appraisal, so may be nervous in the presence of an adult stranger in the classroom. Again, knowing what is expected, and being well prepared, will always be an advantage.

Inspectors look first for evidence of secure subject knowledge and effective lesson planning. Other criteria against which 'quality' will be judged include:

- the teacher's expectations of the pupils and whether or not they are being challenged to deepen their understanding;
- the range of teaching methods and organisational strategies employed;
- the use of time and resources;
- the management of pupils;
- the use of assessment and homework.

Obviously, not all these criteria can be met in one, or even two lessons, but what goes on in the lessons should be 'appropriate for their purpose' – what has been prepared, how it is presented and how pupils are encouraged to be involved in their activities. A geography department will generally be subjected to no more than four days of inspection (the maximum) and for many the anguish may be over in two.

Inspectors face many difficulties when making their judgements: assessing the general level of achievement in a genuinely mixed-ability class, for example, or having to reach conclusions on the basis of only one or two lessons. It is important to bear in mind, however, that experience and accuracy increase as the inspection process builds up casework dossiers. Teachers should also note that no one lesson will be identified in feedback or in the report; the published verdict on attainment represents a cumulative view of what emerges during the course of the whole inspection.

PUPIL ATTAINMENT AND PROGRESS

Inspectors must evaluate and report on what pupils achieve by the end of each key stage, with reference to attainment and to progress in relation to prior attainment. The judgements they make will be based on how pupil attainment relates to national standards. At key stage 4, for example, the relative standards of students can be judged against national data on GCSE results, including trends over the past few years.

Achievement relates to appropriate geographical knowledge, understanding and skills as well as to a range of general skills – numeracy, reading, writing, listening, speaking and IT. Successful lessons are therefore those that offer opportunities for pupils to demonstrate these achievements. Not all lessons can contain everything, but a variety of active learning strategies, including enquiry, will need to be apparent in pupils' exercise books and files, and at the planning stage. As part of their exploration of standards inspectors will also talk and listen to individual pupils.

Pupils must be seen to be making progress in their learning, not only during the lessons observed but also throughout a whole sequence of lessons. This will be evident from pupils' written work and from answers given to questions in lessons. Remember that a pupil's progress is partly dependent on the pace of the lesson.

EVIDENCE OF PLANNING AND PREPARATION

It should be clear from your lessons that you know what you hope to achieve and that your pupils are aware of where they are going. There needs to be evidence of preparation, not only in written notes but in the way the lesson is presented and how it progresses. It should be noted, however, that inspectors are realistic enough to appreciate that experienced teachers will not need the detailed notes that younger or inexperienced teachers may find necessary.

Advance planning is also needed to ensure that pupils of all abilities are able to make progress during lessons, and that all pupils are given opportunities to engage in active learning.

EVIDENCE OF SKILLS AND ATTITUDES TO LEARNING

In geography lessons, inspectors will be looking for evidence that pupils have been taught a range of study skills, and whether or not they can apply their learning to a number of situations; for example, if they are able to draw conclusions, use information to support an argument and use fieldwork skills to solve problems.

Motivation, application and the ability to work co-operatively and productively with others are aspects of pupil behaviour which relate to 'attitudes to learning' and inspectors will comment on these in their subject reports.

EVIDENCE OF GOOD GEOGRAPHY

What constitutes 'good geography' is open to debate, but in the context of the National Curriculum, the following elements can be identified:

> **knowledge and understanding of places** – where they are, what they are like, how people live there;
>
> **an understanding of patterns and processes in human and physical geography;**
>
> **the application of geography to environmental, social and political issues;**
>
> **the ability to carry out geographical enquiry;**
>
> **the ability to apply geographical skills and techniques.**

Place knowledge lies at the core of geographical study yet inspections constantly reveal an absence of such knowledge in pupils of all ages. For example, in an A level class whose task was to analyse indices of deprivation in Bristol, several students did not know where Bristol was. Similarly, pupils studying squatter settlements in Lusaka and São Paulo in a Year 9 class were unable to locate these places on a world map because they did not know which countries they were in. These may be extreme cases, but they do highlight the fact that some pupils may not be making enough use of atlases and maps in their geography lessons. Too often, schemes of work can be found which dismiss skills like map reading in Year 7 and do not require the use of maps thereafter.

EVIDENCE OF GOOD DEPARTMENTAL MANAGEMENT

Evidence of good departmental management will be revealed in a number of different contexts and will be reported on by inspectors under different headings. For example, attendance is regarded as one kind of response which pupils make to school. This will feature in the inspectors' report, so make sure that lesson attendance registers are available for inspection. Also, try to demonstrate that some form of moderation operates across the geography teaching staff.

It is important to establish aims for the geography department which support the general aims of the school, and to have evidence that departmental policies are being implemented (e.g. assessment and marking policies). In the case of marking, make sure it is up-to-date (this ought to be obvious, but it is not always done) and that any variation between teachers' marks is not due to mere accident but to departmental policy.

The inspectors' report: findings and remedies

At the end of an inspection you may be disappointed, or at least surprised, when you realise how little of your teaching time was observed. Inspectors have targets for time to be spent in the classroom and for the number of lessons to be observed so this can mean that observation does not last for a whole lesson. Twenty minutes is the minimum time for lesson observation; double lessons are rarely observed in their entirety. At the other end of the scale, where departments are small, some teachers may be observed five times in one day and almost blanket coverage is experienced.

The optimum length for an inspectors' report is 250 words, though some may be over 400 words. How can all your good work be covered by so few words? As a class teacher, you may receive some feedback for individual lessons, but most benefits come from formal feedback to the head of department at the end of the geography inspection. It is important to make the most of this; you will hear more about the judgements of the inspectors than will be contained in the published report and will be aware of any 'bad news' in advance of its publication.

Inevitably, some reports are less than pleasing. For example, they may observe that able or less able pupils are under-achieving or that none of the pupils is being sufficiently challenged. Advice on how to put things right will not be included in the report but you will certainly need to do something about it. In the case of under-achievement, for example, there is clearly a mismatch between required activities and the abilities of the pupils, and weak differentiation of materials and tasks. Lack of pace in lessons may also be responsible. Such deficiencies can be, and need to be, acted upon.

Another observation in a report may be that pupils seem to lack confidence in enquiry skills and that this is linked to a restriction in the range of teaching styles employed. A surprising number of geographers still equate teaching with talking and feel they must demonstrate skills of oratory for the benefit of inspectors. What is actually needed is evidence of a variety of approaches which closely involve pupils in the learning process and give them opportunities to exercise judgements and take responsibility for their own learning.

Deficiencies in accommodation and resources may be identified in a report as 'issues for action' with no suggestions about how to improve matters. Many heads of geography might welcome such criticism in the hope that the school's response will be to channel additional funds in their direction. Certainly, it is the responsibility of heads and governors to take note of such criticisms and to draw up measures for improvement.

One positive response to the sorts of criticisms outlined above is for a department to devise its own plan of action using a simple grid, with the issues teased out of the report listed in one column and the action to be taken in another. Issues to do with timing, personnel responsible and financial requirements can also be included in the Department Development Plan. The checklist overleaf may help you to survive, and benefit from, the OFSTED process.

To end on a conciliatory note, remember that an inspection only happens once in four years. If you change schools judiciously, you may even avoid inspection altogether (though to do so could land you with a 'rolling-stone' label). Equally, you may be unlucky and have an inspection more than once in four years; some geography teachers have been 'OFSTEDed' twice. Whatever your circumstances, take a positive stance, and remember that nowhere in the report are individuals or single lessons identified.

Checklist for an OFSTED inspection

BEFORE

- Check your documentation – the Departmental Handbook should include:
    - statement of aims
    - outline schemes of work consistent with the National Curriculum
    - staff details and job descriptions
    - appraisal arrangements
    - INSET records
    - departmental timetables
    - policies on ARR, SEN, equal opportunities, charging for fieldwork and any other relevant school policies
    - department development plan
    - spending allocation
- Check that all the departmental staff are familiar with the Handbook and its policies
- Check that all marking is consistent and up-to-date
- Discuss and agree the teaching programme for inspection week
- Make available examples of pupils' work, including field reports
- Check that the departmental minute book is up-to-date
- Check that displays include plenty of pupils' work and remove faded items
- Breathe deeply and relax – it may not be as bad as you fear!

DURING

- Expect to meet the inspector early in the week for an interview
- Inspectors will sit in on lessons without notice. The number of observations will depend on the size of your department
- Do not expect the inspector to give feedback on individual lessons
- Provide the inspector with at least the number of pupils on the class roll, and information regarding the ability range of the class
- Inform the inspector of any departmental meetings you are holding during inspection week
- Inspectors use a prescribed vocabulary. Check with the Framework for obscure meanings
- At the feedback, have an SMT member present to take notes. You are allowed to correct errors of fact

AFTER

- Arrange a celebration
- Discuss the feedback with your department
- When the report is published, analyse the geography paragraph and prepare an action plan
- Adjust your DDP to meet the inspection points

Section Seven

Post-16 geography

SUMMARY OF CHAPTERS

'The starting point is the real world, where the basic components, elements and associated vocabulary may be comprehended. At every stage the real world contributes to the structuring of elements into orderly groupings and relationships which, in turn, support the growth of general concepts, theories and models. These are used to illuminate the real world. The structure of school geography ends, where it begins, in studies of real places...'
Her Majesty's Inspectors of Schools (1972), *New Thinking in School Geography.* Education Pamphlet No 59. HMSO, p.99

Geography is a highly adaptable subject and forms a valuable part of many different subject combinations. This section looks at what students can do with a geography qualification and what post-GCSE courses are available to them.

There is a chapter on developments in teacher education and training, which is increasingly school-based, and a final chapter reviews some of the career paths open to students with geography qualifications.

Chapter 28

The post-16 pre-vocational strand

ALAN SUTTON

Introduction

During the 1980s geographers acquired a deserved reputation for curriculum innovation, producing innovative syllabuses such as the Schools Council Geography for the Young School Leaver Project (GYSL) (Avery Hill), the Bristol Project Geography 14-18, and the Geography 16-19 Project. They also made a contribution to the teaching of a range of qualifications and curriculum initiatives which were intended to 'vocationalise' the curriculum, notably the Certificate of Pre-Vocational Education (CPVE) and the Technical and Vocational Education Initiative (TVEI). The intention of these initiatives was to help prepare young people for adult life and especially work, notably by developing their personal qualities and skills such as initiative, enterprise and problem-solving.

This flurry of creativity has been followed by a transitional period in the development of pre-vocational education; TVEI is ending, CPVE was briefly replaced by the Diploma of Vocational Education (DVE) which has in turn been superseded by the latest pre-vocational initiative, the General National Vocational Qualification (GNVQ), which is probably the most significant development in pre-vocational education in recent years. In deciding on their response to GNVQs, geographers need to consider the following questions:

- Why are GNVQs being introduced?
- What are the advantages of GNVQs for students?
- What do students have to do to be successful?
- What do geographers need to know about GNVQs?
- To what extent are geographers already prepared to teach GNVQs?

The phasing in of GNVQs

GNVQs are broadly-based pre-vocational courses in which students acquire knowledge and skills relevant to a broad vocational area. By September 1996 there will be complete coverage of 14 vocational areas at Foundation, Intermediate and Advanced levels (see Table 1). They are intended to be a preparation for either further education (FE), employment or higher education (HE). The qualification was introduced initially as a post-16 pre-vocational qualification, but from September 1996 it will also be generally

Geography is a way into many kinds of learning

Photo: **The Sheffield College**

available as a Part 1 in key stage 4 to run alongside the reduced statutory core of the National Curriculum. GNVQs are very significant, not least because they are seen by the Government as a way of increasing both participation rates in full-time education post-16 and levels of attainment to meet the National Training and Education Targets (NTETs) which have been endorsed by a wide range of agencies including government departments, the Confederation of British Industry (CBI), the Trade Union Congress (TUC) and the Training and Enterprise Councils (TECs).

From September 1993	From September 1994	From September 1995	From September 1996
Art and Design	Construction and the Built Environment	Distribution	Land-based Industries
Business	Hospitality and Catering	Engineering	
Health and Social Care	Science	Information Technology	
Leisure and Tourism		Management Studies (Advanced)	
Manufacturing		Media: Communication and Production	

Table 1: The phased introduction of GNVQs

The introduction of GNVQs provides a major opportunity to develop an alternative curriculum and qualification to 1-year GCSEs and GCE A/AS levels. GNVQs are intended to be at least as demanding as the alternatives which they replace. So far, GNVQs have been introduced by the National Council for Vocational Qualifications (NCVQ) but the new Part 1 is being developed by NCVQ and the School Curriculum and Assessment Authority (SCAA). NCVQ has been responsible for devising a framework of five levels for all vocational qualifications (see Table 2 below) and for defining national standards of attainment for GNVQs.

Level	NVQ	GNVQ	General Education
5	Professional, Managerial		Higher Education
4	Higher Technician, Junior Management		Higher Education
3	Technician, Supervisor	Advanced	2 GCE A levels
2	Craft	Intermediate	5 GCSEs, A-C
1	Foundation	Foundation	Other GCSEs

Table 2: National qualifications framework (1995)   Source: Smithers and Robinson (1993) p. 43)

NCVQ has also ensured that the assessment of core skills will be an integral part of all GNVQ courses and has developed detailed specifications for five of these skills: communication, numeracy, IT, personal skills and problem-solving, at the five levels in the national qualifications framework. Indeed, communication, numeracy and IT are a mandatory requirement of all GNVQs and accreditation in personal skills is strongly encouraged.

There has been a rapid take-up of GNVQs by schools and colleges since the pilot phase in 1993 introduced them in five vocational areas, and there is already evidence of their contribution to increased participation rates in full-time education post-16 (73% in 1994). The Government's intention is for both participation rates and attainment to continue to improve, but there is some evidence to suggest that participation rates have stabilised. The 'new' further education sector created in 1992 consisting of Further Education, Sixth Form and Tertiary Colleges has been given the key role in increasing participation rates and the colleges will be looking to these new GNVQ courses to attract more students by both the full- and part-time route.

What are the advantages of GNVQs for students?

In contrast to un-modularised academic courses, GNVQs offer a range of potential advantages. Firstly, their unit structure means that students are faced with manageable short-term learning goals and also enables students to acquire credits as they study (credit accumulation). The GNVQ optional units may also allow scope for some student choice, depending on the size of the school or college. Secondly, GNVQs offer students learning experiences which provide a mix of practical skills, theoretical knowledge and real or practical experience of the world of work in a particular vocational context. A third advantage is their equivalence with GCSEs and A levels: a Foundation level GNVQ is equivalent to four to five GCSEs grades D and below; an Intermediate level GNVQ to four to five GCSEs A-C; an Advanced level GNVQ to two GCE A levels. Furthermore, there is an equivalence between GNVQ Advanced level and A level grades: a distinction in GNVQ equates to A level grades A-B; a merit to A level grade C; and a pass to A level grades D and E.

What will students have to do?

The multiple assessment demands of GNVQs are rigorous. Students are required to:

- acquire a range of knowledge and skills across a broad vocational area and develop core skills (communication, application of number and IT) which are not required in GCSE or GCE A level courses;

- develop responsibility for their own work, presenting evidence of their ability to plan ahead, handle information, evaluate their work and synthesise information in order to gain merits or distinctions;

- pass external tests and assemble a portfolio which provides evidence of achievement which is judged against explicit performance criteria.

To what extent are geographers already prepared to teach GNVQs?

Geographers who have already contributed to the teaching of pre-vocational courses, e.g. CPVE, or innovative 16-19 syllabuses, or who have been involved in flexible learning projects, will not find the adjustment to teaching and assessing GNVQs too demanding. Geography teachers who have had some or all of the following experiences will be particularly well placed to adjust to the change in emphasis from teacher to facilitator/manager of GNVQ programmes. These prior experiences could include:

- using student-centred, flexible learning approaches such as action planning, the use of advanced organisers and study guides;

- exploiting the potential of local industrial contacts to develop assignments based on real case study materials;

- developing written guidance to support students in the planning and completion of individual studies or projects;

- using formative profiles in TVEI and CPVE schemes;

- making a conscious effort to build core skills into their schemes of work and lesson plans, particularly information handling and evaluation;

- planning schemes or units of work which require students to be involved in assessing their own work;

- using a wide variety of assessment methods such as surveys, questionnaires, reports, projects, etc.

Some geographers are already teaching a substantial number of GNVQ units, particularly in Leisure and Tourism, or working as members of course teams teaching units for those GNVQ courses where there are topics which they can cover in Business Studies, Manufacturing, Construction and the Built Environment, Information Technology, and Science. These topics include:

- the role of organisations in industry;

- the factors influencing industrial location;

- the environmental impact of industrial processes;

- employment issues such as features of employment, employment trends, external influences on employment and employment opportunities;

- market demands and trends;

- planning issues;

- the use of energy in manufacturing;

- the efficient use of energy.

Geographers have the knowledge base to teach some of the mandatory units of Leisure and Tourism, notably 'Investigating Leisure and Tourism', and optional units associated with travel and tourism. There is a range of options available from each of the three vocational examination boards, such as investigating the UK tourist industry, investigating the travel industry, travel and tourism geography, Third World tourism, and countryside recreation.

What do geographers need to know about GNVQs?

GNVQs are distinctive in their philosophy, structure, content and requirements for teaching, learning and assessment. Students are assessed on the basis of how they work (process skills) as well as on their assembly of a portfolio of work. They are also required to be successful in external tests of knowledge. There are six key features associated with GNVQs which need to be addressed by geography teachers and by school/college management teams, preferably before courses are introduced. The key features are:

(a) student responsibility for learning;

(b) the unit-based structure;

(c) the vocational nature of GNVQs;

(d) managing teaching and learning;

(e) outcome-led assessment;

(f) core skills.

(A) STUDENT RESPONSIBILITY FOR LEARNING

The NCVQ's philosophy for GNVQs is that students should be responsible for their own learning. Hence the requirement that students should produce an action plan for their work; hence also the grading criteria for the award of a merit or a distinction which assess the students' ability to plan ahead, handle information and evaluate their work. Students should also be aware of the competences they are acquiring and be able to monitor their own progress.

(B) THE UNIT-BASED STRUCTURE

At each level – Foundation, Intermediate and Advanced – there are four kinds of units. These are:

Mandatory units which are compulsory at all GNVQ levels. There are eight for an Advanced level, four for an Intermediate and three for a Foundation.

Optional units which provide some degree of choice. Students must do a minimum of these; four at Advanced level, two at Intermediate and three at Foundation.

Core skills units – Communication, Application of Number and IT are compulsory at all three GNVQ levels.

Additional units – such as non-mandatory core skills.

Element 1.3: Explore the UK travel and tourism industry and its development	EVIDENCE INDICATORS
PERFORMANCE CRITERIA A student must: 1 explain the factors which have influenced the development of the UK travel and tourism industry 2 describe the major steps in the development of the UK travel and tourism industry 3 describe, with examples, the products and services available through the UK travel and tourism industry 4 investigate the products and services available in selected travel and tourism facilities	A written report, in two parts, on the UK travel and tourism industry and its development. The first part of the report should explain, in very general terms, the factors which have influenced the development of the UK travel and tourism industry, and describe the major steps in the development of this industry. It should also describe the products and services available through the UK travel and tourism industry. This description should be supported by three examples of travel products/services – one for each range category – and six examples of tourism products/services chosen from the nine categories listed in the range. Between them the examples should cover domestic, outgoing and incoming travel and tourism.
RANGE **UK travel and tourism industry:** travel services (retail travel agencies, business travel agencies, tour operators, principals), tourism (national tourist boards, regional tourist boards, tourist information centres, tourist attractions, guiding services, currency exchange, accommodation, catering, transport)	The second part of the report should be based on an in-depth investigation of travel and tourism products and services available through two selected facilities – one from within the tourism industry and one from the travel industry. The report should identify and describe products and services for each of the facilities.
Factors: increase in individual leisure time, growth of personal disposable income, changing personal needs and expectations, growth of incoming tourism	**Amplification** ***Factors and major steps in development (PC1 and PC2)*** the purpose of exploring the factors which have influenced the development of the industry is to relate economic, social and environmental change since the Industrial Revolution to the growth and nature of the present industry. Because of time constraints students should only consider the major steps.
Major steps: Industrial Revolution, introduction of paid holidays, introduction of Bank Holidays, development of seaside towns, development of road transport, development of rail transport, development of sea transport, development of air transport, development of overseas package tours, Development of Tourism Act, 1969	
Product and services: domestic, outgoing, incoming;	***Products and services (PC3 and PC4)*** exploring and describing products and services made available by the industry should give the student a better understanding of the definition of tourism (see Glossary).
travel (leisure travel, business travel, visiting friends and relatives);	**Guidance** Students could be directed to appropriate sources for information on the development of the industry. Following individual research, students are likely to benefit from a group discussion before writing up their research individually.
tourism (holidays, tours, activities at destination, accommodation, catering, transport, agency and information services, guiding services, currency exchange).	
Investigate: identify products/services available, describe products/services available	Investigation of products and services could be done collaboratively, with students sharing their experiences and supplementing this with individually obtained information. This applies particularly when identifying products and services available in selected facilities.

Figure 1: Advanced level Leisure and Tourism

The structure of a unit is shown in Figure 1, which is an example of one particular element for Advanced level Leisure and Tourism. The specification of these units has recently been revised by the vocational examination boards to provide better guidance for schools and colleges. This supplementary guidance is in the form of a statement of amplification. Each unit consists of a series of elements, assessed by Performance Criteria, which describe what students have to do to be successful. The Range Statement describes what must be included in the study of the unit, and the Evidence Indicators explain the minimum that must be included in the student's portfolio to prove that the required work has been completed.

It is left up to schools and colleges to decide how much time should be allocated to these mandatory and optional GNVQ units, in which sequence they are tackled, and how they are combined. In one Further Education College in the East Midlands, 120 students are following an Advanced GNVQ in Leisure and Tourism. In this programme, the weekly time allocation to GNVQ is 20 hours; of this, 14 hours is allocated to mandatory units, 3 hours for optional units, and 3 hours for core skills units. Mandatory and optional units are allocated an 11-week period. In Year 1 of the course, students study the eight mandatory units and some options and in Year 2 they study further remaining options and some additional units.

(C) THE VOCATIONAL NATURE OF GNVQS

If GNVQs are to have credibility with employers and HE, be motivating for young people, and sufficiently different from their academic alternatives, it is essential that they make reference to the real world of industry, community and commerce. The content of GNVQ courses can be enriched by case study materials drawn from industry, and regular contact with industrialists can improve the quality of work experience by linking in with GNVQ requirements. However, geographers may need to be willing to acquire and/or update their knowledge of a particular vocational area to enable them to develop assignments based on a realistic vocational context. This can be achieved by research visits and/or undertaking a short teacher placement organised by the Teacher Placement Service.

(D) MANAGING LEARNING TO GIVE STUDENTS GREATER RESPONSIBILITY

Geographers must be skilled in the 'flexible learning' methods which characterise the philosophy, structure and assessment requirements of GNVQs. Many geography teachers could benefit from familiarising themselves with the Training Education and Enterprise Directorate (TEED) Flexible Learning Framework which summarises the role of the teacher/tutor and the student under the three headings of managing the teacher/student partnership, managing student route-ways and managing the students' use of resources. For many students, their learning experience pre-16 studying GCSE will generally have been teacher directed with instructions on what to do, when to do it and how to do it, and it will be important for geographers to introduce their students to the new ways of working required by GNVQs. There is an important place for direct instruction on GNVQ courses, particularly in the early stages of the course and probably with students following Intermediate programmes. However, the bulk of the work will have to be carried out through practical investigative activities and assignments where the student is required to work both independently and occasionally with others using the teacher as a tutor to support and facilitate the learning. This requires considerable confidence and expertise on the part of the geography teacher who needs to be proficient in the management of teaching and assessment approaches which clearly resemble these of supported self study and which include a number of competences. These are illustrated in Figure 2.

Action planning

Student action plans can be written in relation to a whole GNVQ programme or, more usually, in relation to a particular assignment or activity or to improve their learning to

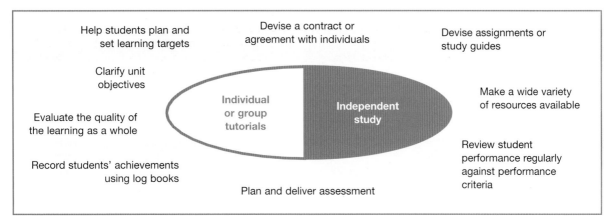

Figure 2: *Managing learning and assessment: a model (after Boardman, 1986)*

learn skills. Action planning involves each student in recording his or her achievements, expressing requirements for future learning, setting learning targets and reflecting upon and reviewing performance. The result is an action plan which is a statement of what the student intends to achieve in the short term. Experience suggests that students find action planning, particularly target setting, difficult, and regular tutorials are necessary to enable students to produce an action plan.

Preparing an action plan is one way for students to demonstrate their ability to meet the grading criteria for a merit or distinction, and geography teachers will need to make students aware of these criteria.

Assignments

Assignments should be devised in such a way that they gradually give students more responsibility for their own learning. This can be done by making tasks progressively more open-ended. Assignments should also enable the students to satisfy the evidence indicators by, for instance, completing a report, survey, video or oral presentation. They should be written in a clear, preferably standardised, format. Geography teachers will need to develop their own assignment-writing skills if they are to enable their students to satisfy the grading criteria. This will involve them in long-term planning to ensure that students achieve all performance criteria for the units and the core skills specifications.

Each assignment should be part of a planned sequence, allowing students to attain one or more of the elements. Some assignments may pick up on a few elements whereas others may be integrated, covering elements across more than one unit.

(E) OUTCOME-LED ASSESSMENT

GNVQ specifications describe outcomes (what students should know, understand and be able to do). Students should be introduced to the course specifications at the beginning of the course, so that they know what they are required to do and how they will be assessed. This must be done not only in the induction period at the beginning of the course but also at the beginning of each GNVQ unit. There are rigorous assessment requirements for students on GNVQ courses which involve both internal assessment and verification by the teacher or lecturer and assessor as well as the external verifier appointed by the vocational examination boards (BTEC, C&G, RSA).

For internal purposes, students have to:

■ achieve the performance criteria for every element in each unit by completing assignments, projects, questionnaires, surveys, etc., which will be assembled in their portfolio of work;

■ demonstrate an ability to meet the performance criteria for core skills units in communication, application of number and IT.

Furthermore, students who wish to gain a merit or distinction grade have to satisfy the grading criteria for planning, information handling, evaluation and synthesis.

There are also regular external assessments in which students have to achieve a satisfactory performance (70% pass mark) in end-of-unit tests in most mandatory units. These unit tests consist of multiple-choice questions which examine the students' knowledge and understanding of each of the units.

In order for assessment to be effective, students must be made aware of the nature and timing of assessment well in advance. During induction, students' abilities in the three core skill areas must be diagnosed and they should be given opportunities to improve their competence. Detailed records of their performance will need to be kept and they need to be encouraged to monitor their own performance.

(F) CORE SKILLS

In contrast to academic courses, where core skills may be taught as part of the normal classroom activities and geography fieldwork, GNVQ teachers have to devise assignments that develop the three core skills of communication, application of number and Information Technology. In addition to the three compulsory core skill units, there are two optional units which can be accredited. These are the personal skills of improving one's learning and performance and working with others.

If the mandatory core skills are to be integrated into the vocational context, geographers will have to ensure that they can work with the core skills specifications. Satisfying the performance criteria for communication skills may be easier than the application of number or IT. In any event, geographers will need to map the opportunities for their students to develop core skills across a range of assignments. This will be particularly important at the Intermediate level, where courses are short and each student is likely to have different levels of ability across the core skills.

Conclusion

GNVQs offer a hitherto unavailable pre-vocational qualification which offers students the possibility of progression from 14-19, and all the indications are that they are here to stay. In addition to the introduction of fourteen vocational areas post-16 at Foundation, Intermediate and Advanced level (see Table 1), there is also the prospect of the Part 1 GNVQ pre-16 which initially was offered in three vocational areas, starting in 1995. This is equivalent to two GCSEs and is intended to take up 20% of curriculum time: Part I Intermediate is equivalent to two GCSEs grades A-C; Part I Foundation to two GCSEs grades D and below.

The Government wants high-quality GNVQ courses, and considerable efforts are being made by NCVQ both to ensure that teachers and lecturers are clear about the standards required and to implement rigorous external quality assurance procedures. The message is that GNVQs are not a soft option; nor can they be if they are to achieve parity of esteem with academic qualifications. With their emphasis as much on the process of teaching and learning as on the content, the introduction of GNVQs into schools and colleges will be a considerable challenge for many teachers and lecturers. Geographers should be in a strong position to take advantage of the opportunity presented by GNVQs, but they should not underestimate the challenge.

References and further reading

Boardman, D. (ed) (1986) *Handbook for Geography Teachers.* The Geographical Association.

BTEC, C&G, RSA, NCVQ, DFE, ED (1995) *Integrating Core Skills. Support Materials for Implementation: A Guide for GNVQ Practitioners.*

Butt, G. (1994) 'Geography, vocational education and assessment' *Teaching Geography,* 79, 4, pp. 182-183.

Department of Employment (DOE) (1991) *Flexible Learning: A Framework for Education and Training in the Skills Decade.*

Further Education Unit (FEU) (1994) *Introducing GNVQs: Planning, Co-ordinating and Managing the GNVQ Curriculum.*

National Council for Vocational Qualifications (NCVQ) (1991) *General National Vocational Qualifications: Proposals for the New Qualifications. A Consultative Paper.*

NCVQ (1995) *Core Skills Specifications: Information Technology; Application of Number; Communication; Personal Skills – working with others and improving own learning and performance.*

NCVQ (1995) *GNVQ Grading Criteria.*

NCVQ (1995) *Assessing Core Skills in GNVQs.*

OFSTED (1995) *GNVQs in Schools: The Introduction of General National Vocational Qualifications.* HMSO.

Smithers, A. & Robinson, P. (1993) *Changing Colleges: Further Education in the Market Place.* The Council for Industry and Higher Education.

Sutton, A. (1994) 'NTETS, GNVQs and flexible learning', *The Curriculum Journal,* 5, pp. 337-353.

Chapter 29

Geography in post-16 colleges

ANDREW POWELL

Geography in post-16 colleges is characterised by a very wide range of courses, students and study methods. As a geographer teaching in a post-16 college you may find yourself in a large geography department with several colleagues sharing the work. More typically, however, you are likely to be a 'department' of only one or two specialists offering geography throughout the college on a variety of courses.

These differences reflect the variety that exists in the types of colleges represented in the post-16 sector and the specific markets which they are serving. The Education Act of 1944 for the first time imposed a statutory duty on local education authorities (LEAs) 'to secure the provision for their area of adequate facilities for further education, that is, full- and part-time education for persons over compulsory school age.' The relative freedom with which local authorities were able to organise this provision resulted in a number of different models emerging. These differed from the traditional school sixth form for the delivery of post-16 academic and vocational work, but led to colleges and schools in some areas being in competition for the same students. A major change occurred with the Further and Higher Education Act (1992) which altered the status of post-16 colleges by removing them from local authority control. As from 1 April 1993 all of the colleges in this sector became, in effect, independent institutions, though they are accountable to the Further Education Funding Council (FEFC) for the purposes of finance, strategic planning and quality inspections. The main types of institution in the post-16 college sector are:

FURTHER EDUCATION (FE) COLLEGES
The term 'FE' is often used to refer to the post-16 sector as a whole. These colleges generally offer a wide range of full- and part-time academic and vocational courses up to A level equivalent. Some are also developing higher-level courses which may be linked with local higher education institutions.

TERTIARY COLLEGES
These are the sole providers of post-16 academic and vocational education in their local catchment area, and pre-16 schools will feed students into them. They have become increasingly popular in recent years as LEAs reorganise post-16 provision on a more efficient basis. They offer a wide range of courses, similar to the FE colleges.

SIXTH-FORM COLLEGES
As with the tertiary colleges, these developed out of LEA reorganisation, where local sixth forms are grouped together to provide mainly academic GCSE/A level-type

Colleges offer geographers many opportunities to contribute to an array of multi-disciplinary courses

Photo: **The Sheffield College**

courses, together with some vocational provision. They could only accept full-time 16-19 students before the 1992 Act, but are now beginning to diversify.

With the new arrangements now firmly in place the differences between the post-16 colleges are lessening, and a unified system is rapidly developing.

The changing place of geography in post-16 colleges

Geography began in many FE colleges as a component of professional courses; the Institute of Bankers, for example, included 'commercial geography' in its exams from 1920. The fact that geography provided essential locational knowledge meant that it was often included in vocational courses during this period, but it was rarely taught, by a specialist, as a subject in its own right.

In 1953 the Further Education Section of the Geographical Association was established to provide a voice for this expanding sector of education. A survey they undertook at this time revealed that there was some geography to be found in over two-thirds of the 535 FE colleges; specialist geography staff (usually just one person) were found in under half the colleges; and many specialist staff relied on part-time non-specialists to help teach the subject. Another interesting finding, still very relevant today, was that if there was a full-time specialist geographer promoting the subject in the college, then the demand for the subject increased.

A more recent college survey by Nuttall (1981) indicated that geography was contributing very little to professional examinations, but was expanding its links with business studies courses by offering economic geography modules. The main area of work for geographers in colleges was on GCE O and A level courses. There was further evidence from a survey by Powell (1986) that geography in colleges was slowly diversifying, particularly as an input to travel and tourism courses and to environmental studies modules on a wide variety of courses, ranging from nursery nursing to access courses for adult returners. At the time of writing, the following range of courses is available:

GCSE GEOGRAPHY

This course is mainly provided for resit students to improve their grades, and maintaining motivation is a key factor in teaching this group. GCSE geography is also frequently offered as a part-time day and/or evening course, catering for a mixed enrolment including first-timers and mature students. The profile of the college GCSE geographer is therefore generally different from the school geography student, and it is important to take this into account when planning and teaching the course. Teaching a GCSE over one year will require you to organise the syllabus carefully to maximise the limited class time available. GCSEs in American and European studies and in travel and tourism may also be taught in some colleges.

A LEVEL GEOGRAPHY

A level courses are generally offered over two years to full-time students following a variety of syllabuses, as found in schools. The student profiles in some colleges will be more mixed than in many schools; most are slightly older and some are mature (over 21). Some colleges also offer one-year A level courses during the day or evening. These are very intensive and attract resit students as well as those who are unable, because of work or cost, to attend a full-time two year course. You will need to plan these courses to reflect the extreme pressure on the time available to cover the content.

A level courses in environmental studies and geology are offered in a few colleges, where teaching may be shared with science colleagues. As in schools, the take-up of AS levels in colleges has been small, although they can be found as part of a mixed diet of GCSE/AS/A level programmes.

VOCATIONAL COURSES (GNVQS)

Geography was once included in many professional courses, particularly as economic geography and travel and tourism in BTEC Diploma courses. Now that vocational courses have been brought under the GNVQ umbrella it is possible to see more clearly where geography is able to make a contribution. The family of GNVQ courses, outlined in Chapter 28, are providing geographers with opportunities for work in many colleges, often by joining multi-disciplinary course teams. A survey carried out by the GA Post-16 Section in 1994/5 revealed a good take-up of GNVQs in leisure and tourism. At **Intermediate level** (GCSE equivalent) units that geographers are teaching include: Investigating Leisure and Tourism, Researching Tourist Destinations and Investigating the Environmental Impact of Leisure and Tourism. At **Advanced level** (A level equivalent) options being taught are: Investigating the UK Holiday Industry, Travel and Tourism Geography, Investigating the Leisure and Tourist Industry, Third World Tourism, and Countryside Recreation.

Some college geographers, especially those with some relevant work experience, teach on travel and tourism degree and HND courses. Geographers may also be able to contribute to options on other GNVQs, in particular those on the Built Environment, Agriculture and Environment, and Information Technology.

GEOGRAPHY AND ENVIRONMENTAL STUDIES ON OTHER COURSES

Opportunities for teaching geography and environmental studies can be found on a variety of other courses in many post-16 colleges. Environmental studies is frequently found on vocational courses, for example it is part of the Nursery Nurses (NNEB) course. General studies programmes can give the geographer a chance to develop a specific interest; in a sixth-form college in York options offered by the geography department include: Japanese studies, statistics, European awareness, foreign travel, British weather, British landscape, and environmental studies.

Access courses for mature student entry to higher education offer opportunities for interesting geographical work through the development of specific syllabuses which relate to the overall course theme. This might be straight geography, environmental studies, or, as in the case of a course developed in a West London college, a module on developing countries for an access bilingual course (see Allchin (1991) for further details).

Being a geographer in a post-16 college

The experience of being a geographer in a post-16 college will depend on:

THE TYPE OF INSTITUTION

This will usually determine how many geographers there are. A few, in particular sixth-form and tertiary colleges, will have large geography departments with up to four or five specialists and several hundred students, mainly taking GCSE and A level courses. The majority will have one or two geographers teaching across a range of courses, although timetables are still likely to be dominated by GCSE and A level work.

THE TYPE OF STUDENTS

Post-16 students will have chosen to attend college courses and, as a consequence, there are usually few discipline problems in colleges, the main job being to motivate students to reach their potential. The range of academic ability may be wider than in schools and mature students will require different teaching approaches.

SELLING THE SUBJECT

Geography does not have a guaranteed position in the curriculum of post-16 colleges. In some, very little or no geography is taught, and there are no geography specialists on the staff. It is important, therefore, for the subject to be pushed within colleges, and for heads of department and course leaders to be made aware of its potential. All the research on post-16 geography suggests that where the subject has a strong position it is because geographers have made a good case for the subject to be included on a variety of courses, and have been innovative in devising appropriate syllabuses. The setting up of a college geographical society would be one way of generating interest, and students and staff could produce their own magazine. Similarly, projects such as 'greening the college' could be undertaken to improve the general environment of the college site, and thus attract attention to the value of geographers within the institution.

OTHER ROLES

In many colleges, geographers are part of a larger department or faculty – usually science, humanities or general education. In such cases, they are often expected to take on other work, such as being a course tutor with a pastoral role. If there is a limited amount of geography available for a full timetable then geography staff could be asked to contribute to other courses, depending on what specialisms can be offered.

Organising geography in colleges

The organisation of the subject in a college will clearly depend on how much geography is offered and how many specialists there are on the staff. Suggestions made in Chapter 24 on departmental management in schools apply equally to the college sector. If you, as a college geographer, are a department of just one or two, then the division of courses and your timetabling could be problematic because of the lack of flexibility. There are several factors that you should consider in your planning:

TYPES OF COURSES

You may well be teaching full- and part-time courses, during the day and evening. The teaching programme for part-time day and evening classes will need to include a large element of set work in order to complete the course, and your teaching style will need to take account of this different type of student group.

If you are devising a specific geographical input for, say, an access course or a travel and tourism module, you will be working with a larger mixed-subject team, and it is important to establish how your geographical input complements the rest of the course. It is also important to remember that students on these courses may well have had a limited geographical education, and you will need to establish the 'group profile' at the beginning of the course.

FIELDWORK

As with all geography courses, it is desirable to carry out some fieldwork if possible, and this will probably be easier to organise for full-time GCSE/A level courses than for part-time classes. Problems relating to cost and time are acute in many colleges, where students often have limited resources, part-time jobs and families. If fieldwork is residential it is particularly important to give early warning about proposed dates so that students can make the necessary arrangements. If cost is a major factor it may restrict your options regarding locations and time spent away, so it is important to recognise this, and other factors, when planning fieldwork provision.

ESTABLISHING LINKS

Post-16 colleges usually have good links with other educational institutions in their area. It is important to establish a working relationship with other geographers in the 11-16 schools that feed your courses, and with local higher education institutions that may be attractive to some of your students, particularly those who are less 'mobile' in their higher education choices. Such links will give some continuity to your planning and will prove invaluable as a source of mutual support.

If there are opportunities for staff industrial placements, this could be useful in enabling you to offer geography on some vocational courses; for example to teach on some travel and tourism courses it is now compulsory to have relevant work experience. You should consider joining a local post-16 colleges 'self-help group' in your area. The GA Post-16 Section has promoted these, and several operate around the country, providing opportunities to exchange ideas and share resources which can be very valuable, particularly if you feel isolated as a geographer in your college. Establishing links with local inspectors, advisers and GA branches is also desirable in that it can involve you in a wider geographical community. You may want to consider organising some specific one-off courses/conferences/meetings at your college to attract local geographers and students and raise the profile of the subject in your area.

RESOURCES

The importance of gathering appropriate resources for your teaching is stressed in other chapters, and for GCSE and A level classes, in particular, there is a wide range of material available. For more specific vocational courses such as GNVQs in tourism and access courses, you may need to use resources that are harder to find. The GA Post-16 Section is a useful source of advice in this context; they will be able to give you information on regional contacts and GA branches as well as help with course planning. The various exam boards publish detailed information on course outlines, and will usually suggest books and other resources that are available for their courses.

INSET

Depending on how many geographers there are in your college, INSET could take the form of in-house activities and/or links with colleagues from other colleges/schools to consider specific issues. Some suggestions for INSET activities are given below:

Departmental planning and structures You will need to share plans and ideas, and it is important to evaluate the department's targets – including student feedback. With FEFC inspections and college quality-assurance systems, effective monitoring and evaluation of courses is increasingly required. Information from these exercises can be usefully fed back into future course planning.

Resources INSET sessions on resource exchanges could include specific work on Information Technology materials suitable for use on geography courses, and developments on GIS and CD-ROM applications could be shared and monitored.

Fieldwork Ideas and approaches which can be applicable to a variety of locations can be discussed and shared. It is important to monitor and develop fieldwork methods and to exchange specific expertise within the subject.

New course developments Keep track of syllabus changes for GCSE and A level courses, and the new courses in areas of vocational education. As GNVQs have been introduced over a long period, INSET sessions to update on the new courses and how geography can be included should be a priority for college geographers.

Conclusion

Your experience of teaching geography in a post-16 college will depend largely on the type of college you are in and the amount of geographical work on the curriculum. The range of students that you will teach and the opportunities for innovative work make teaching in this sector very rewarding, and even if you are a department of one the experience can be very stimulating. The 'adult' environment requires an appropriate teaching method, and working in a large institution means it is important to raise the profile of the subject as much as possible. Maintaining close links with the wider geographical community around the college will create interest, encourage new developments and even help to recruit students onto your courses.

References

The post-16 surveys by Nuttall (1981), Powell (1986), and Allchin (1991) were all carried out as part of unpublished MA theses at the University of London Institute of Education and contain useful background information on geographical courses in colleges.

Chapter 30

Teacher education and training

MARGARET ROBERTS

Teacher education is changing. Since September 1994, all secondary PGCE courses have been subject to new statutory requirements. There are two main changes. Firstly, schools are required to play a larger part in the training of teachers. Schools are now partners with higher education institutes (HEIs) in the planning and management of PGCE courses and selection and assessment of students. PGCE students have to spend two thirds of their time on school-based work, i.e. 24 weeks out of a 36 week course. Secondly, schools, students and institutions are required to focus on the competences of teaching.

How can the new requirements be used to enhance the professional development of new geography teachers? In some ways nothing has changed – the essential question remains: how does anyone learn how to teach? Although the competences provide a list of the desired outcomes of a course of teacher education they do not indicate how they are achieved. Each set of competences, however, can be translated into a set of varied experiences which will encourage professional growth toward those outcomes. This chapter will use the framework provided by the competences to suggest how experiences in both schools and HEIs can contribute to the education of geography teachers.

The framework provided by the competences

SUBJECT KNOWLEDGE

The first group of competences (Figure 1) indicates two types of knowledge needed by teachers: geography teachers need to know about their subject and they need to know about geographical education.

The majority of PGCE geography students have recently studied a substantial amount of geography as part of their degree courses. Geography degree courses, however, vary considerably, and allow for some specialisation. Every PGCE geography student will inevitably demonstrate gaps in the geographical knowledge required for the geography National Curriculum and examination syllabuses. Most students are perfectly capable of filling these gaps on their own, when the need arises, without additional teaching. What schools and HEIs can do is provide guidance on the exact nature of the geographical knowledge required and recommend sources of information.

Too much emphasis on the gaps in students' knowledge would be unfortunate. Many PGCE students start the course with some specialist subject knowledge well

To teach geography is to help pupils make sense of the world. It has never been more difficult or more necessary

Photo: **Margaret Roberts**

> **Subject knowledge**
>
> 2.2   Newly qualified teachers should be able to demonstrate
>
> 2.2.1   an understanding of the knowledge, concepts and skills of their specialist subjects and of the place of these subjects in the school curriculum;
>
> 2.2.2   knowledge and understanding of the National Curriculum and Attainment Targets (NCATs) and the Programmes of Study (PoS) in the subject they are preparing to teach, together with an understanding of the framework of the statutory requirements;
>
> 2.2.3   a breadth and depth of subject knowledge extending beyond PoS and examination syllabuses in schools.

Figure 1: Subject knowledge competences (from Circular 9/92)

beyond the competence level required, and well beyond that of experienced geography teachers and tutors. Recent PGCE students at Sheffield University have between them, for example, worked in India, China, Uganda, USA, Japan, and Peru before starting the course. Others have worked in planning, in publishing, in computing, in a housing department, and in a field studies centre. Most students have up-to-date specialist knowledge, e.g. in ecology, or remote sensing, gained from their degree courses. It is important to identify strengths as well as weaknesses as starting points for professional growth. Particular expertise and enthusiasm can be used by schools and HEIs to help students produce original resources, to revise existing resources, and to inform other PGCE students, thereby increasing their confidence.

LOOKING AT DOCUMENTS	INTERVIEWING AND DISCUSSING	WORKING WITH PUPILS	READING	READING AND DISCUSSING PUPILS' WRITTEN WORK
studying examination syllabuses comparing examination syllabuses looking at past examination papers looking at examiners' reports	finding out why a department chose a particular syllabus and options within it interviewing groups of school pupils about their perceptions of the exam syllabus interviewing individual pupils to become aware of their levels of understanding finding out about coursework procedures discussing examinations with teachers discussing fieldwork with teachers and pupils attending meetings in which exam assignments are set	observing examination classes teaching examination classes going on fieldwork visits	reading about public examinations in books and journals, e.g. in *Teaching Geography*	attending a moderating meeting about exam marking using a marking scheme to mark answers to examination questions reading coursework assignments completed for public examinations

Figure 2: Experiences which will increase knowledge of examination syllabuses

Although students bring to a PGCE course their own knowledge of geographical education based on personal experience they need to extend this considerably during their training. The kind of knowledge which experienced geography teachers and tutors possess on the geography National Curriculum, on examination syllabuses and on geographical education has been built up gradually through a range of experiences. PGCE students could be offered a similar range of experiences to help them increase their knowledge from different sources of information and from different viewpoints. Figure 2 shows examples of such experiences which could increase knowledge of examination syllabuses. A similar range of experiences could help build up knowledge of the geography National Curriculum.

It is not enough for students simply to know the information gained from these various sources of information. They need to be able to use it to understand the situations they encounter, to form their own opinions and to make their own judgements about geographical education. Students will be able to do this more easily if they are given opportunities during the year to discuss their experiences with others and to read widely to explore a range of viewpoints. Many students find that writing essays or reading journals helps them sort out their knowledge and ideas. Given the same range of activities, different students will learn different things, depending on their enthusiasm for the particular aspect of the course, the knowledge and experience they bring with them to the activity and how much time they spend reflecting on the activity.

SUBJECT APPLICATION

Competence in subject knowledge alone would not enable anyone to teach geography. The second group of competences listed in Circular 9/92 is concerned with the skills of applying that knowledge in the classroom (Figure 3).

Subject application

2.3 Newly qualified teachers should be able to:

    2.3.1   produce coherent lessons which take account of NCATs and of the school's curriculum policies;

    2.3.2   ensure continuity and progression within and between classes and in subjects;

    2.3.3   set appropriately demanding expectations for pupils;

    2.3.4   employ a range of teaching strategies appropriate to the age, ability and attainment level of pupils;

    2.3.5   present subject content in clear langugage and in a stimulating manner;

    2.3.6   contribute to the development of pupils' language and communication skills;

    2.3.7   demonstrate ability to select and use appropriate resources, including Information Technology.

Figure 3: Subject application competences (from Circular 9/92)

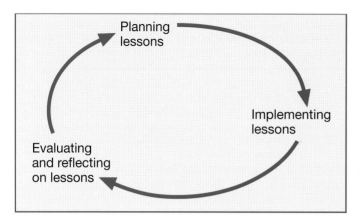

Figure 4: A cycle of learning experiences

The types of experience are directly related to classroom practice and can be expressed in cyclical form (Figure 4) and are shown in detail in Figure 5.

Firstly, lessons have to be **planned**, and this is often a lengthy process for a beginner teacher. Planning demands some knowledge of different ways of planning lessons, and the ability to select strategies, activities and resources. For a beginner teacher selection of resources involves becoming familiar with a wide range of resources, evaluating textbooks, pre-viewing video cassettes and slides, and becoming competent in the use of Information Technology and new equipment. Planning often means considering several possibilities and rejecting some after considerable work. Very few beginner teachers are sufficiently familiar with strategies, activities and resources to plan lessons quickly. Support for planning can come from both sides of the partnership. Schools have the advantage of having on hand equipment and resources, together with detailed knowledge of the pupils to be taught. HEIs can provide access to a wider range of resources and ideas and can help students share ideas with each other.

Secondly, lessons are **implemented**. Although classroom practice is at the core of any geography teacher's initial education it will probably occupy less time than the other experiences. In some ways classroom teaching is the tip of the iceberg, with much hidden time being spent on planning and evaluation. Nevertheless a student has to teach sufficient lessons to experience using a variety of strategies, activities, resources and groupings and of teaching across the age range and across a range of levels of achievement.

Thirdly, lessons are **evaluated**. Evaluations of lessons can take several forms:

TEACHING	PLANNING AND PREPARATION	EVALUATION AND REFLECTION	OBSERVING THE TEACHING OF OTHERS	READING	ACTION RESEARCH ON OWN TEACHING
teaching a small group teaching the whole class being a support teacher teaching individual pupils	using lesson plans and schemes of work devised by others devising own lesson plans and schemes of work discussing alternative plans and strategies beoming familiar with resources and IT packages selecting from a range of resources – books, visual, maps etc.	discussing what happened in lessons and attempting to understand what happened identifying strengths and weaknesses of one's own teaching discussing the reasons for using different resources and different strategies keeping a journal to monitor ideas and feelings	observing whole classes – using observation schedules or field notes discussing observations observing an individual pupil – using field notes observing a small group of pupils – using field notes or video	reading about teaching in books and journals reading about ideas for teaching, e.g. in *Teaching Geography*	tape recording and lessons videoing own lessons obtaining observational data on own lessons

Figure 5: Experiences which help students learn to teach geography

Written evaluations These can be general evaluations or concentrate on what the student wants to write about. Alternatively they can be structured, by a series of headings or by a series of questions, for example:

- What did the pupils learn?
- What did I learn?
- How would I teach that lesson differently?
- How will what I have learned affect my plan for the next lesson for the same class?

Use of competency lists Students could use the list of competences alone, or with a tutor or teacher, to identify what had been achieved in the lesson.

Journals or diaries These include more personal accounts of the experience of the lesson, usually including references to feelings and thoughts before, during and after the lesson as well as reference to what happened in the lesson. Journals can be valuable ways of helping students cope with the stresses and disappointments of teaching as well as celebrating the high points.

Post-lesson discussion with mentor, tutor or fellow student. This can be a very valuable learning process for the student or it can be threatening. Figure 6 shows some guidelines which have been used successfully in the Sheffield University Partnership with geography students.

General principles

i)   The supervisor should endeavour to understand the student's intentions for the lesson.

ii) The student should be encouraged to form his or her own evaluation of the lesson.

iii) Post-lesson discussion should be aimed at helping the student understand what was happening in the lesson as well as evaluating it.

iv) Both participants in the discussion should have opportunities to talk about the lesson. The student should have at least 50% of the talking time.

Procedures

i)   Students should have copies of plans of lessons to give to supervisors. Observers should not suggest amendments immediately before the lesson.

ii) The observer should endeavour to collect objective data on the lesson, rather than evaluative data, either by taking notes, or by recording the lesson on tape or video. Arrangements for collecting these data should be negotiated with the student who might want to identify a focus of attention. (The data is to provide evidence for the post-lesson discussion).

iii) The student should have the opportunity to make the first comments on the lesson and to lead the supervision discussion.

iv) The observer's comments and contribution to the discussion should be sensitive to the student's current needs. Consideration should be given to what kind of comments would help the student's development most and what might be best left unsaid. There are many possible types of contribution:

- questions to probe the student's comments
- questions to find out reasons for the student's actions
- questions about the student's feelings about the lesson
- questions about how the student would re-plan the lesson
- discussion of how to develop from strengths identified by student
- advice on weaknesses identified by student
- identification of strengths and weaknesses not identified by student
- identifying evidence of achievement of competences in the lesson
- advice on alternative ways of teaching the lesson or part of it
- advice on planning the next lesson with the same class
- agreement or disagreement with the student's interpretation of the lesson
- discussion of what the pupils have learned in the lesson.

v)   By the end of the discussion some evaluation of the lesson or parts of it should have been reached, preferably jointly.

Figure 6: Guidelines for observing and discussing lessons with students

---

One of the most effective ways to train teachers is for tutors to work with them in schools

Photo: **School of Education, University of Southampton**

Sympathetic support can enable students to learn a lot from this cycle of experiences. Students learn at each of these three stages, so that as the cycle is repeated the insights gained can be applied in the next cycle.

There are, however, other experiences which will help beginners learn to teach geography and these are shown in Figure 5. Students can learn from adopting a research stance and carrying out investigations into classroom practice. The classroom studied could be their own, with objective data being collected by tutor, teacher or another student. It could be the study of another teacher's lesson. Observation schedules, videos, tape recorders, field notes can be used to collect data. The observations can be general or focused. Figure 7 gives some examples of what might be observed in lessons.

When the data have been collected they can be used to answer a range of questions similar to those used in geographical enquiries:

■ what is happening?

■ who is involved?

■ why is it happening?

■ what ought to happen?

For some students it is this kind of enquiry and action research which helps them learn most, e.g. an analysis of a video recording of a lesson can reveal patterns of classroom talk which can be a starting point for improving classroom discussion.

> ■ teacher's questions: What kind are they? Which get most response? Who answers them? How does the teacher respond to the answers?
>
> ■ pupil's questions: What kind are they? Who asks them? How does the teacher respond?
>
> ■ teacher/pupil interaction: Which kinds of interactions are there during the lesson? How are they distributed among the pupils? Are there some pupils who get much more/less attention than others? (possibly collected on a room plan)
>
> ■ teacher movement: (drawn on a room plan)
>
> ■ pupil/pupil interaction during group work or use of computers (possibly studying one group)
>
> ■ Pupil activity during the lesson: observations of high achieving and low achieving pupils
>
> ■ Pupils use of resources: observation of a small number of pupils

Figure 7: Some examples of data to collect in geography lessons

Last, but not least, reading can help students learn to teach geography. Reading can increase the range of lesson ideas, help students understand them better and raise critical questions about classroom practice.

CLASS MANAGEMENT

The competences on class management (Figure 8) are mostly about maintaining orderly classrooms and apply to all PGCE students. In this particular category (and possibly in some of the others) it would seem important to identify some additional competences which apply to geography teachers. Two seem vital:

    i   an awareness of procedures and guidelines for taking pupils out of school;

    ii an ability to supervise and manage pupils during geography field excursions.

Class management

2.4 Newly qualified teachers should be able to:

    2.4.1   decide when teaching the whole class, groups, pairs or individuals is appropriate for particular learning purposes;

    2.4.2   create and maintain a purposeful and orderly environment for the pupils;

    2.4.3   devise and use appropriate rewards and sanctions to maintain an effective learning environment;

    2.4.4   maintain pupils' interest and motivation.

Figure 8: Class management competences (from Circular 9/92)

Competence 2.4.1 is rather different from the others and demands a range of experiences before students are in a position to achieve it. They need knowledge of ways of organising groups and they need to know about activities which are suitable for group and paired work. They need to experience the cycle (Figure 4) of planning, implementing and evaluating each type of grouping several times. They need opportunities and support in their school experience schools to do this whatever groupings are normally used in those schools. They need opportunities to discuss the merits of using different groupings. Only then are they able to select appropriate groupings. Although the word 'competence' suggests a skill, many of the competences listed, including this one, imply the need for **knowledge**, **understanding** of classroom processes, and the ability to make sound **judgements** as well as management **skills**.

ASSESSMENT AND RECORDING OF PUPILS' PROGRESS

One advantage of the list of competences is that it draws attention to aspects of professional development which have been neglected. Assessing pupils' learning is one of these (Figure 9). Both schools and HEIs can provide a range of experiences (Figure 10) to help students become competent in this area.

Assessment and recording of pupils' progress

2.5 Newly qualified teachers should be able to:

    2.5.1   identify the current level of attainment of individual pupils using NCATs, Statements of Attainment and end-of-key-stage statements where applicable;

    2.5.2   judge how well each pupil performs against the standard expected of a pupil of that age;

    2.5.3   assess and record systematically the progress of individual pupils;

    2.5.4   use such assessment in their teaching;

    2.5.5   demonstrate that they understand the importance of reporting to pupils on their progress and of marking their work regularly against agreed criteria.

Figure 9: Assessment and recording of pupils' progress (from Circular 9/92)

ASSESSING PUPILS' LEARNING	DESIGNING ACTIVITIES TO ASSESS LEARNING	STUDYING DONE BY WIDE RANGE OF PUPILS	READING ABOUT ASSESSMENT
discussing work with pupils marking work done in class or for homework marking test items or examinations using pupil self assessment keeping records of pupils' progress contributing to reports and profiles	building varied assessment opportunities into lesson plans designing a test item to test learning at end of unit of work devising a marking scheme or criteria statements to apply to test items using a data base to analyse test item results	studying video recordings of other geography classrooms, noting pupil progress studying class work and homework done by pupils in other schools (across PGCE group) studying written work provided by SCAA as exemplars studying work done for external examinations provided by examination boards	SCAA documents (GCSE criteria, Level Descriptions etc.) examination board publications articles in newspapers and professional journals, e.g. *Teaching Geography* books and articles in academic journals

Figure 10: Experiences which will help develop assessment and recording competences

The experiences shown in Figure 2 will be useful but there is a lot more to know and understand about assessing learning than knowing about public examinations. Students need to become aware of what all the pupils they teach are learning: they need to diagnose strengths and weaknesses; they need to use their knowledge to plan future lessons; they need to inform pupils and others of their progress. All this can take place in a school, but this experience alone is insufficient. Students need to become aware of how pupils in other schools progress and to become aware of different types and systems of assessment beyond those encountered during their school placements. The HEIs have a vital role here in giving students the range of experiences in the final three columns of Figure 10.

Further professional development

2.6 Newly qualified teachers should have acquired in initial training the necessary foundation to develop:

2.6.1 an understanding of the school as an institution and its place within the community;

2.6.2 a working knowledge of their pastoral, contractual, legal and administrative responsibilities as teachers;

2.6.3 an ability to develop effective working relationships with professional colleagues and parents, and to develop their communication skills;

2.6.4 an awareness of individual differences, including social, psychological developmental and cultural dimensions;

2.6.5 the ability to recognise diversity of talent including that of gifted pupils;

2.6.6 the ability to identify special educational needs or learning difficulties;

2.6.7 self-critical approach to diagnosing and evaluating pupils' learning including a recognition of the effect on that learning of teachers' expectations;

2.6.8 a readiness to promote the moral and spiritual well-being of pupils.

Figure 11: Further professional development competences (from Circular 9/92)

FURTHER PROFESSIONAL DEVELOPMENT

Many of the competences listed in Figure 11 could also appear in one of the other categories, so attention should be drawn to the initial phrase, 'the necessary foundation to develop'. It is not envisaged that every new geography teacher will be completely competent in each of these areas, but that they have had opportunities to make a start. Some of the experiences which are needed would be provided by general tutors and general mentors, but geography tutors and teachers could try to give students opportunities to:

- participate in parent's evenings
- participate in department meetings and INSET days
- teach geography to pupils from different cultural backgrounds
- teach geography to gifted pupils
- teach geography to pupils with a variety of special educational needs.

Assessment of competence

At present different partnerships between schools and HEIs are developing different ways of assessing and recording competences. It would therefore be unhelpful to give specific guidance here, but it is worth making some general comments. The complexity of some of the competences and the developmental nature of the last group of competences (Figure 11) suggest that they cannot be assessed easily at any one point of the course. Students will make progress at different times in different areas, but not necessarily steadily. Students might appear less competent in new circumstances, in a particular class, with a particular topic, in a different school or on a particular day. Competence will be related to the context in which the student is working. Assessment is always based on limited evidence collected in a particular context. Throughout the PGCE course it can be provisional, formative and diagnostic. It should always be sensitive to students' needs and can incorporate their own self-assessment. Some students find it useful to invite their pupils to make assessments of their teaching. By the end of the course, however, using as much evidence as it has been possible to collect, professional judgements have to be made within the new partnerships on whether a student is competent to teach. The competences provide a framework for considering these judgements. In this chapter I am suggesting that they can be also used to provide a framework for thinking about the experiences which beginner geography teachers need in order to become not only competent but also imaginative teachers, able to take geographical education into the twenty-first century.

Reference

Department for Education (1992) *Initial Teacher Training (Secondary Phase)*. Circular 9/92, DFE.

Chapter 31

Where can you go with geography?

PETER FOX

Introduction

This chapter will look at the employment opportunities available to geographers; the routes that can be taken to realise these opportunities; and the type of advice that can be offered to guide young geographers along the way. In the context of this chapter, the term 'geographer' is used to describe someone who is studying or has studied geography in school, college or a higher education institution and who uses or hopes to use, in some form of employment, the skills and/or knowledge which are particular to the subject.

Geography is a popular subject in schools at all levels, and appears regularly among the four or five most popular choices at GCSE and A level. Graduates in the subject have a high success rate in finding employment, a fact which is generally attributed to the 'relevance' of the subject in an ever-changing, environmentally conscious world, and to the broad range of skills (see Table 1) and knowledge which it encompasses. Given the combination of scientific, practical, and artistic elements which characterise most geography courses, it is not surprising that such a wide range of jobs is open to geographers (see Figure 1).

Geography-specific skills	Skills common to other subjects
Information Technology in GIS, satellite images and weather systems	Co-operation, teamwork
Geographical fieldwork and observation skills	Gaining first-hand experience
	Information Technology
Mapwork and cartography	Literacy, numeracy
Recording techniques and data manipulation	Statistics
	Sketching (fieldwork)
Graphicacy – construction of maps and diagrams to aid presentation and argument	Independent study and investigation
	Language development and communication – presenting information
Logistics	Analysis and evaluation of information
Problem-solving, decision-making	Problem-solving

Table 1: Skills specific to geography, and skills which overlap with other disciplines

More than most, a geography qualification leads to a wide variety of possible careers.

Photo: **Mike Hewitt/ Allsport**

Known first destinations (1993)

Men	1,647
Women	1,366
Total	3,013 (100%)

First destination (1993)

A Permanent
    UK employment
B Short-term
    UK employment
C Further academic study
D Teacher training
E Other training
F Overseas employment
G Overseas students
    leaving UK
H Unemployed
I Not available

Type of work (1993)

Men	637
Women	496
Total	1,133 (100%)

Type of work (1993)

The 37.6% of geography graduates whose first destination was permanent UK employment went into the following categories of work:

a Administration and
    operational management
b Research, design, development
c Scientific and engineering
    support
d Environmental planning,
    construction
e Sales, marketing, buying
f Management services,
    computing
g Financial work
h Legal work
i Literacy, entertainment and
    other creative work
j Information, library,
    museum work
k Personnel
l Health and social welfare
m Teaching and lecturing
n Other (including all categories
    with under 3%)

Pie chart (top): a 16.9%, b 3.0%, c 15.4%, g 15.6%, j 3.1%, l 7.9%, n 38%

Pie chart (bottom): A 37.5%, B 11.6%, C 14.7%, D 8.4%, E 6.4%, F 2.5%, G 0.8%, H 11.7%, I 7.0%

Examples of courses and jobs entered by graduates in 1993.

Further full-time study:

PhD: Geography/Ecology
MA: Town Planning
MSc: Applied Remote
Sensing; Environmental
Water Management
Certificates and diplomas:
Education; Horticulture; Law

Employment:

administrators: Adventure
Balloons; Fisher's Seeds;
Friends Provident; Middlesex
University; Wandsworth
Borough Council;
Yorkshire Cable

researchers: Healey & Baker;
Northumbria University;
Sedgemoor District Council;
Yorkshire Environmental
management trainees:
Abbey National; Lillywhites;
Marks & Spencer; Mersey
Regional Health Authority
booksellers: Dillons Bookshop;
Fielders Bookshop;
Sweetens Bookshop
media sales: GIS Progressions;
IPC Magazines;
Macmillan Press
trainee accountants: BOC;
Coopers & Lybrand;
Price Waterhouse
banking trainees:
National Westminster Bank

conservation officer:
Northumberland
environmental technician:
W Halcrow & Partners
information officer:
British Tourist Authority
investment trainee:
Cazenove & Co
IT support: Global Investment;
Techmark Services
pensions trainee:
Prolific Life & Pensions
project worker: Bridgewater
House Association
residential care officer:
Mencap Homes Foundation
statutory and liaison officer:
Thames Water
trainee journalist:
Thompson Group Newspapers

chambermaid: France
computer trainee: British Rail
marketing intern: USA
officer cadet: Army
teacher: Great Marlow School

KEY POINTS

■ The permanent employment
rate has increased by 3%
since 1992 and a very wide
range of careers is entered.

■ Commercial and financial
sectors recruit a considerable
number of geography
graduates.

■ There are limited opportunities
for course-related employment.

Figure 1: The destinations of geography graduates in 1993 (source: What do Graduates Do? published by CRAC)

Making choices

There are several moments in a student's life when choices have to be made which will affect their future. At the end of each key stage, decisions have to be taken on option choices and academic or vocational routes. Students face the same decisions at the age of 18/19 or older; they have the choice of continuing in some form of education or training, finding employment, or taking a year or so off (see Figure 2).

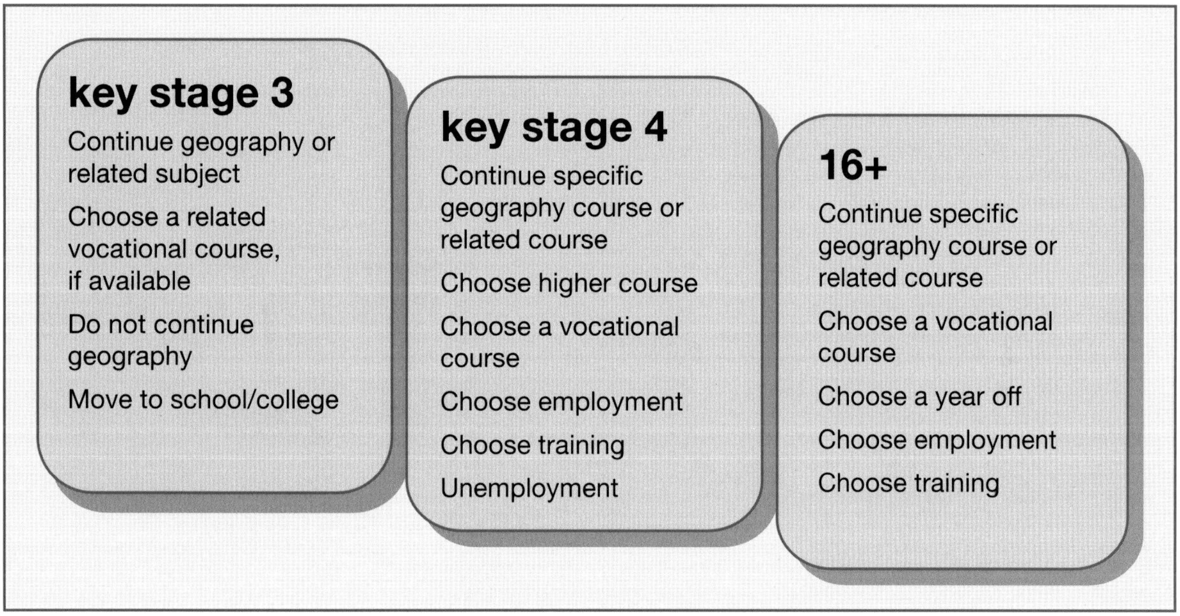

key stage 3

Continue geography or related subject

Choose a related vocational course, if available

Do not continue geography

Move to school/college

key stage 4

Continue specific geography course or related course

Choose higher course

Choose a vocational course

Choose employment

Choose training

Unemployment

16+

Continue specific geography course or related course

Choose a vocational course

Choose a year off

Choose employment

Choose training

Figure 2: Student choices

It is a little glib to say that every student should have a reason for choosing geography at any level. It is quite possible that the student will still be formulating ideas and views on the available alternatives and may not be ready to make clear choices. Some students are not ready to make choices at the end of key stages 3 or 4; nevertheless, it is helpful to encourage them to do so, and to make choices that keep their options open. To an extent, choosing geography enables them to do this.

Students should be encouraged to ask these questions:

- How will I be taught, by whom, and where?
- Why do I wish to start/continue a geography course?
- What will I do if I continue/start a geography course?
- Will I have the necessary qualifications/aptitudes required?
- Where will the study lead in two, three, four or five years' time?
- How long will it take?
- How much will it cost?

Providing advice

Departments and teachers have an important role to play in all these decision-making processes. They must provide correct and fair information about geography which is well-informed and up-to-date, and they must also help students in the decision-making process. Obviously, geography teachers are not alone in this role; they are often supported by colleagues, tutors and specialist guidance teams. Outside the school, support is offered by the Careers Advisory Service which has links with most schools, and local offices which are generally open for longer hours than the school day, as well during school holidays. Good school or college libraries should have a careers section accessible to students of all ages and containing up-to-date information in various

CAREER PROFILES OF THREE SELECTED GEOGRAPHY GRADUATES

Sue Cullum graduated from the University of Bristol with a geography and geology degree. She is now a consultant hydro-geologist for various companies with an expertise in quarrying and landfill. She advises on environmental matters, especially water and gas, and she also lectures occasionally at Imperial College, London. Landform analysis and interpretation and physical geography are important in her work and her IT skills have proved invaluable. Much of her degree work has therefore had direct applicability to her profession. This, of course, is true of other environmentally-related professions and the point will not be laboured.

George Brown is now a reporter on an East Anglian local radio station, having graduated in geography from the University of Hull. His background in economics, physical and social geography has proved invaluable, for instance in the area of job losses and government regional grants. In addition skills developed at university for communicating a case and collating and analysing data have proved very helpful in his professional life.

Jane Hargreaves graduated in geography from Cambridge and went to Emst and Young in the City, becoming a member of the Institute of Chartered Accountants. She now works as a corporate financier at bankers Kleinwort Benson. Jane feels very strongly that her knowledge of urban and industrial geography allied to a logical approach and report writing, data analysis and IT skills (especially spreadsheets and modelling) – all acquired at university – have greatly helped her in her present position.

GEOGRAPHY
LEARNING FOR LIFE

…if you're not into people and places, don't read on!

What is Geography?

Geography studies environments and how people live in them. It explains the location of places and people's activities in these places. Geography encourages us to care for people and the places where they live.

People use geography when making decisions about issues such as:

328

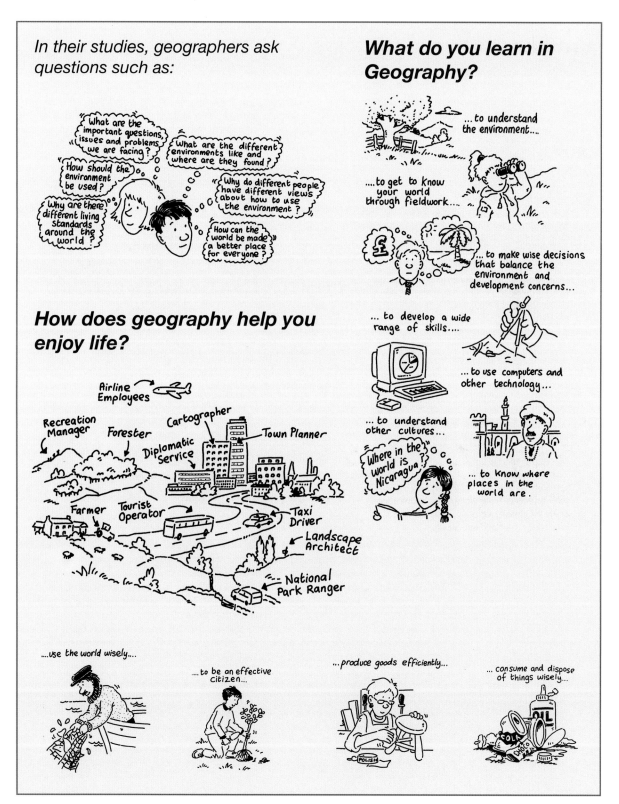

Figure 3: An example of a school leaflet designed to promote geography

forms, including CD-ROM databases and computer software such as MICRODOORS, JIIGCAL, ECCTIS and KUDOS. There should also be a qualified person on hand to offer advice and support, such as current reference material and prospectuses, to both students and staff.

Students who are interested in geography or a related subject will turn to the geography department or teacher for advice on vocational or academic matters. This can be provided in the form of specific leaflets designed by the geography department/teacher and aimed at 'selling' the skills that geography has to offer to students at different levels, as well as illustrating the opportunities that are available to them (see Figure 3). These leaflets can be made available during parents' evenings and/or become

---

━━━ *NRA* ━━━

Produced by: Geography Department, ———— UPTON HEATH ———— School

COURSE CONTENT AND SKILLS RECORD

Name of student: Parminder Aujla   **Date:** May 1996.

Parminder has followed the National Curriculum course in geography which includes the following topics and skills:

(to be completed by the teacher and department)

Parminder has followed a GCSE course in geography and has studied urban geography, hydrology, transport systems, environmental issues, contrasts in development and industrial studies. He has undertaken fieldwork in the local area and at Scarborough.

The department encourages students to undertake their own investigations and problem-solving. Parminder has shown a reasonable competence in this.

The department encourages students to use Information Technology. Parminder has used a word processor, desk top publishing, simulation, graphics, data logging, spreadsheet and database programs as well as CD-ROM.

Parminder can present data in a variety of forms and talk about the data. He has used a laptop computer to collect information about local traffic and has related this to accident black spots on local roads.

Parminder can use Information Technology to find information. He has used the CD-ROM to collect information on acid rain.

Parminder can understand other people's views. He has used a questionnaire to find what views local people have about the widening of the M1 between two local junctions and produced a leaflet using DTP to illustrate his findings.

Parminder can co-operate with others. He had used Metfax and Teletext to obtain weather information and, with a group of students, produced a simulated weather broadcast which was recorded on video and played to the rest of the class.

Parminder knows about local industry. He collected information from a school database and used a computer to draw a coloured map with located proportional pie charts to show employment structure. He has used and had access to the Internet.

Parminder has made use of his OS Mapwork as part of his Duke of Edinburgh expedition into the White Peak of Derbyshire. He has a high standard of map reading skill.

Signed _____   **Head of the Department of Geography**

Figure 4: A sample National Record of Achievement

part of the 'choice' booklets produced by many schools and colleges. A simple wall display in the department can also be very helpful, and it is important that teachers make it clear that they are available to talk to students about options and choices.

One of the most productive and helpful sources of information and advice is people who are already employed in a relevant occupation, or students following 'geographical' courses. Direct contact which such people is particularly productive, and can be instigated by the department/teacher, or the students themselves. Taster courses and Work Experience have an important role to play too, but students need to be well prepared with a list of questions before embarking on these. Asking questions is a key part of the process of information exchange so, in this context, videos and computer programs have only limited value.

What do geographers have to offer?

A geography department in any educational institution can provide lists of skills and the course content for students to include in their National Record of Achievement (NRA). This information is also helpful to college tutors and employers in that it raises their awareness of what geography has to offer (see Figure 4). Promoting the skills and content of the subject is part of the role of any geography department – they must tell students about what they are learning, and about how they can use their knowledge and skills in other contexts.

Which courses and occupations are orientated towards geography?

The development of vocational courses, many of which have substantial geographical components, has widened the range of choices available (see Chapter 28); for example, the Travel and Tourism GNVQ contains a lot of 'traditional geography'. GNVQs differ from GCSE/A level geography in a number of ways, as shown in Table 2.

■ More 'academic' than GCSE	■ Requires self motivation
■ More intensive/focused than GCSE	■ Includes more shared learning and assessment
■ Involves more research, essay writing and reading	■ Has perhaps a more varied and interesting content
■ Involves acquiring more detailed information	■ Links well with other subjects
■ Includes more individual work and self organisation	■ Requires higher level skills in English, maths, Information Technology and information skills

Table 2: *Key differences between GCSE and A level/GNVQ Level 2/3 geography*

A bewildering number of institutions offer vocational courses so it is useful for students to develop a checklist of questions to help them to make choices (see Table 3).

When choosing higher courses, a similar checklist can be developed which sets out criteria (see Table 4). The example in Table 4 could also be used by students when selecting school or college courses. For most universities, candidates have to satisfy a general requirement as well as a course requirement (see Table 5 for a list of degree course subjects including an element of geography).

One of the main strengths of geography (although some would argue it is a weakness!) is the wide range of job opportunities available to geographers. Apart from teaching the subject, there are few jobs that specifically require a geography qualification, but there are some for which study of the subject is clearly an advantage (see Table 6 and Figure 1).

In summary, it is clear from the evidence that geography teachers should have little difficulty convincing their students of the versatility of the subject. Not only does it have direct and indirect links with numerous vocational and other courses, it also provides a sound and relevant base of knowledge and skills which are relevant to a considerable range of job opportunities.

- What will I study? (specifics)
- Can I start this as a new subject from scratch?
- Do courses with similar titles have different content?
- What is the department's attitude to a 'year between' or deferred entry?
- What qualifications will I need to get in? Are there specific qualifications?
- What methods will be used to help me study? What types of teaching methods are used?
- Will there be any practical work/fieldwork – where, when, equipment required, cost?
- What time will there be for supported study?
- What equipment/books and what technical help will be available to me? (library/resources/IT/maps)
- What types of assessment will be used and when? (essays, exams, assessed presentations, fieldwork, practicals)
- Does the final examination give exemption from the academic requirement of other courses/professional bodies?
- Will there be a student guidance system?
- What equipment/books will I need to buy?

- What is the size and nature of the teaching/lecture/seminar/working groups?
- How good do my geography, English, maths, Information Technology skills need to be?
- How many teachers teach the course? What experience have they of teaching this course?
- Will topical/environmental/local issues be dealt with on the course? What optional courses are there?
- Is work experience part of the course?
- By undertaking this course will I be cutting myself off from career options that I might want to leave open?
- Which parts of the course will improve my employability afterwards?
- How much time will I be expected to spend in class and in out-of-class study?
- Will the groups I work with be mixed in terms of age, race, gender, etc?
- Where to get the answers? (Prospectuses, department brochures, alternative/student prospectus, comparative information – publications, CD-ROM. Information from students, open days, tasters, visits, personal recommendations.)

Table 3: Suggested list of questions students might ask about geography and related courses

---

QUALITY

Quality of the Institute/Department in terms of…
Quality of the qualification
Staff:student ratio
Research availability
Availability of resources/IT/study facilities/library
    opening hours
Drop-out rates

COURSES

Range of courses available
Degree of compulsion/choice
Extent of specialisation
Length and number of terms
Vocational experiences

TEACHING STYLES AND ASSESSMENT

Number of staff-student contact hours
Range and quality of teaching methods
Tutorial system

Size of teaching groups
Fieldwork and use of information technology
Assessment methods and frequency of assessment
Student assessment

INSTITUTION

Size
Locality (city, town, campus)
Access from home/accommodation
Accommodation – types/cost?
Popularity
Extra-curricular facilities/activities (social/sport)
Destinations of students
Availability of guidance - student support
Are sponsorships available?

(Based on Geography beyond A-level: A Student's Guide, *edited by G. Malcolm Lewis. The Geographical Association (out of print).)*

Table 4: Criteria checklist for students wishing to follow a geography course

DEGREE COURSE SUBJECTS INCLUDING SOME GEOGRAPHY

Associated courses and combinations. Application for most of these is through the Universities and College Admissions Service (UCAS). In a few cases direct application is required. Check for more details: the list of courses is constantly changing.

Anthropology
African and Asian Studies
Development Studies
Earth Science/Geology
Economics
Environmental Science
European Studies
Green Studies
Information and Library Studies

Languages (Arabic/French/German)
PE/Sports Science
Plant Science
Teaching
Transport
Town and Country Planning
Travel
Urban Studies

Table 5: Degree course subjects including an element of geography

JOBS FOR GEOGRAPHERS!

Geography **QOL**

Travel and Transport
Air Traffic Control **YAB**
Despatch Rider/Courier **YAD**
Diver **YAZ**
Driver **YAD**
Freight Forwarder **YAS**
Merchant Navy **YAL/YAF**
Pilot **YAB**
RAC/AA Work **RAE**
Railway Work **CAM**
Removals **YAT**
Tourist Guide/Courier **GAX**
Transport Work **YAD**
Travel Agency Work **GAX**

Information, History, Law
Advertising **OD**
Archaeologist **FAH**
Author **FAC**
Civil Service **CAB**
History **FAG**
Information Technology Work **CAV**
Journalist **FAC**
Law **L**
Lecturer **FAB**
Legal Executive **LAD**
Library Work **FAF**

Media Work **FAC/GAL**
Teacher **FAB**
Travel Agency Work **GAX**
Translator **FAB**

Armed and Public Services
Army **BAF**
Civil Service **CAB**
Coastguard **YAL**
Diplomatic Service **CAB**
HM Customs **CAB**
Navy **BAB**
Outdoor Pursuits Instructor **GAG**
Post Office Work **YAT**
RAF **BAL**

Environmental, Land, Surveying
Auctioneer **UM**
Countryside Ranger/Warden **WAR**
Conservation Officer **WAR**
Estate Agent/Surveyor **UM**
Farm Manager/Worker **WAB**
Fish Farmer **WAG**
Forester **WAF**
Gamekeeper **WAM**
Horticulture **WAD**
Planning **US**
Surveying **UM**

Retail, Logistics, Statistics
Distribution Manager **OK**
Economist **QOL**
Freight Distribution **OK**
Market Research **OB**
Retail **O**
Warehouse Manager **YAT**

Engineering
Engineer – Civil/Structural **R/U**

Scientific
Archaeologist **FAH**
Conservationist **WAR**
Farming **WAB**
Geologist **QOL**
Meteorologist **QOL**
Oceanography **QOL**

Design
Architect **UB**
Draughtsperson **RAB**
Landscape Architect **UL**
Mapping/Cartography **UT**
Planning **US**
Photographer **EV**

Table 6: Occupations in which a geography qualification is useful. The letters in bold type represent the Careers Library Classification codes (from the 1993 reprint of the codes – COIC)

References and further reading

GEOGRAPHY

Careers in Meteorology (1990). Royal Meteorological Society (leaflet).

COIC (1991) *Working in Geography* (Working In series no 54) ISBN 0 86110 575 3.

Geography Graduates and Employers (1980s). The Geographical Association/Institute of British Geographers/Royal Geographical Society (leaflet).

Hercod, F. & Lenon, B. (eds) (1994) *Directory of University Geography Courses 1995.* Royal Geographical Society. ISBN 0 902447 21 1.

Lewis, G. M. (ed) (1985) *Geography beyond A level: A Student's Guide.* The Geographical Association (now out of print). ISBN 0 900395 92 3 .

Which Degree 1996. Engineering, Technology, Geography (1995). CRAC. ISBN 1 86017 050 1.

GEOGRAPHICAL EDUCATION

Kent, A. (1990) *Selling Geography.* The Geographical Association. ISBN 0 948512 18 0.

Wiegand, P. (ed) (1989) *Managing the Geography Department.* The Geographical Association (now out of print) ISBN 0 948512 13 X.

HIGHER EDUCATION

Allen, T. (1995) *Which University 1996.* CRAC. ISBN 1 86017 041 2.

Casson, D. & Brown, P. (eds) (1994) *The Educational Grants Directory.* *Directory of Social Change publication.* Radius Works, Back Lane, London NW3 1HL. ISBN 1 873860 46 3.

CRAC (published each year) *What Do Graduates Do?* CRAC 1 Distribution Services.

CRAC (1995) *The CRAC Directory of Higher Education 1995-96.* ISBN 1 86017 053 6.

CRAC (1995) *Which Degree 1996.* ISBN 1 86017 048 X.

Ebehard, R. (1995) *Compendium of Higher Education.* Laser. ISBN 0 85394 169 6.

Heap, B. (published each year) *The Complete Degree Course Offers and How to Choose a Course at University and College.* Trotman. (ISBN for 1994 edition 0 85660 216 7.)

Heap, B. (1994) *The Complete Degree Course Offers 1995 on CD-ROM.* Trotman.

Lamley, S. (Fifth edition 1994) *Getting into University and College.* Trotman. ISBN 0 85660 157 8.

CAREERS

The Alternative Guide to the Sixth Form (1994). Trotman. ISBN 0 85660 206 X.

Barlow, H. (1995) *How to Succeed in A levels.* Kogan Page. ISBN 1 85091 655 1.

Boehm, K. & Lees-Spalding, J. (eds) (1994) *The Student Book.* Papermac. ISBN 0 333 59947 0.

Butcher, V. (Second edition 1993) *Taking a Year Off.* Trotman. ISBN 0 84660 206 X.

Central Bureau for Educational Visits and Exchanges (Fifth edition, 1993) *Volunteer Work.* Central Bureau. ISBN 0 900087 92 7.

Chester, C. & Swanson, C. (1992) *Careers in the Travel Industry.* Kogan Page. ISBN 0 7494 0647 X.

COIC (1993) *Careers Library Classification Index 1993.* (Reprint) ISBN 0 86110 644 X.

CRAC (1994) *How to Get a Job in Travel and Tourism.* ISBN 1 85703 113 X.

Institute of Environmental Sciences (1993) *The Environmental Careers Handbook.* ISBN 0 85660 240.

Mature Students' Handbook (1994). Trotman. ISBN 0 85660 162 4.

Taylor, F. (1993) *Careers in Teaching*. Kogan Page. ISBN 0 7494 0978 9.

Vincent, A. (1993) *Your GCSE Decisions*. Trotman. ISBN 0 85660 181 0.

CAREERS REFERENCE GUIDES

CASCAID Computer Software and Guide 1994/5 (14th edition 1994). ISBN 0 85022 354 7.

COIC *MICRODOORS Computer Software*.

COIC (published each year) *Occupations 1995*. ISBN 0 86110 671 7 (1994 edition).

COIC (1993) *Career Builder Computer Software*.

CRAC (1995) *GNVQ: Is it for You?*. ISBN 1 86017 017 X.

CRAC (1995) *CID for Windows on CD-ROM Computer Software*.

ECCTIS (The Educational Counselling and Credit Transfer Information Service) (published each year) *ECCTIS 2000 Ltd* CD-ROM.

Jamieson, A. (1994) *Which Subject, Which Career?* Which Books. ISBN 0 85202 500 9.

JIIG CAL Computer Software and Jobfile 95 (1995). Hodder and Stoughton. ISBN 0 340 62749 2.

KUDOS/SUBJECTWISE Computer software (1994). CASCAID.

Segal, A. & Lea, K. (13th edition 1993) *Careers Encyclopedia*. Cassell. ISBN 0 304 32719 0.

Contact addresses

Careers and Occupational Information Centre
Moorfoot, Sheffield

Careers Research Advisory Council (CRAC)
published under licence by Hobsons Publishing plc, Bateman Street, Cambridge CB2 1LZ

CASCAID
West Annexe, County Hall, Glenfield, Leicester LE3 8YZ

JIIG CAL
University of Edinburgh, 5 Buccleugh Place, Edinburgh EH8 9LW

LASER Advisory Council
21 Bedford Square, London WC1B 3HH

Bibliography

Each section of the *Handbook* includes specific suggestions for further reading. This bibliography lists accessible works of more general interest and practical usefulness for those engaged in geographical education. No attempt has been made to assemble a comprehensive bibliography on geographical education.

Geography in general

Gregory, D. & Walford, R. (eds) (1989) *Horizons in Human Geography.* Macmillan.

Johnston, R.J. (1991) *A Question of Place: Exploring the Practice of Human Geography.* Blackwell.

Unwin, T. (1992) *The Place of Geography.* Longman.

GEOGRAPHY IN THE NATIONAL CURRICULUM FOR ENGLAND AND WALES

Bailey, P. (1991) 'A case hardly won: geography in the national curriculum of English and Welsh schools', *The Geographical Journal*, 158, 1, pp. 65-74.

Wiegand, P. & Rayner, M. (eds) (1989) *Curriculum Progress 5 to 16. School Subjects and the National Curriculum Debate.* Falmer Press.

Primary geography

Blyth, A. & Krause, J. (1995) *Primary Geography: A Developmental Approach.* Hodder and Stoughton.

Foley, M. & Janikoun, J. (1992) *The Really Practical Guide to Primary Geography.* Stanley Thornes.

Marsden, W.E. & Hughes, J. (eds) (1994) *Primary School Geography.* David Fulton.

Wiegand, P. (1992) *Places in the Primary School: Knowledge and Understanding of Places at Key Stages 1 and 2.* Falmer Press.

Wiegand, P. (1993) *Children and Primary Geography.* Cassell.

Geography 8-13

Copeland, G. (1992) *A Teacher's Guide to Geography and the Historic Environment.* English Heritage.

Sebba, J. (1995) *Geography for All.* David Fulton.

Secondary geography

Boardman, D. (ed) (1986) *Handbook for Geography Teachers,* The Geographical Association.

Fien, J., Gerber, R. & Wilson, P. (eds) (1984) *The Geography Teacher's Guide to the Classroom.* Macmillan Australia.

Geography Education Standards Project (1994) *Geography for Life. National Geography Standards 1994.* National Geographic Research and Exploration, Washington DC.

Her Majesty's Inspectors of Schools (1978) *The Teaching of Ideas in Geography.* HMSO.

Her Majesty's Inspectors of Schools (1980) *Geography from 5 to 16. Curriculum Matters 7.* HMSO.

Hacking, E. (1992) *Geography into Practice.* Longman.

Jay, L.J. (1981) *Geography Teaching With a Little Latitude.* Allen and Unwin.

Kent, A., Lambert, D., Naish, M. & Slater, F. (1995) *Geography in Education,* Cambridge University Press.

Lambert, D. (1990) *Geography Assessment: A Guide and Resource for Teachers.* Cambridge University Press.

Marsden, W.E. (1995) *Geography 11-16: Rekindling Good Practice.* David Fulton.

Pike, G. & Selby, D. (1988) *Global Teacher, Global Learner.* Hodder and Stoughton.

Walford, R. & Machon, P. (eds) (1994) *Challenging Times: Implementing the National Curriculum in Geography.* Cambridge Publishing Services.

Geographical Association journals

The Geographical Association publishes the following journals in January, April, July and October:

Geography

Teaching Geography

Primary Geographer

Index